BUILDING *the* PERFECT PC

Robert Bruce Thompson
and Barbara Fritchman Thompson

O'REILLY®

BEIJING · CAMBRIDGE · FARNHAM · KÖLN · PARIS · SEBASTOPOL · TAIPEI · TOKYO

Building the Perfect PC

by Robert Bruce Thompson and Barbara Fritchman Thompson

Published by O'Reilly Media, Inc., 1005 Gravenstein Highway North, Sebastopol, CA 95472.

O'Reilly books may be purchased for educational, business, or sales promotional use. Online editions are also available for most titles (*safari.oreilly.com*). For more information, contact our corporate/institutional sales department: 800-998-9938 or *corporate@oreilly.com*.

Print History:

August 2004:   First Edition.

Editor: Brian Jepson

Production Editor: Emily Quill

Cover Designer: Ellie Volckhausen

Interior Designers: David Futato and Melanie Wang

RepKover. This book uses RepKover™, a durable and flexible lay-flat binding.

0-596-00663-2
[C]

*To Mark Brokering, who came up with the idea
and kept the ball rolling.*

✳

Contents

Foreword

I presume you're reading this because you've either just bought this book, or you're thinking of buying it. So let's get that out the way now. Should you buy this book? Or, having bought it, should you be happy you did? The answer to both questions is yes. If the subject of building your own computer interests you—and why in the world are you reading this if it doesn't?—then you need this book. You won't find anything else like it.

That out of the way, we can look at the broader question of whether you should build your own computers.

As I look around Chaos Manor (*www.jerrypournelle.com*), I see that I have over 20 computers, all networked, and I built nearly every one of them myself. The exceptions are Princess, an ancient Compaq desktop professional workstation running dual Pentium Pro 200 MHz CPUs; a Mac; a TabletPC; and another laptop. No one in his right mind builds his own laptop or Tablet. I keep Princess because I've had her for a decade, and she hasn't been shut down in more than a year, and I haven't the heart to scrap her. Besides, she's still useful for doing long web searches. Until fairly recently I had a Compaq professional workstation (dual 750 MHz Pentium III) as my communications system, but I retired it a few months ago in favor of a new 3 GHz built here, and since then every server and workstation added to the Chaos Manor network was built here. Clearly I must like building systems and using them.

It wasn't always this way. Until a few years ago I had at least as many brand-name systems as home-built "white boxes." Then came the consumerization of the PC industry. Manufacturers were forced into cost reduction after cost reduction. Some of those cost reductions were not wise. Some were disasters. Worse, component makers were themselves competing on cost. It became more and more difficult for computer manufacturers to build a quality line of PCs that they could sell at any realistic price.

It is still possible to buy quality computers, but you'll pay dearly for them. And sometimes, even after having paid an arm and a leg, you still won't be sure of the quality of your system. There are still big companies with mission-critical tasks who are well advised to buy the very best machines from top-of-the-line companies. But most users and small businesses should consider building their own, or having them built to specs by a trustworthy local shop. (And a book like this is indispensable when it comes to sorting through all the possible specifications.)

In general, there are two reasons why you build your own systems.

First is if you want the *highest possible performance,* using only the latest and greatest components. When new and better components come out, it takes a while for commercial system builders to change over. And the first ones to come out with the latest in high-performance command premium prices. If you're interested in building a really screaming machine, you need this book because building that kind of system is tricky. Components like power supplies, cases, and fans are important, and information about *why* they are important is often hard to come by. You'll find all the information you need in this book.

The other reason for building your own system is to get the *best performance and quality for your money,* and to *customize your high-performance system for your specific needs*. You probably don't need the very best performance available, and often you can get more than good-enough systems at dramatically lower prices. These are known as "sweet spot" systems, and once again, if that's your goal, you need this book because that too can be tricky. Sometimes saving money isn't a good idea at all. You can fudge on some components, but you're better off paying a premium for others. Bob and Barbara Thompson offer great advice on which is which.

So if you're thinking of building your own system, you need this book to give you some notion of how difficult it's likely to be and to help you decide if it's a good idea. And if you're determined to build a PC, you need this book because most of us who build PCs have picked up a number of techniques and tricks over the years, and the Thompsons know nearly all of them. Learn from our mistakes. It's a lot easier than paying for your own.

—Jerry Pournelle
Chaos Manor
August 2004

Preface

Building PCs isn't just for techies anymore.

It used to be, certainly. Only gamers and other geeks actually built their PCs from the ground up—everyone else just called the Dell Dude and ordered a system. That started to change a few years ago. The first sign was when general merchandisers like Best Buy started stocking upgrade components. If you wanted to expand the memory in your PC, install a larger hard drive, or add a CD writer, you could now get the components you needed at the local big-box store.

A year or two ago, things changed again. Big-box retailers started carrying PC components like cases and motherboards—parts seldom needed by upgraders, but necessary to build a new PC from scratch. Nowadays, although CompUSA, Best Buy, and other local retailers may not carry as broad a range of PC components as some online specialty retailers, you can get everything you need for a new PC with one visit to a big-box store.

> Specialty PC component superstores like Fry's carry a full range of components at extremely good prices. We wish we had a Fry's within driving distance. Or then again, maybe not. There's too much good stuff there. Our credit cards are smoking already, and a trip to Fry's might be the last straw.

And you can bet that big-box stores don't allocate shelf space to products that aren't selling. Building your own PC has become mainstream. Nowadays, even regular nontechnical people build their own systems and have fun doing it. Instead of settling for a mediocre, cookie-cutter system from Dell or Gateway, they get a PC with exactly the features and components they want, at a good price, and with the pride that comes from knowing they built it themselves. They also get a faster, higher-quality PC with much better reliability than any mass-market system. No small thing, that.

Robert visited Best Buy one day and spent some time hanging out in the PC component aisles. He watched a lot of regular people comparing hard drives, video adapters, DVD writers, and other PC components. Some of them were buying components to upgrade their current systems, but many of them were buying components to build entirely new systems.

Robert watched one grandmotherly woman fill her shopping cart. She chose an Antec case and power supply, a Maxtor hard drive, an Abit motherboard, an AMD Athlon XP processor, an *n*VIDIA graphics adapter, a couple sticks of DDR memory, and a Lite-On DVD writer. He approached her, and the conversation went something like this:

> Robert: "Looks like you're building a new computer."
>
> Woman: "Yes, I'm building my granddaughter a new PC for her birthday."
>
> Robert: "Are you worried about getting everything to work?"
>
> Woman: "Oh, no. This is the third one I've built. You should try it. It's easy."
>
> Robert: "I may do that."

If she'd had this book, she might have made different choices for one or two of her components. Still, Dell may have something to worry about.

Goals of This Book

This book is your guide to the world of building PCs. Its goal is to teach you everything you need to know to select the best components and assemble them into a working PC that matches your own requirements and budget—even if you have no training or prior experience.

We present five projects, in as many chapters. Each chapter details design, component selection, and assembly instructions for a particular type of PC. You can build any or all of these systems as presented, or you can modify them to suit your own requirements.

Rather than using a straight cookbook approach, which would simply tell you *how* to build a PC by rote, we spend a lot of time explaining *why* we made particular design decisions, chose certain components, or did something a certain way. By "looking over our shoulders" as we design PCs and choose components, you'll learn to make good decisions when it comes to designing and building your own PC. You'll also learn how to build a PC with superior quality, performance, and reliability.

Not that we skimped on the how-to. Each project system chapter provides detailed assembly instructions and dozens of photographs that illustrate the assembly process. Even if you've never seen a hard drive, after reading this book you should be completely comfortable sitting down with a bunch of components to build your own PC.

Every project system in this book can be built entirely from components available at your local big-box store. If some of the components we recommend aren't in stock, one or more of the alternative components we recommend almost certainly will be. If you buy this book on a Friday, you can buy your components Saturday morning, assemble the new system Saturday afternoon, test it Sunday, and have it up and running Monday morning.

If you have never built a PC, we hope this book will inspire you to build your first system. If you have some PC building experience, we hope this book will provide the ideas and advice to help make the next PC you build the Perfect PC for your needs.

Audience for This Book

This book is intended for anyone who wants to build a PC for personal or business use. System builders of any experience level will find this book useful because it explains the concepts used to design a PC to fit specific needs and budgets and provides the information needed to choose the best components. First-time system builders will also find this book helpful because it provides detailed step-by-step instructions for building a PC, supplemented by numerous photographs that illustrate each step in detail.

Organization of This Book

The first two chapters of this book comprise a short but comprehensive course in planning the perfect PC and choosing and buying components for it.

Chapter 1, Fundamentals, focuses on things you need to know, things you need to have, and things you need to do before you start to buy components and build your new PC. This chapter explains the advantages of building a PC versus buying one (YOU control the quality, performance, reliability, and quietness of your components), provides design guidelines, and explains the inevitable tradeoffs in performance, price, size, and noise level. We list the tools and software you'll need, and provide a detailed tour of the motherboard, the most important and complex PC component. Finally, we provide detailed troubleshooting information, because it's easier to avoid problems if you know from the beginning what to look out for. After you read this chapter, you'll be prepared for the next step: actually buying the components for your new PC.

Chapter 2, Choosing and Buying Components, tells you everything you need to know about how to select and purchase the components you need to build your new PC.

When you design and build your own PC, you get something that money can't buy if you purchase a preassembled machine: total control of quality, reliability, performance, and noise level.

We explain the important characteristics of each component and how to choose among alternatives. We also recommend specific components by brand and model number, and provide alternative recommendations for those with different requirements or smaller budgets. The original draft of this chapter was more than 40,000 words—far too large for the space available, and nearly a book in itself. As our agent said to Robert, "You're the only author I know who accidentally wrote a book." So we spent most of a week cutting this chapter down to its final size, about half of what it had been. In the process, we ruthlessly eliminated extraneous information, and boiled it down to essentials. After you read this chapter, you will be prepared to choose the optimum components for your new PC and to buy them at a good price.

The final five chapters detail project systems, any of which you can build as-is or modify to suit your particular needs. The introductory section of each project chapter is a design guide that explains the choices we made and how we decided to implement them. Following that is a detailed section on selecting components, with specific products listed by brand name, and a bill of materials. In each case, we list alternative components for those with different needs or budgets. The bulk of each chapter is a detailed guide, with numerous photographs, that shows you step-by-step how to build the system.

Chapter 3, Building a Mainstream PC, teaches you how to build a general-purpose PC that is a jack of all trades and master of...well, quite a few, actually. In the standard configuration, this system combines high performance, top-notch reliability, and moderate cost. Depending on the components you choose—and how much you're willing to spend—you can make this system anything from an inexpensive entry-level box to a do-it-all powerhouse. And it's quiet, particularly if you build it in a midrange configuration. In a normal office or home environment, you can barely hear it running.

Chapter 4, Building a SOHO Server, focuses on building a reliable, high-performance SOHO (Small Office/Home Office) server, appropriate for anything from an inexpensive server for a home office to a serious server for a small-business network. Because these requirements span a vast range, we take particular pains to detail alternative choices and configurations that are appropriate for different environments. We emphasize reliability and data safety regardless of configuration, because a server failure is as disruptive for a home office as for a small business. Accordingly, we emphasize such features as redundant disk storage and reliable backup.

Chapter 5, Building a Kick-Ass LAN Party PC, is all about building a fire-breathing gaming PC with an emphasis on portability. A LAN party happens when a group of people bring their PCs to a central location, hook them up to a network, and start competing. LAN parties are the rage among PC gamers, and most serious LAN partiers build a PC optimized for LAN parties. This chapter shows you how to build a seriously fast PC that's easy to carry around. If you're not a gamer but need speed in a portable package, this system will do the job for you, too.

Further Reading

If you want more information about choosing the best components for your new PC, O'Reilly also publishes *Building the Perfect PC: A Pocket Guide to Choosing and Buying Components*. The pocket guide is a greatly expanded version of Chapter 2, with additional important details. It's small enough to take with you when you prowl the PC component aisles in your local big-box store, and detailed enough to help you buy the right components the first time. Cheap insurance, we think.

Each project chapter is full of tips, many of which are useful no matter what type of system you decide to build. Accordingly, we suggest you read the entire book, including all project chapters, before you start building your new system.

Chapter 6, Building a Home Theater PC, shows you how to build a PC that provides TiVo-like DVR (Digital Video Recorder) functions, without the monthly subscription or the DRM (Digital Restrictions Management) "features" common to commercial PVR units. For about the price of a combination TiVo/DVD writer and program guide subscription, this PC substitutes not only for a commercial DVR unit, but also for an AV receiver, CD-ROM player, DVD-ROM player, DVD recorder, 5.1 home theater speaker system, *and* a gaming console. Talk about bang for the buck.

Chapter 7, Building a Small Form Factor PC, shows you how to build a fully featured PC that is small enough and quiet enough to fit in almost anywhere. Depending on the components you choose, you can make the SFF PC anything from an inexpensive secondary system suitable for a dorm room or child's bedroom to a primary general-purpose system to a home theater or PVR system to a barn-burner of a portable gaming system to a dedicated "appliance" system or small server. We actually built two of these systems, one configured as a satellite DVR system for the master bedroom—with full recording functionality and the ability to play video stored on the main server or home theater PC—and the second as a general-purpose mainstream PC.

Acknowledgments

This book was conceived one day in late 2003, when Robert received a phone call from Mark Brokering, Vice President of Sales and Marketing for O'Reilly. Mark had decided to build a new PC rather than buy one, and he'd picked up a copy of our book, *PC Hardware in a Nutshell*.

Mark had lots of good questions about which components to choose and, later on, questions about assembling his new system. At some point during the back-and-forth of emails and phone calls, Mark commented, "You know, we really need to do a book about building a PC." And so this book was born.

The working title was *Build Your Own Computer*. None of us thought that was a great title, but no one could come up with a better one. Then one day Tim O'Reilly weighed in: "Why don't we call it *Building the Perfect PC*?" Duh. It always seems so obvious after the fact.

In addition to Mark, Tim, and the O'Reilly production staff, who are listed individually in the colophon, we want to thank our technical reviewers: Ron Morse, who's been building PCs for more than 20 years, and Jim Cooley, who's built and repaired computers from San Francisco to Athens (Ohio), with the occasional stop in Bangalore. Both did yeoman duty in finding mistakes we made and in making numerous useful suggestions, all of which helped make this a better book.

Although we tested the configurations we specified for each project system, we did not build and test every permutation with the alternative components we listed. Those alternatives are simply what we might have used if our requirements had been different. That said, we would expect the alternative components we list to work in any combination, and would be very surprised if they didn't.

There are rare exceptions. For example, we built the SOHO Server system around an Intel server board, but listed an Intel desktop board as an alternative. Recent Linux distros should run properly on either of those motherboards, but no Intel desktop board supports Windows Server 2003. When we are aware of a potential conflict or compatibility issue, we say so.

We also want to thank our contacts at the hardware companies, who provided technical help, evaluation units, and other assistance. There are far too many to list individually, but they know who they are. We also want to thank the readers of our web sites and messageboards, many of whom took the time to offer useful suggestions for improvements to the book. Among them, Brian Bilbrey deserves to be singled out. Brian caught several truly egregious errors, and made many helpful suggestions and comments along the way. Thanks, folks. We couldn't have done it without you.

Finally, we want to thank our editor, Brian Jepson, who contributed numerous useful comments and suggestions.

We'd Like to Hear from You

We have tested and verified the information in this book to the best of our ability, but we don't doubt that some errors have crept in and remained hidden despite our best efforts and those of our editors and technical reviewers to find and eradicate them. Those errors are ours alone. If you find an error or have other comments about the book, you can contact the publisher or the authors.

How to contact O'Reilly

Please address comments and questions concerning this book to the publisher:

O'Reilly Media, Inc.
1005 Gravenstein Highway North
Sebastopol, CA 95472
(800) 998-9938 (in the United States or Canada)
(707) 829-0515 (international or local)
(707) 829-0104 (fax)

There is a web page for this book, which lists errata and other information. You can access this page at:

http://www.oreilly.com/catalog/buildpc/

To ask questions or to comment on the book, send email to:

bookquestions@oreilly.com

For more information about books, conferences, Resource Centers, and the O'Reilly Network, go to:

http://www.oreilly.com

How to contact the authors

To contact us directly, send mail to:

barbara@hardwareguys.com
robert@hardwareguys.com

We read all mail we receive from readers, but we cannot respond individually. If we did, we'd have no time to do anything else. But we do like to hear from readers.

There is also a web site for the book, which includes updated hardware recommendations, buying guides, and articles, as well as errata, archived older material, and so on:

http://www.hardwareguys.com

We also maintain a messageboard, where you can read and post messages about PC hardware topics. You can read messages as a guest, but if you want to post messages you must register as a member of the messageboard. We keep registration information confidential, and you can choose to have your mail address hidden on any messages you post.

http://forums.hardwareguys.com/

Finally, we each maintain a personal journal page, updated daily, which frequently includes references to new PC hardware we're working with, problems we've discovered, and other things we think are interesting. You can view these journal pages at:

Barbara: *http://www.fritchman.com/diaries/thisweek.html*
Robert: *http://www.ttgnet.com/thisweek.html*

Disclaimer

Much of the information contained in this book is based on personal knowledge and experience. While we believe that the information contained herein is correct, we accept no responsibility for its validity. The hardware designs and descriptive text contained herein are provided for educational purposes only. It is the responsibility of the reader to independently verify all information. Original manufacturer's data should be used at all times when implementing a design.

The authors, Robert Bruce Thompson and Barbara Fritchman Thompson, and O'Reilly Media, Inc., make no warranty, representation, or guarantee regarding the suitability of any hardware or software described herein for any particular purpose, nor do they assume any liability arising out of the application or use of any product, system, or software, and specifically disclaim any and all liability, including, without limitation, consequential or incidental damages. The hardware and software described herein are not designed, intended, nor authorized for use in any application intended to support or sustain life or any other application in which the failure of a system could create a situation in which personal injury, death, loss of data or information, or damages to property may occur. Should the reader implement any design described herein for any application, the reader shall indemnify and hold the authors, O'Reilly Media, Inc., and their respective shareholders, officers, employees, and distributors harmless against all claims, costs, damages and expenses, and reasonable solicitor fees arising out of, directly or indirectly, any claim of personal injury, death, loss of data or information, or damages to property associated with such unintended or unauthorized use.

Thank You

Thank you for buying *Building the Perfect PC*. We hope you enjoy reading it as much as we enjoyed writing it.

Fundamentals 1

The idea of building a PC for the first time intimidates a lot of people, but there's really nothing to worry about. Building a PC is no more technically challenging than changing the oil in your car or hooking up a VCR. Compared to assembling one of those "connect Tab A to Slot B" toys for your kids, it's a breeze.

PC components connect like building blocks. Component sizes, screw threads, mounting hole positions, cable connectors, and so on are standardized, so you needn't worry about whether something will fit. There are minor exceptions, of course—for example, some small cases accept only half-height or half-length expansion cards. And there are important details, certainly. You must verify, for example, that the motherboard you intend to use supports the processor you plan to use. But overall, there are few "gotchas" involved in building a PC. If you follow our advice in the project system chapters, everything will fit and everything will work together.

> Most compatibility issues arise when you mix new components with older ones. For example, an older video card may not fit the AGP slot in a new motherboard, or a new processor may not be compatible with an older motherboard. If you build a PC from all-new components, you are likely to encounter few such issues. Still, it's a good idea to verify compatibility between the motherboard and other major components, particularly AGP video adapters, processors, and memory. The configurations in this book have been tested for compatibility.

Nor do you need to worry much about damaging the PC, or it damaging you. Taking simple precautions such as grounding yourself before touching static-sensitive components and verifying cable connections before you apply power is sufficient to prevent damage to all those expensive parts you bought. Other than inside the power supply—which you should *never* open—the highest voltage used inside a modern PC is 12V, which presents no shock hazard.

This chapter doesn't cover the nuts-and-bolts details of assembling a PC, because that's covered exhaustively in text and images in the project system chapters. Instead, this chapter explains the fundamentals—everything you need to prepare yourself properly. It examines the advantages of building your own PC and explains how to design a PC that is perfect for your needs. It tells you what you need to know and do before you start the project, and lists the components, hand tools, and software tools you'll need to build your system. Because the motherboard is the heart of a PC, we include a "motherboard tour" section to illustrate each major part of the motherboard. Finally, because the best way to troubleshoot is to avoid problems in the first place, we include a detailed troubleshooting section.

Let's get started.

Why Build a PC?

With entry-level PCs selling for less than $500 and fully equipped mainstream PCs for $1,200, you might wonder why anyone would bother to build a PC. After all, you can't save any money building one, can you? Well actually, you can. In fact, there are many good reasons to build your own PC.

Lower cost

PC makers aren't in business for charitable reasons. They need to make a profit, so they need to sell computers for more than they pay for the components and the labor to assemble them. Significantly more, in fact, because they also need to support such expensive operations as research and development departments, toll-free support numbers, and so on.

But PC manufacturers get big price breaks because they buy components in huge volume, right? Not really. The market for PC components is extremely efficient, with razor-thin margins whether you buy one unit or 100,000. A volume purchaser gets a price break, certainly, but it's a lot smaller than most people think.

Mass-market PCs are inexpensive not because the makers get huge price breaks on quality components, but because they generally use the cheapest components possible. Cost-cutting is a fact of life in mass-market, consumer-grade PCs. If mass-market PC makers can save a few bucks on the case or the power supply, they do it every time, even though spending a few dollars more (or even a few cents more) would have allowed them to build a noticeably better system. If you compare apples to apples—a home-built system versus, say, an equivalent business-class IBM PC—you'll find you can build it yourself for less, sometimes a lot less. Our rule of thumb is that, on average and all other things being equal, you can build a midrange PC yourself for about 75% to 85% of what a major manufacturer charges for an equivalent top-quality system.

Cheaper by the Dozen?

As an example, when Intel announces price reductions or a faster new version of the Pentium 4, the news stories often report "Quantity 1000" pricing for the OEM or "tray" versions. This is what a computer maker who buys processors 1,000 at a time pays; a maker who buys 100,000 at a time may pay a few dollars less. If you buy just one OEM processor, you'll typically pay a couple bucks more than the Quantity 1000 pricing. But you may end up paying even less, because PC makers often order more processors than they need to take advantage of price breaks on larger quantities, and then sell the unneeded processors at a slight loss to distributors who then sell them to retailers.

More choice

When you buy a PC, you get a cookie-cutter computer. You can choose such options as a larger hard drive, more memory, or a better monitor, but basically you get what the vendor decides to give you. If you want something that few people ask for, like a better power supply or quieter cooling fans or a motherboard with more features, you're out of luck. Those aren't options.

And what you do get is a matter of chance. High-volume direct vendors like Gateway and Dell often use multiple sources for components. Two supposedly identical systems ordered on the same day may contain significantly different components, including such important variations as different motherboards or monitors with the same model number but made by different manufacturers. When you build a PC, you decide exactly what goes into it.

Flexible design

One of the best things about building your own PC is that you can optimize its design to focus on what is important to you and ignore what isn't. An off-the-shelf commercial PC is by nature a jack of all trades and master of none. System vendors have to strike a happy medium that is adequate, if not optimum, for the mythical "average" user.

Want a small, quiet PC for your home theater system? There are three options. You can use a standard PC despite its large size and high noise level; you can pay big bucks for a system from a specialty builder that does just what you want; or you can build your own. Need a system with a ton of redundant hard disk storage for editing video or a professional audio workstation? Good luck finding a commercial system that fits your requirements, at least at a reasonable price. When you build your own PC, you spend your money on things that matter to you, and ignore the things that don't.

Better component quality

Most computer vendors cut costs by using cheaper OEM versions of popular components if they're "visible" and no-name components if they're not. By "visible" we mean a component that people might seek out by brand name even in a prebuilt PC, such as an ATi or *n*VIDIA video adapter. Invisible components are ones that buyers seldom ask about or notice, such as motherboards, optical and hard drives, power supplies, and so on.

OEM components may be identical to retail models, differing only in packaging. But even if the parts are the same, there are often significant differences. Component vendors usually do not support OEM versions directly, for example, instead referring you to the system vendor. If that system vendor goes out of business, you're out of luck, because the component maker provides no warranty to end users. Even if the maker

Don't Compare Apples to Oranges

For more than 20 years, Robert's friend Jerry Pournelle has written the Chaos Manor column for BYTE. One month, Jerry decided to build an inexpensive PC as a project system for his column. He wanted to see if he could match the price of a mass-market system he'd seen advertised in the morning paper. So Jerry headed off to Fry's and returned to Chaos Manor with a stack of components.

Shortly afterward, Robert got a phone call from Jerry. Jerry said he'd spent $50 more on components than the mass-market PC would have cost him, "and that doesn't even count the time it'll take me to assemble it." That didn't sound right, so Robert started asking questions. The processor speed, amount of memory, and hard drive size were the same, so Robert started drilling down.

Robert: "What kind of case and power supply did you buy, and how much did they cost you?"

Jerry: "It's an Antec with a 350W power supply. I paid about $70 for it."

Robert: "Was that the cheapest case and power supply Fry's had?"

Jerry: "Well, no. They had a no-name case with a 300W power supply for $14, but I sure wouldn't use something that cheap for any of my systems."

Robert: "How about the motherboard?"

Jerry: "I got an ASUS Athlon XP motherboard for $130. They didn't have that $90 ASUS motherboard you recommended. They had an ECS motherboard for $38, but there was no way I was going to use that."

And so on. Jerry did what most of us would do and what any sensible person would do. He built his "inexpensive" PC using the least expensive high-quality components he could find. But he then compared that top-notch inexpensive system against a mass-market system that was built around the cheapest components available. Would the manufacturer of the mass-market system have used a $14 case and power supply and a $38 motherboard? In a heartbeat.

Jerry couldn't bring himself to take the cost-cutting measures that mass-market PC makers take without a second thought, so he ended up comparing apples to oranges. Jerry spent about $150 more on just the case, power supply, and motherboard, and ended up with a system that cost only $50 more than the piece of junk being advertised in the morning paper. If instead he'd compared the cost of his system against a system of equivalent quality, such as an entry-level IBM business-class system, he might have been surprised at just how much he saved.

does support OEM products, the warranty is usually much shorter on OEM parts, often as little as 30 to 90 days. The products themselves may also differ significantly between OEM and retail-boxed versions. Major PC vendors often use downgraded versions of popular products, for example, an OEM video adapter that has the same or a very similar name as the retail-boxed product but that runs at a lower clock rate. This allows PC makers to pay less for components and still gain the cachet from using the name-brand product.

It's worse when it comes to "invisible" components. We've popped the lid on scores of consumer-grade PCs over the years, and it never ceases to surprise us just how cheaply they're built. Not a one of them had a power supply that we'd even consider using in one of our own systems, for example. They're packed with no-name motherboards, generic memory, the cheapest optical drives available, and so on. Even the cables are often shoddy. After all, why pay a buck more for a decent cable? In terms of reliability, we consider a consumer-grade PC a disaster waiting to happen.

No bundled software

Most purchased PCs include Microsoft Windows, Microsoft Office, or other bundled software. If you don't need or want this software, building a PC allows you to avoid paying the "Microsoft tax."

If you *do* want commercial software, you can buy OEM versions at a bargain price when you buy your hardware components. Buying a hard drive or a motherboard entitles you to buy full OEM versions of the software you need at a large discount. OEM software includes a full license rather than an upgrade license, so you needn't own the product already to benefit from OEM software pricing. OEM software is one of the best-kept secrets in the retail channel. If you need Windows or Office, ask your vendor if they have OEM versions of the titles you want when you order components. OEM versions of Windows and Microsoft applications are "For sale only with a new PC," but Microsoft takes a liberal view of what constitutes a new PC. Buying a hard drive, motherboard, or processor entitles you to buy OEM software.

Warranty

The retail-boxed components you'll use to build your own PC include full manufacturer warranties that may run from one to five years or more, depending on the component. PC makers use OEM components, which often include no manufacturer warranty to the end user; if something breaks, you're at the mercy of the PC maker to repair or replace it. We've heard from readers who bought PCs from makers who went out of business shortly thereafter. When a hard drive or video card failed six months later, they contacted the maker of the item, only to find that they had OEM components that were not under manufacturer warranty.

Not all commercial PCs are poorly built. Most "business-class" systems from IBM and other high-end vendors are well engineered with top-quality components and high build quality. Of course, a business-class system costs a lot more than a consumer-grade system.

OEM Software Pricing

OEM software prices are striking. For example, when we priced motherboards for a new system in mid-2004, we could have bought full OEM versions of Windows XP Home for $82, Windows XP Pro for $133, Office Basic 2003 for $145, or Office Pro 2003 for $220 with the purchase of the motherboard. Full OEM versions generally sell for about two-thirds the price of retail upgrade-only versions and for less than half the price of retail full versions, so if you need the software this is a cheap way to get it. Of course, Microsoft doesn't support OEM versions, which is the main reason for the low price.

Keep receipts together with the "retain this portion" of warranty cards, and put them someplace they can be found if required for future warranty service. This goes for software, too.

Experience

If you buy a computer, your experience with it consists of taking it out of the box and connecting the cables. If you build a computer, you know exactly what went into it, and you're in a much better position to resolve any problems that may occur.

Upgradability

If you design and build your own PC, you can upgrade it later using industry-standard components. That's sometimes not the case with commercial systems, some of which are intentionally designed to be incompatible with industry-standard components. PC makers do this because they want to force you to buy upgrade and replacement components from them, at whatever price they want to charge.

WARNING

These designed-in incompatibilities may be as trivial as nonstandard screw sizes, or as profound as components that are electrically incompatible with standard components. For example, some Dell PCs use motherboards and power supplies with standard connectors but nonstandard pin connections. If you replace a failed Dell power supply with a standard ATX power supply—or if you connect the nonstandard Dell power supply to a standard motherboard—both the power supply and motherboard will be destroyed the moment you apply power to the system.

Designing the Perfect PC

DESIGN PRIORITIES	
Price	☆☆☆☆☆
Reliability	☆☆☆☆☆
Size	☆☆☆☆☆
Noise level	☆☆☆☆☆
Expandability	☆☆☆☆☆
Processor performance	☆☆☆☆☆
Video performance	☆☆☆☆☆
Disk capacity/performance	☆☆☆☆☆

A sign you'll see in many repair shops says, "Good. Cheap. Fast. Pick any two." That's also true of designing a PC. Every choice you make involves a tradeoff, and balancing those tradeoffs is the key to designing a PC that's perfect for your needs. Each of the project system chapters has a graphic that represents the relative importance of different elements and looks something like what's shown to the left.

Ah, if it were only true. Reality, of course, is different. One can't put the highest priority on everything. Something has to give. As Frederick the Great said of designing military defenses, "He who defends everything defends nothing." The same is true of designing a PC.

If you focus on these elements while designing your PC, you'll soon realize that compromises are inevitable. If small size is essential, for example, you must make compromises in expandability, and you may very well have to compromise in other respects. The trick is to decide, *before* you start buying components, which elements are essential, which are important, which would be nice to have, and which can be ignored.

Once you have the priority of those elements firmly fixed in your mind, you can make rational resource allocations and good purchasing decisions. It's worth looking at each of these elements in a bit more detail.

Price

> We put price first, because it's the 900-pound gorilla in system design. If low price is essential, you'll be forced to make compromises in most or all of the other elements. Simply put, high performance, reliability, low noise, small size, and other desirable characteristics cost money. We suggest you begin by establishing a ballpark price range for your new system and then play "what-if" with the other elements. If you've set too low a price, it will soon become clear that you'll need to spend more. On the other hand, you may find that you can get away with spending less and still get everything you want in a system.

Reliability

> We consider high reliability essential in any system, even the least expensive entry-level PC. If a system is unreliable, it doesn't matter how feature-laden it is, or how fast, or how cheap. We always aim for 5-star reliability in systems we design for ourselves and others, although sometimes price and other constraints force us to settle for 4-star reliability. The best mass-market systems may have 3-star reliability, but most deserve only a 1- or 2-star rating.

> What does reliability mean, and how do you design for it? A reliable system doesn't crash or corrupt data. It runs for years with only an occasional cleaning. We are always amused when people claim that Windows is crash-prone. That is true of Windows 9X, of course, but Windows NT/2000/XP has never blue-screened on us except when there was a hardware problem, and that's going back to the early days of Windows NT 4. We're not Microsoft fans—far from it—but the truth is that the vast majority of system crashes that are blamed on Windows are actually caused by marginal or failing hardware. (We just checked the uptime of our Windows NT 4 Server box, which has been running for 322 days without a reboot.)

> There are a few simple rules for designing a reliable system. First, use only top-quality parts. They don't have to be the fastest available—in fact, high-performance parts often run hotter and are therefore less reliable than midrange ones—but top-quality components may be a full order of magnitude more reliable than run-of-the-mill ones. Use a motherboard built around a reliable chipset and made by a top-notch manufacturer; Intel motherboards and chipsets are the standard by which we judge. Use a first-rate power supply and the best memory

Determining Quality

Of course, this raises the question: how does one tell great from good from bad? Discriminating among companies and brands is difficult for someone who doesn't know which companies have an established reputation for quality and reliability, which ones purvey mostly junk, and which ones are too new to have a track record. All of the components and brands we recommend in this book are safe choices, but the proliferation of brands makes it easy to choose inferior components.

If you must use components other than those we recommend, the best way to avoid inferior products is to do your homework. Visit the manufacturers' web sites, check online reviews of products you are considering, and visit discussion forums for the components in question. In the end, trust your own judgment. If a component appears cheap, it probably isn't reliable. If the documentation is sparse or isn't well written, that tells you something about the likely quality of the component as well. If the component has a much shorter warranty than similar components from other manufacturers, there's probably good reason.

Finally, although price is not invariably a perfect predictor of component quality, it's usually a very good indicator. The PC component business is extremely competitive, so if a product sells for much less than similar competing products, it's almost certain to be inferior.

available. Avoid cheap cables. Keep the system cool and be sure to clean out the dust periodically. That's all there is to it. Following this advice means the system will cost a bit more, but it will also be significantly more reliable.

Size

Most people prefer a small PC to a large one, but it's easy to design a system that's *too* small. Albert Einstein said, "Everything should be made as simple as possible, but not simpler." In other words, don't oversimplify. Use the same rule when you choose a size for your PC. Don't over-smallify.

Choosing a small case inevitably forces you to make compromises. A small case limits your choice of components, because some components simply won't fit. It also limits the number of components you can install. For example, you may have to choose between installing a floppy drive and installing a second hard drive. Because a small case can accept fewer (and smaller) fans, it's more difficult to cool the system properly. To move the same amount of air, a smaller fan must spin faster than a larger fan, which generates more noise. The limited volume of the case makes it much harder to work inside it, and makes it more difficult to route cables to avoid impeding airflow. All other things being equal, a small PC will cost more, run slower, produce more heat and noise, and/or be less reliable than a standard-size PC.

For most purposes, the best choice is a standard mini- or mid-tower case. A full-tower case is an excellent choice for a server, or for an office system that sits on the floor next to your desk. Choose a microATX or other small form factor case only if small size is a high priority.

Noise level

Noise level has become a major issue for many people. If you think PCs are getting louder, it's not your imagination. As PCs get faster and faster, they consume more power and produce more heat. The most convenient way to remove heat is to move a lot of air through the case, which requires fans. Fans produce noise.

Just a few years ago, most PCs had only a power supply fan. A typical modern PC may have half a dozen or more fans—the power supply fan, the CPU fan, a couple of supplemental case fans, and perhaps fans for the chipset, video card, and hard drive. All of these fans are needed to keep the components cool, but all of them produce noise. Fortunately, there are methods to cool a PC properly while minimizing noise. We'll look at some of those methods later in this section.

Expandability

Expandability is worth considering when you design a PC. For some systems, expandability is unimportant. You design the system for a particular job, install the components you need to do that job, and never open the case again except for routine cleaning and maintenance. For most general-purpose systems, though, expandability is desirable. For example, if you need more disk space, you might prefer to add a second hard drive rather than replace the original drive. You can't do that unless there's a vacant drive bay. Similarly, embedded video might suffice originally, but you may later decide that you need faster video. If the motherboard you used has no AGP slot, you're out of luck. The only option is to replace the motherboard.

Keep expandability in mind when you choose components so that you don't paint yourself into any corners. Unless size constraints forbid it, choose a case that leaves plenty of room for growth. Choose a power supply that has sufficient reserve to support additional drives, memory, and perhaps a faster processor. Choose a motherboard that provides sufficient expansion slots and memory sockets to allow for possible future expansion. Don't choose less flexible components unless you are certain that you will never need to expand the system.

Processor performance

Most people worry too much about processor performance. Here's the truth. Midrange processors—those that sell for $150 to $225—are noticeably faster than $50 to $100 entry-level processors. The most expensive processors, which sell for up to $1,000, are noticeably faster than midrange processors. Not night-and-day different, but noticeable. For casual use—browsing the Web, checking email, word processing, and so on—a $75 AMD Athlon XP is perfectly adequate. For a general-purpose system, the best choice is a Pentium 4, Athlon XP, or Athlon 64 processor that sells for $150 to $225 in retail-boxed form. It makes little sense to choose a high-end processor unless cost is no object and performance is critical.

Video performance

Video performance, like processor performance, usually gets more attention than it deserves. It's probably no coincidence that processors and video adapters are two of the most heavily promoted PC components. When you design your PC, be careful not to get caught up in the hype. If the PC will be used for intense 3D gaming or similarly demanding video tasks, you need a high-end video adapter. Otherwise, you don't.

Embedded video—a video adapter built into the motherboard—is the least expensive video solution, and is perfectly adequate for most uses. The incremental cost of embedded video ranges from $0 to perhaps $10, relative to a similar motherboard without embedded video. The next step up in video performance is a standalone AGP video adapter, which requires that the motherboard have an AGP slot to accept it. Standalone AGP adapters range in price from $25 or so up to $500 or more. The old 80/20 rule applies to AGP adapters, which is to say that a $100 AGP adapter provides most of the performance and features of a $500 adapter.

More expensive AGP adapters provide incrementally faster 3D video performance and may support more recent versions of Microsoft DirectX; both of these characteristics are of interest to serious gamers. Expensive AGP adapters also run hot and are generally equipped with dedicated cooling fans, which produce additional noise. Some fast AGP adapters, particularly *n*VIDIA models, trade off lower 2D display quality for faster 3D performance.

When you design your PC, we recommend using embedded video unless you need the faster 3D performance provided by an AGP video adapter. If you choose embedded video, make sure the motherboard has an AGP slot available in case you later decide to upgrade the video.

Disk capacity/performance

A mainstream 7,200 RPM ATA or Serial ATA hard drive is the best choice for nearly any system. Such drives are fast, cheap, and reliable. The best models are also relatively quiet and produce little heat. When you design your system, use one of these drives (or two, mirrored for data protection) unless you have good reason to do otherwise. Choose a 15,000 RPM SCSI drive if you need the highest possible disk performance—as for a server or personal workstation—and are willing to pay the price. Avoid 5,400 RPM ATA drives, which cost a few bucks less than 7,200 RPM models but have noticeably poorer performance.

See Chapter 2 for specific component recommendations.

Balanced design

Novice PC builders often ignore the important concept of balanced design. Balanced design means allocating your component budget to avoid bottlenecks. If you're designing a gaming PC, for example, it makes no sense to spend $50 on the processor and $500 on the video card. The resulting system is non-optimal because the slow processor is a bottleneck that prevents the expensive video adapter from performing to its full potential.

The main enemy of balanced design is the constant hype of manufacturer advertising and enthusiast web sites (which sometimes amount to the same thing). It's easy to fixate on the latest "must-have" component, even if its price is much too high to justify. Many people just can't help themselves. Despite their best intentions, they end up spending $250 on the latest super DVD burner when a $100 burner would have done just as well, or they buy a $300 video adapter when a $125 adapter would suffice. If your budget is unlimited, fine. Go for the latest and best. But if you're building a system on a fixed budget, every dollar you spend needlessly on one component is a dollar less you have to spend somewhere else, where it might make more difference.

Balanced design does not necessarily mean giving equal priority to all system components. For example, we have built servers in which the disk arrays and tape backup drive cost more than $10,000 and the rest of the system components totaled less than $2,000. A balanced design is one that takes into account the tasks the system must perform and allocates resources to optimize performance for those tasks.

But balanced design takes into consideration more than simple performance. A truly balanced design accommodates non-performance issues such as physical size, noise level, reliability, and efficient cooling. You might, for example, have to choose a less expensive processor or a smaller hard drive in order to reserve sufficient funds for a quieter case or a more reliable power supply.

The key to achieving a balanced design is to determine your requirements, look dispassionately at the available alternatives, and choose accordingly. That can be tougher than it sounds.

Designing a quiet PC

The ongoing PC performance race has had the unfortunate side effect of making PCs noisier. Faster processors use more power, which in turn requires larger (and noisier) power supplies. Faster processors also produce more heat, which requires larger (and noisier) CPU coolers. Modern hard drives spin faster than older models, producing still more noise and heat. Fast video adapters have their own cooling fans, which add to the din. The days when a high-performance PC sat under your desk making an unobtrusive hum are long gone.

Fortunately, there are steps you can take to reduce the amount of noise your PC produces. No PC with moving parts is completely silent, but significant noise reductions are possible. Depending on your requirements and budget, you can build a PC that is anything from quietly unobtrusive to nearly silent. The key to building a noise-reduced PC is to recognize the sources of noise and to minimize or eliminate that noise at the source.

The major sources of noise are typically the power supply, the CPU cooler fan, and supplementary case fans. Minor sources of noise include the hard drive, the chipset fan, the video adapter fan, and the optical drive. As you design your PC, focus first on major noise sources that can be minimized inexpensively, then on minor noise sources that are cheap to deal with, then on major noise sources that are more expensive or difficult to minimize, and finally (if necessary) on minor noise sources that are expensive or difficult to fix. Use the following guidelines:

Choose a quiet power supply

    In most systems, the power supply is the primary noise source, so minimizing power supply noise is critical.

Monitoring CPU Temperature

Most modern motherboards provide temperature sensors at important points such as the CPU socket. The motherboard reports the temperatures reported by these sensors to the BIOS. You can view these temperatures by running BIOS Setup and choosing the option for temperature reporting, which can usually be found under Advanced Hardware Monitoring, or a similar menu option. Alternatively, most motherboards include a monitoring utility—Intel's, for example, is called the Intel Active Monitor—that allows you to monitor temperatures from Windows rather than having to run BIOS Setup.

CPU temperature can vary dramatically with changes in load. For example, a CPU that idles at 30°C may reach 50°C or higher when it is running at 100% capacity. A hot-running modern processor such as a fast Prescott-core Pentium 4 may reach temperatures of 70°C or higher under load, which is perilously close to the maximum acceptable temperature for that processor. It is therefore very important to verify that your CPU cooler and system fans are doing their jobs properly.

An idle temperature of 30°C or lower is ideal, but that is not achievable with the hottest processors, which idle at 40°C or higher with any but the most efficient CPU coolers. In general, a CPU cooler that produces an idle temperature of 40°C or lower suffices to cool the CPU properly under load.

(continued)

- At the first level, you can choose a standard power supply that is quieter than the norm, such as the Antec TruePower (*http://www.antec-inc.com*) or the PC Power & Cooling Silencer (*http://www.pcpowercooling.com*), which we describe in the next chapter. Such power supplies cost little or no more than equivalent competing models, and are considerably quieter. A system that uses one of these power supplies can be quiet enough to be unobtrusive in a normal residential environment.

- The next step is a power supply that is specifically designed to minimize noise, such as those made by Nexus (*http://www.nexustek.nl*) and Zalman (*http://www.zalmanusa.com*). These power supplies cost a bit more than comparable standard power supplies, but produce as little as 18 dB at idle and not much more under load. A system that uses one of these power supplies (and other similarly quiet components) can be nearly inaudible in a normal residential environment.

- Finally, there are completely silent power supplies, with no moving parts, that use huge passive heatsinks or convective water cooling to dissipate heat. We haven't used any of those, so we can't comment on them.

Choose a quiet CPU cooler

As processor speeds have increased over the last few years, manufacturers have gone from using passive heatsinks to using heatsinks with slow, quiet fans, and finally to using heatsinks with fast, loud fans. Current processors vary in power consumption from less than 30W to more than 100W, with proportionate differences in heat production. At the lower end of that range—30W to 50W—nearly any decent CPU cooler can do the job with minimal noise, including the stock CPU coolers bundled with retail-boxed processors or inexpensive third-party units like those made by Dynatron (*http://www.dynatron-corp.com*). In the middle of the range—50W to 80W—standard CPU coolers begin to produce intrusive noise levels, although specialty quiet CPU coolers can cool a midrange processor with little or no noise. At the upper end of the range, even the quietest fan-based CPU coolers produce noticeable noise.

- For a slow processor, try the stock heatsink/fan unit supplied with the retail-boxed processor. If it produces too much noise, install an inline resistor to reduce the voltage supplied to the fan, which reduces fan speed and noise. Such resistor kits are available from specialty quiet-PC vendors such as QuietPC USA (*http://www.quietpcusa.com*) and Endpcnoise.com (*http://www.endpcnoise.com*).

- For a midrange or fast processor, there are several alternatives. Some of the CPU coolers bundled with Intel Pentium 4 processors are reasonably quiet in stock form, and can be quieted further while still providing adequate cooling by using an inline resistor to drop the supply voltage to 7V. However, Intel uses different CPU cooler models and changes them without notice, so what you end up getting is hit or miss. For the quietest possible fan-based cooler, use the Thermalright SLK-900U/A (*http://www.thermalright.com*) for an Intel Celeron/Pentium 4 or AMD Athlon, or the Zalman CNPS7000A-Cu or CNPS7000A-AlCu for an Intel Celeron/ Pentium 4 or an AMD Athlon/Athlon 64.

- To minimize noise for any processor, install one of the Thermalright or Zalman units listed above. In particular, with slow and mid-range processors (up to the Northwood-core Pentium 4/2.8), Zalman "flower" coolers can be run in silent (fanless) mode, which completely eliminates CPU cooler noise.

WARNING

If you choose an aftermarket CPU cooler, verify that it is physically compatible with your motherboard. Quiet CPU coolers often use very large heatsinks, which may conflict with protruding capacitors and other motherboard components.

Choose quiet case fans

Most modern systems have at least one supplemental case fan, and some have several. The more loaded the system, the more supplemental cooling you'll need to use. Use the following guidelines when selecting case fans:

- Case fans are available in various sizes, from 60mm to 120mm or larger. All other things being equal, a larger fan can move the same amount of air with less noise than a smaller fan because the larger fan doesn't need to spin as fast. Of course, the fan mounting positions in most cases are of fixed size, so you may have little choice about which size fan(s) to use. If you do have a choice—for example if the case has two or three fan positions of different sizes—use the largest fan that fits.

- Case fans vary significantly in noise level, even for the same size and rotation speed. Many factors come into play, including blade design, type of bearings, grill type, and so on. In general, ball bearing fans are noisier but more durable than fans that use needle or sleeve bearings.

- The noise level of a fan can be reduced by running the fan at a lower speed, as long as it still moves enough air to provide proper cooling. The simplest method to reduce fan speed is to install an inline resistor to reduce the supply voltage to 7V. These are available from the sources listed above, or you can make your own with a resistor from Radio Shack or other electronics supply store.

Monitoring CPU Temperature (continued)

If you want to verify temperature under load, run an application that loads the CPU with intense calculations, ideally with lots of floating-point operations. Two such applications we have used are the SETI@home client (*http://setiathome.ssl.berkeley.edu*) and the Mersenne Prime client (*http://mersenne.org*). Run the application for an hour to ensure that the CPU has reached a steady-state temperature, and then use the temperature monitoring application to view the temperature while the application is still running.

What Are dBs, Anyway?

Disclaimer: The following is a gross oversimplification, and we're sure we'll hear about it from people who know more about sound than we do. But here goes.

Sound is measured and specified in deciBels—a tenth of a Bel—which is abbreviated dB. (Some components specify Bels; multiply by 10 to get dB.) Because humans perceive identical sound levels at different frequencies as having different loudness, various weighting schemes are used. The most common, A-weighting, is abbreviated as dB(A). There are also dB(B) and dB(C) scales, but those are not commonly used.

A sound level of 0 dB is defined as the threshold of hearing, a sound level that is just barely perceptible in the absence of any other sound. Here are some reference points:

- 20 dB – A very quiet library or church; rural background noise at night; the quietest possible PC with moving parts

- 25 dB – A whispered conversation; a very quiet PC

- 30 dB – Suburban background noise at night; a quiet PC

- 40 dB – A quiet conversation; a standard PC

- 50 dB – Normal household noise; a normal conversation at 1 meter; a loud PC

- 60 dB – Office conversation; a loud gaming PC or server

(continued)

Some fans include a control panel, which mounts in an available external drive bay and allows you to control fan speed continuously from zero to maximum by adjusting a knob. Finally, some fans are designed to be controlled by the power supply or a motherboard fan connector. These fans vary their speed automatically in response to the ambient temperature, running at high speed when the system is heavily loaded and producing lots of heat, and at low speed when the system is idle.

- The mounting method you use makes a difference. Most case fans are secured directly to the chassis with metal screws. This transfers vibration directly to the chassis panels, which act as sounding boards. A better method is to use soft plastic snap-in connectors rather than screws. These connectors isolate vibration to the fan itself. Better still is to use the soft plastic snap-in connectors in conjunction with a foam surround that insulates the fan frame from the chassis entirely.

The preceding three steps are the main issues to address in quietizing your PC. Once you minimize noise from those major sources, you can also take the following steps to reduce noise from minor sources. Some of these steps cost little or nothing to implement, and all contribute to quieting the PC.

Put the PC on a mat

Rather than putting the PC directly on your desk or the floor, put a sound-deadening mat between the PC and the surface. You can buy special mats for this purpose, but we've used objects as simple as a couple of mouse pads, front and rear, to accomplish the same thing. The amount of noise reduction from this simple step can be surprisingly large.

Choose a quiet hard drive

Once you've addressed the major noise sources, hard drive noise may become more noticeable, particularly during seeks. The best way to reduce hard drive noise is to choose a quiet hard drive in the first place. Seagate Barracuda ATA and S-ATA models are the quietest mainstream hard drives available. To reduce hard drive noise further you can use a Smart Drive Enclosure or the Zalman Hard Drive Heatpipe, both of which are available from the sources listed above.

Choose a video card with a passive heatsink

All video adapter chipsets produce significant heat, but most use a passive heatsink rather than a fan-based cooler. If possible, choose a video adapter with a passive heatsink. If you must use a high-end video adapter with a fan-based cooler, consider replacing that cooler with a Zalman Video Heatpipe. The small fans used on video adapters typically run at high speed and are quite noisy, so replacing the fan with a passive device can reduce noise noticeably.

Choose a motherboard with a passive heatsink

The northbridge chip of modern chipsets dissipates significant heat. Most motherboards cool this chip with a large passive heatsink (see Figure 1-5 for an example), but some use a fan-based cooler. Again, these coolers typically use small, fast fans that produce significant noise. If you have a choice, pick a motherboard with a passive heatsink. If you must use a motherboard with a fan-based chipset cooler, consider replacing that cooler with a Zalman Motherboard Heatsink.

Use an aluminum case

Aluminum conducts heat better than steel, so using an aluminum case makes it easier to cool a system effectively. This has no direct impact on noise level, but it does allow you to use smaller, quieter fans than what you would need with a steel case. In effect, the aluminum case itself becomes a giant heatsink, radiating heat directly. Aluminum cases typically cost more than steel cases and their additional cooling efficiency is relatively minor, so this is probably the last step you should take in designing a quiet mainstream PC.

Silent PC Review (*http://www.silentpcreview.com*) is an excellent source of information about quiet PC issues. The site includes numerous articles about reducing PC noise, as well as reviews of quiet PC components, a forum, and other resources.

Designing a small PC

At the beginning of the millennium, some forward-thinking PC builders and manufacturers began to design and build PCs that were smaller and/or more portable than traditional mini-tower systems. Small PCs have become extremely popular, and it's no wonder. These systems are small, light, easily portable, and fit just about anywhere. In order of decreasing size, small/portable PCs fall into four broad categories:

LAN Party PC

A LAN Party PC is essentially a standard ATX mini- or mid-tower system with a handle and other modifications to increase portability, port accessibility, and other factors important in a "totable" PC. Most LAN Party cases are constructed largely of aluminum to minimize weight and maximize cooling efficiency. LAN Party PCs are often "tricked-out" with colorful motherboards, clear side panels, fluorescent lights, fans, and cables, and other visual enhancements. Despite the customizations, LAN Party PCs are based on industry-standard components and are as capable as any standard PC. Chapter 5 describes the issues involved in designing and building such a system.

What Are dBs, Anyway? *(continued)*

The dB scale is logarithmic, which means that an increase of about 3 dB doubles sound level. For example, if a power supply produces 30 dB and a CPU fan also produces 30 dB, running both at the same time doubles sound level to 33 dB (not 60 dB). Doubling the sound level again by running four 30 dB devices simultaneously increases the sound level by 3 dB again, to 36 dB. Running eight such devices doubles the sound level to 39 dB, sixteen takes it to 42 dB, and so on.

However, because of the way humans perceive sound, a 1 dB difference is barely perceptible, a 3 dB difference is noticeable, and a sound must be about 10 dB louder to be perceived as "twice as loud." For example, if one computer produces 40 dB and another 30 dB, the first computer actually produces more than eight times the sound level of the second, but to human ears it "sounds" only twice as loud.

PC components differ dramatically in sound levels. For example, a very quiet hard drive might produce 25 dB, while another model may produce 30 dB or more. At idle, a standard 400W power supply might produce 40 dB, a quieter model 30 dB (half as loud), and a specialty quiet model only 20 dB (half as loud again). The same differences exist among other noise-producing components, such as CPU coolers, supplemental case fans, optical drives, and so on. Merely by choosing the quietest standard PC components rather than noisier alternatives, you can reduce the noise level of your PC noticeably.

microATX PC

A microATX PC is basically a cut-down version of a standard ATX PC. The microATX case and motherboard are smaller and provide less expandability, but are otherwise comparable in features and functionality to a standard ATX system. The great advantage of microATX PCs relative to the smaller styles described below is that microATX PCs use industry-standard components. microATX cases are available in two styles. Slimline cases are about the size and shape of a VCR. "Cube" cases are typically 8" tall and roughly a foot wide and deep. The relatively small case capacity makes cooling more difficult and puts some restraints on the number and type of hard drives, expansion cards, and other peripherals you can install, but it is possible to build a reliable, high-performance PC in the microATX form factor.

Small Form Factor (SFF) PC

Small Form Factor (SFF) means different things to different people. We use the term here to mean the cube-style form factor pioneered by Shuttle (*http://us.shuttle.com*) with their XPC models. (In fact, Shuttle says that SFF stands for *Shuttle Form Factor.*) Other companies, including Soltek, Biostar, and others, now produce cube-style SFF systems as well. These true SFF systems use proprietary cases, power supplies, I/O templates, and motherboards, which limits their flexibility. In effect, "building" an SFF system consists of buying a "barebones" system with case, power supply, and motherboard, and adding your choice of memory, drives, video adapter, and so on. SFF PCs are typically more expensive, slower, and less reliable than standard size or microATX PCs, but they are noticeably smaller.

The limited space available in cube-style SFF cases restricts component choice. For example, you may have to purchase special low-profile memory modules, and you may not be able to install full-length, standard-height expansion cards. The tiny case volume also makes heat dissipation critical. For example, you may not be able to use the fastest available processors because the case is not capable of cooling them sufficiently.

Mini-ITX PC

Mini-ITX is a semi-proprietary form factor pioneered by VIA Technologies. Although a few minor third-party manufacturers supply Mini-ITX components, VIA products dominate the Mini-ITX market. Mini-ITX motherboards are 170mm (6.7") square, and are in effect smaller versions of microATX motherboards. Although Mini-ITX motherboards are available that accept Socket 370 Pentium III and even Socket 478 Pentium 4 processors, the majority of Mini-ITX systems use VIA motherboards with embedded processors. These processors are very slow relative to modern AMD and Intel processors, and Mini-ITX motherboards are relatively expensive. Even so, Mini-ITX has its place, for systems that do not require high performance but that need to be small and very quiet. Mini-ITX motherboards are so small that they can be built into enclosures as small as a cigar box (literally!), and the flip side to low processor performance is that these processors consume little power and produce little heat. Most Mini-ITX systems use passive cooling and "wall-wart" power supplies, which eliminates fan noise and allows the system to be almost totally silent. Mini-ITX is most appropriate for such "appliance" applications as small Linux servers, routers, and satellite DVR playback-only systems.

Table 1-1 lists the characteristics of each of these system types relative to a standard mini/mid-tower desktop system, using the rankings of Excellent (E), Very Good (VG), Good (G), Fair (F), and Poor (P).

Table 1-1. Small system strengths and weaknesses

	Desktop	LAN Party	microATX	SFF	Mini-ITX
Typical case volume (liters)	35 to 60	25 to 40	12 to 20	8 to 12	2.5 to 9
Size	P to F	F to G	G to VG	VG to E	E
Cost efficiency	E	VG	E	P to F	P to F
Reliability	E	F to VG	VG to E	F to VG	F to VG
Portability	P	VG to E	F to VG	VG to E	VG to E
Noise level	VG to E	F to VG	VG to E	P to VG	E
Cooling	E	G to E	G to VG	P to F	F to E
Upgradability/expandability	E	VG to E	F to VG	F to G	P
Processor performance	E	E	VG to E	VG to E	P
Graphics performance	E	E	VG to E	F to E	P
Disk capacity/performance	E	E	G to VG	G to VG	P

Table 1-1 presents best-case scenarios for each of the form factors. For example, not all standard desktop systems have excellent performance, nor are all of them extremely quiet. Rather, this table presents the best that can be done within the limitations of each form factor, which may vary according to the specific components you select.

If you need to design a small PC, recognize that each step down from standard mini-tower size involves additional compromises in performance, cost, reliability, noise level, and other key criteria. Reducing case size limits the number and type of components you can install and makes it more difficult to cool the system effectively. It also makes it harder to quiet the PC. For example, small cases often use relatively loud power supplies, and because the power supply is proprietary, installing an aftermarket quiet power supply is not an option. Similarly, using a small case forces you to trade off performance against cooling against noise. For example, you may be forced to use a slower processor than you'd like because the necessary

CPU cooler for a faster processor is too large to fit in the available space or is louder than acceptable.

When it comes to designing small PCs, our rule is to use a standard mini-tower system whenever possible. If that's too large, step down to a micro-ATX system. And if that's too large, we suggest you rethink your priorities. Perhaps you could free some additional space by moving things around, or perhaps you could place the PC in a different position. Try hard to avoid using any form factor smaller than microATX.

Then—if and only if you are certain that the tradeoffs are worth it—buy a barebones SFF system and build it out to meet your requirements. We don't think of Mini-ITX systems as direct competitors to traditional PCs at all; they're simply too slow to be taken seriously as a mainstream PC. Instead, we suggest you consider Mini-ITX systems to be special, relatively expensive, low-performance computing appliances that are suitable only for very specialized applications.

Things to Know and Do Before You Start

We've built many systems over the years, and we've learned a lot of lessons the hard way. Here are some things to keep in mind as you begin your project.

Make sure you have everything you need before you start

Have all of the hardware, software, and tools you'll need lined up and waiting. You don't want to have to stop in mid-build to go off in search of a small Phillips screwdriver or to drive to the store to buy a cable. If your luck is anything like ours, you won't find the screwdriver you need and the store will be closed. In addition to tools and components, make sure you have the distribution CDs for the operating system, service packs, device drivers, diagnostics utilities, and any other software you'll need to complete the build.

RTFM

Read the fine manuals, if only the Quick Start sections. Surprisingly, while system manuals are notoriously awful, many component manuals are actually quite good. You'll find all sorts of hints and tips, from the best way to install the component to suggestions on optimizing its performance.

Okay, we admit it. We almost never read the manuals, but we can just about build a system blindfolded. Until you're proficient, reading the manuals before you proceed is the best way to guarantee that your new PC will, um, work.

Don't assume that every box contains what it's supposed to. Before you begin the build, open each box and verify its contents against the packing list. Quite often, we open a new component box only to find that the driver CD, manual, cable, or some other small component that should have been included is missing. On one memorable occasion, we opened a new, shrink-wrapped video adapter box only to find that everything was present except the video adapter itself!

Download the latest drivers

Although PC component inventories turn over quickly, the CDs included with components usually don't contain the most recent drivers. Some manufacturers don't update their driver CDs very often, so the bundled drivers may be a year or more out of date, even if the component itself was made recently. Before you begin building a PC, visit the web site for each of your components and download the most recent driver and BIOS updates. Unpack or unzip them if necessary, burn them to CD, and label the CD. You may choose to install drivers from the bundled CD—in fact, at times it's necessary to do so because the downloadable updates do not include everything that's on the CD—but you want to have those later drivers available so that you can update your system immediately.

Ground yourself before touching components

Processors, memory modules, and other electronic components—including the circuit boards in drives—are sensitive to static shock. Static electricity can damage components even if the voltage is too low for you to see or feel a static spark. The best way to avoid static damage to components is to get in the habit of grounding yourself before you touch any sensitive component. You can buy special anti-static wrist straps and similar devices, but they're really not necessary. All you need to do is touch a metal object like the chassis or power supply before you handle components.

Keep track of the screws and other small parts

Building a PC yields an incredible number of small pieces that need to be kept organized. As you open each component box, your pile of screws, cables, mounting brackets, adapters, and other small parts grows larger. Some of these things you'll need, and some you won't. As we can attest, one errant screw left on the floor can destroy a vacuum cleaner. Worse, one unnoticed screw in the wrong place can short out and destroy the motherboard and other components. The best solution we've found is to use an egg carton or ice cube tray to keep parts organized. The goal is to have all of the small parts accounted for when you finish assembling the PC.

WARNING

Some PCs use a variety of screws that look very similar but are in fact threaded differently. For example, the screws used to secure some case covers and those used to mount some disk drives may appear to be identical, but swapping them may result in stripped threads. If in doubt, keep each type of screw in a separate compartment of your organizer.

While you're at it, download all of the documentation you can find for each component. Quite often, the detailed documentation intended for system builders is not included in the component box. The only way to get it is to download it.

Static Guard

To minimize problems with static, wear wool or cotton clothing and avoid rubber-soled shoes. Static problems increase when the air is dry, as is common in winter when central heating systems are in use. You can reduce or eliminate static with a spray bottle filled with water to which you've added a few drops of dishwashing liquid. Thoroughly spritz your work area immediately before you begin working. The goal is not to get anything wet, but simply to increase the humidity of the air. (Whatever you do, avoid wetting the case or components themselves, especially the connectors and slots, which must be kept clean and dry at all times.)

Use force when necessary, but use it cautiously

Many books tell you never to force anything, and that's good advice as far as it goes. If doing something requires excessive force, chances are a part is misaligned, you have not removed a screw, or there is some similar problem. But sometimes there is no alternative to applying force judiciously. For example, drive power cables sometimes fit so tightly that the only way to connect them is to grab them with pliers and press hard. (Make sure all the contacts are aligned first.) Some combinations of expansion card and slot fit so tightly that you must press very hard to seat the card. If you encounter such a situation, verify that everything is lined up and otherwise as it should be, and that there are no stray wires obstructing the slot. Then use whatever force it takes to do the job, which may be substantial.

Check and recheck before you apply power

An experienced PC technician building a PC does a quick scan of the new PC before performing the "smoke test" by applying power to the PC (if you don't see any smoke, it passes the test). Don't skip this step, and don't underestimate its importance. Most PCs that fail the smoke test do so because this step was ignored. Until you gain experience, it may take several minutes to verify that all is as it should be—all components secure, all cables connected properly, no tools or other metal parts shorting anything out, and so on. Once you are comfortable working inside PCs, this step takes 15 seconds, but it may be the most important 15 seconds of the whole project.

After we build a system, we pick it up and shake it gently. If something rattles, we know there's a screw loose somewhere.

Start small for the first boot

The moment of greatest danger comes when you power up the PC for the first time. If the system fails catastrophically—which sometimes happens no matter how careful you are—don't smoke more than you have to. For example, the SOHO Server project system we built for this book uses four hard drives and two memory modules. When we built that system, we installed only one drive and one memory module initially. That way, if something shorted out when we first applied power, we'd destroy only one drive and memory module rather than all of them. For that reason, we suggest starting with a minimum configuration—motherboard, processor, one memory stick, video, and one hard drive. Once you're satisfied that all is well, you can add your optical and other drives, additional memory, expansion cards, and so on.

Don't let this warning put you off building a PC. If you choose good components, assemble them carefully, and double-check everything before you apply power, the probability of catastrophic failure is probably about the same as getting hit by lightning or winning the lottery.

Leave the cover off until you're sure everything works

Experts build and test the PC completely before putting the lid back on and connecting the external cables. Novices build the PC, reassemble the case, reconnect all the cables, and *then* test it.

The corollary to this rule is that you should *always* put the cover back on the case once everything is complete and tested. Some people believe that leaving the cover off improves cooling. Wrong. Cases do not depend on convection cooling, which is the only kind you get with the cover off. Cases are designed to direct cooling air across the major heat-generating components, processors and drives, but this engineering is useless if you run the PC uncovered. Replace the cover to avoid overheating components.

Another good reason to replace the cover is that running a system without the cover releases copious amounts of RF to the surrounding environment. An uncovered system can interfere with radios, monitors, televisions, and other electronic components over a wide radius.

Things You Need to Have

The following sections detail the items you should have on hand before you actually start building your new system. Make a checklist and make sure you check off each item before you begin. There are few things as frustrating as being forced to stop in mid-build when you belatedly realize you're missing a cable or other small component.

Components

Building a PC requires at least the following components. Have all of them available before you start to build the system. Open each component box and verify the contents against the packing list before you actually start the build.

Case and power supply, with power cord
Motherboard, with custom I/O template if needed
Processor
CPU cooler, with thermal compound or pad
Memory module(s)
Hard drive(s) and cable(s) (and S-ATA power adapter(s), if applicable)
Optical drive with data cable (and audio cable, if applicable)
Floppy drive and cable (if applicable)
Tape drive, cable, and tape cartridge (if applicable)
Card reader and cable (if applicable)

Good Advice for First-Time System Builders

Ron Morse, one of our technical reviewers, has been building PCs for 20 years. He makes the following suggestions for first-time system builders:

- Try to arrange a couple of hours when you can reasonably expect to be free of interruptions when building your first PC. It's a sequential process, and you need to keep track of what you have (and haven't) done.

- Building while this week's NASCAR crashfest or the Padres' latest losing effort plays on the TV isn't a good idea, either. While there's nothing difficult about building a PC, it does take a certain level of concentration. I like to play music, but not Mahler or the Squirrel Nut Zippers, both of which cause me to think too much about the music instead of what I'm doing.

- Most pro shops don't allow food or drink in the assembly area. It's a good rule for the home builder, too. In addition to the obvious concerns about spills and crumbs, condensation from the outside of a cold drink container can drip unnoticed into a sensitive area, and residue from "finger food" can cause problems by contaminating contacts or making small parts hard(er) to grasp and place.

- Pace yourself. Building a PC is amazingly simple...after it's finished. Getting there takes concentration and some physical dexterity. Plan to take short breaks at logical points during the build, then take them.

(21)

Video adapter, unless embedded
Sound adapter, unless embedded
Network adapter, unless embedded
Any other expansion cards (if applicable)
Supplementary case fan(s)
Keyboard, mouse, display, and other external peripherals
Screws, brackets, drive rails, and other connecting hardware

Hand tools and supplies

You really don't need many tools to build a PC. We built one PC using only our Swiss Army Knife, just to prove it could be done. Figure 1-1 shows

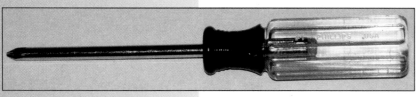

our basic PC building toolkit. Yep. It's true. You can build every PC in this book using only a #1 Phillips screwdriver. It's a bit small for the largest screws and a bit large for the smallest, but it works.

Figure 1-1. A basic PC toolkit

It's helpful to have more tools, of course. Needlenose pliers are useful for setting jumpers. A flashlight is often useful, even if your work area is well lit. A 5mm (or, rarely, 6mm) nut driver makes it faster to install the brass standoffs that support the motherboard. A larger assortment of screwdrivers can also be helpful.

Don't worry about using magnetized tools. Despite the common warnings about doing so, we've used magnetized screwdrivers for years without any problem. They are quite handy for picking up dropped screws and so on. Just use commonsense precautions, such as avoiding putting the magnetized tips near the flat surface of a hard drive or near any floppy disk, tape, or other magnetic media.

You may also find it useful to have some nylon cable ties (not the paper-covered wire twist ties) for dressing cables after you build the system. Canned air and a clean microfiber dustcloth are useful for cleaning components that you are migrating from an older system. A new eraser is helpful for cleaning contacts if you mistakenly grab an expansion card by the connector tab.

Software tools

In addition to hand tools, you should have the following software tools available when you build your system. Some are useful to actually build the system, others to diagnose problems. We keep copies of our standard software tools with our toolkit. That way, we have everything we need in one place. Here are the software tools we recommend:

Operating system distribution discs

OS distribution discs are needed when you build a system, and may also be needed later to update system software or install a peripheral. We always burn copies of the distribution discs to CD-R or DVD+R and keep a copy with our toolkit. If you use Windows or another non-free operating system, remember to record the initialization key, serial number, and other data you'll need to install the software. Use a felt-tip permanent marker to record this data directly onto the disc.

Service packs and critical updates

Rather than (or in addition to) updating Windows and Office online, download the latest service packs and critical updates and burn them to CD-R. In addition to giving you more control over the process, having these updates on CD-R means you can apply them even when the system has no Internet connection, such as when you're building it on your kitchen table.

WARNING

It's a very bad idea to connect an unpatched system to the Internet. Several of our readers have reported having a new system infected by a worm almost instantly when they connected to the Internet, intending to download patches and updates. Unless you have a very good firewall, patch your new system *before* you connect it to the Internet.

Major applications discs

If your system runs Microsoft Office or other major applications that are distributed on CDs, keep a copy of those discs with your toolkit. Again, don't forget to record the serial number, initialization keys, and other required data on the disc itself.

Driver CDs

Motherboards, video adapters, sound cards, and many other components include a driver CD in the box. Those drivers may not be essential for installing the component—the Windows or Linux distribution CD may (or may not) include basic drivers for the component—but it's generally a good idea to use the driver CD supplied with the component (or an updated version downloaded from the web site) rather than using those supplied with the OS, if any.

Pay close attention to the instructions that come with the driver. Most drivers can be installed with the hardware they support already installed. But some drivers, particularly those for some USB devices, need to be installed *before* the hardware is installed.

In addition to basic drivers, the driver CD may include supporting applications. For example, a video adapter CD may include a system tray application for managing video properties, while a sound card may include a bundled application for sound recording and editing. We generally use the bundled driver CD for initial installation and then download and install any updated drivers available on the product web site. Keep a copy of the original driver CD and a CD-R with updated drivers in your toolkit.

CAUTION

Keep original driver CDs stored safely–they may be more valuable than you think. More than once, we've lost track of original driver CDs, thinking we could always just download the latest driver from the manufacturer's web site. Alas, a company may go out of business, or its web site may be down just when you desperately need a driver. Worse still, some companies charge for drivers that were originally freely downloadable. That's one reason we don't buy HP products.

Hard drive installation/diagnostic utility

We're always amazed that so few people use the installation and diagnostic software supplied with hard drives. Perhaps that's because many people buy OEM hard drives, which include only the bare drive. Retail-boxed drives invariably include a utilities CD. Most people ignore it, which is a mistake.

Seagate, for example, provides DiscWizard installation software and SeaTools diagnostic software. If you're building a system, you can use the bootable floppy or bootable CD version of DiscWizard to partition, format, and test the new drive automatically. If you're adding a drive, you can use the Windows version of DiscWizard to install, prepare, and configure the new drive automatically. You can configure the new drive as a secondary drive, keeping the original drive as the boot drive. You can specify that the new drive be the sole drive in the system, and DiscWizard will automatically migrate your programs and data from the old drive. Finally, you can choose to make the new drive the primary (boot) drive and make the old drive the secondary drive. DiscWizard does all of this automatically, saving you considerable manual effort.

All hard drive makers provide installation and diagnostic utilities. Maxtor, for example, distributes MaxBlast installation software and Powermax diagnostic utilities. If you buy an OEM hard drive or lose the original CD, you can download the utilities from the manufacturer's web site. For obvious reasons, many of these utilities work only if a hard drive made by that manufacturer is installed.

Diagnostic utilities

These are a bit of a Catch-22. Diagnostic utilities are of limited use in building a new system because if the PC works well enough to load and run them, you don't need to diagnose it. Conversely, when you do need to diagnose the PC, it's not working well enough to run the diagnostic utility. Duh. (Diagnostic utilities can be helpful on older systems, for example to detect memory problems or a failing hard drive.) The only diagnostic utility we use routinely when building systems is a Knoppix Live Linux CD (*http://www.knoppix.com*). With Knoppix, you can boot and run Linux completely from the CD, without writing anything to the hard drive. Knoppix has superb hardware detection—better than Windows—and can be useful for diagnosing problems on a newly built system that refuses to load Windows.

Many system builders routinely run a memory diagnostic to ensure that the system functions before installing the operating system. One excellent utility for this purpose is MEMTEST86 (*http://www.memtest86.com*). It's free, and either self-boots from a floppy drive or can be run in DOS mode from an optical boot disk. Best of all, it does a great job testing the otherwise difficult-to-diagnose memory subsystem. Microsoft offers a similar free utility (*http://oca.microsoft.com/en/windiag.asp*) that we have not used.

Burn-in utilities

PC components generally either fail quickly or live a long time. If a component survives the first 24 hours, it's likely to run without problems for years. The vast majority of early failures are immediate, caused by DOA components. Something like 99% of the remaining early failures occur within 24 hours, so it's worth "burning in" a new system before you spend hours installing and configuring the operating system and applications.

Many people simply turn on the system and let it run for a day or two. That's better than nothing, but an idling system doesn't stress all components. A better way is to run software that accesses and exercises all of the components. One good (and free) ad hoc way to burn-in a system is to compile the Linux kernel, and we sometimes use that method. We generally use special burn-in software, however, and the best product we know of for that purpose is BurnInTest from PassMark Software (*http://www.passmark.com*).

Getting to Know Your Motherboard

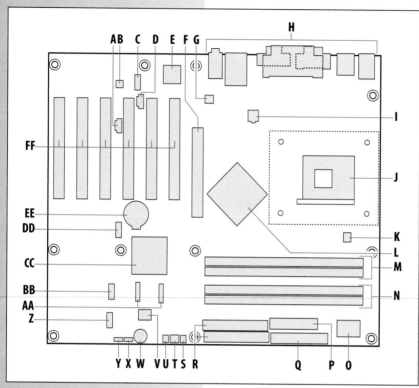

Figure 1-2. Intel D865GBF block diagram (original graphic courtesy Intel Corporation)

The motherboard is the most complex component in a PC. All of the other components connect to and are controlled by the motherboard, so it's important to be able to identify its major parts.

Figure 1-2 shows the major components present on a representative modern motherboard, in this case an Intel D865GBF for a Pentium 4 processor. The rest of this section includes photographs of each of these components to help you visually identify items. The details and layout vary from model to model, but all modern motherboards include these or similar components. Once you're able to locate and identify the major components on one motherboard, you should be able to do the same on any other motherboard.

Most motherboards include a reference label to show the location of connectors, jumpers, and other key components. Place this label inside the case after assembly so you'll have key configuration information readily available if you open the case to install additional components or troubleshoot problems.

- **A** Auxiliary line-in connector
- **B** Audio codec
- **C** Front-panel audio connector
- **D** ATAPI CD-ROM connector
- **E** Ethernet PLC device (optional)
- **F** AGP connector
- **G** Rear chassis fan connector
- **H** Back-panel connectors
- **I** +12V power connector (ATX12V)
- **J** mPGA478 processor socket
- **K** Processor fan connector
- **L** Intel 82865G GMCH
- **M** DIMM Channel A sockets
- **N** DIMM Channel B sockets
- **O** I/O controller
- **P** Power connector
- **Q** Diskette drive connector
- **R** Parallel ATA IDE connectors
- **S** SCSI hard drive activity LED connector (optional)
- **T** Front chassis fan connector
- **U** Chassis intrusion connector
- **V** 4 Mbit Firmware Hub (FWH)
- **W** Speaker
- **X** BIOS Setup configuration jumper block
- **Y** Auxiliary front-panel power LED connector
- **Z** Front-panel connector
- **AA** Serial ATA connectors
- **BB** Front-panel USB connector
- **CC** Intel 82801EB I/O Controller Hub (ICH5)
- **DD** Front-panel USB connector
- **EE** Battery
- **FF** PCI bus add-in card connectors

Most of these items are reasonably self-explanatory, but a few deserve comment:

Intel D82865G GMCH (Item L)

The Intel D82865G GMCH is the Graphics and Memory Controller Hub, which in a non-Intel chipset would be called the northbridge. The GMCH provides the link between the processor and memory, and also includes the circuitry for the embedded video.

4 Mbit Firmware Hub (Item V)

The Intel Firmware Hub (FWH) stores the BIOS code and BIOS Setup configuration data in nonvolatile read/write memory. When you update the main system BIOS, the new BIOS code is written to the FWH.

Intel 82801EB I/O Controller Hub (Item CC)

The Intel 82801EB I/O Controller Hub (ICH5) is what would be referred to as the southbridge in a non-Intel chipset. The ICH provides an interface between the GMCH, the BIOS, and major system communication peripherals, including the PCI bus, USB, and the ATA and S-ATA interfaces. It also provides the circuitry for the embedded audio.

Figure 1-3 shows the relationship between the GMCH, the ICH, and other major system components.

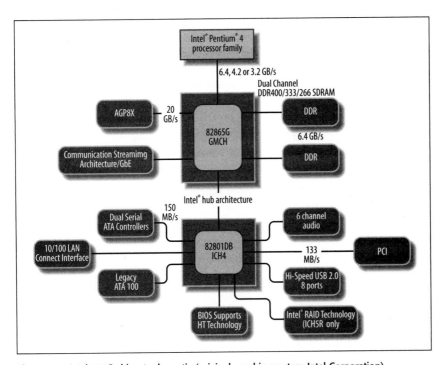

Figure 1-3. Intel 865G chipset schematic (original graphic courtesy Intel Corporation)

Figure 1-4. Left rear quadrant of the Intel D865GBF

Figure 1-4 shows the left rear quadrant of the D865GBF motherboard. The six light-colored PCI bus add-in card connectors (Item FF)—also called simply "PCI slots"—dominate this image. The auxiliary line-in connector (A), which can be used to route analog audio from an optical drive, is visible between PCI slots 3 and 4, near the top. The audio codec (B), which processes audio data, is the small surface-mount chip just above the gap between PCI slots 3 and 4. The ATAPI CD-ROM connector (D) nestles between the top edges of PCI slots 4 and 5, with the front-panel audio connector (C), shown with two jumpers installed, immediately above it. The optional Ethernet PLC device (E), which provides the embedded Ethernet adapter, is the rectangular black chip just above PCI slot 6. The AGP connector (F) is the dark slot to the lower right of PCI slot 6. The rear chassis fan connector (G) is the small white plastic connector with three pins, visible above and to the right of the AGP slot. The battery (EE) is partially visible at the bottom center of the image, and the heatsink for the Intel 82865G GMCH (L) is partially visible at the lower right.

Figure 1-5 shows the right rear quadrant of the D865GBF motherboard. The back-panel connectors (H) are grouped on the upper right edge of the motherboard. The Pentium 4 processor socket (J) is the light-colored rectangle at the lower right of the image, with the processor fan connector (K) visible as a small, white, plastic three-pin connector at the extreme lower right of the image, to the right of the label. The ATX12V supplementary power connector (I) is the small connector block visible immediately to the left of the row of cylindrical capacitors above the processor socket. The Intel 82865G GMCH (L) is actually concealed by a heatsink, the large, finned object directly to the left of the processor socket.

Figure 1-5. Right rear quadrant of the Intel D865GBF

Figure 1-6 shows the right front quadrant of the D865GBF motherboard. The dark slots immediately below the heatsink and processor socket are the DIMM Channel A sockets (M) and the DIMM Channel B sockets (N). The I/O controller (O) is the rectangular black surface-mount chip at the extreme lower right. To its left are the translucent plastic 20-pin main ATX power connector (P) above, with the black 34-pin diskette drive connector (Q) below. The two connectors adjacent to the diskette drive connector and main ATX power connector are the parallel ATA IDE connectors (R). The lower, black connector is the primary ATA IDE connector. The white connector immediately above it is the secondary ATA IDE connector.

Figure 1-6. Right front quadrant of the Intel D865GBF

Figure 1-7 shows the left front quadrant of the D865GBF motherboard. Near the lower right corner of the image, adjacent to the mounting hole, is where the optional SCSI hard drive activity LED connector (S) would be if we had ordered that option. We didn't, so the position for it is simply an empty solder pad. Immediately to the left of the nonexistent SCSI activity connector is the front chassis fan connector (T), the white plastic connector with three pins visible. To its left is the chassis intrusion connector (U), a two-pin black plastic connector.

The round object at the bottom center of the image is the speaker (W), and the 4 Mbit Firmware Hub (V) is the rectangular black surface-mount chip visible just above it. To the left of the speaker is the BIOS Setup configuration jumper block (X), shown jumpered in the 1-2 position. To the left of the jumper block is the auxiliary front-panel power LED connector (Y), a three-position jumper with pin 2 absent. The front-panel connector (Z) is the white plastic connector block with several pins, visible above and to the left.

Figure 1-7. Left front quadrant of the Intel D865GBF

The Intel ICH5 82801EB I/O Controller Hub (CC) is the large, square black chip at the upper center of the image, with two Serial ATA connectors (AA) immediately beneath it. There are two front-panel USB connectors. One of those (BB) is directly to the left of the Serial ATA connectors, adjacent to two cylindrical capacitors. The second (DD) is at the upper left of the image, adjacent to the battery (EE).

Troubleshooting

Many first-time system builders are haunted by the question, "What if it doesn't work?" Or, worse still, "What if it goes up in flames the first time I turn it on?" Set your mind at ease. This isn't rocket surgery. Any reasonably intelligent person can build a system with a high degree of confidence that it will work normally the first time it is turned on. If you use good components and assemble them carefully, you're actually less likely to encounter problems with a home-built system than with a prebuilt mail-order system or with a system off the shelf from your local superstore.

Shipping can be tough on a computer. We always pop the cover of PCs that have been shipped, and often find that something has been jarred loose. Our editor reports that when he shipped a PC to his parents, it arrived with the AGP card completely out of its slot. Not good.

Even worse, shipping can cause the CPU cooler to break loose, particularly on AMD Athlon XP systems. A heavy heatsink rattling around can do some serious damage to other components, but even that's not the major concern. Running a system without a CPU cooler causes an Athlon XP to go up in smoke in seconds, literally. If someone ships a system to you, *always* open it up and verify that everything is properly connected before you apply power to the system.

Still, problems can happen. So, while it would take a whole book to cover troubleshooting in detail, it's worth taking a few pages to list some of the most likely problems and solutions. Fortunately, it's easier to troubleshoot a newly built system than a system that's been in use for some time. Fewer things can go wrong with a new system. You can be certain that the system is not infected with a virus or malware, for example, and driver problems are much less likely on a new system because you have all the latest drivers installed.

The best time to troubleshoot is while you're building the system. A good carpenter measures twice and cuts once. Take the same approach to building your system, and you're unlikely to need any of this troubleshooting advice. As you build the system, and then again before you apply power for the first time, verify that all cables are oriented and connected correctly. Make sure expansion cards, memory modules, the processor, and so on are fully seated, and that you haven't left a tool in the patient. Each project system chapter includes a final checklist. Verifying the items on that checklist eliminates about 99% of potential problems.

Possible problems fall into one of four categories: easy versus hard to troubleshoot, and likely versus unlikely. Always check the easy/likely problems first. Otherwise, you may find yourself replacing the video card before you notice that the monitor isn't plugged in. After you exhaust the easy/likely possibilities, check the easy/unlikely ones, followed by hard/likely, and, finally, hard/unlikely.

Other than sheer carelessness—to which experienced system builders are more prone than are novices—most problems with new systems result from one or more of the following:

- Cable problems. Disconnected, mis-connected, and defective cables cause more problems than anything else. The plethora of cables inside a PC makes it very easy to overlook a disconnected data cable or to forget to connect power to a drive. It's possible to connect some cables backward. Ribbon cables are a particularly common problem because some can be connected offset by a row or column of pins. And the cables themselves cannot always be trusted, even if they are new. If you have a problem that seems inexplicable, always suspect a cable problem first.

One of our technical reviewers observes: "A good flashlight with a tight beam (I use a mini Maglight) really helps to spot offset ribbon connector problems, even if workspace lighting is otherwise adequate. I've done systems where a hand-held magnifier became an indispensable tool."

Fortunately, most problems with defective cables involve ribbon cables, and those are pretty easy to come by. For example, when we recently assembled a new PC, the motherboard came with two IDE cables and a floppy drive cable. The floppy drive came with a cable, the hard drive with another IDE cable, and the optical drive with still another IDE cable. That gave us four IDE cables and two floppy cables, so we ended up with two spare IDE cables and a spare floppy cable. Those went into our spares kit, where they'll be available if we need to swap cables to troubleshoot another system.

- Configuration errors. Years ago, motherboards required a lot more manual configuration than modern motherboards do. There were many switches and jumpers, all of which had to be set correctly or the system wouldn't boot. Modern motherboards auto-configure most of their required settings, but may still require some manual configuration, either by setting physical jumpers on the motherboard or by changing settings in CMOS Setup.

Motherboards use silk-screened labels near jumpers and connectors to document their purposes and to list valid configuration settings. These settings are also listed in the motherboard manual. Although it is rare, we have encountered errors in the silk-screened motherboard labels or the manuals. (On one notable occasion, the motherboard labels and the manual agreed and were *both* wrong, which cost us several hours of aggravation.) Always check both the motherboard labels and the manual to verify configuration settings. If the motherboard maker posts updated manuals on the Web, check those as well.

- Incompatible components. In general, you can mix and match modern PC components without worrying much about compatibility. For example, any hard drive or optical drive works with any IDE interface, and any ATX12V power supply is compatible with any ATX12V motherboard (although the power supply may not have adequate power). Most component compatibility issues are subtle. For example, you may install a 1 GB memory module in your new system, but when you power it up, the system sees only 256 MB or 512 MB because the motherboard doesn't recognize 1 GB memory modules properly. All of the components we recommend in the project system chapters are compatible with one another, but if you use other components it's worth checking the detailed documentation on the manufacturers' web sites to verify compatibility.

- Dead-on-arrival components. Modern PC components are extremely reliable, but if you're unlucky one of your components may be DOA. This is the least likely cause of a problem, however. Many first-time system builders think they have a DOA component, but the true cause is almost always something else—usually a cable or configuration problem. Before you return a suspect component, go through the detailed troubleshooting steps we describe. Chances are the component is just fine.

A healthy PC finishes the POST (Power-On Self-Test) with one happy-sounding beep. If you hear some other beep sequence during startup, there is some sort of problem. BIOS beep codes provide useful troubleshooting information, such as identifying the particular subsystem affected. Beep codes vary, so check the motherboard documentation for a description of what each code indicates.

Here are the problems you are most likely to encounter with a new system, and what to do about them.

Problem: When you apply power, nothing happens.

1. Verify that the power cable is connected to the PC and to the wall receptacle, and that the wall receptacle has power. Don't assume. We have seen receptacles in which one half worked and the other didn't. Use a lamp or other appliance to verify that the receptacle to which you connect the PC actually has power. If the power supply has its own power switch, make sure that the switch is turned to the "On" or "1" position. If your local mains voltage is 110/115/120V, verify that the power supply voltage selector switch, if present, is not set for 220/230/240V. (If you need to move this switch, disconnect power before doing so.)

2. If you are using an outlet strip or UPS, make sure that its switch (if it has one) is on and that the circuit breaker or fuse hasn't blown.

3. If you installed an AGP video adapter, pop the lid and verify that the AGP adapter is fully seated in its slot. Even if you were sure that it seated fully initially—and even if you thought it snapped into place—the AGP adapter still may not be properly seated. Remove the AGP card and reinstall it, making sure it seats completely. If the motherboard has an AGP retention mechanism, make sure the notch on the AGP card fully

engages the mechanism. Ironically, one of the most common reasons for a loose AGP card is that the screw used to secure it to the chassis may torque the card, pulling it partially out of its slot. This problem is rare with high-quality cases and AGP cards, but quite common with cheap components.

4. Verify that the main ATX power cable and the ATX12V power cable are securely connected to the motherboard and that all pins are making contact. If necessary, remove the cables and reconnect them. Make sure the latch on each cable plug snaps into place on the motherboard jack.

5. Verify that the front-panel power switch cable is connected properly to the front-panel connector block. Check the silkscreen label on the motherboard and the motherboard manual to verify that you are connecting the cable to the right set of pins. Very rarely, you may encounter a defective power switch. You can eliminate this possibility by temporarily connecting the front-panel reset switch cable to the power switch pins on the front-panel connector block. (Both are merely momentary on switches, so they can be used interchangeably.) Alternatively, you can carefully use a small flat-blade screwdriver to short the power switch pins on the front-panel connector block momentarily. If the system starts with either of these methods, the problem is the power switch.

6. Start eliminating less likely possibilities, the most common of which is a well-concealed short circuit. Begin by disconnecting the power and data cables from the hard, optical, and floppy drives, one at a time. After you disconnect each one, try starting the system. If the system starts, the drive you just disconnected is the problem. The drive itself may be defective, but it's far more likely that the cable is defective or was improperly connected. Replace the data cable and connect the drive to a different power supply cable.

If you have a spare power supply—or can borrow one temporarily from another system—you might as well try it as long as you have the cables disconnected. A new power supply being DOA is fairly rare, at least among good brands, but if you have the original disconnected it's not much trouble to try a different one.

7. If you have expansion cards installed, remove them one by one, except for the AGP adapter. If the motherboard has embedded video, temporarily connect your display to it and remove the AGP card as well. Attempt to start the system after you remove each card. If the system starts, the card you just removed is causing the problem. Try a different card or install that card in a different slot.

8. Remove and reseat the memory modules, examining them to make sure they are not damaged, and then try to start the system. If you have two memory modules installed, install only one of them initially. Try it in both (or all) memory slots. If the module doesn't work in any slot, it may be defective. Try the other module, again in every available memory slot. By using this approach, you can determine if one of the memory modules or one of the slots is defective.

9. Remove the CPU cooler and the CPU. Check the CPU to make sure there are no bent pins. If there are, you may be able to straighten them using a credit card or a similar thin, stiff object, but in all likelihood you will have to replace the CPU. Check the CPU socket to make sure there are no blocked holes or foreign objects present.

WARNING

Before you reinstall the CPU, always remove the old thermal compound and apply new compound. You can generally wipe off the old compound with a paper towel, or perhaps by rubbing it gently with your thumb. (Keep the processor in its socket while you remove the compound.) If the compound is difficult to remove, try heating it gently with a hair dryer. Never operate the system without the CPU cooler installed.

---

10. Remove the motherboard and verify that no extraneous screws or other conductive objects are shorting the motherboard to the chassis. Although shaking the case usually causes such objects to rattle, a screw or other small object may become wedged so tightly between the motherboard and chassis that it will not reveal itself during a shake test.

11. If the problem persists, the most likely cause is a defective motherboard.

Problem: The system seems to start normally, but the display remains black.

1. Verify that the display has power and the video cable is connected. If the display has a non-captive power cable, make sure the power cord is connected both to the display and to the wall receptacle. If you have a spare power cord, use it to connect the display.

2. Verify that the brightness and contrast controls of the display are set to midrange or higher.

3. Disconnect the video cable and examine it closely to make sure that no pins are bent or shorted. Note that the video cable on some monitors is missing some pins and may have a short jumper wire connecting other pins, which is normal. Also check the video port on the PC to make sure that all of the holes are clear and that no foreign objects are present.

4. If you are using a standalone AGP adapter in a motherboard that has embedded video, make sure the video cable is connected to the proper video port. Try the other video port just to make sure. Most motherboards with embedded video automatically disable it when they sense that an AGP card is installed, but that is not universally true. You may have to connect the display to the embedded video, enter CMOS Setup, and reconfigure the motherboard to use the AGP card.

5. Try using a different display if you have one available. Alternatively, try using the problem display on a known-good system.

6. If you are using an AGP card, make certain it is fully seated. Many combinations of AGP card and motherboard make it very difficult to seat the card properly. You may think the card is seated, and may even feel it snap into place. That does not necessarily mean it really is fully seated. Look carefully at the bottom edge of the card and the AGP slot, and make sure the card is fully in the slot and parallel to it. Verify that installing the screw that secures the AGP card to the chassis did not torque the card, forcing one end up and out of the slot.

7. If the system has PCI expansion cards installed, remove them one by one. (Be sure to disconnect power from the system before you remove or install a card.) Each time you remove a card, restart the system. If the system displays video after you remove a card, that card is either defective or is conflicting with the AGP adapter. Try installing the PCI card in a different slot. If it still causes the video problem, the card is probably defective. Replace it.

Problem: When you connect power (or turn on the main power switch on the back of the power supply), the power supply starts briefly and then shuts off.

WARNING
All of the following steps assume that the power supply is adequate for the system configuration. This symptom may also occur if you are using a grossly underpowered power supply. Worse still, doing that may damage the power supply itself, the motherboard, and other components.

---

1. This may be normal behavior. When you connect power to the power supply, it senses the power and begins its startup routine. Within a fraction of a second, the power supply notices that the motherboard hasn't ordered it to start, so it shuts itself down immediately. Press the main power switch on the case and the system should start normally.

2. If pressing the main power switch doesn't start the system, you have probably forgotten to connect one of the cables from the power supply or front panel to the motherboard. Verify that the power switch cable is connected to the front-panel connector block, and that the 20-pin main

ATX power cable and the 4-pin ATX12V power cable are connected to the motherboard. Connect any cables that are not connected and press the main power switch, and the system should start normally.

3. If the preceding steps don't solve the problem, the most likely cause is a defective power supply. If you have a spare power supply or can borrow one from another system, install it temporarily in the new system. Alternatively, connect the problem power supply to another system to verify that it is bad.

4. If none of the preceding steps solves the problem, the most likely cause is a defective motherboard. Replace it.

Problem: When you apply power, the floppy drive LED lights solidly and the system fails to start.

1. The FDD cable may be misaligned. Verify that the FDD cable is properly installed on the FDD and on the motherboard FDD interface. You may have installed the FDD cable backward or installed it offset by one row or column of pins.

2. If the FDD cable is properly installed, it may be defective. Disconnect it temporarily and start the system. If the system starts normally, replace the FDD cable.

3. If the FDD cable is known-good and installed properly, the FDD itself or the motherboard FDD interface may be defective. Replace the FDD. If that doesn't solve the problem and you insist on having an FDD, either replace the motherboard or disable the motherboard FDD interface and install a PCI adapter that provides an FDD interface.

Problem: The optical drive appears to play audio CDs, but no sound comes from the speakers.

1. Make sure the volume/mixer is set appropriately, i.e., the volume is up and CD Audio isn't muted. There may be multiple volume controls in a system. Check them all.

2. Try a different audio CD. Some recent audio CDs are copy-protected in such a way that they refuse to play on a computer optical drive.

Few optical drives or motherboards include an analog audio cable, so you will probably have to buy a cable. In the past, audio cables were often proprietary, but modern drives and motherboards all use a standard ATAPI audio cable.

3. If you have tried several audio CDs without success, this may still be normal behavior, depending on the player application you are using. Optical drives can deliver audio data via the analog audio-out jack on the rear of the drive or as a digital bit stream on the bus. If the player application pulls the digital bit stream from the bus, sound is delivered to your speakers normally. If the player application uses analog audio, you must connect a cable from the analog audio-out jack on the back of the drive to an audio-in connector on the motherboard or sound card.

4. If you install an audio cable and still have no sound from the speakers, try connecting headphones or amplified speakers directly to the headphone jack on the front of the optical drive (if present). If you still can't hear the audio, the drive may be defective. If you can hear audio via the front headphone jack but not through the computer speakers, it's likely the audio cable you installed is defective or installed improperly.

Problem: S-ATA drives are not recognized.

1. How S-ATA drives are detected (or not detected) depends on the particular combination of chipset, BIOS revision level, S-ATA interface, and the operating system you use. Failing to recognize S-ATA devices may be normal behavior.

2. If you use a standalone PCI S-ATA adapter card, the system will typically not recognize the connected S-ATA drive(s) during startup. This is normal behavior. You will have to provide an S-ATA device driver when you install the operating system.

3. If your motherboard uses a recent chipset, e.g., an Intel 865 or later, and has embedded S-ATA interfaces, it should detect S-ATA devices during startup and display them on the BIOS boot screen. If the drive is not recognized, update the BIOS to the latest version if you have not already done so. Restart the system and watch the BIOS boot screen to see if the system recognizes the S-ATA drive. Run BIOS Setup and select the menu item that allows you to configure ATA devices. If your S-ATA drive is not listed, you can still use it, but you'll have to provide a driver on diskette during OS installation.

4. Recognition of S-ATA drives during operating system installation varies with the OS version and the chipset. The original release of Windows 2000 does not detect S-ATA drives with any chipset. To install Windows 2000 on an S-ATA drive, watch during the early part of Setup for the prompt to press F6 if you need to install third-party storage drivers. Press F6 when prompted and insert the S-ATA driver floppy. Windows XP may or may not recognize S-ATA drives, depending on the chipset the motherboard uses. With recent chipsets, e.g., the Intel 865 series and later, Windows XP recognizes and uses S-ATA drives natively. With earlier chipsets, e.g., the Intel D845 and earlier, Windows XP does not recognize the S-ATA drive natively, so you will have to press F6 when prompted and provide the S-ATA driver on floppy. Most recent Linux distributions (those based on the 2.4 kernel or later) recognize S-ATA drives natively.

5. If the S-ATA drive is still not recognized, pop the lid and verify that the S-ATA data and power cables are connected properly. Try removing and reseating the cables and, if necessary, connecting the S-ATA drive to a different motherboard interface connector. If the drive still isn't accessible, try replacing the S-ATA data cable. If none of this works, the S-ATA drive is probably defective.

Problem: The monitor displays BIOS boot text, but the system doesn't boot and displays no error message.

1. This may be normal behavior. Restart the system and enter BIOS Setup (usually by pressing Delete or F1 during startup). Choose the menu option to use default CMOS settings, save the changes, exit, and restart the system.

2. If the system doesn't accept keyboard input and you are using a USB keyboard and mouse, temporarily swap in a PS/2 keyboard and mouse. If you are using a PS/2 keyboard and mouse, make sure you haven't connected the keyboard to the mouse port and vice versa.

3. If the system still fails to boot, run BIOS Setup again and verify all settings, particularly CPU speed, FSB speed, and memory timings.

4. If the system hangs with a DMI pool error message, restart the system and run BIOS Setup again. Search the menus for an option to reset the configuration data. Enable that option, save the changes, and restart the system.

5. If you are using an Intel motherboard, power down the system and reset the configuration jumper from the 1-2 (Normal) position to the 2-3 (Configure) position. Restart the system, and BIOS Setup will appear automatically. Choose the option to use default CMOS settings, save the changes, and power down the system. Move the configuration jumper back to the 1-2 position and restart the system. (Actually, we do this routinely any time we build a system around an Intel motherboard. It may not be absolutely required, but we've found that it minimizes problems.)

6. If you are still unable to access BIOS Setup, power down the system, disconnect all of the drive data cables, and restart the system. If the system displays a Hard Drive Failure or No Boot Device error message, the problem is a defective cable (more likely) or a defective drive. Replace the drive data cable and try again. If the system does not display such an error message, the problem is probably caused by a defective motherboard.

Problem: The monitor displays a Hard Drive Failure or similar error.

1. This is almost always a hardware problem. Verify that the hard drive data cable is connected properly to the drive and the interface and that the drive power cable is connected.

2. Use a different drive data cable and connect the drive to a different power cable.

3. Connect the drive data cable to a different interface.

4. If none of these steps corrects the problem, the most likely cause is a defective drive.

Problem: The monitor displays a No Boot Device, Missing Operating System, or similar error message.

1. This is normal behavior if you have not yet installed an operating system. Error messages like this generally mean that the drive is physically installed and accessible, but the PC cannot boot because it cannot locate the operating system. Install the operating system.

2. If the drive is inaccessible, verify that all data and power cables are connected properly. If it is a parallel ATA drive, verify that the master/slave jumpers are set correctly and that the drive is connected to the primary interface.

Problem: The system refuses to boot from the optical drive.

1. All modern motherboards and optical drives support the El Torito specification, which allows the system to boot from an optical disc. If your new system refuses to boot from a CD, first verify that the CD is bootable. Most, but not all, operating system distribution CDs are bootable. Some OS CDs are not bootable, but have a utility program to generate boot floppies. Check the documentation to verify that the CD is bootable, or try booting the CD in another system.

2. Run CMOS Setup and locate the section where you can define boot sequence. The default sequence is often (1) floppy drive, (2) hard drive, and (3) optical drive. Sometimes, by the time the system has decided it can't boot from the FDD or hard drive, it "gives up" before attempting to boot from the optical drive. Reset the boot sequence to (1) optical drive and (2) hard drive. We generally leave the system with that boot sequence. Most systems configured this way prompt you to "Press any key to boot from CD" or something similar. If you don't press a key, the system then attempts to boot from the hard drive, so make sure to pay attention during the boot sequence and press a key when prompted.

3. Some high-speed optical drives take several seconds to load a CD, spin up, and signal the system that they are ready. In the meantime, the BIOS may have given up on the optical drive and gone on to try other boot devices. If you think this has happened, try pressing the reset button to reboot the system while the optical drive is already spinning and up to speed. If you get a persistent prompt to "press any key to boot from CD," try leaving that prompt up while the optical drive comes up to speed. If that doesn't work, run CMOS Setup and reconfigure the boot sequence to put the FDD first and the optical drive second. (Make sure there's no diskette in the FDD.) You can also try putting other boot device options (e.g., a Zip drive, network drive, or boot PROM) ahead of the optical drive in the boot sequence. The goal is to provide sufficient delay for the optical drive to spin up before the motherboard attempts to boot from it.

4. If none of these steps solves the problem, verify that all data cable and power cable connections are correct, that master/slave jumpers are set correctly, and so on. If the system still fails to boot, replace the optical drive data cable.

5. If the system still fails to boot, disconnect all drives except the primary hard drive and the optical drive. If they are parallel ATA devices, connect the hard drive as the master device on the primary channel and the optical drive as the master device on the secondary channel, and restart the system.

6. If that fails to solve the problem, connect both the hard drive and the optical drive to the primary ATA interface, with the hard drive as master and the optical drive as slave.

7. If the system still fails to boot, the optical drive is probably defective. Try using a different drive.

Problem: When you first apply power, you hear a continuous high-pitched screech or warble.

1. The most likely cause is either that one of the system fans has a defective bearing, or that a wire is contacting the spinning fan. Examine all the system fans—CPU fan, power supply fan, and any supplemental fans—to make sure they haven't been fouled by a wire. Sometimes it's difficult to determine which fan is making the noise. In that case, use a cardboard tube or rolled-up piece of paper as a stethoscope to localize the noise. If the fan is fouled, clear the problem. If the fan is not fouled but still noisy, replace the fan.

2. Rarely, a new hard drive may have a manufacturing defect or may have been damaged in shipping. If so, the problem is usually obvious from the amount and location of the noise and possibly because the hard drive is vibrating. If necessary, use your cardboard-tube stethoscope to localize the noise. If the hard drive is the source, the only alternative is to replace it.

Choosing and Buying Components

2

The components you choose for your system determine its features, performance level, and reliability. How and where you buy those components determines how much the system costs.

Sometimes it is a good idea to spend more for additional features or performance, but often it is not. The trick is to figure out where to draw the line—when to spend extra money for extra features and performance, and when to settle for a less expensive component. Our years of experience have taught us several lessons in that regard:

- Benchmarks lie. Buying PC components based solely on benchmark results is like buying a car based solely on its top speed. It's worse, actually, because no standards exist for how benchmarks measure performance, or what aspect of performance they measure. Using one benchmark, Component A may be the clear winner, with Component B lagging far behind. With another benchmark, the positions may be reversed. When you select components for your new system, we suggest you regard benchmarks with suspicion and use them only as very general guidelines, if at all.

- Performance differences don't matter if it takes a benchmark to show them. Enthusiast web sites wax poetic about a processor that's 10% faster than its competitor or a video card that renders frames 5% faster than its predecessor. Who cares? A difference you won't notice isn't worth paying for.

- It's easy to overlook the really important things and focus on trivialities. The emphasis on size and speed means that more important issues are often ignored or given short shrift. For example, if you compare two hard drives, you might think the faster drive is the better choice. But the faster drive may also run noticeably hotter and be much louder and less reliable. In that situation, the slower drive is probably the better choice.

- Integrated (or embedded) components are often preferable to stand-alone components. Many motherboards include integrated features such as video, audio, and LAN. The integrated video on modern motherboards suffices for most purposes. Only hardcore gamers and others with special video requirements need to buy a separate video adapter. The best integrated audio—such as that on motherboards that use Intel and *n*VIDIA chipsets—is good enough for almost anyone. Integrated LAN adapters are more than good enough for nearly any desktop system.

The advantage of integrated components is threefold: cost, reliability, and compatibility. A motherboard with integrated components costs little or no more than a motherboard without such components, and can save you $100 or more by eliminating the cost of inexpensive standalone equivalents. Because they are built into the motherboard, integrated components are usually more reliable than standalone components. Finally, because the motherboard maker has complete control over the hardware and drivers, integrated components usually cause fewer compatibility issues and device conflicts.

Finding the Sweet Spot

To find the sweet spot, just compare the price of a component to its performance or capacity. For example, if one processor costs $175 and the next model up is 10% faster, it should cost at most 10% more. If it costs more than that, you've reached the wrong part of the price/performance curve, and you'll be paying a premium for little additional performance. Similarly, before you buy a hard drive, divide the price by the capacity. At the low end, you may find that a small hard drive costs more per gigabyte than a larger drive. At the high end, a very large drive probably costs significantly more per gigabyte than a medium-capacity model. The sweet spot is in the middle, where the cost per gigabyte is lowest. Make sure, though, that you compare apples to apples. Don't compare a Pentium 4 processor to a Celeron or a 5,400 RPM hard drive to a 7,200 RPM model.

- Buying at the "sweet spot" is almost always the best decision. The sweet spot is the level at which the price/performance ratio is minimized—where you get the most bang for your buck. For example, Intel sells a broad range of processors, from $75 Celerons to $1,000 Pentium 4 Extreme Editions. Celerons are cheap but slow; P4/EE processors are fast but hideously expensive. There must be a happy medium. The sweet spot for Intel processors is around $175 for a retail-boxed CPU. If you spend much less, you get less performance per dollar spent. If you spend much more, you get only a slight performance increase. This sweet spot has stayed the same for years. That $175 buys you a faster processor every time Intel cuts prices. But that $175 processor has always been the bang-for-the-buck leader.

- It's almost always worth paying more for better quality and reliability. If the specs for two components look very similar but one sells for less than the other, it's a safe bet that someone cut corners to reduce the price of the cheaper component. The cheaper component may use inferior materials, have shoddy build quality or poor quality control, or the manufacturer may provide terrible tech support or a very short warranty. If it's cheaper, there's a reason for it. Count on it. The best way to avoid the trap of poor-quality components is to be willing to pay a bit more for quality. The difference between a mediocre product and a top-quality one can be surprisingly small. Throughout this book, we recommend only high-quality products. That's not to say that products we don't list are bad, but those we do recommend are good.

- Brand names really do mean something, but not all brands are good ones. Brand names imply certain performance and quality characteristics, and most manufacturers take pains to establish and maintain those links in consumers' minds. Different brand names are often associated with different quality and/or performance levels in a Good/Better/Best hierarchy, in the same way that General Motors sells their inexpensive models as Chevrolets and their most expensive models as Cadillacs.

For example, ViewSonic makes several lines of CRT monitors, including their high-end Pro Series, their midrange Graphics Series, and their entry-level E2 Series. Like many vendors, ViewSonic also maintains a separate brand name for their cheapest products, which they call OptiQuest. If you buy a Pro Series monitor, you know it's going to cost more than the lower-end models, but you also know it's going to have excellent performance and will likely be quite reliable. Conversely, if you buy an OptiQuest monitor, you know it's going to be cheap and not very good. Some manufacturers also have a "high-end" brand name, although that practice has declined as margins have eroded throughout the industry.

- If you're on a tight budget, shop by brand name rather than by performance specifications. For the same price, it's usually better to choose a component that has less impressive specifications but a better brand name rather than a component with better specifications but a poor brand name. For example, if you can't afford a Plextor PX-712A 12X DVD writer, and your choices are a Plextor PX-708A 8X DVD writer and a similarly priced Brand-X 12X DVD writer, go with the 8X Plextor. It may be a bit slower than the Brand X drive, but it will probably be a lot less picky about what brand of discs it will use and will almost certainly be more reliable. In other words, if you have to choose between better quality and higher performance, choose quality every time.

In this chapter, we tell you what we've learned based on 20 years of buying PC hardware components. Throughout the chapter, we focus on recommending products and brand names that are reliable and offer good value for your money. If you hew closely to our advice when you make your buying decisions, you won't go far wrong.

Finally, with so many alternatives, it's easy to buy the right part from the wrong source. Accordingly, the last part of this chapter distills what we've learned about how and where to buy PC hardware components. When you finish reading this chapter, you'll have all the information you need to make the right buying decisions.

Choosing Components

The biggest advantage of building your own PC is that you can choose which components to use. If you buy a cookie-cutter system from Dell or HP, most of the decisions are made for you. You can specify a larger hard drive, more memory, or a different monitor, but the range of options is quite limited. Want a better power supply, a quieter CPU cooler, and a mother-

Same Factory, Different Brands

It's not uncommon for several manufacturers to relabel identical or closely similar products from the same Pacific Rim factory. For example, the factory that makes many of the cases that Antec sells under its brand names also makes similar cases that are sold under other brand names such as Chieftec and Chenming. Contrary to web wisdom, that doesn't mean that those similar products are identical to the Antec case. Different companies can specify different levels of finish, quality control, and so on. A case with the Antec name on it meets Antec's quality standards. An "identical" case with a different brand name may not be of the same quality.

board with built-in FireWire and RAID 0+1 support? Tough luck. Those options aren't on the table.

When you build from scratch, you get to choose every component that goes into your system. You can spend a bit more here and a bit less there to get exactly the features and functions you want at the best price. It's therefore worth devoting some time and effort to component selection, but there are so many competing products available that it's difficult to separate the marketing hype from reality.

On your own, you might find yourself struggling to answer questions like, "Should I buy a Seagate hard drive or a Western Digital?" (hint: Seagate) or "Does Sony or HP make the best DVD writers?" (hint: neither; go with a Plextor.) We've done all that research for you, and the following sections distill what we've learned in testing and using hundreds of products over many years.

We recommend products by brand name, and we don't doubt that some people will take issue with some of our recommendations. We don't claim that the products we recommend are "best" in any absolute sense, because we haven't tested every product on the market and because "best" is inherently subjective. However, although what's "best" for us may be just "very good" from your point of view, it almost certainly won't be "awful."

So, keeping all of that in mind, the following sections describe the products we recommend.

For more detailed selection criteria and in-depth explanations of technical issues related to choosing components, see *Building the Perfect PC: A Pocket Guide to Choosing and Buying Components* (O'Reilly).

Case

The case (or *chassis*) is the foundation of any system. Its obvious purpose is to support the power supply, motherboard, drives, and other components. Its less obvious purposes are to contain the radio-frequency interference produced by internal components, to ensure proper system cooling, and to subdue the noise produced by the power supply, drives, fans, and other components with moving parts.

A good case performs all of these tasks well and is a joy to work with. It is strongly built and rigid. Adding or removing components is quick and easy. All the holes line up, and there are no sharp edges or burrs. On the other hand, a bad case is painful to work with, sometimes literally. It may have numerous exposed razor-sharp edges and burrs that cut you even if you're careful. It is cheaply constructed of flimsy material that flexes excessively. Tolerances are very loose, sometimes so much so that you have to bend sheet metal to get a component to fit, if that is even possible. Using a cheap case is a sure way to make your system building experience miserable.

Use the following guidelines when choosing a case:

- Choose the proper size case, taking into account the original configuration and possible future expansion. For a general-purpose system, choose a mini- or mid-tower case. For a small PC, choose a microATX case. Choose a case that leaves at least one drive bay—ideally a 5.25" external bay—free for later expansion.

- Get a case with supplemental cooling fans or with enough space to add them. Heat is the enemy of processors, memory, drives, and other system components. Cooler components last longer and run more reliably.

Power supply

The power supply is one of the most important components in a PC, and yet most people give it little consideration. In addition to providing reliable, stable, closely regulated power to all system components, the power supply draws air through the system to cool it. A marginal or failing power supply can cause many problems, some of which are very subtle and difficult to track down. Most problems are not subtle, however. A poor or marginal power supply is likely to cause system crashes, memory errors, and data corruption, and may fail catastrophically, taking other system components with it.

Use the following guidelines to choose a power supply appropriate for your system:

- Above all, make sure the power supply you buy fits your case and has the proper connectors for your motherboard. Most cases use ATX power supplies, and any ATX power supply fits any ATX case. SFF and microATX cases often use SFX or proprietary power supplies. We avoid using those whenever possible.

- Size your power supply according to the system configuration. (The wattages we specify are for power supplies that are rated at 40°C, such as Antec and PC Power & Cooling units. For power supplies that are rated at 25°C, multiply these wattages by 1.5 or 150%.) For an entry-level system, install a 230W or larger power supply. For a mainstream system, install a 300W or larger power supply. For a high-performance system, install a 400W or larger power supply. For a heavily loaded system, install a 500W or larger power supply.

- Buy only an ATX12V-compliant power supply.

- Make sure the power supply provides Serial ATA power connectors.

Processor

Most people spend too much time dithering about which processor to install. There are really only two choices you need to make: first, Intel versus AMD, and second, how much you should spend. Here are the considerations for each of the processor price ranges:

Low end (under $150)
At the bottom of this range—sub-$100 processors—inexpensive Athlon XP models simply mop the floor with comparably priced Celerons. At the upper end of this range are the least expensive processors that we consider mainstream models—the fastest Celerons, fast Athlon XPs, and the slowest Pentium 4s. Around the $150 mark, Intel begins to achieve performance parity, or nearly so.

Midrange ($150 to $250)
This is the mainstream. The bottom half of this range includes the fastest Athlon XPs and the midrange Pentium 4s, any of which are good choices for a mainstream system. At the upper end of this range are fast Pentium 4s and Athlon 64s. Midrange processors as a group are generally noticeably faster than low-end processors and cost only a little more, while at the same time being only a bit slower than high-end processors and costing a lot less.

High end ($250+)
At the lower end, this range is the realm of the fastest Pentium 4 and Athlon 64 processors. At the high end—which may approach or exceed $1,000—you'll find the Intel Pentium 4 Extreme Edition and the Athlon 64 FX. This range is characterized by a rapidly decreasing bang-for-the-buck ratio. A $150 processor might be 50% faster than a $75 processor, but a $400 processor may be only 10% faster than a $200 processor, and a $1,000 processor only 5% faster than a $400 one.

Also consider the following issues when you choose a processor:

- Even the slowest current processor more than suffices for office productivity applications. If you never load the system heavily, you won't notice

The New Celerons

As we went to press, Intel began shipping a new series of Celerons, the so-called "Celeron D" processors, which are based on the Prescott-core Pentium 4. We didn't expect much from these new Celerons, but we were wrong. Intel turned the tables on AMD. The Celeron D is fully competitive in price and performance with inexpensive Athlon XP models. On that basis, we withdraw our blanket condemnation of the Celeron. If you do buy a Celeron, though, make certain it's a D model. Celerons based on the older Northwood core are still dogs.

Processor

 When price is a high priority, we recommend the fastest retail-boxed AMD Athlon XP you can find for $75 to $100. For midrange systems, choose the fastest retail-boxed Intel Pentium 4 or AMD Athlon 64 you can find for $185 or so. If multimedia/AV is important to you, choose the Pentium 4. If gaming is your priority, choose the Athlon 64. If you need the fastest possible processor and are willing to pay the price, choose the Intel Pentium 4 Extreme Edition or the AMD Athlon 64 FX.

 Dollar for dollar, the Intel Celeron simply cannot compare to the AMD Athlon XP, and we see no reason to ever use one.

much difference between an inexpensive processor and a more expensive model.

- Low-end processors are hampered by small secondary caches. These cripple performance, particularly if you work with large data sets, such as multimedia, graphics, or video.

- In the midrange and high-end segments, Intel processors cost more than AMD processors with comparable performance. However, Athlon 64 motherboards usually cost more than comparable Pentium 4 motherboards and often have fewer features, so the overall cost for comparable AMD and Intel systems is usually quite close.

- Processors in the "sweet spot" range—$150 to $200 for a retail-boxed processor—usually represent the best bang for the buck.

- Buy the processor you need initially, rather than buying a slower processor now and planning to upgrade later. Processor upgrades, AMD and Intel, are a minefield of compatibility issues.

Heatsink/fan units (CPU coolers)

Modern processors consume 50W to 100W or more. Nearly all systems deal with the resulting heat by placing a massive metal heatsink in close contact with the processor and using a small fan to draw air through the heatsink fins. This device is called a heatsink/fan (HSF) or CPU cooler. Use the following guidelines when choosing an HSF:

- Make certain the HSF is rated for the exact processor you use. An HSF that physically fits a processor may not be sufficient to cool it properly. In particular, be careful with Prescott-core Pentium 4 processors, which produce much more heat than the earlier Northwood-core P4s running at the same speed.

- Make sure the HSF is usable with your motherboard. Some HSFs are incompatible with some motherboards because

Heatsink/Fan Units

 In general, we recommend using the HSFs that are bundled with retail-boxed processors. These are generally midrange in performance and noise level.

 If you use an OEM processor, we recommend Dynatron HSFs for general usage (*http://www.dynatron-corp.com*).

 If you need a very quiet heatsink/fan, use a Zalman "flower" HSF, which allows you to run fast processors with nearly no fan noise (*www.zalman. co.kr/english/intro.htm*).

 We generally use the thermal compound or phase-change medium that is provided with the heatsink/fan unit, assuming it is approved by the processor maker. (AMD is very specific about which thermal transfer media are acceptable for its processors.) When we reinstall an HSF, we use Antec Silver Thermal Compound (*http://www.antec-inc.com*), which is as good as "premium" silver thermal compounds and costs much less.

 Avoid the generic "no-name" HSFs you'll find on bargain tables in some computer stores or computer fairs for as little as $4. Anyone who installs a no-name $4 HSF on a $200 CPU deserves whatever happens. Also avoid premium HSFs that are so beloved by overclockers—you can easily spend $50 or more on such a unit, and it provides little benefit relative to the stock HSF or an inexpensive Dynatron unit. For example, we tested an $18 Dynatron unit against a "big-name" unit that sold for $58, using the same processor and thermal compound. The CPU temperature with the Dynatron stabilized at 33° C, versus 32° C with the premium unit. BFD.

clamping the HSF into position may crush capacitors or other components near the processor socket.

- Pay attention to noise ratings. Some high-efficiency HSFs designed for use by overclockers and other enthusiasts have very noisy fans. Other HSFs are nearly silent.

- Use the proper thermal compound. When you install an HSF, and each time you remove and replace it, use fresh thermal compound to ensure proper heat transfer. Thermal compound is available in the form of viscous thermal "goop" and as phase-change thermal pads, which melt as the processor heats up and solidify as it cools down. Make sure that the thermal compound you use is approved by the processor maker.

Motherboard

The motherboard is the main logic board around which a PC is built. It is the center of the PC in the sense that every system component connects to the motherboard, directly or indirectly. The motherboard you choose determines which processors are supported, how much and what type of memory the system can use, what type of video adapters can be installed, the speed of communication ports, and many other key system characteristics.

Use the following guidelines when choosing a motherboard:

- For a general-purpose system, choose an ATX motherboard. For a small system, a microATX motherboard may be a better choice, although using the smaller form factor has several drawbacks—notably, giving up several expansion slots and making it more difficult to route cables and cool the system.

- For a Pentium 4 or Celeron system, choose a Socket 478 (current technology) or Socket 775 (the new Socket T) motherboard. The former is less expensive and more widely available; the latter incorporates newer chipsets, provides additional features such as PCI Express support, and provides a better upgrade path. For an Athlon XP system, choose a Socket A motherboard. For an Athlon 64 system, choose a Socket 939 motherboard.

- For an Intel processor, choose a motherboard that uses an Intel 865- or 875-series chipset (Socket 478) or an Intel 9-series chipset (Socket T), depending on your budget and priorities. For an Athlon XP processor, choose a motherboard that uses an *n*VIDIA *n*Force2-series chipset. For an Athlon 64 processor, choose a motherboard that uses an *n*VIDIA *n*Force3-series chipset.

- Make sure the motherboard supports the *exact* processor you plan to use. Just because a motherboard supports a particular processor family doesn't mean that it supports all members of that family. You can find this information on the motherboard maker's web site or in the release notes to the BIOS updates. It's also important to know exactly what revision of the motherboard you have, because processor support may vary by motherboard revision level.

- Choose a motherboard that supports at least the host bus speeds you need now and expect to need for the life of the board. For example, if you install a 533 MHz FSB Celeron initially, choose a motherboard that also supports 800 MHz FSB Pentium 4 processors.

- Make sure the motherboard supports the type and amount of memory you need. Any motherboard you buy should support PC3200 DDR-SDRAM. Do not make assumptions about how much memory a motherboard supports; check the documentation to find out what specific memory configurations are supported.

- Before you choose a motherboard, check the documentation and support that's available for it, as well as the BIOS and driver updates available. Frequent updates indicate that the manufacturer takes support seriously.

Memory

The only real decisions here are how much memory to install, what size modules to use, and what brand to buy. For entry-level systems, we recommend no less than 256 MB, although Windows XP is happier with more. For mainstream systems, 512 MB may suffice, but 1 GB is better. For performance systems, workstations, and multimedia/graphics systems, install at least 1 GB, and more is better. Consider the following factors when choosing memory modules:

- Use PC3200 DDR-SDRAM memory modules.

- It's generally less expensive to buy a given amount of memory in one module rather than two or more modules. However, the largest-capacity modules often sell at a substantial premium. For example, a 1 GB DIMM may cost three times as much as a 512 MB DIMM, rather than only twice as much.

- For higher performance, use DIMMs in pairs if your motherboard has a dual-channel memory controller, as do all current Intel motherboards and some AMD motherboards.

Motherboards

 For Intel processors, we recommend Intel motherboards. The D865GBFL is our usual choice. The build quality is very high, and the board is fast and as stable as any we've used. The embedded video, audio, and LAN are good enough for most purposes. The D865PERL is a D865GBFL without video, and is equally good. Choose the D865PERL if you want to use a separate AGP 3D graphics adapter. The D865GLC is essentially a microATX variant of the D865GBF. The D875PBZ is a good choice when top performance is necessary. ASUS also manufactures top-notch P4 motherboards. We can recommend any of their P4P800-series boards based on the 865P/PE or 875P chipset, including the microATX P4P800-VM.

 For AMD processors, we recommend motherboards based on *n*VIDIA *n*Force2- and *n*Force3-series chipsets. For the Athlon XP, the best of these are ASUS A7N8X-series motherboards. For the Athlon 64, choose the ASUS SK8N.

 We avoid motherboards from ABIT, Adtran, Albatron, Biostar, Chaintech, DFI, ECS (Elitegroup Computer Systems), FIC, Iwill, Leadtek, Shuttle, Soyo, Vantec, and others we haven't listed. We also avoid motherboards that use a VIA Technologies chipset or a PC Chips chipset, even if the motherboard was made by one of our preferred manufacturers.

Memory

 We use Crucial and Kingston PC3200 memory almost exclusively, and recommend that others do the same. Crucial produces CL3 memory, which we almost always use. Kingston produces CL3 and CL2.5 modules. We use the latter when memory performance is critical.

 Avoid generic "white-box" memory. Such modules often use chips that failed testing by reputable manufacturers or were pulled from rejected modules, and are likely to cause data corruption and stability problems. We also generally avoid so-called "premium" or "performance" modules, which cost more but seldom provide much real increase in system performance.

Floppy Disk Drive

 If you want an FDD, buy any brand. FDDs are commodity items, and the brand makes little difference.

 If you're short on external drive bays and want both an FDD and a card reader, install a combination FDD/card reader. We'd use the $25 Mitsumi FA402A.

• Verify the memory configurations supported by your motherboard. For example, a particular motherboard may support 256 MB DIMMs but not 512 MB DIMMs. One motherboard may support 512 MB DIMMs in all four of its memory slots, but another may support 512 MB DIMMs in only two of its four slots. Check the motherboard documentation to determine the memory configurations your chosen motherboard supports. You can also visit the Crucial web site (*http://www.crucial.com*) and use their memory configurator to verify compatibility.

• Non-parity memory modules provide no error detection or correction. ECC modules detect and correct most memory errors, but are slower and more expensive than non-parity modules. Use ECC memory if you install more than 2 GB of memory and the motherboard supports ECC memory. For 2 GB or less, use non-parity modules.

• PC3200 memory is available in CL3 versions and faster CL2.5 versions. CL2.5 memory is typically only 3% or so faster than CL3, so using CL2.5 memory seldom provides any real benefit to overall system performance. If CL2.5 memory is available for the same price as CL3 memory, go ahead and buy it, but don't pay more for it.

Floppy disk drive

Every time we build a PC without a floppy disk drive (FDD), we end up regretting it when we need to load a driver from floppy. Accordingly, we recommend installing an FDD. At $8 or so, it's cheap insurance.

Hard drive

It's easy to choose a good hard drive. Various manufacturers produce high-quality drives at similar price points for a given size and type of drive. That said, we use only Seagate and Maxtor drives because we have had reliability problems with drives made by some other manufacturers.

Within a given grade of drive, however, drives from different manufacturers are usually closely comparable in features, performance, and price, if not necessarily in reliability. Compatibility is not an issue. Any recent ATA hard disk coexists peacefully with any other recent ATA/ATAPI device, regardless of manufacturer. The same is generally true of SCSI drives.

Use the following guidelines when you choose a hard drive:

- The first consideration in choosing a hard drive is whether to use standard ATA (parallel ATA or P-ATA), Serial ATA (S-ATA), or SCSI. P-ATA and S-ATA drives are inexpensive, fast, capacious, and reliable, and are the best choice for most general-purpose systems. SCSI hard drives cost significantly more and require adding an expensive SCSI host adapter, but provide the best performance, particularly under heavy load.

  — Choose a P-ATA drive if your motherboard lacks S-ATA interfaces. Choose an ATA/100 or an ATA/133 model. Only Maxtor produces ATA/133 drives, which are no faster than ATA/100 drives. A motherboard with ATA/100 interfaces can use ATA/133 drives and vice versa, but the disk subsystem runs as ATA/100 in either case.

  — S-ATA drives are generally a bit faster than similar P-ATA models, and use thin cables that improve system cooling relative to wide P-ATA ribbon cables. If your system has S-ATA interfaces and the S-ATA drive you want costs only $5 or $10 more than the P-ATA model, choose S-ATA. But if the price differential is much larger, or if you would have to buy a separate S-ATA interface card to use the S-ATA drive, use P-ATA.

  — If disk performance is critical, buy an Ultra320 SCSI host adapter and a 15,000 RPM Ultra320 SCSI drive. Note that you will pay a large premium, both for the drive itself and for the required SCSI host adapter. Purchase a drive and host adapter that comply with the SCAM (SCSI Configured AutoMagically) standard. We recommend and use only Adaptec SCSI host adapters.

- It's tempting to buy the largest drive available, but large drives often cost more per gigabyte than mid-size drives, and the largest drives are often slower. Decide what performance level and capacity you need, and then buy a drive that meets those requirements. Choose the model based on cost per gigabyte. You may need to buy the largest drive avail-

---

RECOMMENDATIONS

Hard Drive

 If you need an S-ATA or P-ATA hard drive, choose a Seagate model of the appropriate size and speed. We use Seagate Barracuda 7200.7 S-ATA drives almost exclusively in our own systems. Maxtor drives are also excellent, although they are noisier and run hotter than the Seagate Barracuda drives.

 If you need the faster performance of SCSI, choose a 15,000 RPM Ultra320 SCSI Seagate Cheetah drive and an Adaptec Ultra320 SCSI host adapter.

 We no longer use Western Digital hard drives because we have experienced multiple premature drive failures with various models. Although we have never had a premature drive failure with IBM (now Hitachi) ATA hard drives, enough of our readers have reported problems with some IBM/Hitachi models that we avoid them as well. We don't have sufficient data to judge the reliability of Samsung models.

---

able despite its high cost per gigabyte and slower performance, simply to conserve drive bays and ATA channels.

- Choose a 7,200 RPM P-ATA or S-ATA drive for a general-purpose system. 5,400 RPM ATA drives are a few bucks cheaper, but much slower. 10,000 RPM ATA drives cost much more than 7,200 RPM models and are not all that much faster.

- Get the model with a larger buffer/cache if it doesn't cost much more. Some drives are available in two versions that differ only in buffer size. One might have a 2 MB buffer and the other an 8 MB buffer. The larger buffer is worth paying a few dollars extra for.

- The quietest mainstream drives, the Seagate Barracuda ATA and S-ATA models, are literally half as loud as some competing models, and also run cooler. When you have a choice, always choose quiet and cool over noisy and hot.

Optical drive

Every system needs an optical drive of some sort, if only for loading software. There are several types of optical drives available. Some can use only CDs, which typically store about 700 MB of data; others can use DVDs, which typically store about 4,700 MB of data. CD-ROM and DVD-ROM drives are read-only (the "ROM" part of the name). CD writers and DVD writers (also called burners or recorders) can write optical discs as well as read them. DVD is backward compatible with CD, which means that a DVD drive can also read CD discs, and nearly all DVD writers can also write CD discs.

CD drive speeds are specified as a multiple of the 150 KB/s audio CD rate, which is called 1X. For example, a 52X CD drive transfers data at 52 times 150 KB/s, or 7,800 KB/s. DVD drives use a different "X-factor." A 1X DVD drive transfers data at about 1.321 MB/s, or about nine times faster than a 1X CD drive.

Choose an optical drive for your system based on the capabilities you need and the price you are willing to pay. Roughly in order of increasing price and usefulness, your choices are:

CD-ROM drive. A CD-ROM drive provides basic functionality at minimum cost. CD-ROM drives read only CD-DA (audio) discs, CD-ROM (data) discs, and (usually) CD-R/CD-RW writable discs, and cannot write discs. CD-ROM drives are $15 commodity items. There is little reason to choose a brand other than by price and manufacturer reputation.

DVD-ROM drive. DVD-ROM drives read CD-DA, CD-ROM, CD-R/RW, and DVD discs, and cannot write discs. DVD-ROM drives are $30 commodity items. Choose by price and manufacturer reputation.

CD-RW drive. CD-RW drives, also called CD writers or CD burners, read the same formats as CD-ROM drives, but can also write data to inexpensive CD-R (write-once) and CD-RW (rewritable) discs. CD writers typically sell for a bit more than DVD-ROM drives, generally $30 to $40. CD writers provide a means to copy audio and data CDs, and are also an inexpensive backup solution. Nearly all current CD-RW drives have similar features and speed, so there is little reason to choose a brand other than by price and manufacturer reputation.

DVD-ROM/CD-RW drive. DVD-ROM/CD-RW "combo" drives combine the functionality of a DVD-ROM drive and a CD-RW drive, and sell for a few dollars more than CD writers, typically $45 to $60. Because they can read nearly any optical disc and write CDs, we consider them the best compromise for an inexpensive system. Once again, there is little reason to choose a brand other than by price and manufacturer reputation.

DVD writer. DVD writers do it all—they both read and write both CDs and DVDs. Basic DVD writers sell for $75, but high-end models cost $150 or more. Most high-end and many mid-range models can use DVD+R, DVD+RW, DVD-R, and DVD-RW discs interchangeably, which offers the most flexibility. Inexpensive models may support only DVD+R/RW or DVD-R/RW. (We recommend using DVD+R/RW discs rather than DVD-R/RW discs whenever possible, because "plus" discs have better error correction than "minus" discs.) Current mainstream DVD writers support 8X or 12X writes on DVD+R discs, either of which is fast enough for most purposes. Inexpensive writers often support only 4X writes, which requires patience.

RECOMMENDATIONS

Optical Drive

 For a CD-ROM drive, any current model made by Lite-On, Mitsumi, NEC, Samsung, or Sony is acceptable. All are reliable, so buy on price.

 For a DVD-ROM drive, choose any current model made by Lite-On, Mitsumi, NEC, Samsung, Sony, or Toshiba. If you need to read writable DVD discs, make sure the model you choose explicitly lists compatibility with the formats you use. If you need to read DVD-RAM discs, buy a Toshiba model. Otherwise, buy on price.

 For the most reliable CD-RW drive available with the best digital audio extraction (for "ripping" audio CD tracks to your hard drive), choose the Plextor Premium, as long as it remains available. Otherwise, choose any 48X, 52X, or 54X model from Lite-On, Mitsumi, Samsung, or Sony, based on price.

 For a combination DVD-ROM/CD-RW drive, choose any current model made by Lite-On, Samsung, Sony, Teac, or Toshiba that supports 16X DVD reads and 48X or higher CD-R writes. If you need to read writable DVD discs, make sure the model you choose explicitly lists compatibility with the formats you use. If you need to read DVD-RAM discs, buy a Toshiba model. Otherwise, all are reliable and priced similarly, so buy the least expensive.

 For a DVD±R/RW drive, choose the 8X Plextor PX-708A or the 12X Plextor PX-712A (ATA) or PX-712SA (S-ATA). Our second choice is the Sony DRU-530A. For those on a tight budget, the NEC ND-2500A is the best inexpensive 8X DVD±R/RW drive.

 Avoid optical drives from any manufacturer other than those named above. External USB optical drives can be a pain in the butt. Avoid them in favor of an internal drive unless portability is paramount.

Video adapter

The video adapter, also called a graphics adapter or graphics card, renders video data provided by the processor into a form that the monitor can display. Many motherboards include embedded video adapters. You can also install a standalone video adapter in a motherboard expansion slot. Keep the following in mind when you choose a video adapter:

- Unless you run graphics-intensive games, 3D graphics performance is unimportant. Any recent video adapter is more than fast enough for business applications and casual gaming.

- Choose embedded video unless there is good reason not to. Embedded video adds little or no cost to a motherboard, and generally suffices for anyone except hardcore gamers or those with other special video requirements. Make sure any motherboard you buy allows embedded video to be disabled and provides an AGP slot. That way, you can upgrade the video later if you need to.

- If you need a 3D graphics adapter, don't overbuy. A $400 video adapter is faster than a $100 adapter, but nowhere near four times faster. As with other PC components, the bang-for-the-buck ratio drops quickly as the price climbs. If you need better 3D graphics performance than embedded video provides but you don't have much in the budget for a video adapter, look at "obsolescent" 3D video adapters—those a generation or two out of date. If you buy an older adapter, make sure that the level of DirectX it supports is high enough to support the games you play.

- If you choose a standalone video adapter, buy only a 1.5V AGP 4X (AGP 2.0) or 0.8V AGP 4X/8X (AGP 3.0) adapter. Check the motherboard manual to verify which type or types of AGP adapter it supports, and then buy accordingly.

- Display quality is subjective, but a real issue nonetheless. The three major video chipset companies are ATi and *n*VIDIA—both of which provide chipsets that are used both for standalone AGP adapters and for embedded video—and Intel, whose Extreme Graphics 2 is available only as embedded video.

  — ATi produces a wide range of video chipsets. 3D performance ranges from moderate in inexpensive models to extremely high in expensive ones. 2D video quality is excellent across the entire line and at any resolution. ATi drivers balance 3D performance and 2D image quality, favoring neither at the expense of the other.

  — *n*VIDIA produces a wide range of video chipsets. 3D performance ranges from moderate in inexpensive models to extremely high in expensive models. 2D video quality ranges from mediocre in older adapters, particularly high-performance models, to good in some recent models. We consider *n*VIDIA 2D image quality acceptable at low resolutions, but less so at 1280 × 1024 and higher. *n*VIDIA drivers tend to favor 3D performance at the expense of 2D image quality.

— Intel Extreme Graphics 2 video is built into some Intel chipsets and is available only in embedded form. 3D performance is low to moderate, although it is acceptable for casual gaming. 2D display quality is very good to excellent.

• Make sure that the adapter you choose has drivers available for the operating system you intend to use. This is particularly important if you run Linux or another OS with limited driver support.

• Make sure the video adapter provides the interface(s) you need. Most analog CRT monitors use the familiar high-density DB15 "VGA" connector, although a few high-end models also support RGB component video. Flat-panel displays (FPDs) use a variety of connectors, including the analog DB15VGA connector (typically used by low-end FPDs), or one of three different types of Digital Visual Interface (DVI) connectors. Midrange and higher FPDs normally provide a DVI-D digital connector, and may also provide a DB-15 analog connector and/or a DVI-A analog connector. If you plan to use an FPD, whenever possible choose an FPD and a video adapter that both provide DVI-D connectors.

RECOMMENDATIONS

Video Adapter

 For a general-purpose system, choose embedded video based on an ATi, Intel, or *n*VIDIA chipset. Make sure the motherboard you select has an AGP 2.0 or higher slot so that you can upgrade the video later if necessary.

 If you need a standalone video adapter, buy an ATi RADEON model that fits your needs and budget. Buy either a "Built by ATi" RADEON adapter, which is actually made by ATi, or a "Powered by ATi" RADEON adapter, which is made by a third-party company using an ATi chipset. In the latter category, we have had good experience with RADEON video adapters made by Crucial Technology. ATi and other companies produce various RADEON models in two variants. Standard models are pure graphics cards. All-In-Wonder (AIW) models include a television tuner and software for recording video.

 Avoid embedded video based on anything other than an ATi, Intel, or *n*VIDIA chipset. Avoid generic or off-brand video adapters, even if they use an ATi or *n*VIDIA chipset.

Display

You'll spend a lot of time looking at your display, so it's worth devoting some time and effort to choosing a good one. The first decision to make when you choose a display is whether to buy a traditional "glass bottle" CRT monitor or an LCD flat-panel display (FPD).

FPDs have several advantages over CRT monitors. FPDs are brighter than CRTs and have better contrast. Short of direct sunlight impinging on the screen, a good FPD provides excellent images under any lighting conditions. FPDs are much lighter than CRTs and are only a few inches deep, which makes them more convenient when space is limited. Finally, FPDs consume only 20% to 60% as much power as typical CRTs.

FPDs also have many drawbacks relative to CRTs. Not all FPDs suffer from all of these flaws—newer models are less likely than older models to suffer from any particular flaw, and inexpensive models are more likely than premium models to suffer from these flaws, both in number and in degree.

The primary drawback of FPDs is their hideously high price, literally two to three times as much as comparable CRTs. FPDs are optimized for one resolution, usually 1024 × 768 for 14" and 15" FPDs, and 1280 × 1024 for 17", 18", and 19" FPDs. FPDs backlight the image with an array of cold cathode ray tubes (CCRTs), which are similar to fluorescent tubes and are subject to failure. An out-of-warranty CCRT failure means you might as well buy a new FPD, because it's very costly to repair.

FPDs have other drawbacks as well. Even the best FPD is marginal for displaying fast-motion video and games because the image smears and ghosts. FPDs have a limited viewing angle. Most graphic artists we've spoken to refuse to use FPDs because the appearance of colors and the relationship between colors change depending on the viewing angle. FPDs provide less vibrant color than a good CRT monitor. This is particularly evident in the darkest and lightest ranges, where the tones seem to be compressed; this limits subtle gradations between light tones or dark tones that are readily evident on a good CRT. Also, many FPDs add a color cast to what should be neutral light or dark tones. FPDs, particularly inexpensive models, suffer from image persistence, which causes temporary "ghost images."

Finally, most FPDs have one or more defective pixels. These defective pixels may be always-on (white), always-off (black), or a color. People vary in their reaction to defective pixels. Many people won't even notice a few defective pixels, while others, once they notice a defective pixel, seem to be drawn to that pixel to the exclusion of everything else. Most manufacturer warranties specifically exclude some number of defective pixels, typically between five and ten, although the number may vary with display size and, sometimes, with the location of the defective pixels and how closely they are clustered. As long as the display meets those requirements, the manufacturer considers the display to be acceptable. You may or may not find it so.

Our opinion is that FPDs should be used only if their size, weight, low power consumption, or portability outweighs their much higher cost and other disadvantages. Otherwise, we recommend you choose a good CRT and allocate the money you save to other system components.

Use the following guidelines when choosing a CRT monitor:

- A good monitor is a long-term purchase. Even with heavy use, a good monitor should last five years or more, whereas inexpensive monitors often fail within a year or two.

Good Name Brands

Deciding which are the "good" name brands is a matter of spirited debate. We consider NEC-Mitsubishi, Samsung, and ViewSonic to be the "Big Three" CRT monitor makers. Their monitors, particularly midrange and better models, provide excellent image quality and are quite reliable. Many people also think highly of EIZO/Nanao monitors. You're likely to be happy with a monitor from any of these manufacturers, although we buy only NEC-Mitsubishi monitors for our systems.

Further down the ladder are "value" brands like Mag Innovision, Princeton, and Optiquest. Our experience with value brands has not been good. Their display quality is mediocre, and they tend not to last long.

- Check physical dimensions and weight carefully before you buy, and verify that the monitor fits your desk or workstation furniture. Large monitors may weigh 50 lbs. or more, and some exceed 100 lbs. That said, if you find yourself debating between one size and the next size up, go with the larger monitor. But if your decision is between a low-end larger monitor and a high-end smaller one for about the same price, you may be happier with the smaller monitor.

- Avoid reduced-depth monitors whenever possible. Space constraints may force you to choose a short-neck model, but be aware that you will pay more for such a monitor, and its image quality will be lower.

- Stick with good name brands. Doing so won't guarantee that you'll get a good monitor, but it does increase your chances. The monitor market is extremely competitive. If two similar models differ greatly in price, the cheaper one likely has significantly worse specs. If the specs are similar, the maker of the cheaper model has cut corners somewhere.

- Buy the monitor locally if possible. You'll save on shipping costs, of course, but that is not the main reason why it's a good idea. Buying locally gives you the opportunity to examine the exact monitor you are buying. Monitors vary more between samples than other computer components. Also, monitors are sometimes damaged in shipping, often without any external evidence on the monitor itself or even the box. Damaged monitors may arrive DOA, but more frequently they have been jolted

RECOMMENDATIONS

CRT Monitor

 We do not recommend buying any 15" CRT monitor. A 17" model costs only a few dollars more and provides a much larger display area. If for some reason you must have a 15" CRT monitor, choose the NEC AS500 (*http://www.necmitsubishi.com*).

 For a budget 17" CRT monitor, choose the NEC AS700. The AS700 is the best inexpensive 17" monitor we have used. It supports 1024 × 768 resolution at 85 Hz, which is more than adequate, and provides NEC's typical high display quality. It'd be hard to find a better 17" budget monitor. One good indication of monitor quality is the length of the warranty. The NEC AccuSync AS700 has a three-year parts and labor warranty, which is extraordinary for an inexpensive 17" monitor. Many competing models have only a one-year parts and labor warranty, and some have only a one-year parts/90-days labor warranty.

 Do not buy a premium 17" CRT monitor. Although high-end 17" monitors are available, we see no point in paying $175 or more for a 17" monitor. For little or no more than the cost of a premium 17" monitor, you can instead buy an entry-level 19" monitor from a first-tier maker. That 19" monitor supports the same or higher resolutions as the premium 17" monitor. The image scale at those resolutions will actually be large enough to use, and the image quality of the entry-level 19" will be more than good enough for general use.

 For a budget 19" CRT monitor, choose the NEC AS900. The AS900 is a superb entry-level model. It supports 85 Hz refresh at 1280 × 1024, which is perfectly adequate for normal use. It can also run 76 Hz at 1600 × 1200, which may come in handy for special purposes. Like the other AccuSync monitors, the AS900 has a three-year warranty, which is much better than the warranties on most no-name displays.

 For a mainstream 19" CRT monitor, the NEC FE991SB is hard to beat. It supports 1280 × 1024 resolution at 89 Hz, 1600 × 1200 at 76 Hz, and (rather uselessly, we think) 1792 × 1344 at 68 Hz. The images are extremely bright and have the trademark NEC crispness and contrast.

severely enough to cause display problems and perhaps reduced service life, but not complete failure. Buying locally allows you to eliminate a "dud" before you buy it, rather than having to deal with shipping it back to the vendor or manufacturer.

- Most monitor manufacturers produce no 15" models (there's no profit in them), and usually three—Good, Better, and Best—models in 17", 19", and 21". In general, the Good model from a first-tier maker corresponds roughly in features, specifications, and price to the Better or Best models from lower-tier makers. For casual use, choose a first-tier Good model, most of which are very good indeed. If you work with graphics, the Better model from a first-tier maker is usually the best choice. The Best models from first-tier makers are usually overkill, although they may be necessary if you use the monitor for CAD/CAM or other demanding tasks.

- Choose the specific monitor you buy based on how it looks to you. Comparing specifications helps narrow the list of candidates, but nothing substitutes for actually looking at the image displayed by the monitor. For example, monitors with Sony Trinitron tubes have one or two fine horizontal internal wires whose shadows appear on the screen. Most people don't even notice the shadow, but some find it intolerable.

- Make sure the monitor has sufficient reserve brightness. Monitors dim as they age, and one of the most common flaws in new monitors, particularly those from second- and third-tier manufacturers, is inadequate brightness. A monitor that is barely bright enough when new may dim enough to become unusable after a year or two. A new monitor should provide a good image with the brightness set no higher than 50%.

If you have weighed the tradeoffs carefully and decided that an FPD is right for you, use the following guidelines when choosing one:

- Current FPDs are available in analog-only, digital-only, and hybrid analog/digital models. Analog input is acceptable on 15" models running 1024 × 768, but on 17" models running 1280 × 1024, analog video noise becomes an issue. At that level of resolution, analog noise isn't immediately obvious to most users, but if you use the display for long periods the difference between display with a clean digital signal and one with a noisy analog signal will affect you on an almost subconscious level. At 1024 × 768, we regard an analog signal as acceptable. At 1280 × 1024, we regard a digital signal as very desirable but not essential for most users. Above 1280 × 1024, we regard digital signaling as essential.

- Insist on 24-bit color support. Most current FPDs support true 24-bit color, allocating eight bits to each of the three primary colors, which allows 16.7 million colors to be displayed. Many early FPDs and some inexpensive current models support only 18-bit color, with six bits per color, and use extrapolation to simulate full 24-bit color support, which results in poor color quality. Avoid FPDs described as "24-bit compatible," which means they aren't 24-bit displays.

- Some FPD makers produce two or three lines of FPDs. Entry-level models are often analog-only and use standard panels. Midrange models usually have analog and digital inputs, and may use enhanced panels. Professional models may be analog/digital hybrids or digital-only, and use enhanced panels with IPS (In-Plane Switching) or MDVA (Multi-Domain Vertical Alignment). Choose an entry-level model only if you are certain you will never use the display for anything more than word processing, web browsing, and similarly undemanding tasks. If you need a true CRT-replacement FPD, choose a midrange or higher model. For the best possible image quality, choose a high-end model with IPS that is made by a top-tier manufacturer.

- Decide what panel size and resolution is right for you. When you choose an FPD, you are also effectively choosing the resolution that you will always use on that display.

- Verify the rated CCRT life. For an entry-level FPD that will not be used heavily, a 25,000-hour CCRT life is marginally acceptable. If you will use the FPD heavily, insist on CCRTs rated at 50,000 hours.

- Buy the FPD locally if possible. And whether or not you buy locally, insist on a no-questions-asked return policy. FPDs are more variable than CRT monitors, both in unit-to-unit varia-

---

RECOMMENDATIONS

FPD Monitor

 For an entry-level 15" FPD, choose the Hitachi CML158B. Although it is an analog-only FPD, the CML158B has excellent display quality. It provides 1024 × 768 native resolution with a 0.297mm pixel pitch. The viewing angles are acceptable, at 130° horizontal and 100° vertical. Brightness, at 250 nit, is excellent, as is contrast at 400:1. At 35ms, the response time is middling, so you probably won't want to use this FPD for fast-motion video.

 For a general-purpose 17" FPD, choose the Hitachi CML174B or the similar CML175B, which adds built-in speakers but is otherwise identical. The CML174B has analog and DVI-D connectors and provides superb image quality. It supports 1280 × 1024 native resolution with a 0.264mm pixel pitch. The viewing angles are excellent, at 160° horizontal and vertical. Brightness, at 260 nit, is excellent, as is contrast at 400:1. At 16ms, the response time is fast enough to support fast-motion video reasonably well, although the CML174B still exhibits some ghosting and smearing when displaying graphics-intensive games. (Of course, that's true of any FPD, so you can't hold it against the CML174B.) Color rendition on the CML174B is as good as it gets on an FPD, which is to say good enough to satisfy anyone except the most demanding graphics artists. The CML174B costs only $150 or so more than the CML158B, and we think it's the best choice for an FPD for a general-purpose system.

 For a general-purpose 19" FPD, choose the Hitachi CML190B. It has analog and DVI-D connectors and provides superb image quality. It supports 1280 × 1024 native resolution with a 0.294mm pixel pitch. The viewing angles are wider even than the CML174B, at 170° horizontal and vertical. Brightness, at 250 nit, is a bit lower than the CML174B, but still excellent. Contrast, at 500:1, is superb. At 25ms, the response time is a bit slower than the CML174B, but still fast enough for most purposes other than fast-motion video and gaming. Color rendition on the CML190B is excellent. The CML190B costs $250 or so more than the CML174B, but that extra money buys you a "big" FPD, with a VIS similar to that of a 20" CRT.

---

tion and in usability with a particular graphics adapter. This is particularly important if you are using an analog interface. Some analog FPDs simply don't play nice with some analog graphics adapters. Also, FPDs vary from unit to unit in how many defective pixels they have and where they are located. You might prefer a unit with five defective pixels near the edges and corners rather than a unit with only one or two defective pixels located near the center of the screen. In return for the higher price you pay at a local store, ask them to endorse the manufacturer's warranty—that is, to agree that if the FPD fails you can return it to the store for a replacement rather than return the FPD to the manufacturer.

- If possible, test the exact FPD you plan to buy (not a floor sample) before you buy it. Ideally (and particularly if you will use the analog interface), you should test the FPD with your own system, or at least with a system that has a graphics adapter identical to the one you plan to use. Choose the specific FPD you buy based on how it looks to you. Comparing specifications helps narrow the list of candidates, but nothing substitutes for actually looking at the image displayed by the FPD.

- Make sure the FPD has a good warranty. Inexpensive FPDs may have a one-year parts and labor warranty, which is inadequate. Or they may have a three-year warranty on parts and labor, but warrant the CCRTs for only one year; in effect, that's just a one-year warranty with window dressing, because the CCRTs are by far the most likely component to fail. Insist on a three-year parts and labor warranty that covers all parts, including CCRTs. If the manufacturer offers an extended warranty that covers all parts, consider buying it.

The best choices for flat-panel displays are more limited than for CRT monitors. We consider the first tier in flat-panel displays to include only Hitachi and Fujitsu, with Samsung straddling the low first-tier/high second-tier boundary.

We favor Hitachi FPDs based on their image quality and their dead-pixel warranty, which at zero dead pixels and five dead subpixels is the best in the industry. Also, all of the Hitachi FPD models we recommend are warranted for three years, including the backlight.

We have not seen the 20" Hitachi CML200B FPD, but based on our experience with other Hitachi products we would expect it to be an excellent choice for those who can afford it. For $500 or so more than the CML190B, the CML200B buys you only one extra inch, but it is the best choice we know of in a 20" FPD that supports 1600 × 1200 native resolution.

Audio adapter

Audio adapters, also called sound cards, are a dying breed. Nearly all motherboards provide embedded audio that is more than good enough for most people's needs. In particular, the embedded audio provided by *n*VIDIA and Intel chipsets is excellent, with good support for six-channel audio. Only gamers, those who work professionally with audio, and those who have purchased a motherboard without embedded audio need consider buying a standalone audio adapter.

NOTE

Gamers dislike embedded audio not because it lacks features or sound quality but because it puts a small burden on the main system processor, which can reduce graphics frame rates slightly.

RECOMMENDATIONS

Audio Adapter

We won't presume to advise audio professionals, but for others who need a standalone audio adapter here are the ones we recommend:

 For an inexpensive general-purpose audio adapter, choose the Turtle Beach Santa Cruz (*http://www. turtlebeach.com*). Although it's been on the market for years, the Santa Cruz still provides absolutely top-notch audio quality and is a decent choice for gaming as well. At about $55, the Santa Cruz has excellent features and sound quality at a reasonable price.

We haven't yet had the opportunity to test two new audio adapters from Turtle Beach. The Catalina is their new performance sound card. It sells for about $70 and is targeted at serious gamers. The Riviera is their new entry-level sound card. It sells for $40 or so, and is targeted at people who have older motherboards with unsatisfactory embedded audio and who want to upgrade to better audio at low cost. Given our experience with earlier Turtle Beach products, we expect both of these to have superior sound quality for their price points and to provide excellent value for the money.

 For an audio adapter with good sound quality and better gaming support than the Santa Cruz, choose the M-Audio Revolution 7.1 (*http://www.m-audio. com*). At $95 or so, the Revolution 7.1 costs more than the Santa Cruz and has somewhat inferior sound quality, at least to our ears. But there is no doubt that the Revolution 7.1 is very popular among gamers who don't want to pay the price for a high-end Sound Blaster Audigy2 card.

 For serious gamers, the Sound Blaster Audigy2 ZS is the gold standard (*http://www.soundblaster.com*). It is available in several models, from the basic $90 Audigy2 ZS to the $200 Audigy2 ZS Platinum Pro, with various software bundles, optional connectors, and controllers. The Audigy2 ZS has very good sound quality, although to our ears it is slightly inferior to the M-Audio Revolution 7.1 and particularly to the Turtle Beach cards. There is no doubt, though, that the Audigy2 series cards have better gaming support than any competitor.

 Avoid house-brand and no-name audio adapters.

Speakers

Computer speakers range from $10 pairs of small satellites to $500+ sets of six or seven speakers that are suitable for a home theater system. Personal preference is the most important factor in choosing speakers.

Speakers that superbly render a Bach concerto are often not the best choice for playing a first-person shooter game like Unreal Tournament. For that matter, speakers that one person considers perfect for the Bach concerto (or the UT game), someone else may consider mediocre at best. For that reason, we strongly suggest that you listen to speakers before you buy them, particularly if you're buying an expensive set.

RECOMMENDATIONS

Speakers

 For a basic 2.0 speaker set, buy the $15 Creative Labs SBS250 (*http://www.creative.com*) or the Logitech X-120 (*http://www.logitech.com*). They have only 2.5W per channel, but that is sufficient for listening to music and casual gaming. The sound quality is surprisingly good for the price, much better than no-name 2.0 sets that typically sell for $8 or $10. If you need a bit more power, go with the Creative SBS270 set, which sells for a few dollars more and provides 5W per channel, but is otherwise similar to the SBS250 set.

 For a basic 2.1 speaker set, buy the $35 Logitech X-220, which provides 5.8W to each of the two satellites and a 20.4W subwoofer. For a step up in power and sound quality, go with the $70 Logitech Z-3 set, which is what Robert uses on his desk. For a premium 2.1 set, buy the $115 Logitech Z-2200, which boasts THX certification and 200W RMS total power, or the Klipsch Promedia GMX A-2.1, which has only 78W RMS total power, but provides stunningly good sound quality for the price (*http://www.klipsch.com*).

 For a basic 4.1 speaker set, buy the $45 Creative SBS450, which provides 6W to each of the four satellites and 17W to the subwoofer. For more power and better sound quality, go with the $130 Logitech Z-560 set, which provides 53W to each of the four satellites and 188W to the subwoofer.

 For a basic 5.1 speaker set, buy the $60 Logitech Z-640, which provides 7.3W to each of the four satel-lites, 16.3W to the center-channel speaker, and 25.7W to the subwoofer. For more power and better sound, go with the $150 THX-certified Logitech Z-5300 set, which provides 35.25W to each of the four satellites, 39W to the center-channel speaker, and 100W to the subwoofer. For a premium 5.1 set, choose the $275 Logitech Z-680, which is THX-certified and provides Dolby Digital & DTS hardware decoding, along with 62W to each of the four satellites, 69W to the center-channel speaker, and 188W to the subwoofer. We use a Logitech Z-680 set for our Home Theater PC. Also consider the $325 Klipsch Promedia Ultra 5.1 set, which provides five 60W satellites (any of which can be used as the center-channel speaker) and a 170W subwoofer.

The Logitech Z-680 and Promedia Ultra 5.1 are both top-notch speaker systems. Both have superb sound quality and as much power as anyone could need. We slightly prefer the Klipsch Promedia Ultra 5.1 speakers for listening to classical music, and we slightly prefer the Logitech Z-680 speakers for gaming.

 For a basic 6.1 speaker set, buy the $70 Logitech X-620, which provides 7.4W to each of the two front satellites, 7.5W to each of the two rear satellites, 8W to each of the two center-channel speakers, and 24.3W to the subwoofer. For more power and better sound quality, go with the $250 THX-certified Creative Megaworks THX 6.1 set, which provides 70W to each of the five satellites (any of which can be used as the rear center-channel speaker), 75W to the front center-channel speaker, and 150W to the subwoofer.

Speaker sets are designated by the total number of satellite speakers, followed by a period and a "1" if the set includes a subwoofer (also called a low-frequency emitter or LFE). A speaker set that includes only two satellites is called a 2.0 set. One that adds a subwoofer is called a 2.1 set. A 4.1 speaker set has four satellites—left and right, front and rear—and a subwoofer. A 5.1 set adds a center-channel speaker, which is useful for watching movies on DVD. A 6.1 set adds a rear center-channel speaker, which is primarily useful for gaming.

The price of a speaker set doesn't necessarily correspond to the number of speakers in the set. For example, there are very inexpensive 5.1 speaker sets available, and some 2.1 sets that cost a bundle. We recommend that you decide on the number of speakers according to your budget. If you have $75 to spend, for example, you're better off buying a good 2.1 speaker set than a cheesy 5.1 set.

Keyboards

The best keyboard is a matter of personal preference. We may really like a keyboard that you dislike intensely, and vice versa. Ultimately, your own preferences are the only guide.

Keyboards vary in obvious ways like layout, size, and style, and in subtle ways like key spacing, angle, dishing, travel, pressure required, and tactile feedback. People's sensitivity to these differences varies. Some people are keyboard agnostics who can sit down in front of a new keyboard and, regardless of layout or tactile response, be up to speed in a few minutes. Others have strong preferences about layout and feel. If you've never met a keyboard you didn't like, you can disregard these issues and choose a keyboard based on other factors. If love and hate are words you apply to keyboards, test out a keyboard for at least an hour before you buy it.

That said, here are several important characteristics to consider when you choose a keyboard:

- Keyboards are available in two styles, the older straight keyboard and the modern ergonomic style. Some people strongly prefer one or the other; other people don't care. If you've never used an ergonomic keyboard, give one a try before you buy your next keyboard. You may hate it—everyone does at first—but after you use it for an hour you may decide you love it.

- The position of the alphanumeric keys is standard on all keyboards other than those that use the oddball Dvorak layout. What varies, sometimes dramatically, is the placement, size, and shape of other keys, such as shift keys (Shift, Ctrl, and Alt), function keys (which may be across the top, down the left side, or both), and cursor control and numeric keypad keys. If you are used to a particular layout, purchasing a keyboard with a similar layout makes it easier to adapt to the new keyboard.

- Most current keyboards use the USB interface natively, and are supplied with an adapter for connecting to a PS/2 keyboard port. We use mostly USB keyboards, but it's a good idea to have at least one PS/2 keyboard available (or a PS/2 adapter) for those times when Windows shoots craps and won't recognize USB devices.

- Some keyboards provide dedicated and/or programmable function keys to automate such things as firing up your browser or email client or to allow you to define custom macros that can be invoked with a single keystroke. These functions are typically not built into the keyboard itself, but require loading a driver. To take advantage of those functions, make sure a driver is available for the OS you use.

- The weight of a keyboard can be a significant issue for some people. The lightest keyboard we've seen weighed just over a pound, and the heaviest nearly eight pounds. If your keyboard stays on your desktop, a heavy keyboard is less likely to slide around. Conversely, a heavy keyboard may be uncomfortable if you work with the keyboard in your lap.

- Some manufacturers produce keyboards with speakers, scanners, and other entirely unrelated functions built in. These functions are often clumsy to use, are fragile, and have limited features. If you want speakers or a scanner, buy speakers or a scanner. Don't get a keyboard with them built in.

- Wireless keyboards are ideal for presentations, TV-based web browsing, or just for working with the keyboard in your lap. Wireless keyboards use a receiver module that connects to a USB port or to the PS/2 keyboard port on the PC. The keyboard and receiver communicate using either radio frequency (RF) or infrared (IR). IR keyboards require direct line-of-sight between the keyboard and receiver, while RF keyboards do not. Most IR keyboards and many RF keyboards provide limited range—as little as five feet or so—which limits their utility to working around a desk without cables tangling. Any wireless keyboard you buy should use standard AA, AAA, or 9V alkaline or NiMH batteries rather than a proprietary battery pack.

RECOMMENDATIONS

Keyboard

 Logitech and Microsoft both produce a wide range of excellent keyboards, one of which is almost certainly right for you. Even their basic models are well built and reliable. The more expensive models add features such as RF or Bluetooth wireless connectivity, programmable function keys, and so on. We used Microsoft keyboards almost exclusively for many years, and continue to recommend them. However, when we tested several Logitech keyboards some months ago, we found that we actually preferred their features and feel. We currently use Logitech keyboards on most of our primary systems, although we continue to use various Microsoft keyboards on several older systems.

 Avoid inexpensive, no-name keyboards.

Mice

Choosing a mouse is much like choosing a keyboard. Personal preference is by far the most important consideration. If possible, try a mouse before you buy it.

Use the following guidelines when choosing a mouse:

- Mice are available in various sizes and shapes, including small mice intended for children, notebook-size mice, the formerly standard "Dove bar" size, the mainstream ergonomic mouse, and some oversize mice that have many buttons and extra features. Most people find standard-size mice comfortable to use for short periods, but if for longer periods small differences in size and shape often make a big difference in comfort and usability. Although oversize mice provide attractive features and functions, people with small hands may find such mice too large to use comfortably. Pay particular attention to mouse shape if you are left-handed. Although Microsoft claims that their asymmetric ergonomic mice are equally usable by left- and right-handers, many lefties find them uncomfortable and resort to right-handed mousing. Other manufacturers, including Logitech, produce symmetric ergonomic mice.

Don't assume that hand size and mouse size are necessarily related. For example, Barbara, who has small hands, prefers the Microsoft IntelliMouse Explorer, which is an oversize mouse. She found that using a standard or small mouse for long periods caused her hand to hurt. Changing to a large mouse solved the problem.

- Get a wheel mouse. Although some applications do not support the wheel, those that do are the ones most people are likely to use a great deal—Microsoft Office, Internet Explorer, Mozilla, and so on. Using the wheel greatly improves mouse functionality by reducing the amount of mouse movement needed to navigate web pages and documents.

- Standard two-button mice (three, counting the wheel) suffice for most purposes. However, five-button mice are ideally suited to some applications, such as games and web browsing. For example, the two extra buttons can be mapped to the Back and Forward browser icons, eliminating a great deal of extraneous mouse movement.

- Mice have cords ranging in length from less than four feet to about nine feet. A short mouse cord may be too short to reach the system, particularly if it is on the floor. If you need a longer mouse cord, purchase a PS/2 keyboard extension cable, available in nearly any computer store.

- Consider buying a cordless mouse. The absence of a cord can make a surprising difference.

- Buy an optical mouse. Optical mice use a red LED light source and do not require any special mousing surface. Because they are sealed units, optical mice seldom need cleaning. Robert had to take his mechanical mice apart and clean them literally every few days, but his optical mice go for months without cleaning.

Network adapters

A network adapter—also called a LAN (Local Area Network) adapter, or NIC (Network Interface Card)—is used to connect a PC to a home or business network. A network adapter provides a relatively fast communication link—from 10 to 1,000 megabits per second (Mb/s)—between the PC and other devices connected to the network. Network adapters are available in wired and wireless versions. A network may use all wired network adapters, all wireless network adapters, or some combination of the two.

Wired network adapters

In a typical wired network, the network adapters in each PC connect to a central hub or switch that allows any connected device to communicate with any other connected device. In a home or SOHO setting, a wired network adapter may also be used to connect an individual PC directly to a cable modem or xDSL modem.

Nearly all wired network adapters support one or more of a family of networking standards that are collectively referred to as *Ethernet*. Current Ethernet adapters use unshielded twisted pair (UTP) cable, which resembles standard telephone cable, and communicate at 10 Mb/s (10BaseT), 100 Mb/s (100BaseT or "Fast Ethernet"), or 1,000 Mb/s (1000BaseT or "Gigabit"). Wired Ethernet adapters use an 8-position, 8-connector (8P8C) jack that resembles an oversized telephone jack, and is usually (although incorrectly) called an "RJ-45" connector.

Many motherboards include embedded wired Ethernet adapters, which are typically 10/100 or 10/100/1000 hybrid devices. You can add wired Ethernet to a system that lacks an embedded NIC by installing an inexpensive PCI expansion card. Embedded network adapters are reliable and add

(Not Always) Backward Compatible

Most Ethernet adapters are backward compatible with slower Ethernet versions. For example, most 100BaseT adapters can also communicate with 10BaseT devices, and most 1000BaseT adapters can also communicate with 100BaseT and 10BaseT devices. This is not invariably true, however. Some Ethernet devices support only one or two standards. That can cause problems if, for example, you connect a 10BaseT adapter to a hub or switch that supports only 100BaseT or 100BaseT and 1000BaseT. Although the devices can be physically connected, they do not communicate. Components that support multiple speeds, called *hybrid components*, are usually labeled in the form 10/100BaseT, 100/1000BaseT, or 10/100/1000BaseT.

little or nothing to the cost of a motherboard, but they do extract a small performance penalty because they use the main system CPU for processing. Standalone desktop PCI network adapters typically cost from $15 to $40, depending on manufacturer and speed. PCI network adapters place little or no load on the main system CPU, and are often more efficient and fully featured than embedded adapters.

The best rule of thumb for most desktop systems is to use an embedded network adapter, if your chosen motherboard offers that option and if you do not require the additional management and other features available only with standalone adapters. For servers, use a standalone 100BaseT PCI network adapter unless you are using a special server motherboard that incorporates one or more server-class 100BaseT or 1000BaseT network adapters. For 1000BaseT on a server, use only an embedded adapter. A PCI 1000BaseT adapter simply consumes too much of the available PCI bandwidth to be usable in such an environment.

Wireless network adapters

Wireless network adapters—also called WLAN (Wireless LAN) cards, 802.11 cards, or Wi-Fi (Wireless Fidelity) cards—use radio waves to communicate. WLAN adapters communicate with a central device called an access point (AP) or wireless access point (WAP). In a mixed wired/ wireless network, the AP connects to the wired network and provides an interface between the wired and wireless portions of the network. One AP can support many WLAN adapters, but all of the adapters must share the bandwidth available on the AP. In a large network, multiple APs may be used to extend the physical reach of the wireless network and to provide additional bandwidth to computers that connect to the network with WLAN adapters.

WLAN adapters are commonly used in notebook computers, either in embedded form or as a PC card. WLAN adapters are also available as PCI expansion cards that can be installed in desktop systems to provide a network link when it is difficult or expensive to run a cable to a system. The original 1997-era WLAN adapters used the 802.11 standard, which supported a maximum data rate of only 2 Mb/s. Those adapters are long obsolete. Current WLAN adapters support one or more of the following standards.

802.11b

802.11b supports a maximum data rate of 11 Mb/s, comparable to 10BaseT Ethernet, and has typical real-world throughput of 5 Mb/s. 802.11b uses the unlicensed 2.4 GHz spectrum, which means it is subject to interference from microwave ovens, cordless phones, and other devices that share the 2.4 GHz spectrum. The popularity of 802.11b is waning because components that use the faster 802.11g standard, described below, are now available at low cost. Millions of 802.11b adapters remain in use, primarily as embedded or PC card adapters in notebook computers.

802.11a

802.11a supports a maximum data rate of 54 Mb/s and has typical real-world throughput of 25 Mb/s. It uses a portion of the 5 GHz spectrum that was licensed until late 2003, but is now unlicensed. 5 GHz signals have shorter range and are more easily obstructed than 2.4 GHz signals, but are also less likely to interfere with other nearby devices. 802.11a is incompatible with 802.11b because they use different frequencies. The higher cost for 802.11a devices means they are used almost exclusively in business environments. Most 802.11a components have business-oriented features, such as remote manageability, that add cost but are of little interest to home users.

802.11g

The most recent WLAN standard is 802.11g, which combines the best features of 802.11a and 802.11b. Like 802.11b, 802.11g works in the unlicensed 2.4 GHz spectrum, which means it has good range but is subject to interference from other 2.4 GHz devices. Because they use the same frequencies, 802.11b WLAN adapters can communicate with 802.11g APs, and vice versa. Like 802.11a, 802.11g supports a maximum data rate of 54 Mb/s and has typical real-world throughput of about 25 Mb/s. That is sufficient to support real-time streaming video, which 802.11b cannot. 802.11g devices now sell for little more than 802.11b devices, so 802.11g has effectively made 802.11b obsolete.

"802.108g"

Several manufacturers, including D-Link and NetGear, produce APs that claim to provide 108 Mb/s bandwidth. And in fact they do, but only by "cheating" on the 802.11g specification. Such APs, colloquially called "802.108g" devices, work as advertised, but using them may cause conflicts with 802.11g-compliant devices operating in the same vicinity.

802.11g defines 11 channels (13 in Europe), each with 22 MHz of bandwidth. Each 22 MHz channel can support the full 54 Mb/s bandwidth of 802.11g. But these channels overlap, as shown in Figure 2-1. Three of the channels—1, 6, and 11—are completely non-overlapping, which means that three 802.11g-compliant APs in the same vicinity—one assigned to each of the three non-over-

Wireless Interoperability

802.11b and 802.11g components are standards-based, so devices from different manufacturers should interoperate. In practice, that is largely true, although minor differences in how standards are implemented can cause conflicts. In particular, some high-end 802.11b/802.11g components include proprietary extensions for security and similar purposes. Those components do generally interoperate with components from other vendors, but only on a "least common denominator" basis—that is, using only the standard 802.11 features. The best way to ensure that your wireless network operates with minimal problems is to use WLAN adapters and APs from the same vendor.

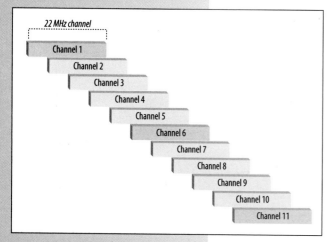

Figure 2-1. 802.11g channels

lapping channels—can share the 2.4 GHz spectrum without conflicts. Alternatively, two 802.11g-compliant APs can be assigned to two channels that do not overlap each other, for example, channels 2 and 8.

An 802.108g device claims two of the three completely non-overlapping channels, typically either 1 and 6 or 6 and 11, although it could in theory use 1 and 11. That leaves only one channel available for other 802.11g devices. To make matters worse, although 802.11g APs detect other nearby 802.11g APs and adjust themselves to use nonconflicting channels, many 802.11g APs fail to detect 802.108g APs operating nearby. The 802.11g devices wrongly assume that the channels being used by the 802.108g devices are available, and so may choose to operate on those "available" channels. The upshot is that it's possible, even likely, to end up with an 802.11g device and an 802.108g device attempting to use the same channel at the same time, which means that neither device works properly.

RECOMMENDATIONS

Network Adapters

 For a wired network adapter, try to choose a motherboard that includes an embedded 10/100, 100/1000, or 10/100/1000 network interface. 10/100 is acceptable for most people's current needs, but Gigabit models provide "future-proofing" at small additional cost.

Make sure you know what you're getting when you order a motherboard. Many motherboards are available in several variants, only some of which may include embedded LAN. For example, the excellent Intel D865PERL motherboard is available in three models, one without embedded LAN (D865PERL), one with embedded 10/100 LAN (D865PERLL), and one with embedded Gigabit (1000) LAN (D865PERLK).

 If your motherboard does not provide an embedded LAN adapter or if you prefer to use a separate LAN adapter, choose a 10/100 PCI LAN adapter from Intel or D-Link.

A PCI 1000 Mb/s LAN adapter can saturate the 133 MB/s PCI bus, or nearly so. Accordingly, we use PCI Gigabit LAN adapters only if there is no alternative. We prefer to use embedded Gigabit LAN that keeps LAN traffic off the PCI bus. For example, Intel motherboards with embedded Gigabit LAN route LAN traffic across the dedicated CSA (Communications Streaming

Architecture) bus, leaving the PCI bus free for other purposes.

 If you are building a new wireless network, use a D-Link 802.11g or 802.108g WLAN adapter and AP. Choose 802.11g if channel conflicts are possible, e.g., if you live in an apartment or if your business is in close proximity to other businesses. Choose 802.108g if there are no 802.11b/g APs nearby, but note that you may have to replace 2.4 GHz cordless phones with models that use a different frequency band. If you are expanding a wireless network, use an 802.11g adapter from the same company that made the existing components.

If you need to purchase an 802.11g or 802.108g AP, consider buying a model that also incorporates a hardware firewall/router. Using a hardware firewall/router on a home or SOHO network is the single most important thing you can do to improve security and reduce the likelihood that your systems will be infected by a worm.

 Avoid no-name network adapters and other components. If possible, avoid mixing components from different manufacturers, particularly in a wireless network. Avoid 802.11a unless you need SNMP remote manageability and other business-oriented features.

> **WARNING**
>
> If you use wireless networking, remember that you are broadcasting data omni-directionally. The range of 802.11b/g is up to several hundred feet with a normal antenna, and can be extended to several miles using a simple antenna built from a soup or potato-chip can. In fact, rumor has it that U.S. surveillance satellites can easily receive 802.11b/g broadcasts from orbit.
>
> Unless you enable encryption, which is usually disabled by default, anyone nearby who has a WLAN adapter can intercept your data. Worse still, people can connect to your network and use it as though they were wired into it. Nor is this a merely theoretical danger. Wardriving—cruising around looking for unsecured access points—has been a popular pastime since 802.11b became popular. If you run an unsecured 802.11* network, it *will* be compromised.
>
> Various forms of wireless encryption and authentication are available, some standard and some proprietary to certain brands of gear. At a minimum, enable WEP (Wired-Equivalent Privacy). WEP is not secure in any real sense, but it is enough to discourage all but the most sophisticated intruders, and also ensures that others don't innocently connect to your network—if you're in a densely populated area and your AP is in range of a library, café, or other public space, it's likely to be mistaken for a public hotspot. Read the manual for your WLAN gear and visit the maker's web site to determine what security measures are right for you and how to implement them.

Modems

A modem—a contraction of the term MOdulator/DEModulator—converts data from the digital form used by your computer to an analog form that can be transferred across an ordinary voice telephone line, and vice versa. A modem—also called a "dial-up modem" to differentiate it from cable modems and DSL modems—is typically used to connect via a POTS (Plain Old Telephone Service) line to an Internet Service Provider (ISP) or similar data service. Most current modems also support inbound and outbound faxing.

Modems are a mature market segment. They reached their maximum possible speed—"56K," which is actually limited by law to 53K—several years ago, and modem manufacturers have since devoted few development resources to them. Most current modems use one of a handful of chipsets, so the similarities between modems from different manufacturers are much greater than their differences. Most have very similar features and performance, so choosing the best model for your needs is usually a matter of deciding what type of modem you need and then balancing minor price differences against manufacturer reputations.

Use the following criteria when choosing the type of modem appropriate for your needs:

- All current modems support the so-called 56K data rate using V.90 or V.92 protocols. With perfect line and external network conditions, a

V.90 modem can in theory transmit data at 31,200 bits/s and receive data at 56,000 bits/s ("56K"). In practice, regulatory limits on power levels limit the receive speed to 53,000 bits/s, and line conditions often limit it to even lower data rates. V.92 is a minor upgrade of the V.90 standard and maintains the 53,000 bits/s receive speed of V.90, but increases transmit speed to 48,000 bits/s. Again, the theoretical data rates are seldom achieved on real-world telephone lines. V.92 also extends the V.90 standard to add the following convenience features:

QuickConnect

> Anyone who has used a dial-up modem is familiar with the series of tones that the sending and receiving modems exchange. During this "handshake" procedure, the two modems negotiate their fastest shared protocols and test the line to determine the fastest usable data rate. With V.90 modems, this handshake can require as much as 30 seconds to complete. The V.92 QuickConnect feature reduces the time necessary to establish the connection by up to 50% by storing information about modems it has previously connected to and the line conditions it experienced during earlier connections.

Modem-on-Hold

> In the Bad Old Days, if you forgot to disable call-waiting on your modem line, your data connection was unceremoniously dropped if another call came in while you were using the modem. The V.92 Modem-on-Hold feature is designed to work with call-waiting. If you are using the modem and a voice call comes in on that line, the data connection is placed on hold. You can then pick up the phone and talk to the caller. When you complete the voice call, you hang up and re-establish the data connection where you left off. Note that using the Modem-on-Hold feature requires explicit support by the ISP, and many ISPs have not chosen to implement it.

Although a few V.90 modems remain on the market, the vast majority of currently available modems support V.92. The differences between V.90 and V.92 are so minor that many existing V.90 modems can be upgraded to V.92 via a simple firmware update.

Although V.92 modems ordinarily connect to V.90 modems without any problem, we have had reports from readers who upgraded their V.90 modems to V.92 and subsequently experienced problems connecting to their ISPs. Accordingly, before you upgrade to V.92 we suggest that you make sure you can later downgrade back to V.90 if necessary.

- A true modem contains a CPU or controller that processes outbound data before delivering it to the telephone line interface and processes inbound data from the telephone interface before delivering it to the computer. Several years ago, various manufacturers began shipping controllerless modems, which are also referred to as soft modems, software modems, or Winmodems. These devices are not true modems at all, but are simple hardware interfaces between the computer and the telephone line. A soft modem has no internal CPU. Instead, it uses the main system CPU to do all the processing. The only advantage of a soft modem is low cost. The disadvantages of soft modems are that they consume CPU power, which may cause degraded performance; that they can be used only with an operating system that supports them, which typically means only recent versions of Windows; and that they frequently drop connections and crash the computer. Don't use a soft modem, no matter how little it costs.

- Modems are available in internal and external versions. External modems cost a bit more than comparable internal modems because they require a case and power supply, but it's usually worth spending those few extra dollars for the additional flexibility an external modem provides. Most internal modems are installed in a PCI expansion slot. A few are designed to fit the dedicated AMR (audio/modem riser) or CNR (communications and networking riser) slot present on some motherboards. Internal modems may be controller-based or controllerless. External modems connect to either a serial port or a USB port. All external modems are controller-based. External modems provide status lights, which can be invaluable when you are troubleshooting connection problems. Also, external modems can be power-cycled independently of the PC if they lock up, which at times can keep you from losing all of the unsaved data in files that are open when the modem shoots craps.

RECOMMENDATIONS

Modems

 For general use, buy an external V.90 or V.92 controller-based modem. If you want the best modem available, bar none, buy the $250 U.S. Robotics Courier 56K V.92 Business Modem, which can establish and maintain connections under line conditions so bad that other modems don't even attempt to connect. For a less expensive but still excellent external modem, buy the $50 U.S. Robotics USR5633A 56K USB Faxmodem. If for some reason you must have an internal modem, choose the $35 U.S. Robotics USR5699B 56K V.92 Internal Faxmodem PCI.

 Avoid internal modems, whether they are controller-based or controllerless. Avoid no-name modems of any description.

Buying Components

We've bought hundreds of thousands of dollars worth of PC components over the last 20 years, for ourselves and on behalf of employers and clients. In the following sections, we'll tell you what we learned along the way.

Buying guidelines

Until the early 1990s, most computer products were bought in computer specialty stores. Retail sales still make up a significant chunk of computer product sales—although the emphasis has shifted from computer specialty stores to local "big box" retailers like Best Buy, CompUSA, Fry's, Wal*Mart, and Costco—but online resellers now account for a large percentage of PC component sales.

Should you buy from a local brick-and-mortar retailer or an online reseller? We do both, because each has advantages and disadvantages.

Local retailers offer the inestimable advantage of instant gratification. Unless you're more patient than we are, when you want something, you want it Right Now. Buying from a local retailer puts the product in your hands instantly, instead of making you wait for FedEx to show up. You can also hold the product in your hands, something that's not possible if you buy from an online reseller. Local retailers also have a big advantage if you need to return or exchange a product. If something doesn't work right, or if you simply change your mind, you can just drive back to the store rather than dealing with the hassles and costs of returning a product to an online reseller.

Online resellers have the advantage in breadth and depth of product selection. If you want the less expensive OEM version of a product, for example, chances are you won't find it at local retailers, most of which stock only retail-boxed products. If an online reseller stocks a particular manufacturer's products, they tend to stock the entire product line, whereas local retailers often pick and choose only the most popular items in a product line. (Of course, popular products are usually popular for good reasons.) Online resellers are also more likely to stock niche products and products from smaller manufacturers. Sometimes, if you must have a particular product, the only option is to buy it online.

Online resellers usually advertise lower prices than local retailers, but it's a mistake to compare only nominal prices. When you buy from a local retailer, you pay only the advertised price plus any applicable sales tax. When you buy from an online retailer, you pay the advertised price plus shipping, which may end up costing you more than buying locally.

WARNING

Ah, but you don't have to pay sales tax when you buy online, right? Well, maybe. In most jurisdictions, you're required by law to pay a use tax in lieu of sales tax on out-of-state purchases. Most people evade use taxes, of course, but that free ride is coming to an end. States faced with increasing budget problems (which is to say all of them) are starting to clamp down on people who buy from online resellers and don't pay use tax. States are using data-mining techniques to coordinate with each other and with credit card companies and online retailers to uncover unpaid use taxes. If you don't pay use taxes, one day soon you're likely to hear from the audit division of your state department of revenue, asking what these credit card charges were for and why you didn't report the use taxes due on them. Count on it.

Although online resellers *may* have a lower overall price on a given component, it's a mistake to assume that is always the case. Local retailers frequently run sales and rebate promotions that cut the price of a component below the lowest online price. For example, we bought a spindle of 100 CD-R discs on sale from a local retailer for $19.95 with a $10 instant rebate and a $20 mail-in rebate. After the cost of the stamp to mail in the rebate form, they *paid* us $9.68 to carry away those 100 discs, which is pretty tough for an online reseller to match. Similarly, we bought an 80 GB hard drive for $79.95, with a $15 instant rebate and a $30 mail-in rebate. Net cost? About $35 for a retail-boxed 80 GB hard drive, which no online vendor could come close to matching.

In particular, local retailers are usually the best place to buy heavy and/or bulky items, such as monitors, cases, UPSs, and so on. Local retailers receive these items in pallet loads, which makes the cost of shipping an individual item almost nothing. Conversely, online resellers have to charge you, directly or indirectly, for the cost of getting that heavy item to your door.

Whether you purchase your PC components from a local brick-and-mortar store or a web-based retailer, here are some guidelines to keep in mind:

- Make sure you know exactly what you're buying. For example, a hard drive may be available in two versions, each with the same or a similar model number but with an added letter or number to designate different amounts of cache. Or a hard drive maker may produce two models of the same size that differ in price and performance. Always compare using the exact manufacturer model number. Before you buy a product, research it on the manufacturer's web site and on the numerous independent web sites devoted to reviews. We usually search Google with the product name and "review" in the search string.

- Vendors vary greatly. Some we trust implicitly, and others we wouldn't order from on a bet. Some are always reliable, others always unreliable, and still others seem to vary with the phases of the moon. We check *http://www.resellerratings.com*, which maintains a database of customer-reported experiences with hundreds of vendors.

- The list price or Suggested Retail Price (SRP) is meaningless. Most computer products sell for a fraction of SRP, others sell for near SRP, and for still others the manufacturer has no SRP, but instead publishes an Estimated Selling Price (ESP). To do meaningful comparisons, you need to know what different vendors charge for the product, and fortunately there are many services that list these prices. We use *http://www.pricescan.com*, *http://www.pricewatch.com*, and *http://www.pricegrabber.com*. These services may list 20 or more different vendors, and the prices for a particular item may vary dramatically. We discard the top 25% and the bottom 25% and average the middle 50% to decide a reasonable price for the item.

- Many components are sold in retail-boxed and OEM forms. The core component is likely to be similar or identical in either case, but important details may vary. For example, Intel CPUs are available in retail-boxed versions that include a CPU cooler and a three-year warranty. They are also available as OEM components (also called *tray packaging* or *white box*) that do not include the CPU cooler and have only a 90-day warranty. OEM items are not intended for retail distribution, so some manufacturers provide no warranty to individual purchasers. OEM components are fine as long as you understand the differences and do not attempt to compare prices between retail-boxed and OEM.

- The market for PCs and components is incredibly competitive, and margins are razor-thin. If a vendor advertises a component for much less than other vendors, it may be a "loss leader." More likely, though, and particularly if its prices on other items is similarly low, that vendor cuts corners, whether by using your money to float inventory, by shipping returned product as new, by charging excessive shipping fees, or, in the extreme case, by taking your money and not shipping the product. If you always buy from the vendor with the rock-bottom prices, you'll waste a lot of time hassling with returns of defective, used, or discontinued items and dealing with your credit card company when the vendor fails to deliver at all. Ultimately, you're likely to spend more money than you would have by buying from a reputable vendor in the first place.

- The actual price you pay may vary significantly from the advertised price. When you compare prices, include all charges, particularly shipping charges. Reputable vendors tell you exactly how much the total charges will be. Less reputable vendors may forget to mention shipping charges, which may be very high. Some vendors break out the full manufacturer pack into individual items. For example, if a retail-boxed hard drive includes mounting hardware, some vendors will quote a price for the bare drive without making it clear that they have removed the mounting hardware and charge separately for it. Also be careful when buying products that include a rebate from the maker. Some vendors quote the net price after rebate without making it clear that they are doing so.

- Some vendors charge more for an item ordered via their 800 number than they do for the same item ordered directly from their web site. Some others add a fixed processing fee to phone orders. These charges reflect the fact that taking orders on the Web is much cheaper than doing it by phone, so this practice has become common. In fact, some of our favorite vendors do not provide telephone order lines at all.

- It can be very expensive to ship heavy items such as CRTs, UPSs, and printers individually. This is one situation in which local big-box stores like Best Buy have an advantage over online vendors. The online vendor has to charge you for the cost of shipping, either directly or indirectly, and that cost can amount to $50 or more for a heavy item that you need quickly. Conversely, the big-box stores receive inventory items in truckloads or even in railcar shipments, so their delivery cost for any individual item is quite small and they can pass that reduced cost on to buyers. If you're buying a heavy item, don't assume that it will be cheaper online. Check your local Best Buy or other big-box store and you may find that it actually costs less there, even after paying sales tax. And you can carry it away with you instead of waiting for FedEx to show up.

- Most direct resellers are willing to sell for less than the price they advertise. All you need do is tell your chosen vendor that you'd really rather buy from them, but not at the price they're quoting. Use lower prices you find with the price comparison services as a wedge to get a better price. But keep in mind that reputable vendors must charge more than fly-by-night operations if they are to make a profit and stay in business. If we're ordering by phone, we generally try to beat down our chosen vendor a bit on price, but we don't expect them to match the rock-bottom prices that turn up on web searches. Of course, if you're ordering from a web-only vendor, dickering is not an option, which is one reason why web-only vendors generally have better prices.

- Using a credit card puts the credit card company on your side if there is a problem with your order. If the vendor ships the wrong product, a defective product, or no product at all, you can invoke charge-back procedures to have the credit card company refund your money. Vendors who live and die on credit card orders cannot afford to annoy credit card companies, and so tend to resolve such problems quickly. Even your threat to request a charge-back may cause a recalcitrant vendor to see reason.

- Some vendors add a surcharge, typically 3%, to their advertised prices if you pay by credit card. Surcharges violate credit card company contracts, so some vendors instead offer a similar discount for paying cash, which amounts to the same thing. Processing credit card transactions does cost money, and we're sure that some such vendors are quite reputable, but our own experience with vendors that surcharge has not been good. We always suspect that their business practices result in a high percentage of charge-back requests, and so they discourage using credit cards.

- Good vendors allow you to return a defective product for replacement or a full refund (often less shipping charges) within a stated period, typically 30 days. Buy only from such vendors. Nearly all vendors exclude some product categories, such as notebook computers, monitors, printers, and opened software, either because their contracts with the manufacturer require them to do so or because some buyers commonly abuse return periods for these items, treating them as "30-day free rentals." Beware of the phrase "All sales are final." That means exactly what it says.

Nearly all retailers refuse to refund your money on opened software, DVDs, etc., but will only exchange the open product for a new, sealed copy of the same title. One of our readers tells us how he gets around that common policy. He returns the open software in exchange for a new, sealed copy of the same product, keeping his original receipt. He then returns the new, sealed copy for a refund. That's probably unethical and may be illegal for all we know, but it does work.

- Check carefully for any mention of restocking fees. Many vendors who trumpet a "no-questions-asked money-back guarantee" mention only in the fine print that they won't refund all your money. They charge a restocking fee on returns, and we've seen fees as high as 30% of the purchase price. These vendors love returns because they make a lot more money if you return the product than if you keep it. Do not buy from a vendor that charges restocking fees on exchanges (as opposed to refunds). For refunds, accept no restocking fee higher than 10% to 15%, depending on the price of the item.

- If you order by phone, don't accept verbal promises. Insist that the reseller confirm your order in writing, including any special terms or conditions, before charging your credit card or shipping the product. If a reseller balks at providing written confirmation of their policies, terms, and conditions, find another vendor. Most are happy to provide written confirmation. If you're ordering from a vendor that uses web-based ordering exclusively, use a screen capture program or your browser's save function to grab copies of each screen as you complete the order. Most vendors send a confirming email, which we file in our "Never Delete" folder.

- File everything related to an order, including a copy of the original advertisement; email, faxed, or written confirmations provided by the reseller; copies of your credit card receipt; a copy of the packing list and invoice; and so on. We also jot down notes in our PIM regarding telephone conversations, including the date, time, telephone number and extension, person spoken to, purpose of the call, and so on. We print a copy of those to add to the folder for that order.

- Make it clear to the reseller that you expect them to ship the exact item you have ordered, not what they consider to be an "equivalent substitute." Require they confirm the exact items they will ship, including manufacturer part numbers. For example, if you order an ATi RADEON 9800 XT graphics card with 256 MB of RAM, make sure the order confirmation specifies that item by name, full description, and ATi product number. Don't accept a less detailed description such as "graphics card," "ATi graphics card," or even "ATi RADEON graphics card." Otherwise, you'll get less than you paid for—a lesser RADEON card, an OEM card with a slower processor or less memory, or even a "Powered by ATI" card (which is to say a card with an ATI processor made by another manufacturer) rather than a "Built by ATI" card. Count on it.

- Verify warranty terms. Some manufacturers warrant only items purchased from authorized dealers in full retail packaging. For some items, the warranty begins when the manufacturer ships the product to the distributor, which may be long before you receive it. OEM products typically have much shorter warranties than retail-boxed products—sometimes as short as 90 days—and may be warranted only to the original distributor rather than to the final buyer. Better resellers may *endorse the manufacturer warranty* for some period on some products, often 30 to 90 days. That means that if the product fails, you can return the item to the reseller, who will ship you a replacement and take care of dealing with the manufacturer. Some resellers disclaim the manufacturer warranty, claiming that once they ship the item, dealing with warranty claims is your problem, even if the product arrives DOA. We've encountered that problem a couple of times. Usually, dropping phrases like "merchantability and fitness for a particular purpose" and "revocation of acceptance" leads them to see reason quickly. We usually demand that the reseller ship us a new replacement product immediately and include a prepaid return shipping label if they want the dead item back. We don't accept or pay for dead merchandise under any circumstances, and neither should you.

- Direct resellers are required by law to ship products within the time period they promise. But that time period may be precise (e.g., "ships within 24 hours") or vague (e.g., "ships within three to six weeks"). If the vendor cannot ship by the originally promised date, they must notify you in writing and specify another date by which the item will ship. If that occurs, you have the right to cancel your order without penalty. Be sure to make clear to the reseller that you expect the item to be delivered in a timely manner. Reputable vendors ship what they say they're going to ship when they say they're going to ship it. Unfortunately, some vendors have a nasty habit of taking your money and shipping whenever they get around to it. In a practice that borders on fraud, some vendors routinely report items as "in stock" when in fact they are not. Make it clear to the vendor that you do not authorize them to charge your credit card until the item actually ships, and that if you do not receive the item when promised you will cancel the order.

Of course, even if you follow all of these guidelines, you may still run into problems. Even the best resellers sometimes drop the ball. If that happens, don't expect the problem to go away by itself. If you encounter a problem, remain calm and notify the reseller first. A good reseller will be anxious to resolve it. Find out how the reseller wants to proceed and follow their procedures, particularly for labeling returned merchandise with an RMA number. If things seem not be going as they should, explain to the vendor why you are dissatisfied and tell them that you plan to request a charge-back from your credit card company. Finally, if the reseller is entirely recalcitrant and if any aspect of the transaction (including, for example, a confirmation letter you wrote) took place via the U.S. Postal Service, contact your postmaster about filing charges of mail fraud. That really gets a reseller's attention, but use it as a last resort.

Recommended sources

The question we hear more often than any other is, "What company should I buy from?" When someone asks us that question, we run away, screaming in terror. Well, not really, but we'd like to. Answering that question is a no-win proposition for us, you see. If we recommend a vendor and that vendor treats the buyer properly, well, that's no more than was expected. But Thor forbid that we recommend a vendor who turns around and screws the buyer.

Yes, it's true. Robert is of Viking extraction. On government forms, he describes himself as "Viking-American." And, no, he doesn't wear a funny helmet. Except among friends. And he hasn't pillaged anything in months. Years, maybe.

So, which online resellers do we buy from? Over the years, we've bought from scores of online vendors, and our favorites have changed. For the last few years, our favorite has been NewEgg (*http://www.newegg.com*). NewEgg offers an extraordinarily good combination of price, product selection, support, shipping, and return and replacement policies. We know of no other direct vendor that even comes close.

NewEgg's prices aren't always rock-bottom, but they generally match any other vendor we're willing to deal with. NewEgg runs daily specials that are often real bargains, so if you're willing to consider alternatives and to accumulate components over the course of a few weeks you can save a fair amount of money. NewEgg ships what they say they're going to ship, when they say they're going to ship it, and at the price they agreed to ship it for. If there's a problem, they make it right. It's hard to do better than that.

WARNING
All of that said, if you buy from NewEgg and subsequently your goldfish dies and all your teeth fall out, don't blame us. All we can say is that NewEgg has always treated us right. But things can change overnight in this industry, and though we don't expect NewEgg to take a sudden turn for the worse, it could happen.

As to local retailers, we buy from—in no particular order—Best Buy, CompUSA, Target, Office Depot, OfficeMax, and our local computer specialty stores, depending on what we need and who happens to have advertised the best prices and rebates in the Sunday ad supplements. Wal*Mart used to sell only assembled PCs, but has recently started stocking PC components, such as ATi video adapters, so we'll add Wal*Mart to our list as well.

If you buy from a local retailer, open the box from the bottom rather than the top. If you need to return a non-defective item, that makes it easier to repackage the product with the manufacturer's seals intact, which can help avoid restocking fees.

Final Words

We've done our best in this chapter to tell you what components to buy for your new PC and where and how to buy them. The specific components you need will differ according to the type of system you plan to build. We describe how to make component-specific decisions in later chapters in this book. So before you actually start ordering components, you might want to read some (or all) of those chapters.

When the components arrive, restrain yourself. Don't start building your system before the FedEx truck even pulls out of your driveway, particularly if this is your first system build. Read or reread the relevant project chapter.

One thing you *should* do immediately, though, is to check the contents of the boxes that were just delivered. Verify what you ordered against the packing list and invoice, and verify what's actually in the box against those documents. Usually everything will be right, but if you have components coming from different sources, you don't want to wait a week before you find out that an early shipment was wrong or incomplete.

Take it a step further. Once you've verified that everything is correct with the order, start opening the individual component boxes. Look for a packing list in the front of the manual, and make sure that you actually received everything that was supposed to be in the box. It's not uncommon for small parts—mounting hardware, cables, driver CDs, and so on—to be missing. If that happens, call the vendor immediately and tell them what's missing from your order.

At this point, you should have everything you need to start building your new PC. It's kind of like being a kid again, on Christmas morning.

Building a
Mainstream PC
3

Cost-effectiveness	Expandability
▮▮▮▮▮▮▮▮▮▮▯▯▯▯▯	▮▮▮▮▮▮▮▯▯▯▯▯▯▯
Reliability	Processor performance
▮▮▮▮▮▮▮▮▮▮▮▮▮▮▮	▮▮▮▮▮▮▮▮▮▯▯▯▯▯
Compactness	Video performance
▮▮▮▯▯▯▯▯▯▯▯▯▯▯▯	▮▮▮▮▮▮▮▮▮▯▯▯▯▯
Quietness	Disk capacity/performance
▮▮▮▮▮▮▯▯▯▯▯▯▯▯▯	▮▮▮▮▮▮▮▮▮▯▯▯▯▯

A Mainstream PC is a PC that seeks balance at a reasonable price point. It uses top-quality (but midrange-performance) components throughout, because that is where you find the best value for your dollar. What differentiates a Mainstream PC from an Entry-Level PC is that the former makes fewer compromises. Whereas budget is always a very high priority for an Entry-Level PC, it is less important for a Mainstream PC. If spending more money yields better performance or reliability, a Mainstream PC gets those extra dollars, whereas an Entry-Level PC probably doesn't.

This means that, relative to the Entry-Level PC, the Mainstream PC gets more, better, and faster everything. A better case and power supply, more memory, a faster processor, better video, a larger hard drive, a more capable optical drive, better mouse, keyboard, speakers, and so on. Considered individually, the incremental cost of better components is typically quite small. But taken collectively, the difference adds up fast. Depending on which components you choose, a Mainstream system may cost 50% to 100% more than an Entry-Level system. That extra money buys you higher performance now and down the road, and extends the period between upgrades. If an Entry-Level PC will meet your needs for 12 to 18 months without upgrades, a Mainstream PC may suffice for 24 to 36 months or longer, depending on the demands you put on it.

In this chapter, we'll design and build the perfect Mainstream PC.

Determining Functional Requirements

We sat down to think through our own requirements for a Mainstream PC. Here's the list of functional requirements we came up with:

Reliability

> First and foremost, the Mainstream PC must be reliable. We expect it to run all day, every day, for years without complaint. The key to reliability is choosing top-quality components, particularly motherboard, memory, hard drive, and power supply. Those components don't need to be the largest or fastest available, but they do need to be of high quality.

Balanced performance

> A Mainstream PC is a jack of all trades. We expect it to perform any task we might give it at least competently, if not better. But, because this is not a cost-no-object system, we need to balance component performance against price. For example, although this system is not suitable for a hardcore gamer, we expect it to provide adequate 3D graphics performance to play mainstream 3D games. That means striking a compromise between low-cost embedded video and a $400 fire-breathing gaming video adapter. Similarly, we expect this system to be capable of serious number crunching, but the fastest processors cost more than we can justify for this system. Accordingly, we aim for a balanced design that allows the system to do most things very well and everything else at least acceptably well.

Noise level

> Most Mainstream PCs are used in environments where noise is an issue. Accordingly, we'll design this system for quiet operation, but not spend much extra money to do so. That means, for example, that we'll take noise level into account when choosing the hard drive and power supply, but we won't spend $50 extra to replace the stock CPU cooling fan with a silent unit. Our goal is a quiet PC, not a silent PC (if there can truly be such a thing).

This Mainstream PC is destined to be Barbara's primary office desktop system. Her office is located directly across the hall from our master bedroom, so we do not take noise reduction lightly.

Hardware Design Criteria

With the functional requirements determined, the next step was to establish design criteria for the Mainstream PC hardware. The facing page sidebar shows the relative priorities we assigned for our Mainstream PC. Your priorities may differ.

Many consumer-grade systems, particularly those sold in office superstores and big-box stores and by some large OEMs, masquerade as Mainstream PCs but are really Entry-Level PCs with a few extra bells and whistles. These PCs have faster CPUs and more memory—components whose specifications are easily visible—but use the same low-end motherboards, marginal power supplies, and no-name optical drives found in their less expensive Entry-Level lines. True Mainstream PCs, at least as we define them, are a vanishing breed. Marketers believe that spending $5 more on a better power supply or $10 more on a better motherboard will only boost the price of their systems, making them uncompetitive with other brands, without increasing sales or profit. From their point of view, consumers are too ignorant to appreciate the difference between cheap components and good components that cost only slightly more. The best way to prove them wrong is to build your own Mainstream PC from top-notch components.

As you can see, this is a well-balanced system. Other than reliability, which we regard as critical for any system, all of the other criteria are of similar priority. Here's the breakdown:

Price

Price is moderately important for this system, but value is more so. We won't attempt to match the low price of commercial systems built with low-end components, but we won't waste money, either. If spending a bit more noticeably improves performance, reliability, or usability, we won't begrudge the extra cost.

Reliability

Reliability is the single most important criterion. A Mainstream PC that is not built for reliability is not worthy of the name.

Size

Size is unimportant in the sense that we will not compromise other criteria in exchange for smaller size. A standard mini/mid-tower chassis is appropriate for most Mainstream PCs.

Noise level

Noise level is moderately important for a Mainstream PC. Our goal is to build a reasonably quiet PC at little or no incremental cost, rather than a very quiet PC using expensive special components. Accordingly, we'll keep noise level in mind when we choose components, but we won't pay much extra for a marginally quieter component.

Expandability

Expandability is relatively unimportant for a Mainstream PC. Fewer than 5% of commercial Mainstream PCs are ever upgraded, and those upgrades are usually of a minor nature such as adding memory or replacing a video card or hard drive. Self-built Mainstream PCs are more likely to be upgraded, but even then the upgrades are unlikely to require more than perhaps a spare drive bay or two, an expansion slot, or a couple of available memory sockets. We'll choose a case, power supply, and motherboard that are adequate to support such minor upgrades.

Processor performance

Processor performance is moderately important for a Mainstream PC, both initially and to ensure that the system can run new software versions without requiring a processor upgrade. Slow and midrange mainstream processors are the "sweet spot" in price/performance ratio. Although economy processors such as the Intel Celeron and AMD Athlon may suffice initially, spending a bit more on a mainstream processor buys you more horsepower and a larger cache, both of which increase the time during which the processor will provide subjectively adequate performance. The slowest variants of the Intel Prescott-core Pentium 4 processors, introduced in February 2004, are the most

DESIGN PRIORITIES	
Price	★★★☆☆
Reliability	★★★★★
Size	★★☆☆☆
Noise level	★★★☆☆
Expandability	★★☆☆☆
Processor performance	★★★☆☆
Video performance	★★★☆☆
Disk capacity/performance	★★★☆☆

cost-effective processors available. They are aggressively priced and fast enough that you probably won't need to upgrade the processor anytime soon.

Video performance

3D video performance is important for a Mainstream PC only if you use it to run 3D games. Otherwise, embedded video suffices. On the other hand, 2D video quality is important for any Mainstream PC because it determines display clarity and sharpness for browsers, office suites, and similar 2D applications. Intel embedded video provides good 2D quality and mediocre 3D performance. Because we want our Mainstream PC to have reasonably good 3D performance, we'll use a separate 3D video adapter. Otherwise, we'd have used a motherboard with embedded video.

Disk capacity/performance

Disk capacity and performance are moderately important for a Mainstream PC. Fortunately, this is an easy criterion to meet, because current ATA hard drives are huge, fast, cheap, and reliable.

Component Considerations

With our design criteria in mind, we set out to choose the best components for the Mainstream PC system. The following sections describe the components we chose and why we chose them.

WARNING

Although we tested the configuration we used to build our own Mainstream PC, we did not test permutations with the listed alternatives. Those alternatives are simply the components we would have chosen had our requirements been different. That said, we know of no reason the alternatives we list should not work perfectly.

Case and power supply

Antec Sonata Mid-Tower Case (http://www.antec-inc.com)

The Antec Sonata is our favorite case of all time. In fact, it is so good that we recommend it unless there's very good reason to use something else. There may not be such a thing as a perfect case, but the Sonata comes closer than any other case we know of.

The Sonata seems larger inside than outside. Although it's standard mini-tower size, the Sonata provides nine drive bays—three 5.25" external, two 3.5" external, and four 3.5" internal. The internal bays use rubber grommets to absorb hard-drive vibrations and minimize noise.

Fit and finish are excellent. All edges are deburred and/or rolled, with no sharp edges anywhere. You don't have to worry about cutting yourself when you work on a Sonata. The Sonata also provides numerous convenience features, including a washable air filter and front-panel USB, IEEE-1394 (FireWire), and audio ports.

> Barbara, whose office is across the hall from our master bedroom, uses a Sonata for her primary system, not least because it is so quiet. The Sonata front bezel has two bright blue LEDs, which are sometimes the only indication that the system is running. One of our older dogs is afraid of the dark, so we've always had to keep a nightlight on for him. We found that the Sonata's blue LEDs were an excellent substitute for a nightlight.

The Sonata comes standard with the excellent TruePower 380 power supply. This power supply is extremely well regulated, robust enough to support any reasonable system configuration, and so quiet you can barely tell it's running. In addition to the power-supply fan, the Sonata includes one very quiet, low-speed, 120mm supplemental fan standard, with the option to add a second 120mm fan. Cooling is not a problem with the Sonata.

The Sonata is finished in a high-gloss black that Antec calls "Piano Black." Although the finish is beautiful, it's relatively easy to scratch, so the Sonata requires careful handling. Gloss black also shows dust readily, which Antec appears to have considered—they include a treated cloth for polishing.

Motherboard

Intel D865PERL (http://www.intel.com)

For our Mainstream PC, we wanted a Pentium 4 motherboard made by Intel. Intel motherboards set the standards by which we judge all other motherboards for construction quality, stability, and reliability. We chose the rock-solid Intel D865PERL, which supports any current Intel Pentium 4 or Celeron processor that uses a 400, 533, or 800 MHz FSB.

The D865PERL has four DIMM slots—which makes future memory upgrades easy—and supports up to 4 GB of PC3200 DDR-SDRAM. It also provides a plethora of interfaces and ports, including five PCI slots, a Universal 0.8/1.5 V AGP 3.0 (4X/8X) slot, two parallel ATA-100 interfaces, two Serial ATA interfaces, an FDD interface, PS/2 mouse and keyboard ports, serial and parallel ports for compatibility with legacy peripherals, eight USB 2.0 ports, and a partridge in a pear tree.

The only thing missing from the D865PERL is embedded video. Although embedded video is suitable for Entry-Level and some Mainstream systems, we wanted better 3D performance for this system. There's no point in paying for embedded video we won't use, so we chose the video-less D865PERL as the foundation for this system.

Motherboard Variants

If you buy a D865PERL, make sure you know exactly what you're getting. Like many Intel motherboards, the D865PERL is available retail-boxed, OEM, or bulk in various models. Retail-boxed and OEM boards are sold individually; bulk boards are sold only in pallet-loads to PC makers. All D865PERL models include the excellent ADI AD1985-based embedded audio. Some models include various combinations of 10/100 Ethernet, Gigabit Ethernet, IEEE-1394 (FireWire), or S-ATA RAID support. Interestingly, it's easy to identify models with S-ATA RAID, FireWire, or Gigabit Ethernet support because they use black printed-circuit boards (PCBs). Audio-only and audio plus 10/100 Ethernet models use green PCBs. Three of the four D865PERL models are available only retail-boxed or bulk. The fourth model is also available in OEM form. For available configurations, see *http://developer. intel.com/design/motherbd/rl/rl_ available.htm*.

ALTERNATIVES: MOTHERBOARD

If embedded video is sufficient, use the Intel D865GBF. In effect, this is a D865PERL with embedded Intel Extreme Graphics 2, but lacks options for FireWire or S-ATA RAID.

Processor

Intel Pentium 4/3.2E (*http://www.intel.com*)

A Mainstream PC deserves a mainstream processor. Relative to economy processors such as the Intel Celeron and AMD Duron and Athlon, mainstream processors are faster and have larger caches, both of which provide higher performance and greater longevity between upgrades.

We consider the Intel Prescott-core Pentium 4, introduced in February 2004, to be the best choice for a Mainstream PC. Relative to the older Northwood-core processors, Prescott processors (recognizable by their "E" suffixes) have twice the L2 cache (1 MB versus 512 KB) and add SSE-3 support that accelerates multimedia performance.

In our testing, Prescott processors were evenly matched overall with Northwood processors running at the same clock speed. Although Northwood processors won some benchmarks by small percentages, Prescott processors won about the same number of benchmarks by slightly larger percentages, and the processors finished in a dead heat on many benchmarks. Overall, we rate the Prescott as the same speed or slightly faster than Northwood.

Architectural improvements in Prescott processors provide increasing benefits as the clock rate increases. For example, we tested a 2.8 GHz Prescott against a 2.8 GHz Northwood and found that the Northwood averaged slightly faster in most benchmarks. Conversely, when we tested the two processors at 3.2 GHz, Prescott was slightly faster in most benchmarks.

Our tests ignored SSE-3, because few SSE-3 benchmarks were available when we ran the tests. As more applications gain SSE-3 support throughout 2004 and into 2005, Prescott will become the processor of choice for running such applications.

The one negative about Prescott is its high power consumption and accordingly high heat dissipation. If you're used to processor temperatures in the 35° C range, the 50° C to 60° C temperatures that Prescott reaches under load can be scary. Don't let that put you off, though. Prescott is designed to run at what in the past would have been considered very high temperatures. Use a good heatsink/fan unit that is rated for the speed of the processor you use, and you'll be fine.

For a Mainstream PC, we recommend using the fastest Prescott-core Pentium 4 processor you can buy for less than $200. Buy the retail-boxed version rather than the OEM version. The retail-boxed version costs only a few dollars more, and includes a three-year warranty and a bundled heatsink/fan unit that is both quiet and effective.

ALTERNATIVES: PROCESSOR

No good ones. The aging AMD Athlon XP can't keep up with the Pentium 4. The Athlon 64, while an excellent processor, is hampered by the lack of motherboards that we consider sufficiently robust and stable for a Mainstream PC. If you must have an AMD Athlon XP, we recommend the 3200+ in an ASUS A7N8X-E Deluxe motherboard. It will be slower than the Pentium 4, but fast enough for most purposes. If you insist on an AMD Athlon 64, use the fastest retail-boxed Athlon 64 you can find for less than $200 in an ASUS K8V Deluxe motherboard.

Memory

Crucial PC3200 DDR-SDRAM (http://www.crucial.com)

Memory is inexpensive enough that it is senseless to hamper a Mainstream PC by installing too little. We consider 512 MB appropriate for most Mainstream PCs, although you may want more if you run memory-intensive applications like Photoshop on your system.

The Intel D865PERL motherboard has four DIMM slots and a dual-channel memory controller that provides faster memory performance when DIMMs are installed in pairs. Installing a pair of 256 MB DIMMs, for a total of 512 MB, leaves two DIMM slots available for future expansion. In a year or two, you can fill that second pair of DIMM slots with 256 MB, 512 MB, or 1 GB modules, taking the system to 1.0 GB, 1.5 GB, or 2.5 GB of total memory, doubling to quintupling the amount of main memory. That should suffice for the expected lifetime of the system.

Crucial memory is fast, reliable, inexpensive, and readily available. We've used Crucial memory for more than a decade in hundreds of systems, and it's never let us down. Accordingly, we chose two Crucial PC3200 256 MB DIMMs for this system.

Video adapter

ATi RADEON 9200 (http://www.ati.com)

A Mainstream PC needs excellent 2D video quality and, if it is to be used at all for gaming, 3D graphics performance adequate for all but the most intensive games. Embedded Intel video meets the first requirement, but its 3D graphics performance is sedate, to put it politely. If you'll never use the system for gaming, go with embedded video; otherwise, choose an entry-level 3D video adapter.

You needn't buy an expensive graphics adapter to get reasonable 3D performance. Hardcore gamers willingly pay $400 or more for the latest, fastest 3D graphics adapters, but those are overkill for a Mainstream PC. A Mainstream PC needs a sub-$100 3D graphics adapter that provides competent 3D acceleration with top-notch 2D display quality. Fortunately, the least expensive ATi RADEON video adapter, the RADEON 9200, meets those requirements exactly.

The ATi RADEON 9200 has the best 3D performance in its price range and provides excellent 2D display quality. Comparably priced *n*VIDIA adapters provide 3D performance a half-step behind the RADEON, but have noticeably inferior 2D display quality. We think the ATi RADEON 9200 is better in every important respect, so that's what we decided to use. If you want a step up in video performance, an ATi RADEON 9600-series card is also an excellent choice.

Hard disk drive

Seagate Barracuda 7200.7 SATA 160GB (http://www.seagate.com)

A Mainstream PC needs a mainstream hard drive, and you can't get much more mainstream than a Seagate Barracuda 7200.7 SATA drive. The Barracuda 7200.7 is inexpensive, fast, very quiet, and extremely reliable.

When we wrote this, Seagate Serial ATA drives were the only native S-ATA drives available. So-called S-ATA drives from Maxtor and other makers were bridged S-ATA models, which means they were actually standard parallel ATA drives with circuitry to convert the S-ATA protocols used by the interface to the P-ATA protocols used by the drive. Such conversion always incurs overhead that slows performance. In our testing, the Barracuda 7200.7 SATA drive was in fact faster than competing models, due no doubt to its native S-ATA interface and large 8 MB buffer.

The Seagate drive was available in 80, 120, 160, and 200 GB capacities. At the time we built this system, the 200 GB model was still selling at a substantial premium, so we went with the 160 GB unit.

Optical drive

Plextor PX-708A DVD writer (http://www.plextor.com)

No real decision here. A Mainstream PC needs a "do-it-all" optical drive, and nothing we know of comes close to the Plextor PX-708A. It writes CD-R/RW, DVD+R/RW, and DVD-R/RW—all at high speeds—and reads nearly any optical disc except DVD-RAM.

We chose a DVD writer rather than a CD writer for maximum flexibility and functionality. In particular, the gigantic size of modern hard drives makes backing up problematic. Back when a 10 GB hard drive was huge, a CD writer was a viable backup device. One could back up the entire hard drive to less than a dozen CDs, and most people's active data fit on one CD.

Nowadays, hard drives have jumped in capacity by an order of magnitude, and many people have much larger active data sets to back up. With roughly seven times the capacity of a CD-R disc and media costs dropping every month, writable DVDs are now an excellent inexpensive backup solution.

WARNING

If you need to read burned DVDs, check the compatibility. Most DVD drives read any type of DVD disc, except perhaps DVD-RAM. Others will not read DVD+R/RW or DVD-R/RW discs. Check the technical specs on the web site to verify that the drive you intend to buy is listed as compatible with the types of DVD discs you intend to use.

Keyboard

Logitech Elite (http://www.logitech.com)

Personal preference outweighs all else when choosing a keyboard. So many personal factors determine the usability of a keyboard—straight versus ergonomic, layout, key size, cup depth, angle, stroke length, corded versus cordless, and so on—that no one can choose the "best" keyboard for someone else.

That said, we had to pick a "mainstream" keyboard for our Mainstream PC, and our favorite mid-priced keyboard is the Logitech Elite. For several years we'd been using Microsoft keyboards almost exclusively. In the course of writing this book, we decided it was time to take another look at Logitech models. Although Microsoft keyboards are as good as ever and remain on our recommended list, when we did head-to-head comparisons we found we usually preferred the feel of the Logitech models.

Mouse

Logitech Click! Optical Mouse (http://www.logitech.com)

Personal preference is the most important factor in choosing a mouse as well. Subtle differences in size, shape, button position, and so on can have a major effect on how comfortable a mouse is to use. What someone else loves, you may hate, and vice versa.

Conventional wisdom is not always reliable. For example, because Barbara has small hands, most ergonomics experts would recommend a small mouse for her. She used a small mouse for years, but began experiencing hand pain when using it. On a whim, she decided to try a Microsoft Explorer 5-button mouse, which is one of the largest standard mice on the market. Her hand pain went away, and she's been using large mice ever since. The moral is that if you're at all unhappy with your current mouse, try something else. You may well like it much better.

Years ago, Microsoft sent us prototype samples of their first "red light" optical mouse. We fell in love with optical mice, and used Microsoft optical mice exclusively for years. When we were evaluating Logitech keyboards for this book, we decided we might as well look at their new line of optical mice as well. We're glad we did. At the midrange and high end, we actually prefer the feel of the Logitech models, particularly the MX-series mice. They feel more precise than the Microsoft models, and seem to fit our hands better. At the low end, Logitech and Microsoft optical mice seem comparable, but the Logitech models generally cost a bit less for models with features similar to competing Microsoft models.

ALTERNATIVES: KEYBOARD

Many. Decide which features and layout you want, and then choose the appropriate Logitech model. If Logitech doesn't offer a model that meets your needs, look next to one of the many models sold by Microsoft.

ALTERNATIVES: MOUSE

Many. We used a Logitech Click! Optical Mouse for the Mainstream PC based on price and feel, but you might prefer another model. We recommend limiting your choices to Logitech and Microsoft. Whatever you do, get an optical mouse rather than a mechanical model. Also, consider a wireless model—the absence of a mouse cord is a convenience that many people consider worth the small additional cost.

Speakers

Logitech Z-3 speaker system (http://www.logitech.com)

A Mainstream PC deserves a decent set of speakers, but we realistically don't want to spend more than $100. There are scores of speaker systems available within that range, including sets with 5, 6, or even 7 speakers. We decided it was better to spend our $100 on a good 2.1 system—two satellites and a subwoofer—rather than spending the same amount on a cheesy, tinny-sounding speaker system with a half dozen satellites.

At 23W RMS for the subwoofer and 8.5W RMS for each satellite, the Z-3 won't rattle the walls, but the sound quality is excellent for the price, and the volume is more than sufficient for casual gaming or listening to music. In fact, as Robert was writing this, Barbara just yelled from the other end of the house for him to turn down the volume. We tested the Z-3 with everything from shoot-'em-up games to the Rolling Stones to Bach concertos, and the Z-3 did well with all of them. The satellites do a good job on the midrange and highs, and the subwoofer provides excellent bass response for this price level.

The Z-3 speakers are solidly built, and attractive enough to use in your living room or den. The satellites each use one 2" midrange/tweeter driver, and are brushed aluminum with wood-grain vinyl and removable grilles. The subwoofer is a 9" cube with an 8" driver and built-in amplifier.

Our only criticism of the Z-3 speaker system is that the cable that links the subwoofer to the satellites is too short. That won't be a problem for most people, but Robert ended up with the subwoofer sitting on top of his desk rather than underneath it because the cable wasn't long enough to reach.

Display

NEC MultiSync FE991SB 19" CRT (http://www.necmitsubishi.com)

A Mainstream PC should have a 19" display. Budget limits us to a CRT monitor rather than a flat-panel LCD display, but that's not really a problem because the FE991SB outperforms LCD displays that sell for two to three times its price. It supports 1280 × 1024 resolution at 89 Hz, 1600 × 1200 at 76 Hz, and (rather uselessly, we think) 1792 × 1344 at 68 Hz. The images are extremely bright and have the trademark NEC crispness and contrast.

ALTERNATIVES: SPEAKERS

The Logitech Z-3 is our favorite sub-$100 2.1 speaker system, but the Altec-Lansing 2100LA is also an excellent choice. We listened to several sub-$100 4.1, 5.1, 6.1, and 7.1 speaker systems, and decided none of them were worth having. We prefer decent sound from three speakers to terrible sound from 5, 6, or 7 speakers.

ALTERNATIVES: DISPLAY

The FE991SB is an aperture-grill CRT, which uses two horizontal wires to stabilize the grill. Most people don't notice these wires, but they are sometimes visible, particularly on a white background. If you find these wires intolerable, we recommend the NEC MultiSync FE990, which uses a shadow mask rather than an aperture grill. The FE990 image is not quite as bright or contrasty as the FE991SB image, but the FE990 doesn't use the wires. If you're on a tight budget, we recommend the NEC AccuSync 900.

Whatever you do, don't buy a cheap monitor. Remember, you'll be staring at it a lot. The joy of saving a few bucks is soon forgotten, but the agony of poor display quality lasts for the lifetime of the cheap monitor, which fortunately tends to be short.

UPS

APC Back-UPS LS 700 (http://www.apc.com)

Some people consider a UPS a luxury, but we won't run a system without one. We have power outages frequently around here, particularly during spring thunderstorms and winter ice storms. We've used scores of American Power Conversion (APC) UPSes over the years, and have seldom had a problem with them, something we can't say for some of APC's competitors. (And, yes, we say that despite the fact that APC recalled 2 million UPSes early in 2003, which they did voluntarily because of a handful of problem units.)

In addition to protecting against the obvious problem—complete power loss—a UPS contributes to system stability. People who begin using a UPS are often surprised by how infrequently their systems lock up. Many lock-ups blamed on Windows are in reality caused by power blips too short to make the lights flicker, but more than long enough to crash a computer. If your work is worth anything, it's worth the small cost of a UPS.

Component summary

Table 3-1 summarizes our component choices for the Mainstream PC system.

Table 3-1. Bill of Materials for Mainstream PC

Component	Product
Case	Antec Sonata Mid-Tower Case
Power supply	Antec TruePower 380 (bundled)
Motherboard	Intel D865PERL
Processor	Intel Pentium 4/3.2E (Prescott-core)
CPU cooler	(bundled with retail-boxed CPU)
Memory	Crucial PC3200 DDR-SDRAM (two 256 MB DIMMs)
Video adapter	ATi RADEON 9200
Hard disk drive	Seagate Barracuda 7200.7 SATA (160 GB)
Optical drive	Plextor PX-708A DVD writer
Keyboard	Logitech Elite
Mouse	Logitech Click! Optical Mouse
Speakers	Logitech Z-3 2.1 speaker system
Display	NEC MultiSync FE991SB 19" CRT monitor
UPS	APC Back-UPS LS 700

Dynatron CPU cooler? Didn't you guys list a retail-boxed Prescott-core Pentium 4 with a bundled CPU cooler? Yep, but we had to change our plans slightly. When we started to build this system, we did our usual component compatibility check. On the Intel processor compatibility web page for the D865PERL, we found that the Prescott-core P4 requires a motherboard with a revision number of C27650-209, C27646-210, C26719-211, C27648-208, C40926-202, or later. Our motherboard had a revision number of C27646-209. Rats.

That particular D865PERL wouldn't support the Prescott-core P4, so we had to use a different processor or a different motherboard. We happened to have a 3.2 GHz Northwood-core P4 on our workbench, so we decided to use it instead. Our Northwood was an OEM model that didn't include the heatsink/fan unit, so we needed a third-party HSF. We chose a Dynatron Dallas-series D62 DC1207BM-X cooler, with which we've had excellent experience in the past.

You're unlikely to have a problem of this nature. We got our motherboard long before we got the Prescott-core processor. Most mail-order places have very fast inventory turnover, so if you order all your components at the same time they'll almost certainly be very recent stock. It is worth checking, though. Installing a fast recent processor in an older motherboard can cause problems ranging from boot failures to damaging the motherboard and/or processor. If we were ordering parts for this system today, we'd buy the Prescott rather than the Northwood.

Building the System

Figure 3-1 shows the major components of the Mainstream PC. The Intel D865PERL motherboard is on top of the Antec Sonata case, with the Plextor PX-708A DVD burner and the ATi RADEON 9200 video adapter to the left and the Logitech keyboard and mouse to the right. In front, left to right, are the Seagate Barracuda hard drive, two 256 MB sticks of Crucial PC3200 memory, the Pentium 4 processor, and the Dynatron CPU cooler.

Figure 3-1. Mainstream PC components, awaiting construction

Before you proceed, make sure you have everything you need. Open each box and verify the contents against the packing list. Oh, yeah—and make sure your processor is compatible with your motherboard. We didn't do that until we started building our system, and it bit us in the ass.

Although by necessity we describe building the system in a particular order, you don't need to follow that exact sequence when you build your own system. Some steps—for example, installing the processor and memory before installing the motherboard in the case—should be taken in the sequence we describe because doing otherwise makes the task more difficult or risks damaging a component. Other steps—such as installing the video adapter after you install the motherboard in the case—*must* be taken in the order we describe because completing one step is a prerequisite for completing another. But for most steps, the exact sequence is unimportant. As you build your system, it will be obvious when sequence matters.

Preparing the case

The first step in building any system is always to make sure that the power supply is set to the correct input voltage. Some power supplies set themselves automatically. Others, including the Antec True380 power supply in this system, must be set manually using a slide switch to select the proper input voltage, as shown in Figure 3-2.

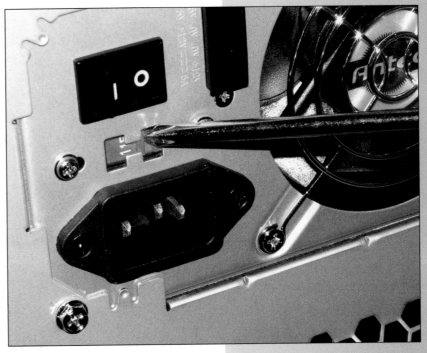

Figure 3-2. Verify that the power supply is set for the proper input voltage

---

WARNING

If you connect a power supply set for 230V to a 115V receptacle, there's no harm done. The PC components will receive only half the voltage they require, and the system won't boot. But if you connect a power supply set for 115V to a 230V receptacle, the PC components will receive *twice* the voltage they're designed to use. If you power up the system, that overvoltage will destroy the system instantly, in clouds of smoke and showers of sparks.

After you've verified that the power supply is set correctly, remove the two shipping screws that secure the side panel, as shown in Figure 3-3. We call them "shipping screws" because they're there primarily to keep the side panel securely in place during shipping. Although you can insert these screws after you finish building the system, it really isn't necessary. The side-panel latch is sufficient to secure the side panel during routine use.

Figure 3-3. Remove the shipping screws

Figure 3-4. Press the latch and lift the side panel off

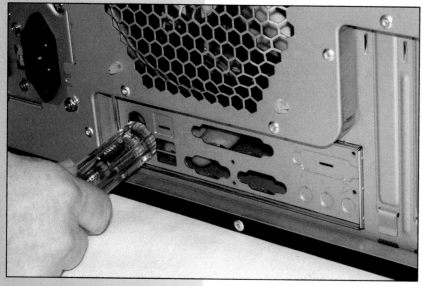

Figure 3-5. Remove the I/O template supplied with the case

After you remove the shipping screws, press the side-panel latch and remove the panel, as shown in Figure 3-4.

Every case we've ever seen, including the Antec Sonata, comes with an I/O template. So does every motherboard. The generic I/O template supplied with the case never seems to fit the I/O panel of the motherboard, so you need to remove the stock I/O template and replace it with the one supplied with the motherboard.

I/O templates are made of thin metal that is easily bent. The best way to remove an I/O template without damaging it, as shown in Figure 3-5, is to use a tool handle to press gently against the panel from outside the case, while using your fingers to support the panel from the inside. (We don't know why we care about damaging the generic I/O template supplied with the case. We have a stack of them sitting around, and have never needed one.)

Most motherboards, including the Intel D865PERL, come with a custom ATX I/O template designed to match the motherboard I/O panel. Before you install the custom I/O template, compare it to the motherboard I/O panel to make sure the holes in the template correspond to the connectors on the motherboard.

Once you've done that, press the custom I/O template into place. Working from inside the case, align the bottom, right, and left edges of the I/O template with the matching case cutout. When the I/O template is positioned properly, press gently along the edges to seat it in the cutout, as shown in Figure 3-6. It should snap into place, although getting it to seat properly sometimes requires several attempts. It's often helpful to press gently against the edge of the template with the handle of a screwdriver or nut driver.

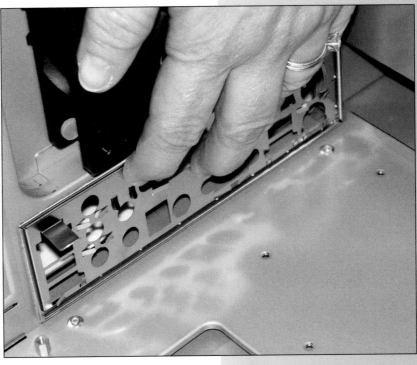

Figure 3-6. Snap the custom I/O template into place

> **WARNING**
>
> Be careful not to bend the I/O template while seating it. The template holes need to line up with the external port connectors on the motherboard I/O panel. If the template is even slightly bent it may be difficult to seat the motherboard properly.

After you install the I/O template, carefully slide the motherboard into place, making sure that the back panel connectors on the motherboard are firmly in contact with the corresponding holes on the I/O template. Compare the positions of the motherboard mounting holes with the standoff mounting positions in the case. One easy method is to place the motherboard in position and insert a felt-tip pen through each motherboard mounting hole to mark the corresponding standoff position beneath it.

> If you simply look at the motherboard, it's easy to miss one of the mounting holes in all the clutter. We generally hold the motherboard up to a light, which makes the mounting holes stand out distinctly.

The Intel D865PERL motherboard has eleven mounting holes. The Antec Sonata, like many cases, is shipped with several standoffs preinstalled. All of the standoffs preinstalled in the Sonata corresponded with motherboard mounting holes, so we needed to install standoffs at only a few remaining mounting-hole locations.

Figure 3-7. Install a brass standoff in each mounting position

Figure 3-8. Verify that a standoff is installed for each motherboard mounting hole and that no extra standoffs are installed

Install additional brass standoffs until each motherboard mounting hole has a corresponding standoff. Although you can screw in the standoffs using your fingers or needlenose pliers, it's much easier and faster to use a 5mm nut driver, as shown in Figure 3-7. Tighten the standoffs finger-tight, but do not overtighten them. It's easy to strip the threads by applying too much torque with a nut driver.

Once you've installed all the standoffs, do a final check to verify that (a) each motherboard mounting hole has a corresponding standoff, and (b) that no standoffs are installed that don't correspond to a motherboard mounting hole. As a final check, we usually hold the motherboard in position above the case, as shown in Figure 3-8, and look down through each mounting hole to make sure there's a standoff installed below it.

Another method we've used to verify that all standoffs are properly installed is to place the motherboard flat on a large piece of paper and use a felt-tip pen to mark all motherboard mounting holes on the paper. We then line up one of the marks with the corresponding standoff and press down until the standoff punctures the paper. We do the same with a second standoff to align the paper, and then press the paper flat around each standoff. If we've installed the standoffs properly, every mark will be punctured, and there will be no punctures where there are no marks.

Preparing and populating the motherboard

It is always easier to prepare and populate the motherboard—that is, to install the processor and memory—while the motherboard is outside the case. In fact, you must do it this way with some systems, because installing the heatsink/fan unit requires access to both sides of the motherboard. Even if it is possible to populate the motherboard while it is installed in the case, we always recommend having the motherboard outside the case and lying flat on the work surface. More than once, we've tried to save a few minutes by replacing the processor without removing the motherboard. Too often, the result has been bent pins and a destroyed processor.

WARNING

Each time you handle the processor, memory, or other static-sensitive components, first touch the power supply to ground yourself.

Figure 3-9. The standard Intel Socket 478 heatsink/fan retaining bracket

Preparing the motherboard

Intel Socket 478 motherboards include a standard heatsink/fan retaining bracket, shown in Figure 3-9, which fits HSF units supplied by Intel as well as those sold by many third-party vendors. The Intel bracket is well engineered. Unlike the inferior AMD Socket A method, which requires clamping a heavy HSF unit to two fragile plastic tabs that are part of the socket itself, Intel uses a robust bracket that clamps to the motherboard using four connectors. The HSF mounts to this bracket, which removes the weight of the HSF from the plastic CPU socket.

The Dynatron heatsink/fan unit we chose uses its own bracket, which is better than the standard Intel bracket. However, this means that you must remove the standard Intel bracket. To do so, use a small flat-blade screwdriver to lift the four white posts, as shown in Figure 3-10. Lifting the posts releases the pressure on the plastic expansion clamps on the underside of the motherboard, allowing the bracket to be pulled free. If the bracket does not pull free easily, use the flat part of the screwdriver blade to press gently on the expansion clamps until they release. With the standard retaining bracket removed, the mounting holes are visible, as shown in Figure 3-11.

Figure 3-10. Lift the white plastic posts to release the standard bracket

Figure 3-11. With the standard bracket removed, the four mounting holes are visible

Figure 3-12. The baseplate for the Dynatron heatsink/fan unit

We detail the process of installing the Dynatron heatsink/fan unit and its retaining bracket because this is the HSF we recommend if you use an OEM processor rather than a retail-boxed model. If you use the retail-boxed processor, the supplied HSF simply snaps into place in the standard Intel retaining bracket.

The Dynatron HSF includes a metal baseplate, shown in Figure 3-12, that mounts beneath the motherboard. (Note the white plastic insulating pad that prevents the metal baseplate from contacting the motherboard.) The baseplate includes four threaded mounting studs that protrude through the mounting holes and provide a place to secure the Dynatron HSF retaining bracket.

To mount the Dynatron baseplate, turn the motherboard over, align the threaded mounting studs with the mounting holes, and press the baseplate into place, as shown in Figure 3-13. With some motherboards, the baseplate fits snugly and will stay in place against its own weight. With others, including the Intel D865PERL, the baseplate is a loose fit, so you'll need to support its weight as you turn the motherboard face up to keep it from dropping out.

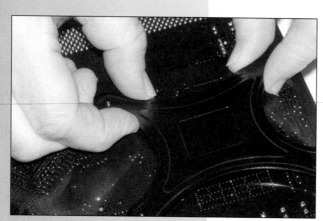

Figure 3-13. Working from the bottom of the motherboard, press the Dynatron baseplate into position

With the baseplate in position, fit the four holes in the Dynatron retaining bracket over the threaded studs of the baseplate, as shown in Figure 3-14.

Use the four screws supplied with the Dynatron HSF unit to secure the retaining bracket to the baseplate, as shown in Figure 3-15. Tighten the screws firmly. The Dynatron heatsink is a heavy chunk of copper. The motherboard mounts vertically in the Sonata case, and the last thing you want is a pound or so of heatsink vibrating loose and flopping around inside the case.

Figure 3-14. Drop the Dynatron retaining bracket into place over the four threaded posts in the Dynatron baseplate

Figure 3-15. Insert the four screws provided to secure the Dynatron bracket to the baseplate

Installing the processor

To install the Pentium 4 processor, lift the arm of the ZIF (zero insertion force) socket, as shown in Figure 3-16, until it reaches vertical. In this position, there is no clamping force on the socket holes, which allows the processor to drop into place without requiring any pressure.

Pin 1 is indicated on the processor and socket by a small triangle. With the socket lever vertical, align pin 1 of the processor with pin 1 of the socket and drop the processor into place, as shown in Figure 3-17. The processor should seat flush with the socket just from the force of gravity. If the processor doesn't simply drop into place, something is misaligned. Remove the processor and verify that it is aligned properly and that the pattern of pins on the processor corresponds to the pattern of holes on the socket. *Never* apply pressure to the processor—you'll bend one or more pins, destroying the processor.

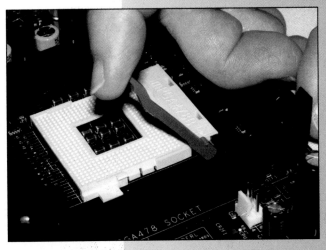

Figure 3-16. Lift the socket lever to prepare the socket for the processor

> Yes, we label our processors with a Sharpie® or other felt-tip marker. We build so many systems and move components around so much that that we need some way to keep track of which processor is which. This one is a 3.2 GHz Northwood-core Pentium 4 with 512 KB L2 cache, as indicated by the label.

Figure 3-17. Drop the processor in place

With the processor in place and seated flush with the socket, press the lever arm down and snap it into place, as shown in Figure 3-18. You may have to press the lever arm slightly away from the socket to allow it to snap into a locked position.

> Closing the ZIF lever sometimes causes the processor to lift slightly out of its socket. Once you are sure the processor is fully seated, it's safe to maintain gentle finger pressure on it to keep it fully seated as you close the ZIF lever.

Figure 3-18. Lock the processor in place

Installing the heatsink/fan (HSF)

Modern processors draw as much as 100W of power, and must dissipate a correspondingly large amount of heat. Our Northwood-core Pentium 4/3.2 has a peak draw of 89W and must dissipate the resulting heat over the surface of its heat spreader, which is about the size of a large postage stamp. Without a good heatsink/fan (HSF) unit, the processor would almost instantaneously shut itself down to prevent damage from overheating.

Using a proper HSF is critical. Retail-boxed processors include an Intel HSF unit that is perfectly adequate for the task. If you buy an OEM processor, it's up to you to install an HSF unit that is sufficient to keep the processor operating within the design temperature range. Just because an HSF fits doesn't guarantee that it's usable. Faster processors consume more power and generate more heat. An HSF designed and rated for a Pentium 4/2.4 may be—and probably is—woefully inadequate for a Pentium 4/3.2. HSFs designed for faster processors are generally larger and heavier, use copper instead of aluminum fins, and have more powerful fans. The Dynatron unit we used is rated for a Pentium 4 up to 3.2 GHz. If we had installed a Pentium 4/3.4 or faster, we'd have chosen a different model.

To install the HSF unit, begin by polishing the heat spreader surface on top of the processor with a paper towel or soft cloth, as shown in Figure 3-19. The goal is to remove any grease, grit, or other material that might prevent the heatsink from making intimate contact with the processor surface.

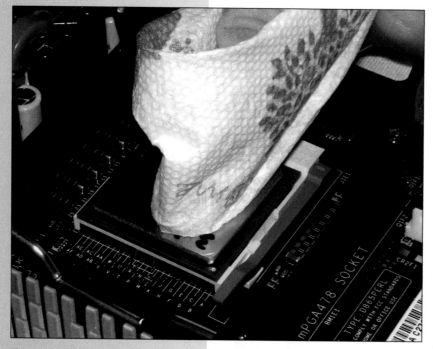

Figure 3-19. Polish the processor with a paper towel before installing the HSF

As long as you're polishing, check the surface of the heatsink. If the heatsink base is bare, that means it's intended to be used with thermal compound, usually called "thermal goop." In that case, also polish the heatsink base. Some heatsinks have a square or rectangular pad made of a phase-change medium, which is a fancy term for a material that melts as the CPU heats and resolidifies as the CPU cools. This liquid/solid cycle ensures that the processor die maintains good thermal contact with the heatsink. If your heatsink includes such a pad, you needn't polish the base of the heatsink. (Heatsinks use *either* a thermal pad *or* thermal goop, not both.)

The Dynatron heatsink/fan unit includes a single-serving packet of standard silicone thermal goop. Cut the corner of the packet and squeeze the thermal goop into a pile on the center of the processor, as shown in Figure 3-20. You don't have to get all of the thermal goop onto the processor; getting most of it is good enough.

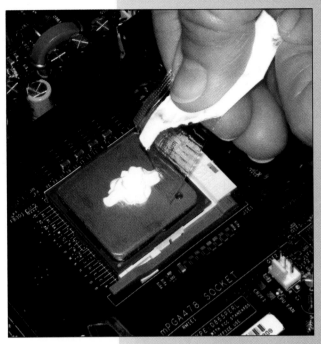

Figure 3-20. Apply the provided thermal compound

Yes, polishing the processor removed our handwritten label, but we can tell what type of processor is installed in a working system. It's just when the processor is lying on the bench that we need the label. If we remove this processor, we'll relabel it before we return it to our inventory shelf.

WARNING

If you remove the heatsink, you must replace the thermal compound or pad when you reinstall it. Before you reinstall, remove all remnants of the old thermal pad or compound. This can be difficult, particularly for a thermal pad, which can be very tenacious. We use an ordinary hair dryer to warm the thermal material enough to make it easy to remove. Sometimes the best way is to warm up the compound and rub it off with your thumb. (Use rubber gloves or a plastic bag to keep the gunk off your skin.)

Alternatively, one of our technical reviewers says that rubbing gently with 0000 steel wool works wonders in removing the gunk, and the steel wool is fine enough not to damage the surface. Another of our technical reviewers tells us that he uses Goof-Off or isopropyl alcohol to remove the remnants of the thermal goop or thermal pad. Whatever works for you is fine. Just make sure to remove the old thermal compound and replace it with new compound each time you remove and reinstall the processor.

When we replace a heatsink, we use Antec Silver Thermal Compound, which works well and is widely available and inexpensive. Don't pay extra for "premium" brand names like Arctic Silver. They cost more than the Antec product, and our testing shows little or no difference in cooling efficiency.

Figure 3-21. Align the HSF unit over the processor and seat it

Orient the HSF above the processor, keeping it as close to horizontal as possible, as shown in Figure 3-21. Slide the HSF unit down into the retaining bracket. Press down gently and use a small circular motion to spread the thermal goop evenly over the surface of the processor.

If you apply thermal goop liberally, as we have done here, excess goop squoosh- es out from between the HSF base and the processor surface when you put the heatsink in place. Good practice suggests removing excess goop from around the socket, but that may be impossible with a large heatsink because the heatsink blocks access to the socket area. Standard silicone thermal goop does not con- duct electricity, so there is no danger of excess goop shorting anything out.

If you're a neatnik, use your finger (covered with a latex glove or plastic bag) to spread thin layers of goop on the processor surface and heatsink base before you install the HSF. We do that with silver-based thermal compounds, which we don't trust to be electrically nonconductive, despite manufacturers' claims to the contrary.

Figure 3-22. Clamp the HSF into place

With the HSF resting loosely in place, the next step is to clamp it tightly against the processor to ensure good thermal transfer between the CPU and heatsink. To do so, press down the locking clamps on each side of the HSF unit until the free end of each clamp snaps into the hook on the retaining bracket base. It's easier to press the first locking clamp into place because there isn't yet any pressure on the HSF, so we generally do the less-accessible clamp first. In this case, that was the clamp nearer the center of the motherboard. The clamp at the edge of the motherboard, shown in Figure 3-22, is easily accessible, so we locked that one into place second.

The thermal mass of the heatsink draws heat away from the CPU, but the heat must be dissipated to prevent the CPU from eventually overheating as the heatsink warms up. To dispose of excess heat as it is transferred to the heatsink, most CPU coolers use a small muffin fan to continuously draw air through the fins of the heatsink. Some CPU fans use a drive power con-nector, but most are designed to attach to the dedicated CPU fan connector on the motherboard. Using a motherboard fan power connector allows the motherboard to control the CPU fan, reducing the speed for quieter opera-tion when the processor is running under light load and not generating much heat, and increasing the speed when the processor is running under heavy load and generating more heat. The motherboard can also monitor fan speed, which allows it to send an alert to the user if the fan fails or begins running sporadically.

Figure 3-23. Connect the CPU fan cable to the CPU fan connector

To connect the CPU fan, locate the three-pin header connector on the motherboard labeled CPU Fan and plug in the keyed cable from the CPU fan, as shown in Figure 3-23.

Installing the memory

Installing memory is easy enough, but before you begin plugging in memory modules willy-nilly, take a moment to determine the best memory configuration. The Intel D865PERL motherboard has a dual-channel memory controller that provides better memory performance than a single-channel controller, but it's possible to force the motherboard to operate in single-channel mode if you're not careful about where you install the memory modules. Dual-channel operation requires using DIMMs in pairs, one per channel.

Examining the D865PERL motherboard, we see that it has four DIMM slots in two pairs. The slot nearest the processor is Channel A DIMM0, followed by Channel A DIMM1, Channel B DIMM0, and Channel B DIMM1. We want to install one memory module in Channel A and the second in Channel B. We could use either slot, but as a matter of good practice we decided to install our DIMMs in the first (DIMM0) slot of each channel. Also, the Channel B DIMM1 slot is nearer the main ATX power connector, so using it reduces the clearance available when you connect power to the motherboard. Having decided where to install the memory modules, the first step in actually installing them is to pivot the locking tabs on both sides of the DIMM socket outward, as shown in Figure 3-24.

Figure 3-24. Pivot the locking tabs on both sides of the DIMM socket outward

To install the first DIMM, first find the notch in the contact area of the DIMM and align the DIMM so that the notch lines up with the raised plastic tab in the Channel A DIMM0 slot. Then slide the DIMM into place, as shown in Figure 3-25.

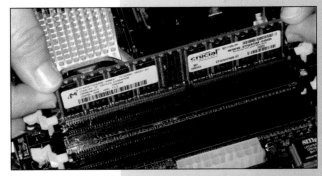

Figure 3-25. Orient the first DIMM with the notch aligned properly with the socket

With the DIMM properly aligned with the Channel A DIMM0 slot and oriented vertically relative to the slot, use both thumbs to press down on the DIMM until it snaps into place, as shown in Figure 3-26. The locking tabs should automatically pivot back up into the locked position when the DIMM snaps into place. If they don't, close them manually to lock the DIMM into the socket.

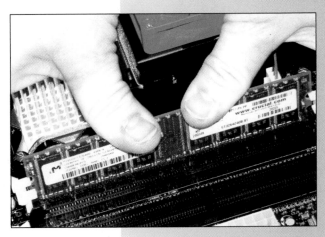

Figure 3-26. Seat the DIMM by pressing firmly until it snaps into place

Figure 3-27. Orient the second DIMM with the notch aligned properly with the socket

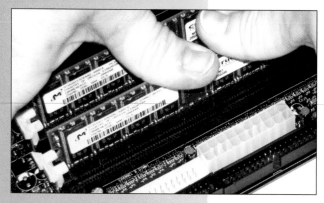

Figure 3-28. Seat the DIMM by pressing firmly until it snaps into place

Figure 3-29. Slide the motherboard into position

To install the second DIMM, first find the notch in the contact area of the DIMM and align the DIMM so that the notch lines up with the raised plastic tab in the Channel B DIMM0 slot. Then slide the DIMM into place, as shown in Figure 3-27.

With the DIMM properly aligned, use both thumbs to press down until it snaps into place, as shown in Figure 3-28. Make sure the locking tabs pivot into the locked position.

With the processor and memory installed, you're almost ready to install the motherboard in the case. Before you do that, check the motherboard documentation to determine if any configuration jumpers need to be set. The Intel D865PERL has only one jumper, which sets operating mode. On our motherboard, that jumper was set correctly by default.

Installing the motherboard

Installing the motherboard is the most time-consuming step in building the system because there are so many cables to connect. It's important to get all of them connected right, so take your time and verify each connection before and after you make it.

Seating and securing the motherboard

To begin, slide the motherboard into the case, as shown in Figure 3-29. Carefully align the back-panel I/O connectors with the corresponding holes in the I/O template, and slide the motherboard toward the rear of the case until the motherboard mounting holes line up with the standoffs you installed earlier.

> Check one more time to make sure that there's a brass standoff installed for each mounting hole, and that no brass standoff is installed where there is no mounting hole. One of our technical reviewers suggests installing white nylon standoffs, trimmed to length, in all unused standoff positions covered by the motherboard, particularly those near the expansion slots. Doing so provides more support to the motherboard, making it less likely that you'll crack it while seating a recalcitrant expansion card.

Before you secure the motherboard, verify that the back-panel I/O connectors mate properly with the I/O template, as shown in Figure 3-30. The I/O template has metal tabs that ground the back-panel I/O connectors. Make sure that none of these tabs intrudes into a port connector. An errant tab at best blocks the port, rendering it unusable, and at worst may short out the motherboard.

After you position the motherboard and verify that the back-panel I/O connectors mate cleanly with the I/O template, insert a screw through one mounting hole into the corresponding standoff, as shown in Figure 3-31. You may need to apply pressure to keep the motherboard positioned properly until you have inserted two or three screws.

If you have trouble getting all the holes and standoffs aligned, insert two screws but don't tighten them completely. Use one hand to press the motherboard into alignment, with all holes matching the standoffs. Then insert one or two more screws and tighten them completely. Finish mounting the motherboard by inserting screws into all standoffs and tightening them.

> People sometimes ask us why we don't use power screwdrivers. Because they're large, clumsy, and the batteries always seem to be dead when we want to use them. Worse still, we once watched someone crack a motherboard by overtorqueing the mounting screws with a power screwdriver. A clutched driver eliminates that objection, but we still find power screwdrivers too clumsy to use, even when we've built many identical systems on an ad hoc production line.

With first-rate products like the Antec Sonata case and the Intel D865PERL motherboard, all the holes usually line up perfectly. With second- and third-tier brands, that's not always the case. At times, we've been forced to use only a few screws to secure the motherboard. We prefer to use all of them, both to physically support the motherboard and to ensure that all of the grounding points are in fact grounded, but if you simply can't get all of the holes lined up, simply install as many screws as you can.

Figure 3-30. Verify that the back-panel connectors mate cleanly with the I/O template

Figure 3-31. Install screws in all mounting holes to secure the motherboard

Connecting the front-panel switch and indicator cables

Once the motherboard is secured, the next step is to connect the front-panel switch and indicator cables to the motherboard. Before you begin connecting front-panel cables, examine the cables. Each is labeled descriptively, e.g., "Power," "Reset," and "HDD LED." Match those descriptions with the front-panel connector pins on the motherboard to make sure you connect the correct cable to the appropriate pins. Figure 3-32 shows the pinouts for the Power Switch, Reset Switch, Power LED, and Hard Drive Activity LED connectors.

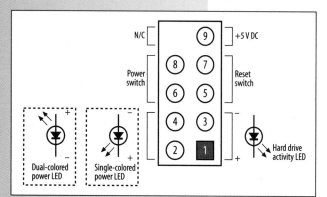

Figure 3-32. Front-panel connector pinouts (original graphic courtesy Intel Corporation)

- The Power Switch and Reset Switch connectors are not polarized, and can be connected in either orientation.

- The Hard Drive Activity LED is polarized, and should be connected with the ground (black) wire on pin 3 and the signal (red) wire on pin 1.

- There are two Power LED connectors on the Intel motherboard, one on the main front-panel connector block that accepts a two-position Power LED cable, and a supplementary Power LED connector adjacent to the main front-panel connector block that accepts a three-position Power LED cable with wires in positions one and three (the latter being the type of Power LED cable supplied with the Antec Sonata case). The Power LED connectors are dual-polarized, and can support a single-color (usually green) Power LED, as is provided with the Antec Sonata case, or a dual-color (usually green/yellow) LED. For the Sonata, connect the green wire to pin 1 on the supplementary Power LED connector, and the black wire to pin 3. If you are using a case that has a two-wire Power LED cable and/or a dual-color Power LED, check the case documentation to determine where and how to connect the Power LED cable.

Although Intel has defined a standard front-panel connector block and uses that standard for its own motherboards, few other motherboard makers adhere to that standard. Accordingly, rather than provide an Intel-standard monolithic connector block that would be useless for motherboards that do not follow the Intel standard, most case makers, including Antec, provide individual one-, two-, or three-pin connectors for each switch and indicator.

Once you determine the proper orientation for each cable, connect the Power Switch, Reset Switch, Power LED, and Hard Drive Activity LED, as shown in Figure 3-33. Not all cases have cables for every connector on the motherboard, and not all motherboards have connectors for all cables provided by the case. For example, the Antec Sonata case provides a speaker cable. The Intel D865PERL motherboard has a built-in speaker but no connector for an external speaker, so that cable goes unused. Conversely, the Intel D865PERL has a Chassis Intrusion Connector for which no corresponding cable exists on the Antec Sonata case, so that connector goes unused.

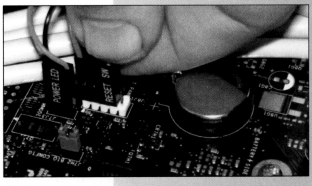

Figure 3-33. Connect the front-panel switch and indicator cables

When you're connecting front-panel cables, try to get it right the first time, but don't worry too much about getting it wrong. Other than the power switch cable, which must be connected properly for the system to start, none of the other front-panel switch and indicator cables is essential, and connecting them wrong won't damage the system. Switch cables—power and reset—are not polarized. You can connect them in either orientation, without worrying about which pin is signal and which is ground. LED cables may or may not be polarized, but the worst thing that happens if you connect a polarized LED cable backward is that the LED won't light. Most cases use a common wire color, usually black, for ground, and a colored wire for signal.

Connecting the front-panel USB ports

The Antec Sonata case provides two front-panel USB 2.0 ports, for which the Intel D865PERL motherboard provides corresponding internal connectors. To route USB to the front panel, you must connect a cable from each front-panel USB port to the corresponding internal connector. Figure 3-34 shows the pinouts for the dual front-panel internal USB connectors.

The D865PERL actually provides four internal USB 2.0 connectors in two sets of two header-pin groups. We decided to connect both front-panel USB ports to the same group of header pins, leaving the second set of header pins free in case we ever decide to run additional USB ports to the rear of the system.

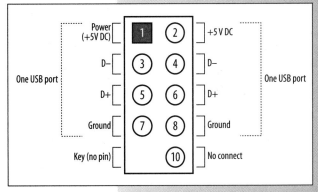

Figure 3-34. Front-panel USB connector pinouts (original graphic courtesy Intel Corporation)

Some Antec cases, including the Overture case we used for the Home Theater PC, provide a monolithic 10-pin USB connector that mates to motherboard USB header pins that use the standard Intel layout. With such a case, connecting the front-panel USB ports is a simple matter of plugging that monolithic connector into the header pins on the motherboard. Unfortunately, the Antec Sonata front-panel USB connector cable uses eight individual wires, each with a single connector. Figure 3-35 shows Robert (finally) getting all eight of the individual wires connected to the proper pins.

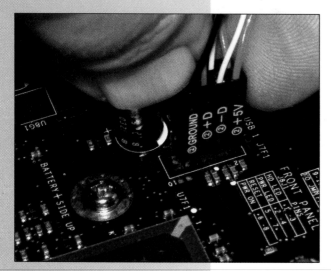

Figure 3-35. Connect the front-panel USB cables

Yes, we know it looks as though Robert is sliding a single four-pin connector onto the header pins, but trust us, those are four individual wires. Arrghh. The best way Robert found to get all the wires connected properly was to clamp the four wires between his fingers, aligned as a single connector would be, and then slide the group of connectors onto the header pins. And the second group of four is much harder to get onto the pins than the first set.

Antec *really* needs to provide a combination cable, with both a monolithic connector and individual wires, as they do for the front-panel audio connector. Perhaps they already do. One of our technical reviewers says his recently purchased Antec Sonata case came with a monolithic block on the front-panel USB cable.

Connecting the front-panel IEEE-1394a (FireWire) port

The Antec Sonata case provides one front-panel FireWire (IEEE-1394a) port, for which the Intel D865PERL motherboard provides a corresponding internal connector (actually, it provides two). To route FireWire to the front panel, you must connect a cable from the front-panel FireWire port to this internal connector. Figure 3-36 shows the pinouts for the internal FireWire connector.

For the FireWire cable, the Antec Sonata case again provides individual wires, this time six of them. That turns out to be fortunate. The monolithic FireWire connector provided with the Antec Overture case uses a different physical connector and different pinouts than the header-pin connector on

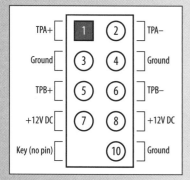

Figure 3-36. Front-panel IEEE-1394a (FireWire) connector pinouts (original graphic courtesy Intel Corporation)

the Intel motherboard, which would have required building or buying an adapter cable. The individual wires are labeled somewhat differently from the labels used on the motherboard, as follows:

TPA+ (blue wire) to TPA+ (motherboard pin 1)
TPA- (yellow wire) to TPA- (motherboard pin 2)
VG (black wire) to Ground (motherboard pin 3, 4, or 10)
TPB+ (green wire) to TPB+ (motherboard pin 5)
TPB- (salmon wire) to TPB- (motherboard pin 6)
VP (white wire) to +12 V DC (motherboard pin 7 or 8)

Connect the six wires, as shown in Figure 3-37. The position of the internal FireWire connector near the edge of the motherboard makes it extremely difficult both to connect the wires and to see which pin you're connecting the wire to. A strong light, a good pair of bent-nose pliers, and (unless you have excellent vision) a magnifying glass help considerably.

Figure 3-37. Connect the front-panel FireWire cables

Connecting the front-panel audio ports

The next decision is whether to route audio to the front-panel audio connectors. The Intel D865PERL motherboard has a set of header pins, the front-panel audio connector/jumper block, that serves two functions:

- With jumpers installed, the pins serve as a jumper block that routes audio line-out to the rear-panel audio line-out connector, and mic-in to the rear-panel mic-in connector.

- With jumpers removed, the pins serve as a connecting block for the front-panel audio cable, routing audio line-out and mic-in signals to the front-panel audio connectors. In this configuration, the rear-panel audio line-out and mic-in connectors are disabled.

We decided to leave all audio functions connected to the rear panel, primarily because we find it disconcerting to have cables dangling from the front of our systems. If you prefer to have front-panel audio, remove the jumpers and install the front-panel audio connecting cable supplied with the Sonata case. This cable has a monolithic, keyed, 10-pin connecting block that is compatible with the standard Intel front-panel audio connector.

For more information about configuring the front-panel audio connector/jumper block, see Table 41 in section 2.9.1 on page 75 of the Intel Desktop Board D865PERL Technical Product Specification, available on the Intel web site at *http://www.intel.com*.

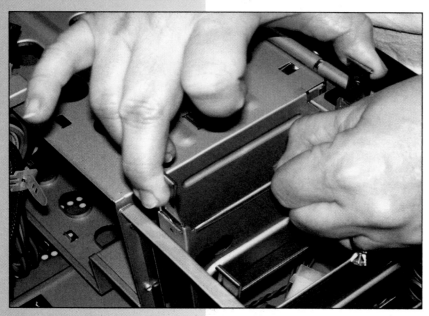

Figure 3-38. Remove an internal drive bay

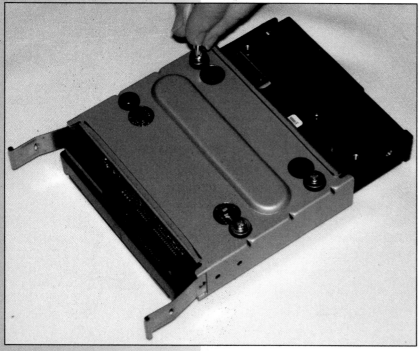

Figure 3-39. Secure the drive in the bay using four screws

Installing the hard drive

The Antec Sonata has three external 5.25" drive bays, two external 3.5" drive bays, and four internal 3.5" drive bays. The external bays are for devices like optical drives and floppy disk drives that use removable media. The four internal 3.5" bays can each hold one hard drive, and can be snapped in and out individually. To mount the hard drive, begin by removing an internal drive bay. As you press in on the two locking tabs, slide the bay out of the chassis, as shown in Figure 3-38.

Before you install the hard drive in the drive bay, verify that the drive is configured properly. We are using a Serial ATA hard drive in this system. Serial ATA drives do not require configuration because each S-ATA drive connects to a dedicated interface. If we had used a standard ATA hard drive, we'd have checked the jumpers on the drive to verify it was set as master.

The Antec drive bay uses rubber shock-mounting pads to isolate the drive, which reduces the amount of vibration and noise transferred from the hard drive to the chassis. One of those pads is visible as a small black circle to the lower left of the screw being driven. Secure the drive to the bay by installing four of the provided screws with oversized heads, as shown in Figure 3-39. Drive the screws finger-tight, but do not over-torque them.

With the hard drive secured in the bay, the next step is to reinstall the bay in the chassis, as shown in Figure 3-40. To do so, align the drive-bay rails with the chassis slots and slide the drive bay into the chassis. Press down firmly until the two locking tabs snap into place.

With the drive bay reinstalled, the next step is to connect the Serial ATA data cable to the drive. It doesn't matter which end of the Serial ATA cable you connect to the drive; the two ends are interchangeable. The Serial ATA data cable is keyed with a notch at one end that slides over a corresponding tab on the drive connector. Align the cable connector to the drive connector and press down firmly until the cable connector slides into place, as shown in Figure 3-41.

The next step is to connect the Serial ATA data cable to the motherboard Serial ATA interface. The motherboard provides two Serial ATA interfaces, labeled SATA 0 and SATA 1. Although the drive functions properly connected to either interface, best practice is to connect the primary hard drive to the first interface, SATA 0. The motherboard SATA connector is keyed in the same fashion as the hard-drive SATA connector. Orient the Serial ATA data cable so that its keying slot corresponds to the keying tab on the motherboard connector and press the cable into place, as shown in Figure 3-42.

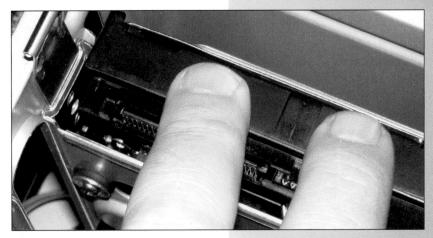

Figure 3-40. Slide the drive bay into the chassis and press until it snaps into place

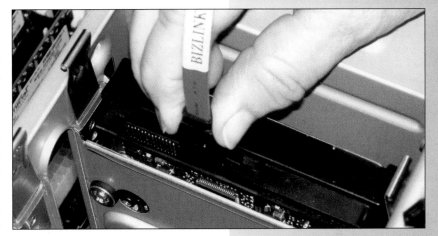

Figure 3-41. Connect the Serial ATA cable to the hard drive

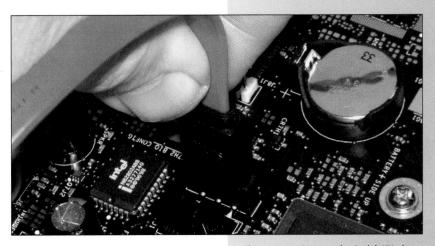

Figure 3-42. Connect the Serial ATA data cable to the motherboard interface

Figure 3-43. Connect the Serial ATA power cable to the drive

Figure 3-44. Insert the RADEON 9200 video adapter

The final hard-drive installation step is to connect power to the hard drive. To do so, examine the various cables coming out of the power supply to locate a Serial ATA power cable. The Serial ATA power connector is keyed similarly to the Serial ATA data cable, using a slot and tab arrangement. Align the keying slot on the cable with the keying tab on the drive and slide the power cable into place, as shown in Figure 3-43.

Installing the video adapter

As long as we have the system on its side, we might as well install the RADEON 9200 video adapter now. To begin, align the adapter with the motherboard AGP slot—the brown slot nearest the processor—to determine which slot cover you need to remove (it's not always obvious). For a D865PERL motherboard installed in a Sonata case, it's the slot cover nearest the processor.

Remove the correct slot cover. You may also need to loosen the screw for the adjacent slot cover temporarily in order to free the slot cover you want to remove. Carefully slide the rear bracket of the RADEON into place, making sure that the external connectors on the bracket clear the edges of the slot. Carefully align the AGP connector on the RADEON with the AGP slot and use both thumbs to press the RADEON down until it snaps into the slot, as shown in Figure 3-44.

WARNING

When a newly built system fails to boot, the most common cause is that the AGP adapter is not fully seated. Some combinations of adapter, case, and motherboard make it devilishly hard to install the adapter properly. It may seem that the adapter is fully seated. You may even hear it snap into place. That's no guarantee. Always verify that the card contacts have fully penetrated the AGP slot, and that the base of the adapter is parallel to the slot and in full contact with it. Many motherboards, including the D865PERL, have an AGP retaining bracket, visible here as two tabs to the lower right of the heatsink. This bracket mates with a corresponding notch on the video adapter, snapping into place as the adapter is seated. If you need to remove the adapter later, remember to press those tabs to unlock the retaining bracket before you attempt to pull the card.

After you are certain that the video adapter is fully seated, secure it by inserting a screw through the bracket into the chassis, as shown in Figure 3-45.

Figure 3-45. Secure the RADEON 9200 video adapter

Installing the optical drive

The Antec Sonata case provides three external 5.25" bays, each of which is covered by a snap-in plastic bezel. We decided to install the Plextor DVD writer in the middle bay. Before installing the drive, you have to remove the bezel for the selected drive bay. The easiest way to do that on the Sonata case is to insert a small flat-blade screwdriver in the gap between bezels and pop the bezel out. The back of the bezel holds two drive mounting rails. Remove those from the bezel and install one on each side of the optical drive, as shown in Figure 3-46.

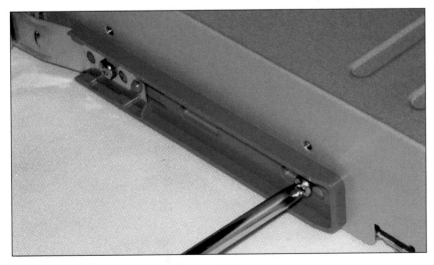

Figure 3-46. Install mounting rails on the optical drive

What, No Floppy Drive?

We decided against installing a floppy disk drive (FDD) in this system, although we may come to regret it. We didn't skip the FDD to save money—they only cost $8 or so—but to avoid having one more dust collector and one more ribbon cable to block airflow.

Some years ago, Intel and Microsoft started telling everyone that the humble FDD was a "legacy" device. We doubted the wisdom of that statement at the time, and over the years we've frequently had cause to regret not installing an FDD. More than once, we've had to open up a system and install an FDD to load a driver that wouldn't load from CD or to update the BIOS.

But things have changed, and we now consider the FDD passé for new systems. It's as easy to sneakernet files on CDs as on floppies, and many files nowadays are too large to fit on a floppy anyway. Intel's Express BIOS Update runs from within Windows, which eliminates the main reason for installing an FDD. Installing Windows 2000 or XP on a motherboard that uses the Intel 865 or later chipset does not require a supplemental driver on floppy disk. We used to use FDD-based diagnostics, but nowadays we just boot the Knoppix live Linux distro from CD. In fact, we can't think of a thing we need an FDD for.

So, although we won't install an FDD in our Mainstream PC, we won't give you a hard time if you decide to install one in yours.

Vertical alignment and seating depth within the drive bay are both important. If vertical alignment is off, the drive may be too high or too low within the bay. You may not be able to seat the drive because other drives or bezel covers block it. If mounting depth is off, the drive may seat too far in or too far out rather than flush with other drives and bezel covers. You can adjust vertical alignment and seating depth by choosing different holes in the drive rails and drive body. The alignment shown is proper for the Plextor PX-708A drive in the Antec Sonata case. Other drives and other cases may require different alignments to seat properly.

Before you install the drive, verify the jumper settings. The Plextor PX-708A DVD writer ships with a jumper installed in the rightmost position, as shown in Figure 3-47. This default jumper setting configures the drive as master. We plan to use the optical drive as the secondary master, so the default jumper setting is correct.

Figure 3-47. Verify the jumper settings on the optical drive

We almost did a Very Bad Thing. The leftmost jumper position on the Plextor PX-708A is labeled "DMA" but has no jumper installed by default. Our first reaction was, "Of course we want DMA enabled," so we were about to install a jumper block on those pins. Fortunately, we checked the manual first. As it turns out, the default setting enables UltraDMA. We're not sure what installing a jumper block would have done, but it wouldn't have been anything good.

It's usually easier to connect the ATA cable to the drive before you install the drive in the case. The Plextor PX-708A includes a standard 40-wire ATA cable, which we used. Because optical drives have relatively slow transfer rates, they can use the older 40-wire ATA cable rather than the 80-wire Ultra-ATA cable used for ATA hard drives. (An 80-wire cable works fine if that's all you have, but it's not necessary.)

To connect the cable, locate pin 1 on the drive connector, which is usually nearest the power connector. The pin 1 side of the cable is indicated by a red stripe. Align the cable connector with the drive connector, making sure the red stripe is on the pin 1 side of the drive connector, and press the cable into place, as shown in Figure 3-48.

To mount the drive in the case, feed the loose end of the ATA cable through the drive bay from the front, align the drive rails with the corresponding slots in the case, and press the drive firmly into place until the drive rails snap into the locked position. If you mounted the drive rails correctly, the drive should seat flush with the bezels that cover the vacant drive bays. Working from the rear of the drive, feed the ATA cable down into the case, placing the loose end near the front right edge of the motherboard.

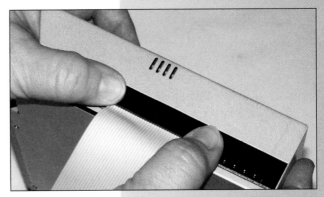

Figure 3-48. Connect the ATA cable to the optical drive

We want to connect the Plextor PX-708A optical drive as the master device on the secondary ATA channel. (We'll leave the primary ATA channel unused, because Windows can become confused if the primary hard drive is Serial ATA and there is a master device on the primary ATA channel.)

The primary ATA and secondary ATA interfaces are located near the right front edge of the motherboard near the DIMM slots. The primary ATA interface is the black connector nearest the edge, and the secondary ATA interface is a white connector immediately adjacent. Locate pin 1 on the secondary ATA interface, align the ATA cable with its red stripe toward pin 1 on the interface, and press the connector into place, as shown in Figure 3-49.

After you connect the ATA cable, don't just leave it flopping around loose. That not only looks amateurish, but can impede airflow and cause overheating. Tuck the cable neatly out of the way, using tape, cable ties, or tie wraps to secure it to the case. If necessary, temporarily disconnect the cable to route it around other cables and obstructions, and reconnect it once you have it positioned properly.

Figure 3-49. Connect the optical drive ATA cable to the secondary ATA interface on the motherboard

About the Audio Cable

Years ago, connecting an analog audio cable from the optical drive to the motherboard audio connector or sound card was necessary to play audio from the drive. Recent optical drives and motherboards use digital audio, which is delivered across the bus rather than via a separate cable. Few optical drives or motherboards include an analog audio cable nowadays, because one is seldom needed.

To verify the setting for digital audio, use Windows 2000/XP Device Manager to display the Device Properties sheet for the optical drive. The "Enable digital CD audio" checkbox should be marked. If not, mark it to enable digital audio. If the checkbox is grayed out, does not appear, or refuses to stay checked after a reboot, that means your optical drive and/or motherboard does not support digital audio. In that case, use an MPC analog audio cable to connect the drive to the CD-ROM audio connector on the motherboard or sound card. Some old audio programs do not support digital audio, and so require an analog audio cable to be installed even if the system supports digital audio.

The Plextor PX-708A DVD writer provides two audio connectors. In addition to the four-pin MPC analog audio connector, the PX-708A includes a two-pin digital audio connector that you can connect to a Sony Philips Digital Interface (SP/DIF) audio connector or a Digital In audio connector on your motherboard or sound card.

We suggest you install an audio cable only if needed. Otherwise, you can do without.

The final step in installing the optical drive—one we forget more often than we should—is to connect power to the drive. Choose one of the power cables coming from the power supply and press the Molex connector onto the drive power connector, as shown in Figure 3-50. It may require significant pressure to get the power connector to seat, so use care to avoid hurting your fingers if the connector seats suddenly. The Molex power connector is keyed, so verify that it is oriented properly before you apply pressure to seat the power cable.

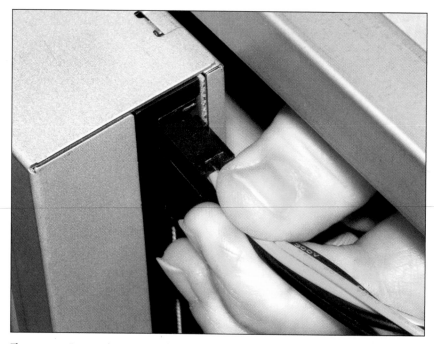

Figure 3-50. Connect the power cable to the optical drive

Connecting the ATX power connectors

The next step in assembling the system is to connect the two power connectors from the power supply to the motherboard. The main ATX power connector is a 20-pin connector located near the right front edge of the motherboard. Locate the corresponding cable coming from the power supply. The main ATX power connector is keyed, so verify that it is aligned properly before you attempt to seat it.

Once everything is aligned, press down firmly until the connector seats, as shown in Figure 3-51. It may take significant pressure to seat the connector, and you should feel it snap into place. The locking tab on the side of the connector should snap into place over the corresponding nub on the socket. Make sure the connector seats fully. A partially seated main ATX power connector may cause subtle problems that are very difficult to troubleshoot.

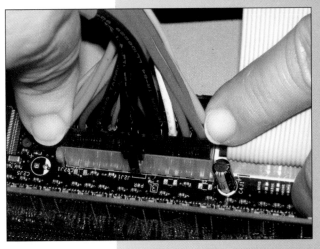

Figure 3-51. Connect the main ATX power connector

Pentium 4 systems require more power to the motherboard than the standard main ATX power connector supplies. Intel developed a supplementary connector, called the ATX12V connector, that routes additional +12V current directly to the VRM (Voltage Regulator Module) that powers the processor. On most Pentium 4 motherboards, including the D865PERL, the ATX12V connector is located very near the processor socket. The ATX12V connector is keyed. Orient the cable connector properly relative to the motherboard connector, and press the cable connector into place until the plastic tab locks, as shown in Figure 3-52.

WARNING

Failing to connect the ATX12V connector is one of the most common causes of initial boot failures on newly built Pentium 4 systems. If nothing happens the first time you power up the system, chances are you forgot to connect the ATX12V connector.

Figure 3-52. Connect the ATX12V power connector

Final assembly steps

Congratulations! You're almost finished building the system. Only a few final steps remain, and those won't take long.

Connect the supplemental case fan

The Sonata has one rear-mounted 120mm supplemental fan. To enable it, connect a four-pin Molex connector from the power supply to the connector on the fan. If you are concerned about heat, connect the fan to one of the standard power supply connectors, which causes the fan to run at full speed as long as the system is running. If you are concerned about noise level, connect the fan to one of the power connectors labeled "Fan Only." These connectors are controlled by the power supply, which varies the speed of the fan according to the temperature level inside the case.

Connect the fan-signal connector (optional)

The True380 power supply has a fan-signal connector cable that allows the power supply to report its current fan speed to the motherboard. That speed can be monitored by the BIOS and reported by the Intel Active Monitor software that is bundled with the motherboard.

The fan-signal connector cable can be hard to locate. It's only a few inches long, and is tied off and tucked in among the numerous other cables coming out of the power supply. It's the cable with a three-pin connector with black and blue wires.

To enable this function, connect the fan-signal connector cable to a fan connector on the motherboard. We chose the VRM fan connector, which is a standard three-pin fan connector located near the edge of the motherboard between the processor socket and the rear I/O panel. With the processor installed and the motherboard already in place, it's hard to get to this connector. Your best bet is to use your needlenose pliers to install the connector.

WARNING

You may not want to enable this function. The True380 power supply fan can spin at as little as 1,500 RPM under light load conditions. The BIOS may misinterpret that low speed as a fan failure and generate frequent false alarms.

Connect the front-panel LEDs (optional)

The Sonata case includes two large, bright blue LEDs, one on either side of the flip-up door that conceals the front-panel USB, FireWire, and audio connectors. When we say "bright," we mean bright enough to serve as a night light, which in fact is how Barbara uses these LEDs on the Sonata in her office. These LEDs have nothing to do with system functions; they exist for decorative purposes only. If you connect them, they remain lit as long as the system is running. To enable the LEDs, locate the male power connector coming from the front bezel and plug it into one of the standard Molex connectors from the power supply.

Dress the cables

The final step in assembling the system is to dress the cables. That simply means routing the cables away from the motherboard and other components and tying them off so they don't flop around inside the case. Chances are that no one but you will ever see the inside of your system, but dressing the cables has several advantages other than making the system appear neater. First and foremost, it improves cooling by keeping the cables from impeding airflow. It can also improve system reliability. More than once, we've seen a system overheat and crash because a loose cable jammed the CPU fan or case fan. (See Figures 4-50 and 5-62 for examples of properly dressed cables.)

After you've completed these steps, take a few minutes to double-check everything. Verify that all cables are connected properly, that all drives are secured, and that there's nothing loose inside the case. Check one last time to verify that the power supply is set for the correct input voltage. It's a good idea to pick up the system and tilt it gently from side to side to make sure that there are no loose screws or other items that could cause a short. Use the following checklist:

___ Power supply set to proper input voltage
___ No loose tools or screws (shake the case gently)
___ Heatsink/fan unit properly mounted; CPU fan connected
___ Memory modules fully seated and latched
___ Front-panel switch and indicator cables connected properly
___ Front-panel I/O cables connected properly
___ Hard drive data cable connected to drive and motherboard
___ Hard drive power cable connected
___ Optical drive data cable connected to drive and motherboard
___ Optical drive power cable connected
___ Optical drive audio cable(s) connected (if applicable)
___ Floppy drive data and power cables connected (if applicable)
___ All drives secured to drive bay or chassis
___ Expansion cards fully seated and secured to the chassis
___ Main ATX power cable and ATX12V power cable connected
___ Front and rear case fans installed and connected (if applicable)
___ All cables dressed and tucked

Once you're certain that all is as it should be, it's time for the smoke test. Leaving the cover off for now, connect the power cable to the wall receptacle and then to the system unit. Unlike many power supplies, the Antec True380 has a separate rocker switch on the back that controls power to the power supply. By default, it's in the "0" or off position, which means the power supply is not receiving power from the wall receptacle. Move that switch to the "1" or on position. Press the main power button on the front of the case, and the system should start up. Check to make sure that the power supply fan, CPU fan, and case fan are spinning. You should also hear the hard drive spin up and the happy beep that tells you the system is starting normally. At that point, everything should be working properly.

When you turn on the rear power switch, the system will come to life momentarily and then die. That's perfectly normal behavior. When the power supply receives power, it begins to start up. It then quickly notices that the motherboard hasn't told it to start, and so it shuts down again. All you need to do is press the front-panel power switch and the system will start normally.

Turn off the system, disconnect the power cord, and take these final steps to prepare the system for use:

Set the BIOS Setup configuration jumper to Configure mode

The BIOS Setup configuration jumper block on the Intel D865PERL motherboard is used to set the operation mode. This jumper is located on the left front of the motherboard, near the SATA 0 connector. By default, the jumper is in the 1-2 or "normal" position. Move the jumper block to the 2-3 or "configure" position.

Reconnect the power cord and restart the system

When the configuration jumper is set to Configure mode, starting the system automatically runs BIOS Setup and puts the system in maintenance mode. This step allows the motherboard to detect the type of processor installed and configure it automatically. When the BIOS Setup screen appears, clear all BIOS data and reset the system clock. Save your changes and exit. The system automatically shuts down. Disconnect the power cord.

Set the BIOS Setup configuration jumper to Normal mode

With the power cord disconnected, move the BIOS Setup configuration jumper block from 2-3 (Configure mode) to 1-2 (Normal mode).

Replace the side panel and reconnect power

With the jumper set for Normal operation, replace the side panel and reconnect the power cord. Your system is now completely assembled and ready for use.

Final Words

This system went together like a dream. It took us less than an hour to build, or four days, depending on how you look at it. Counting only actual construction time, it took about 45 minutes from start to finish. Counting the time to shoot images, re-shoot images, re-re-shoot images, tear down for re-shoots and re-re-shoots, re-build and re-re-build after the re-shoots and re-re-shoots, and so on, it took four days. We think a first-time system builder should be able to assemble this system in an evening with luck, and certainly over a weekend.

Installing software

Software installation went smoothly with only two problems, one minor and one major. The minor problem was our own fault. As we installed Windows, we got to the screen that displays the license agreement and prompts you to press F8 to accept it. We pressed F8 and nothing happened.

We pressed F8 again and then again. Nothing. Finally, we noticed a key labeled "F-Lock" at the top left of the Logitech Elite keyboard. Aha! By default, the Elite shifts function keys to provide custom functions. Pressing that key lit the F-Lock LED and enabled the function keys to operate normally. Duh. Reading the manual might have helped.

The major problem resulted from the temporary insanity that sometimes afflicts us when it's time to install the OS on a new system. Ordinarily, we'd have installed Windows 2000 Pro without a second thought. We dislike Windows XP for many reasons, but particularly for its forced product activation and its numerous DRM (Digital Restrictions Management) features. We'd sworn never to install XP on a production system. Windows 2000 is good enough for what we do, and we plan to keep using it until Linux is sufficiently mature as a desktop OS to meet our needs.

For some reason, this time we decided to install Windows XP Professional. Big mistake. With Setup nearly complete, Windows XP tried to connect to our internal network, which currently runs a Windows NT Server 4 domain controller (soon to be replaced with a Linux server running Samba). We have never had any problems installing Windows 2000 clients, which detect the domain controller and join the domain without further ado.

However, one of the "improvements" in Windows XP is that it apparently no longer detects Windows NT 4 domain controllers. The detailed help suggested that perhaps Windows XP couldn't find the domain controller because it was using a NetBIOS computer name, which of course it was, and recommended adding the invisible domain controller to our WINS Server. The problem is, WE DON'T RUN A WINS SERVER, YOU STUPID EXCUSE FOR AN OPERATING SYSTEM.

Windows 2000 clients can locate the domain controller using NetBIOS-over-TCP/IP (NetBT) broadcasts. That function is apparently unsupported in Windows XP. That left us with two obvious choices: to install a WINS Server, or to install a different OS on the new system. We certainly didn't want to install a WINS Server, so we shut down the system, inserted a Windows 2000 Professional distribution CD, and restarted Setup.

Three hours later, the 160 GB hard drive had finished formatting for the second time that day, and we began installing Windows 2000 Professional. Soon thereafter, we had a functioning network client that, *mirabile dictu*, could actually see our domain controller. To prevent further heartache, we broke all of our Windows XP Professional distribution CDs into many small pieces. (Well, we wanted to do that. What we really did was stick them on the shelf as proof of license. There's no reason we can't "downgrade" to Windows 2000 using those licenses.)

One of our technical reviewers has a different view. He says, "I understand why you feel the way you do about Windows XP. But, for this particular class of machine I think your recommendation of Windows 2000 is a disservice. It's quickly becoming a boutique OS and the readers of this book don't need boutique anything, as you point out in your own criteria. Besides, I don't know anyone except you and Pournelle who run domains at home (I don't get out much) and I doubt very many of the people who will use this book to build a mainstream PC will be so configured. For the rest of us, XP is better supported and will have a longer useful life, and is 'more mainstream' than Win2K both now and into the future. I urge you to reconsider."

And he makes some good points. Choose Windows XP if it's the best operating system for your particular needs. Just don't be surprised if Microsoft shows up one day to claim your first-born child.

With Windows 2000 Pro and Service Pack 4 installed, it was time to install and update drivers. Intel lists a specific sequence for installing drivers. Following that sequence is important for system stability. In particular, it's important to run the Intel Chipset Software Installation Utility (formerly called the INF Update Utility) before installing other drivers.

Although it's possible to install the drivers manually, Intel makes it easy by including an Express Installer CD with their motherboards. Running the Express Installer CD displays the dialog shown in Figure 3-53. After you mark the checkboxes for the utilities you want to install and click the Install Now button, the Express Installer automatically loads the drivers in the proper sequence without further user intervention.

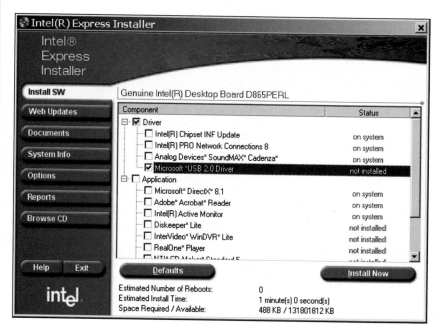

Figure 3-53. The Intel Express Installer

The Express Installer refused to install the Microsoft USB 2.0 driver, despite our efforts to force installation. We found by searching the Intel and Microsoft sites that there's a licensing issue involved in using the USB 2.0 driver on Windows 2000, although Windows XP Service Pack 1/1a includes it. We do know it is possible (somehow) to install the driver on Windows 2000, because we've done it before. Lack of USB 2.0 support isn't a problem for us because we don't plan to connect any high-speed USB devices to this system in the near future. But when we have a spare moment we will resolve the problem, simply because we don't like loose ends.

After the Express Installer installs the Intel-provided drivers and utilities, install any necessary third-party drivers. For this system, the ATi RADEON drivers were the only third-party drivers needed. Rather than using the driver CD included with the adapter, we downloaded and installed the latest RADEON drivers, which are provided as a single large executable file. After installing the drivers and rebooting, the system was ready to roll.

Some components include what we call "optional drivers." For example, we generally don't install the drivers available for the Logitech keyboard and mouse, although they are required to support enhanced functions such as programming the keyboard. We seldom use those enhanced functions, so we just use the default Microsoft drivers. If you want to enable those enhanced functions on your system, install the drivers.

With all of the drivers installed, we restarted the system and installed our standard suite of applications, including Office 2000, Mozilla, OpenOffice. org, WebWasher, IrfanView, and WinZIP.

Updating the BIOS

"If it ain't broke, don't fix it" is a good rule when it comes to updating the main system BIOS. We generally don't update the main system BIOS unless the later BIOS fixes a problem that actually affects us. But when we checked the Intel web site, we found that the most recent BIOS available was several versions later than the BIOS installed on our motherboard. Reading the cumulative list of changes from our old BIOS to the current version, we learned that many significant fixes had been made. Accordingly, we decided to update the BIOS to the most recent version.

Intel provides two methods to update the main system BIOS. The first, called the Iflash BIOS Update, uses the traditional floppy-based method. You download the BIOS update as a binary file, and copy it and the updater program to a floppy disk. Booting that floppy disk transfers the updated BIOS code to the system. The second method, shown in Figure 3-54, is called the Intel Express BIOS Update and runs from within Windows. To update the BIOS using this method, simply click on the Express BIOS Update executable and follow the prompts.

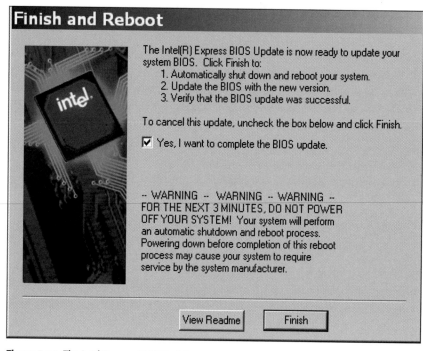

Figure 3-54. The Intel Express BIOS Update

WARNING

Never interrupt the system while a BIOS update is in progress. If you turn off the system (or if the power fails) during a BIOS update, the motherboard may be left in an unbootable state. For that reason, we recommend using a UPS when updating the BIOS. Fortunately, Intel makes provision for recovering from a failed BIOS update. If the update fails, download the current version of the Intel Recovery BIOS and copy it to a floppy disk. Disconnect power from the system and remove the jumper from the BIOS Setup Configuration jumper block, which puts the system in BIOS Recovery Mode. Put the Recovery BIOS floppy disk in the drive, reconnect the power, and start the system. After a few minutes, the system beeps to indicate that the BIOS has been recovered successfully. Disconnect the power, replace the configuration jumper in the Normal (1-2) position, reconnect the power, and restart the system. It should boot normally.

Possible future upgrades

Overall, we're extremely happy with this system. One of our few issues is that it is a bit louder than we had hoped it would be. The problem doesn't seem to be the Sonata case fan or power supply, both of which are nearly inaudible, nor the Seagate Barracuda hard drive, which is nearly inaudible even during seeks. The problem seems to be the Dynatron CPU cooler, which generates a high-pitched noise that's audible outside the case even with the cover on. Not that we blame the Dynatron CPU cooler—it's no louder than other CPU coolers we've tried that are rated for a Pentium 4/3.2 processor.

We're considering two possible solutions for the problem. First, the noise level isn't a problem when we're actually using the system, so we may simply enable power-saving mode to put the system to sleep when it's not being used. Second, we're looking at the quiet CPU coolers made by Zalman and other companies. Most of these coolers are huge, heavy, and expensive, but if it's possible to cool this system while keeping the noise level acceptable for a living area, it may be worth the tradeoff.

Otherwise, the system is as nearly perfect for our needs as a PC can possibly be. Although "enthusiast" sites like AnandTech and Tom's Hardware sneer at the performance of the ATi RADEON 9200, we find that it provides excellent 3D graphics performance for the games we play. The display quality is superb, and we don't think we'll be replacing it anytime soon. In fact, this system should serve our needs for the next three years or so without any upgrades except possibly adding some memory. We have 512 MB now, and two slots free for adding more.

For updated component recommendations, commentary, and other new material, visit *http://www.hardwareguys.com/guides/mainstream.html*.

Building a
SOHO Server

4

Cost-effectiveness

Reliability

Compactness

Quietness

Expandability

Processor performance

Video performance

Disk capacity/performance

One day in early 2004, our server started making funny noises. It was no big deal, as it turned out. A bearing in the supplemental case fan was failing. That was cheap and easy to fix, but it got us thinking.

Our server, that anonymous beige box where all our data lives, was an antique. As we blew the dust off it, literally and figuratively, we took stock of the hardware upon which so much of our working lives depended. An ancient Intel RC440BX motherboard. A Slot 1 Pentium III/550 processor with 128 MB of Crucial PC133 memory (we could have sworn we'd upgraded that to 256 MB). A 10 GB 7,200 RPM hard drive that Maxtor had sent us for evaluation before that drive was commercially available. A Travan tape drive from Tecmar, a company that departed the tape drive business years ago. And Windows NT Server 4. Ugh.

Although we'd made a few minor upgrades—including mirroring the 10 GB Maxtor to a larger Seagate drive—we realized that we were several years into the 21st century and still depending on a server that dated from the late 20th century. That was good in the sense that a server *should* be so reliable that one simply forgets it's there. And, despite all the nasty things people say about Windows stability, that server often ran for months on end without a reboot. That's what happens when you build a machine with top-notch components, put it on a good UPS, and blow out the dust dinosaurs from time to time.

But although that box had been a good and faithful servant, it was clearly time for a change. So we set out to design and build a server that would meet our needs now and (we hope) for several years to come. We decided from the start that we would look to the future rather than to the past. Accordingly, our server will run Linux rather than a legacy Microsoft OS. Linux is fast, free, easier to install and maintain than Windows, and immensely stable, and suffers from few of the security flaws endemic to Microsoft operating systems.

We work in a typical "SOHO" (Small Office/Home Office) environment—half a dozen desktop systems, some printers and other shared peripherals, and a cable-modem Internet connection. Of necessity, we designed our new SOHO server to meet our own needs. Your needs may differ from ours, though, and a SOHO server isn't a one-size-fits-all proposition. Accordingly, we've made every attempt to explain why we chose to configure our new server as we did, and how you might want to alter our configuration to suit your own requirements. In this chapter, you'll look over our shoulders as we design and build the perfect SOHO server.

If yours is a typical SOHO environment, you may wonder if you need a dedicated server. After all, it's easy enough to set up a share on a desktop system and use that box as a shared desktop/server. If you have only a couple users and make few demands on a network, that may be a viable alternative. Otherwise, the security, reliability, and other advantages of a dedicated server are worth the relatively low cost.

Determining Functional Requirements

The problem with defining a "SOHO server" is that both words mean different things to different people. SOHO might encompass anything from one to 25 or more users, and a simple file and print server has very different requirements from a system that also functions as an application, database, web, and/or email server. In short, a SOHO server can be just about anything.

At one extreme, a SOHO server can simply be a repurposed older desktop system, perhaps with a larger hard drive added. At the other extreme, a SOHO server can be a $15,000 box that uses such technologies as multiple processors, ECC memory, SCSI RAID, redundant power supplies, and so on.

As much as we believe in the advantages of building your own, we think it's a mistake to build the latter type of server, except perhaps for medium or large companies that will have several such servers in use. A small company can no more afford extended server downtime than can a larger company, and avoiding downtime means having spares on hand. If you're running a dozen such servers, it's no great hardship to maintain a reasonable spares kit. If you're running only one server, the cost of spares can nearly double the cost of building the server.

Accordingly, for a "larger" small company that requires a powerful, sophisticated server, we recommend buying rather than building. Call IBM, buy a server that meets your requirements, and sign up for the best on-site service plan they offer. The cost of 20 people sitting around drawing their salaries while they're unable to work adds up quickly. Even a short server outage may cost the company more than you "saved" by building your own server.

> If you're going to do it, do it right. Don't buy from Dell or another second-tier server vendor. Don't buy HP. Buy IBM, period. We know we'll get mail from people with horror stories about their IBM servers. It happens, but not often. And we'd hear lots more horror stories if we recommended anything but IBM servers.

Most SOHO servers fall between the extremes, and it's such servers that this chapter focuses on. Tables 4-1 and 4-2 list some starting points for configuring a SOHO file or application server appropriate for your own requirements.

Table 4-1. Suggested SOHO file server configurations

	1–5 users	6–10 users	11–20 users	20+ users
CPU	Celeron or Pentium 4	Pentium 4/2.0G	Pentium 4/2.4G	Pentium 4/3.0G
Memory	256 MB or more	384 MB or more	512 MB or more	1024 MB or more
Disk subsystem	ATA RAID 1	ATA RAID 1, 5, or 0+1	SCSI RAID 1 or 5	SCSI RAID 5
Ethernet interface	100BaseT	100BaseT	100BaseT	1000BaseT
Backup hardware	DVD+R, Travan, or external hard drive	DVD+R, Travan, or external hard drive	Travan, DDS-4, DAT 72, or AIT	DDS-4, DAT 72, or AIT

Table 4-2. Suggested SOHO application server configurations

	1–5 users	6–10 users	11–20 users	20+ users
CPU	Pentium 4/3.0G	Pentium 4 EE	Xeon or Dual Xeon	Dual Xeon
Memory	1024 MB	1024 to 2048 MB	App-dependent	App-dependent
Disk subsystem	ATA RAID 1 or 5	ATA RAID 5 or 0+1	SCSI RAID 1 or 5	SCSI RAID 5 or 0+5
Ethernet interface	100BaseT	100BaseT	100BaseT or 1000BaseT	1000BaseT
Backup hardware	Travan or DDS-4	Travan or DDS-4	DDS-4, DAT 72, or AIT	DDS-4, DAT 72, or AIT

Dust Removal

The best method for removing dust is hotly debated among PC builders. (Yeah, every one of us needs to get a life.) Some use a brush. Others use canned air or a vacuum cleaner, or some combination. We loosen the dust with a camel-hair brush we got at an art supply store, and suck up the dust using an ordinary vacuum cleaner with a set of PC hoses and nozzles we got at a computer store. We've heard it said that standard vacuum cleaners can create static charges simply by moving so much air around, but we've never had that problem. If you're concerned, you can buy a static-safe vacuum cleaner from Jensen Tools (*http://www.jensentools.com*), Specialized Products (*http://www.specialized.net*), or a similar tool supplier. For particularly filthy power supplies, we sometimes carry the unit down to the local gas station and blow it out with the air compressor hose.

All of these configurations assume you are running Linux, which for most situations is the best OS choice for a SOHO server. If for some reason you must run a Microsoft Server OS, these configurations may be marginal, particularly CPU and memory. There's no getting around it—Windows Server is a pig. When it comes to server hardware, Linux takes tiny sips, while Windows Server takes great gulps.

Although we specify number of users, all users are not equal. One user who runs a CPU-intensive, server-based application may put more load on an application server than a dozen users who occasionally retrieve and save a document or spreadsheet. The type of load also varies. A shared database that resides on the server may stress the disk subsystem but place fewer demands on CPU and memory. A client/server application that ships large amounts of data to clients may stress the network interface. A server-based application may hammer the CPU and memory but not the disk subsystem. And so on.

When you design a SOHO server, it's important to determine which server subsystems are likely to be bottlenecks and design accordingly. For example, if the server functions primarily as a database server, you might spend a significant part of your budget on a stacked SCSI RAID disk subsystem and lots of memory, and correspondingly less on CPU, the network interface, and other components. If network throughput is the bottleneck, you might install multiple Gigabit Ethernet adapters on the server and use Gigabit Ethernet switches rather than 100BaseT hubs. Designing a SOHO server is all about balance—allocating your budget to eliminate the most important bottlenecks. Of course, each time you eliminate one bottleneck, you uncover another.

We sat down to think through our own requirements for a SOHO server. Here's the list of functional requirements we came up with:

Reliability

First and foremost, the SOHO server must be reliable. Our server runs 24/7/365. Other than periodic downtime to blow out the dust, upgrade hardware, and so on, we expect our server to take a licking and keep on ticking.

Data safety

We've never lost any data other than by our own stupidity, and we want to keep it that way. We're paranoid about backup. We use one of our desktop clients to do weekly full backups and daily differential backups of the server to tape, as well as monthly full backups to DVD+R. We run a batch file several times a day to back up changed files to other network volumes. That's all well and good, but the fact remains that if the server fails between backups we might lose hours of work. That's unacceptable, so we'll use redundancy in the disk subsystem.

Flexibility

Initially, our SOHO server will be almost exclusively a file and print server. It will run Linux, though, so it's likely that at some point it will transmogrify to an application server of some sort. To allow for that possibility with minimum disruption, we'll initially configure the server with enough processor, memory, and disk space to allow adding functions incrementally without upgrading the hardware.

Expandability

When we first considered building a new SOHO server, we planned to build an "appliance" system with a microATX board in a small case such as the Antec Minuet. There are a lot of advantages to such a server. It's small and so can be put anywhere. It doesn't consume much power, produces little heat, and doesn't make much noise. But as we thought about it, we realized that for us the disadvantages of a small system outweighed the advantages. However flexible our initial configuration, it's likely that at some point we will want to expand the server. We may decide to install a SCSI RAID disk subsystem, for example, or install a tape drive in the server. The microATX form factor is simply too limiting. With a full ATX motherboard and a mini-tower case, we have room to grow.

Those who put limited demands on a server may be better served by a microATX "appliance" server. Conversely, those who need more expandability may opt for a full-tower server case that accepts dual motherboards, redundant power supplies, piles of hard drives, and so on.

Hardware Design Criteria

With the functional requirements determined, the next step was to establish design criteria for the SOHO server hardware. Here are the relative priorities we assigned for our SOHO server. Your priorities may differ.

Here's the breakdown:

Price

Price is moderately important for this system. We don't want to spend money needlessly, but we will spend what it takes to meet our other criteria.

Reliability

Reliability is the single most important consideration.

Size

Size is unimportant. Our SOHO server will sit in a server closet that has room to spare.

DESIGN PRIORITIES	
Price	★★★☆☆
Reliability	★★★★★
Size	★☆☆☆☆
Noise level	★☆☆☆☆
Expandability	★★★☆☆
Processor performance	★★☆☆☆
Video performance	★☆☆☆☆
Disk capacity/performance	★★★★☆

Noise level

Noise level is unimportant, again because the server will reside in a closet, far from our ears.

Expandability

Expandability is moderately important. Our server will initially have four hard drives and an optical drive installed, but we may want to expand the storage subsystem later. Similarly, although we'll use the embedded video, S-ATA, and network interfaces initially, we may eventually install one or two SCSI host adapters, additional network interfaces, and so on.

Processor performance

Processor performance is relatively unimportant, at least initially. Our SOHO server will run Linux for file and print services, which place little demand on the CPU. However, we expect that the server will eventually run at least some server-based applications, perhaps X11 apps that display on workstations or server-based applications such as mailman or squirrelmail. The incremental cost of installing a moderately fast Pentium 4 is small enough that we'll do it now and have done with it.

Video performance

Video performance is of no importance. In fact, other than for initial configuration, we'll probably run our SOHO server headless—that is, we'll temporarily install a monitor while we install and configure Linux, but subsequently manage the server from a desktop system elsewhere on the network. Our only requirement for the video adapter is that it run X, because we prefer to use the Linux GUI installation utilities rather than doing everything at the command line. (Yes, yes, we know. Real Men don't run X on servers. What can we say? We're wimps.)

Disk capacity/performance

Disk capacity and performance are secondary only to reliability. Back when our old server had only one ATA drive and Robert happened to be doing something very disk intensive on the server, Barbara sometimes used to shout, "What are you doing to the server?" as she waited (and waited) for a document to load on her system. We found that mirroring a pair of 7,200 RPM ATA disks killed two birds with one stone. It mostly solved the disk contention problem—having two spindles speeds up reads considerably—and also provided disk redundancy. If one drive failed, the other contained everything written to the mirror set right up to the instant of failure. Based on our own experience, we decided that although a mirrored pair of ATA drives would probably suffice, we might just as well install a full ATA RAID and have done with it.

RAID for SOHO servers

RAID is an acronym for *Redundant Array of Inexpensive Disks*. A RAID stores data on two or more physical hard drives, thereby reducing the risk of losing data when a drive fails. Some types of RAID also increase read and/or write performance relative to a single drive.

Five levels of RAID are defined, RAID 1 through RAID 5. RAID levels are optimized to have different strengths, including level of redundancy, optimum file size, random versus sequential read performance, and random versus sequential write performance. RAID 1 and RAID 5 are commonly used in PC servers; RAID 3 is used rarely; And RAID 2 and RAID 4 are almost never used. The RAID levels typically used on SOHO servers are:

RAID 1

> RAID 1 uses two drives that contain exactly the same data. Every time the system writes to the array, it writes identical data to each drive. If one drive fails, the data can be read from the surviving drive. Because data must be written twice, RAID 1 writes are a bit slower than writes to a single drive. Because data can be read from either drive in a RAID 1, reads are somewhat faster. RAID 1 is also called *mirroring*, if both drives share one controller, or *duplexing*, if each drive has its own controller.

> RAID 1 provides very high redundancy, but is the least efficient of the RAID levels in terms of hard drive usage. For example, with two 160 GB hard drives in a RAID 1 array, only 160 GB of total disk space is visible to the system. RAID 1 may be implemented with a physical RAID 1 controller or in software by the operating system. Some motherboards have embedded ATA or S-ATA interfaces that offer native RAID 1 support.

RAID 5

> RAID 5 uses three or more physical hard drives. The RAID 5 controller divides data that is to be written to the array into blocks and calculates parity blocks for the data. Data blocks and parity blocks are interleaved on each physical drive, so each of the three or more drives in the array contains both data blocks and parity blocks. If any one drive in the RAID 5 fails, the data blocks contained on the failed drive can be recreated from the parity data stored on the surviving drives.

> RAID 5 is optimized for the type of disk usage common in an office environment—many random reads, and fewer random writes of relatively small files. RAID 5 reads are faster than those from a single drive because RAID 5 has three spindles spinning and delivering data simultaneously. RAID 5 writes are also typically a bit faster than single-drive writes. RAID 5 uses hard drive space more efficiently than RAID 1.

In effect, although RAID 5 uses distributed parity, a RAID 5 array can be thought of as dedicating one of its physical drives to parity data. For example, with three 160 GB drives in a RAID 5 array, 320 GB—the capacity of two of the three drives—is visible to the system. With RAID 5 and four 160 GB drives, 480 GB—the capacity of three of the four drives—is visible to the system. RAID 5 may be implemented with a physical RAID 5 controller or in software by the operating system. Few motherboards have embedded RAID 5 support.

RAID 3

RAID 3 uses three or more physical hard drives. One drive is dedicated to storing parity data, and user data is distributed among the other drives. RAID 3 is the least common RAID level used for PC servers because its characteristics are not optimal for the disk usage patterns typical of small-office LANs. RAID 3 is optimized for sequential reads of very large files, and so is used primarily for applications such as streaming video.

Then there is the so-called RAID 0, which isn't really RAID at all because it provides no redundancy:

RAID 0

RAID 0, also called *striping*, uses two physical hard drives. Data written to the array is divided into blocks, which are written to each drive in an alternating manner. For example, if you write a 256 KB file to a RAID 0 that uses 64 KB blocks, the first 64 KB block may be written to the first drive in the RAID 0. The second 64 KB block is written to the second drive, the third 64 KB block to the first drive, and the final 64 KB block to the second drive. The file itself exists only as fragments distributed across both physical drives, so if either drive fails all data on the array is lost. That means that data stored on a RAID 0 is *more* at risk than data stored on a single drive, so in that sense a RAID 0 can actually be thought of as less redundant than the zero redundancy of a single drive. RAID 0 is used because it provides the fastest possible disk performance. Reads and writes are very fast, because they can use the combined bandwidth of two drives.

Finally, there is *stacked RAID*, which is an "array of arrays" rather than an array of disks. Stacked RAID can be thought of as an array that replaces individual physical disks with subarrays. The advantage of stacked RAID is that it combines the advantages of two RAID levels. The disadvantage is that it requires a lot of physical hard drives.

Stacked RAID

The most common stacked RAID used in PC servers is referred to as *RAID 0+1*, *RAID 1+0*, or *RAID 10*. A RAID 0+1 uses four physical drives arranged as two RAID 1 arrays of two drives each. Each RAID 1 array would normally appear to the system as a single drive, but RAID 0+1 takes things a step further by creating a RAID 0 array from the two RAID 1 arrays. For example, a RAID 0+1 with four 160 GB drives comprises two RAID 1 arrays, each with two 160 GB drives. Each RAID 1 is visible to the system as a single 160 GB drive. Those two RAID 1 arrays are then combined into one RAID 0 array, which is visible to the system as a single 320 GB RAID 0. Because the system "sees" a RAID 0, performance is very high. Because the RAID 0 components are actually RAID 1 arrays, the data is very well protected. If any single drive in the RAID 0+1 array fails, the array continues to function, although redundancy is lost until the drive is replaced and the array is rebuilt.

Until a few years ago RAID 0+1 was uncommon on small servers because it required SCSI drives and host adapters, and therefore cost thousands of dollars to implement. Nowadays, thanks to inexpensive ATA drives, the incremental cost of RAID 0+1 is very small. Instead of buying one $200 ATA hard drive for your small server, you can buy four $100 ATA hard drives and a $50 ATA RAID adapter. You may not even need to buy the ATA RAID adapter because some motherboards include native RAID 0+1 support. Data protection doesn't come much cheaper than that.

Component Considerations

With our design criteria in mind, we set out to choose the best components for the SOHO server system. The following sections describe the components we chose and why we chose them.

Although we tested the configuration we used to build our own SOHO server, we did not test permutations with the listed alternatives. Those alternatives are simply the components we would have chosen had our requirements been different. That said, we know of no reason the alternatives should not work perfectly.

Case and power supply

Intel Server Chassis SC5250-E (http://www.intel.com)

Most so-called SOHO server cases are simply thinly disguised mini-tower cases with perhaps a lockable swing-out front bezel. The Intel Server Chassis SC5250-E is different. It was designed from the ground up as an entry-level server case, and includes such features as a padlock loop (so your hard drives don't walk away) and such options as an active Ultra-320 SCSI backplane. In addition to two 5.25" and one 3.5" externally accessible drive bays, the standard SC5250-E configuration supports six hard drives, with the option to install hot-swappable bays for five SCSI or four S-ATA drives. The SC5250-E also includes an industrial-strength 450W power supply that more than suffices for our needs. The SC5250-E is our first choice for a serious SOHO server.

If you're building a SOHO server on a tighter budget, we know of no better case than the Antec PLUS1080AMG. Although it is a standard mid-tower case, the PLUS108AMG acts like a full tower. It accepts oversize Extended ATX motherboards and has drive bays galore—four 5.25" and two 3.5" externally accessible bays and four 3.5" internal bays.

Antec designed this case with accessibility in mind, and it is very easy to work on. The lockable side panel swings out and lifts off. The 5.25" bays use snap-in drive rails that mount from the front, and the 3.5" bays use removable snap-in drive cages, making it easy to install or remove drives. There are no sharp edges, burrs, or other signs of cost-cutting.

The PLUS1080AMG has server-class cooling. It comes standard with three 80mm fans, two in the rear and one in the side panel. There are positions for two more 80mm fans, one in front and one to cool the hard drive. Fans snap in and out. To help keep the interior clean, Antec includes a front-mounted washable air filter that's easy to remove, clean, and reinstall. The PLUS1080AMG case includes an Antec TruePower 430W power supply, which is more than adequate for most SOHO server configurations.

For a microATX "appliance" server, we'd use the Antec Aria, which provides one externally accessible 5.25" drive bay and three 3.5" internal bays. That's enough for a DVD writer and a pair of mirrored ATA hard drives, which suffices for a typical small server.

If you're on a tight budget, use an Intel D865GBF instead. The GBF is marketed as a desktop board, but it's quite suitable for a small server. The GBF isn't as fast as the D875/S875. It lacks the S-ATA RAID controller, but you can install an inexpensive S-ATA RAID card if you need RAID. The embedded LAN controller is desktop-class, and the embedded audio is useless on a server. Despite all of that, the GBF is rock-solid and a good compromise if the budget is tight.

If you need multiple processors, choose one of the Intel workstation- or server-class Xeon boards and install one or two Xeon processors. Remember what we said earlier in the chapter, though. If you really need multiple processors, you should probably be buying a server instead of building one.

Any current Northwood- or Prescott-core Pentium 4 is fast enough for any Linux-based SOHO file and print server we can imagine. If we were determined to build an AMD-based SOHO server, we'd use a fast Athlon XP in an ASUS A7N8X Deluxe, which is the most stable AMD Athlon motherboard we've found.

Motherboard

Intel S875WP1 (http://www.intel.com)

Although motherboards for AMD processors are much more reliable than they used to be, Intel defines the ultimate in reliability. For our SOHO server, we wanted a Pentium 4 motherboard made by Intel. Video performance is unimportant for a server, so we wanted integrated video. Embedded 100BaseT Ethernet is acceptable for our environment. Although we plan to use only 512 MB of memory initially, support for 2 GB or more of PC3200 dual-channel DDR-SDRAM is desirable for expandability. We may eventually add SCSI drives, a tape drive, and other storage devices to this system, so a full ATX motherboard with plenty of expansion slots was a plus. Finally, we wanted embedded S-ATA interfaces and plenty of USB 2.0 ports for external peripherals.

We could have used an Intel D-series desktop motherboard, but there was a better option. In addition to its familiar D-series motherboards, Intel makes various S-series server motherboards. The Intel S875WP1 is the server version of their high-end D875PBZ desktop motherboard. The S875WP1 differs from the D875PBZ in several respects, but the most important are the addition of embedded video, an optional four-drive S-ATA RAID controller, and dual server-class Ethernet controllers, including one 100BaseT and one 1000BaseT. The S875WP1 is in every respect an ideal entry-level server motherboard, so that's what we chose.

Processor

Intel Pentium 4 (http://www.intel.com)

Processor performance is a minor consideration for a file and print server. In fact, if this server were to be used only for file and print duties, even a slow Celeron or Duron would do the job with Linux. But although this server will provide only file and print services initially, we expect it to last for years with few upgrades, and we may eventually run some applications on it. Accordingly, it made sense to choose a faster processor that would give us some horsepower in reserve.

At the time we built this server, Intel had just introduced the Prescott-core Pentium 4 processors. Older Northwood-core processors were going at fire-sale prices as vendors cleared inventory. We chose a 3 GHz Northwood for our server. Any Northwood, including the slowest 1.8 GHz model, would have been more than adequate for our current requirements, so choosing the 3 GHz model bought us lots of headroom for future needs.

We chose the retail-boxed model, which comes with a three-year warranty and a high-quality heatsink/fan unit. For an OEM Pentium 4, we would have installed a Dynatron DC1207MB-X heatsink/fan (*http://www. dynatron-corp.com*).

Memory

Crucial PC3200 DDR-SDRAM (http://www.crucial.com)

We could analyze the memory requirements of a Linux SOHO server all day long, but what's the point? Memory costs little, so it makes no sense to compromise. In our 20 years of dealing with servers, we've never heard anyone complain that his server had too much memory.

Our small SOHO server running Linux would probably be happy with 256 MB. In fact, if we ran Linux at the command line, 128 MB would suffice. But our crystal ball is notoriously unreliable, so we really don't know what demands we'll put on our server next year or even next month. On that basis, we decided to install 512 MB initially.

> Memory stability is paramount for a server. Don't even think about using cheap, no-name, unreliable memory on a server, nor, for that matter, using fast memory timings even with high-grade memory. Install the highest-quality memory you can buy, and run it at the default memory timing.

We could install one 512 MB DIMM—which actually costs less than two 256 MB DIMMs—but the dual-channel memory controller on the S875WP1 motherboard provides better memory performance if DIMMs are installed in pairs. We therefore decided to use two 256 MB DIMMs, which leaves two memory slots free for future expansion. If our server needs more memory in a year or two, we can do a five-minute upgrade to 1 GB of total memory simply by installing another pair of 256 MB DIMMs.

In theory, we could later upgrade to 1.5 GB by installing two 512 MB DIMMs, or to 2.5 GB by installing two 1 GB DIMMs, but we won't do that. We're using non-parity memory modules, for which we consider 1 GB the cutoff. If we install more than 1 GB, we use ECC memory modules. ECC memory is slower and more expensive than non-parity memory, but ECC memory detects and corrects memory errors, which non-parity memory cannot. Like most motherboards, the Intel S875WP1 can use mixed non-parity and ECC modules, but using a non-parity module disables ECC for all installed modules.

Hard disk drive

Seagate Barracuda 7200.7 SATA (http://www.seagate.com)

The disk subsystem of our SOHO server must be capacious, fast, and reliable. Capacious, because this server will store all of the data we want to keep online, including large video files. Fast, because the server will sometimes be hammered by several clients accessing large amounts of data. Reliable, because we have never lost any data—other than by our own stupidity—and we don't intend to start now.

Capacity

Our target for capacity was between 300 and 500 GB. The largest hard drives available when we built this system held 250 GB, so clearly we needed multiple hard drives to meet our capacity requirement. Considering only capacity, we could meet our requirement by installing two ATA hard drives, each with a capacity of 150 to 250 GB. If we needed the entire capacity of both drives to appear as one volume, we could use the operating-system disk management utilities or a RAID 0 controller to concatenate those two physical drives into one logical volume. If multiple volumes were acceptable, we could simply install the two drives normally and partition and format them as separate volumes.

Configuring a RAID 0 array may or may not require identical drives. In general, software-based RAID 0 permits striping a smaller drive to a partition on a larger drive. Hardware-based RAID 0 controllers often require that both drives in the array be of identical capacity.

Performance

A 7,200 RPM ATA hard drive performs well with only one person accessing it, but bogs down badly when several people access it simultaneously. A 10,000 or 15,000 RPM SCSI drive performs well in a small multiuser environment, but such drives are very expensive and have small capacities. The only affordable option for a small server that requires high disk performance and large capacity is to use 7,200 RPM ATA drives in a RAID 0.

Reliability

Using two 7,200 RPM ATA drives in a RAID 0 meets our capacity and performance requirements, but not the reliability requirement. If either drive in a RAID 0 fails, all data on both drives is lost. In effect, that means a RAID 0 is half as reliable as a single drive, which is unacceptable. Reliability requires redundancy, using either RAID 1 mirroring or RAID 5 disk striping with parity. Unfortunately, neither of those RAID levels is fast enough for our requirements.

So, SCSI costs too much, ATA RAID 0 isn't reliable enough, and ATA RAID 1 or RAID 5 isn't fast enough. What's a system designer to do? Fortunately, we can meet all of our requirements by using a stacked RAID. Instead of choosing one RAID level, we'll combine two RAID levels in one array—RAID 0 for performance and capacity, and RAID 1 for reliability. This configuration is referred to as RAID 0+1.

If you've been paying attention, you might object that using RAID 0+1 means we need four hard drives. True enough. But our RAID 0+1 uses inexpensive S-ATA drives. When we wrote this, four 160 GB S-ATA drives (640 GB of drive space) cost about the same as one 73 GB 15K SCSI drive,

Backing Up the Beast

If you're concerned about how to back up a 320 GB disk array, you're not alone. Optical drives are neither large enough nor fast enough to back up this amount of disk space. At first glance, a tape drive may appear to be the solution. It's not, at least not for a typical SOHO server. Affordable tape technologies have neither the speed nor the capacity to back up such large amounts of data. And, if you attempt to use them for backing up data on that scale, you find that they're no longer affordable at all.

Travan, for example, seems affordable only until you consider the number of tapes you'd need to back up a 320 GB array. Even if you were willing to spend $2,000 or so for a Travan drive and the scores of tapes you'd need for a reasonable tape rotation scheme, a full backup to Travan tapes would take literally days. Nor can you use Travan for an unattended backup, because you'd need to switch tapes several times.

DDS-3 and DDS-4 drives use less expensive tapes, but the drives are expensive enough to rule out DDS on cost alone. DDS also has insufficient capacity for unattended backups. DDS tape libraries are large and fast enough, but cost thousands. AIT, 8mm, and other large-capacity tape technologies have similar disadvantages. None is appropriate for an inexpensive SOHO server.

So what's left? External FireWire/USB 2.0 hard drives, which we suggest you look at not as hard drives, but as funny-looking backup tapes. With compression, a 160 GB or 200 GB external hard drive can store the entire contents of a 320 GB disk array. If the array is smaller or the amount of stored data does not exceed the capacity of the external drive, you can make an exact copy without compression, which makes it trivially easy to restore. FireWire and USB 2.0 are fast enough to copy 320 GB from the array to an external hard drive in a few hours, which means you can do a full backup overnight. The media cost per gigabyte stored is comparable to that of Travan tape, and you needn't buy an expensive tape drive.

We recommend buying at least two or three external USB 2.0 hard drives and using them, just as you would tapes, to do weekly full backups of the array. If you gulp at spending a few hundred dollars on external drives, just think for a moment about the cost of losing all your data. You might think the RAID 0+1 is sufficient protection for your data. It isn't. RAID prevents

against drive failures, period. It doesn't prevent accidental deletions, corrupted files, or catastrophic data loss caused by fire or theft. The only way to protect against such dangers is to have an offline, offsite copy of your data, ideally multiple copies. FireWire/USB 2.0 external hard drives are the only affordable solution we know of for backing up a large SOHO array.

But external hard drives are only part of the solution. A weekly full backup is a good start, but a proper backup plan requires backing up changed files daily or more often. Such incremental backups are much smaller than full backups, but are essential to recovering files changed since the previous full backup. As for full backups, it is important that these incremental backups be stored offline and offsite. We recommend one of the following methods, depending on how much data you need to back up daily:

- **CD writer**. A CD writer stores about 700 MB natively, or 1.0 GB to 1.5 GB with compression, to a $0.20 CD-R disc. A 52X writer, such as the Plextor Premium, takes three minutes or so to fill a disc. A CD writer is appropriate for incremental backups if your array has only a few relatively small files changed or added daily.

- **DVD writer**. A DVD writer stores more than 4 GB natively, or 6 GB to 8 GB with compression, to a $1 DVD+R disc. An 8X writer fills a DVD+R disc in less than 10 minutes. A DVD writer is appropriate for incremental backups if your array has many files or several relatively large files changed daily.

- **Travan tape drive**. A Travan NS/20 tape drive stores 10 GB natively, or 15 GB to 20 GB with compression, to a $30 tape at about 3.5 GB per hour. A Travan 40 tape drive stores 20 GB natively, or 30 GB to 40 GB with compression, to a $50 tape at about 7 GB per hour. Accordingly, a Travan tape drive is most appropriate for incremental backups if your array has many large files changed every day. Because of its relatively low speed, a Travan backup is normally run overnight.

When it comes to preventing data loss, we use the belt-and-suspenders method. In addition to backing up to external hard drives, optical discs, and tape, we frequently copy changed files to other network volumes using Windows batch files or rsync. If you value your data, you should do the same. The following sections detail the backup hardware we recommend.

even ignoring the cost of a SCSI host adapter. For the same amount of money, then, an S-ATA RAID 0+1 provides more than four times as much disk capacity as the single SCSI drive. Read performance under typical SOHO loads is similar. The SCSI drive provides faster writes, but most of the activity on a SOHO server consists of reads, so that's a minor issue. The RAID also provides data redundancy, which the single drive does not.

The Intel S875WP1 motherboard is available in two models. The basic model provides two S-ATA connectors, each of which supports one drive. The model we chose provides the standard two S-ATA connectors, and four additional S-ATA connectors that can be configured for RAID 0, RAID 1, or RAID 0+1. We'll connect our four hard drives to those four S-ATA connectors, and configure them in a RAID 0+1.

We chose Seagate Barracuda 7200.7 SATA hard drives for several reasons. Although the Seagate Barracuda performs very respectably in desktop benchmarks, it is sometimes slightly slower than similar drives from Maxtor, Western Digital, and other manufacturers. But in server benchmarks, the Barracuda outperforms the other 7,200 RPM ATA drives we tested, sometimes by significant margins. Barracudas are also much quieter than competing drives, which can be an issue even for a server when several drives are running. Finally, our impression, along with those of our readers and several hard drive recovery companies we've spoken with, is that Seagate ATA drives are significantly more reliable than competing models.

External hard drive

Seagate External Hard Drive (http://www.seagate.com)

We don't know why Seagate doesn't use a better name for their external hard drives than Seagate External Hard Drive. Seagate uses the names of fast animals for their other products—Barracuda, Cheetah, and so on. You'd think they could have named their external hard drive the Greyhound or the Hare or the Falcon or something. Anything. Oh, well.

Despite the generic name, the Seagate External Hard Drive is an excellent product. It's basically a Barracuda hard drive in an external enclosure with USB 2.0 and FireWire interfaces. It's small, light, fast, cool-running, and quiet. We can't think of another thing we'd want in an external hard drive.

Well, maybe one thing. Like all of its competitors, the Seagate External Hard Drive is designed for use with a Windows or Mac computer. It includes CMS BounceBack Express software, which provides one-button backup. The first time you press the button, the software does a full backup of your internal hard drive. Once the full backup is done, pressing the button backs up only the changes. Although one-touch backup isn't supported for Linux, any recent Linux distribution can recognize the drive and back up data to it.

ALTERNATIVES: EXTERNAL HARD DRIVE

Although we prefer the Seagate External Hard Drive, the largest model available is 160 GB. Maxtor offers several lines of external hard drives, including the OneTouch series, the Personal Storage 5000 series, and the Personal Storage 3000 series, all of which are available in capacities from 40 GB to 300 GB in USB 2.0 and FireWire interfaces. You can also "roll your own" by buying an external USB 2.0 or FireWire enclosure and installing a standard ATA hard drive, although we and several of our readers have had less than satisfactory experience with some of these external drive enclosures. As with most things, you get what you pay for.

Our editor, Brian Jepson, comments, "I have seen these wonderful non-enclosures (*http://www.wiebetech. com/products.html*) that are nothing more than the FireWire to ATA bridge, no case. So, if you're buying a pile of drives and want to avoid paying for an enclosure for each of them, you can just snap the drive into the drive dock when you need to use it and put the drive on the shelf when you're done."

CD writer

Plextor PlexWriter Premium CD writer (http://www.plextor.com)

Most SOHO servers need larger differential backup capacity than what a CD writer provides. The incremental cost of a DVD writer is relatively small and DVD writers can also write CDs, so it seldom makes sense to limit yourself to CD capacities by installing a CD writer. But if your environment is such that a CD writer is sufficient and likely to remain so, you can save $100 or so by installing a top-notch CD writer rather than a DVD writer of comparable quality. The Plextor PlexWriter Premium is the best CD writer you can buy, period.

DVD writer

Plextor PX-708A DVD writer (http://www.plextor.com)

For most SOHO servers, a DVD writer is the best choice for differential backups. Although its native capacity is limited to about 4.5 GB, it is far faster than a tape drive and uses much less expensive media. The Plextor PX-708A is the best, fastest, most reliable DVD writer we know of. It costs only $100 or so more than a CD writer of comparable quality, and can also do backups to inexpensive CD-R discs for those times when you don't need the larger capacity of a writable DVD disc.

We recommend using top-quality DVD+R discs for backup. The PX-708A drive can fill a DVD+R disc in less than 10 minutes; writing to DVD+RW takes about twice as long. Although the PX-708A can also write DVD-R and DVD-RW, we don't recommend using those for data backups. DVR+R and DVD+RW provide excellent error detection and correction, which DVD-R and DVD-RW do not.

CD-ROM or DVD-ROM drive

Lite-On LTN-526/S 52X CD-ROM drive
Lite-On XJ-HD166X DVD-ROM drive (http://www.liteonit.com.tw)

If you plan to do differential backups to a tape drive, the SOHO server doesn't need an optical writer, but it does need a read-only optical drive for loading software and so on. Reliability is much less important for a read-only optical drive because you seldom use it. Adequate CD-ROM drives sell for $15 to $20, and DVD-ROM drives for twice that. We'd be inclined to choose the later, if only because DVD-ROM is becoming a common software distribution media.

ALTERNATIVES: CD WRITER

None. Sure, you can buy a Lite-On CD writer for $30, but spending an extra $50 or so on Plextor's best CD writer is worth it if only for peace of mind. Backup hardware is the worst place to compromise on cost versus quality. When you need a backup of your data, you need it badly. We trust Plextor to deliver when the chips are down.

ALTERNATIVES: DVD WRITER

As we went to press we received samples of the 12X Plextor PX-712A (ATA) and PX-712SA (S-ATA) drives, which are even faster than the PX-708 models. If we were building this system now, we'd use a PX-712 drive.

ALTERNATIVES: CD-ROM/DVD-ROM

Any Japanese brand CD-ROM or DVD-ROM drive is acceptable, including Mitsumi, NEC, Pioneer, Sony, Teac, and Toshiba. Among Korean makers, we consider Samsung and Lite-On models to be reliable, but we avoid products from LG (Lucky Goldstar) Electronics.

Mass-market resellers such as Staples, Best Buy, Office Depot, and CompUSA aggressively push house-brand or no-name drives, often with rebates that make the final price of the drive almost zero. Most of those drives are made by Lite-On or LG Electronics. If you can identify the drive as one made by Lite-On, consider buying it. Otherwise, avoid house-brand drives.

Tape drive

Certance Travan 20 and NS/20 tape drives (http://www.certance.com)

Certance (formerly Seagate) Travan 20 and NS20 tape drives are an excellent choice for doing differential backups of a large disk array. We consider them to be the most reliable inexpensive tape drives available. Certance produces multiple variants of this drive, including ATAPI and SCSI-2 versions, both of which are available as bare drives or as TapeStor models (bundled with software). The more expensive Travan NS20 models support read-while-write and hardware compression, while the entry-level Travan 20 models do not. Otherwise, all use the same basic drive mechanism and have similar specifications. For the SOHO server, an ATAPI Travan 20 model suffices.

Keyboard, mouse, and display

Because this SOHO server runs Linux, we need a keyboard, mouse, and display only for initial installation and configuration. Once the server is running, we can manage it remotely from one of our desktop systems.

Yes, we know about Windows Remote Desktop, but it's not the same. Remote Desktop provides limited remote management functions, but some management tasks must still be done from a monitor and keyboard physically connected to the server. Linux remote management tools allow us to do almost anything remotely that doesn't require changing hardware.

UPS

APC Smart-UPS SU700NET

Running a server without a UPS is foolish. Even a momentary power glitch can corrupt open databases, trash open documents, and crash server-based apps, wiping out the work of everyone connected to the server. A UPS literally pays for itself the first time the power fails.

We chose a 700 VA APC unit for our SOHO server. The APC Smart-UPS SU700NET is very reliable, is designed specifically for small servers, and costs less than $300. Its 700 VA rating is adequate for our SOHO server, and it has sufficient runtime to allow an orderly shutdown.

We considered using an APC Back-UPS Pro unit, but decided the Smart-UPS was worth the additional cost. Relative to the Back-UPS Pro, the Smart-UPS provides true sine-wave output, longer runtime, shorter recharge times, more extensive status displays, greater expandability, and various remote management options.

**ALTERNATIVES:
TAPE DRIVE**

None, really. Inexpensive tape drives are a dying breed, as evidenced by the bankruptcy of Onstream and other companies who attempted to make a go of this market. People who would formerly have bought an inexpensive tape drive nowadays buy a DVD writer instead. Several other companies produce Travan 20 drives, but the Seagate/Certance models are the best choice.

**ALTERNATIVES:
UPS**

If you're on a tight budget, choose the APC Back-UPS LS 700 or the Belkin F6C800-UNV 800 VA Universal UPS. Neither has the features of the APC Smart-UPS, but both provide plenty of capacity and runtime at less than half the price of the Smart-UPS 700.

Component summary

Table 4-3 summarizes our component choices for the SOHO server system. Only one of the optical drives listed is needed, and the tape drive is optional. (See the explanation earlier in this chapter.) For our own SOHO server, we installed the Plextor PX-708A DVD writer, but not a CD writer, CD/DVD-ROM drive, or tape drive.

Table 4-3. Bill of Materials for the SOHO server

Component	Product
Case	Intel Server Chassis SC5250-E
Power supply	Intel 450W (bundled)
Motherboard	Intel S875WP1
Processor	Intel Pentium 4 (retail-boxed)
CPU cooler	(bundled with processor)
Memory	Crucial PC3200 DDR-SDRAM (two 256 MB DIMMs)
Video adapter	(embedded)
Sound adapter	(none)
Hard drive	Seagate Barracuda 7200.7 SATA (four)
S-ATA power adapters	Antec Serial ATA Power Adapter (four)
External hard drive	Seagate 160GB External Hard Drive (at least two)
CD writer	Plextor PlexWriter Premium
DVD writer	Plextor PX-708A, PX-712A, or PX-712SA
CD/DVD-ROM drive	Lite-On LTN-526/S 52X CD-ROM drive Lite-On XJ-HD166X DVD-ROM drive
Tape drive	Certance Travan 20 or Travan NS/20
Keyboard	(none)
Mouse	(none)
Speakers	(none)
Display	(none)
UPS	APC Smart-UPS SU700NET

Building the System

Figure 4-1 shows the major components of the SOHO server. The Intel Server Chassis SC5250-E is flanked on the left by the Plextor PX-708A DVD writer and a Seagate External Hard Drive, and on the right by the Intel S875WP1-E server motherboard. In front of them, left to right, are four Seagate Barracuda 7200.7 SATA hard drives and the retail-boxed Pentium 4 CPU. Two 256 MB sticks of Crucial memory are located front and center.

Figure 4-1. SOHO server components, awaiting construction

Make sure you have everything you need before you start building the system. Open each box and verify the contents against the packing list. Once again, we failed to follow that advice, and once again we got bit. This time, it was because we made what seemed at the time to be a reasonable assumption. The Intel SC5250-E specifications list support for four Serial ATA hard drives. We foolishly assumed that meant the power supply provided power connectors for at least four S-ATA drives. Wrong.

The Intel power supply provides *zero* S-ATA power connectors. For some S-ATA drives, that wouldn't matter, because they have both S-ATA power connectors and standard (Molex) power connectors. Alas, the Seagate S-ATA drives have only S-ATA power connectors. We were stuck until we could come up with adapter cables to connect the Seagate S-ATA drives to the standard connectors on the Intel power supply.

> As it turns out, we can't blame Intel for not including S-ATA power connectors. The SC5250-E case has many options, one of which is an S-ATA backplane that supports hot-swapping S-ATA hard drives. We didn't order that option because it cost more than $100 and we had no real need for hot-swap support. If we had ordered that option, we would have had no problem powering our S-ATA drives.

You might think that S-ATA power adapter cables would be easy to come by. You'd be wrong. We called the local computer stores, Best Buy, Office Depot, and every other place we could think of that might stock such adapter cables. No luck. Most of them didn't even know what we were talking about. Those that did had none in stock and no idea where to get them. We then searched several of our usual online vendors and found that they didn't have what we needed either. We couldn't even find any on the Belkin and Cables-to-Go web sites.

We were surprised, to say the least. This isn't rocket surgery. S-ATA hard drives are becoming common, and only the newest power supplies provide S-ATA power connectors. One would think these adapter cables would be available everywhere. Nope. We wasted hours trying to find four lousy $3 cables.

Antec to the rescue! We finally thought to check the Antec web site, where we found the Antec Serial ATA power adapter cables shown in Figure 4-2. We needed four adapters. They come two to a package, so we ordered five packages. We're not going to go through this again. We'll scatter Serial ATA power adapter cables throughout our tool kits, on our workbench, and with our spare S-ATA drives in the inventory room. Never again.

Figure 4-2. Antec Serial ATA power adapters

As always, you needn't follow the exact sequence of steps we describe when you build your own SOHO server. Always install the processor before you install the motherboard in the case, because doing otherwise risks damaging the processor, but the exact sequence doesn't matter for most other steps. Some steps must be taken in the order we describe because completing one step is required for completing the next, but as you build your system it will be obvious when sequence matters.

Preparing the case

The first step in building any system is always to make sure that the power supply is set to the correct input voltage. Some power supplies—including the Intel 450W unit supplied with the SC5250-E case—set themselves automatically. Others must be set manually using a slide switch to select the proper input voltage.

WARNING

If your power supply must be set manually for input voltage, make absolutely certain you've set the proper voltage before you connect anything to the power supply. If your power receptacle provides 115V and the power supply is set to 230V, the system won't boot, but nothing will be damaged. But if you connect a power supply set for 115V to a 230V receptacle, turning on the system will destroy all components instantly.

To begin preparing the SC5250-E case, remove the two screws that secure the side panel, as shown in Figure 4-3. We call them "shipping screws" because they're there primarily to keep the side panel securely in place during shipping. Although you can insert these screws again after you finish building the system, it really isn't

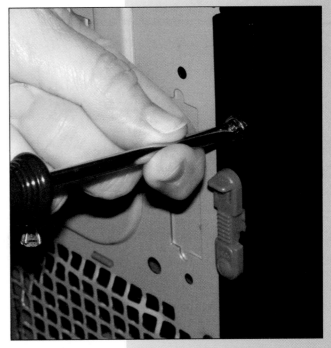

Figure 4-3. Remove the screws that secure the side panel

necessary. The side-panel latch by itself is sufficient to secure the side panel during routine use.

After you remove the screws that secure the side panel, slide the two blue plastic locking tabs to the unlocked position, as shown in Figure 4-4, and lift the side panel off.

With the side panel removed, remove the two screws that secure the hard drive bay to the side of the case, as shown in Figure 4-5.

The next step is to remove the front bezel. To do so, place the case in a vertical position and press the two plastic locking tabs on the left side of the bezel, as shown in Figure 4-6. Then swing the bezel to the right and lift it off, as shown in Figure 4-7.

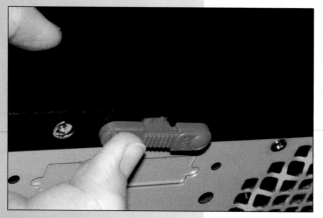

Figure 4-4. Unlock the two locking tabs and lift the side panel off

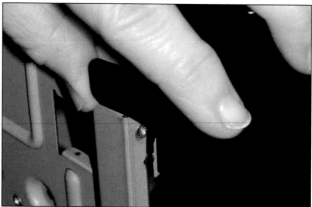

Figure 4-6. Press the two locking tabs to release the front bezel

Figure 4-5. Remove the two screws that secure the removable hard drive bay to the side of the case

Figure 4-7. After unlatching the bezel, swing it to the right and lift it off

With the bezel removed, remove the two screws that secure the hard drive bay to the front of the case, as shown in Figure 4-8. Grasp the hard drive bay firmly and slide it out of the chassis, as shown in Figure 4-9.

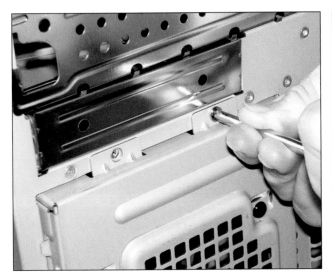

Figure 4-8. Remove the two screws that secure the removable hard drive bay to the front of the case

Figure 4-9. Slide the drive bay out of the chassis

The Intel SC5250-E chassis is one of very few cases that come without a standard I/O template. That saves us the usual step of removing the standard template, which almost never matches the back-panel I/O ports of whatever motherboard we happen to be installing, and replacing it with the template supplied with the motherboard.

Locate the I/O template in the S875WP1 motherboard box, and compare it to the back-panel I/O ports on the motherboard to verify that it's the correct template. Align the template with the I/O template cutout in the case, as shown in Figure 4-10.

With the template aligned, press gently along the edges until it snaps into place. If you have trouble getting the template to seat, you're not alone. Some easily snap right into place, but others simply refuse to seat without extraordinary effort. Just as you get one side popped into place, another pops free. Or you get three of them

Figure 4-10. Align the I/O template in the chassis cutout

Figure 4-11. Snap the custom I/O template into place (may be easier said than done)

aligned, and the fourth just refuses to seat. The best way we've found to seat recalcitrant templates is to work our way toward one corner, getting everything aligned as we go. Once everything but that one corner is in place, we press gently with a tool handle, as shown in Figure 4-11, until the final corner seats.

WARNING

Be careful not to bend the I/O template while seating it. The template holes need to line up with the external port connectors on the motherboard I/O panel. If the template is even slightly bent it may be difficult to seat the motherboard properly.

After you install the I/O template, carefully slide the motherboard into place, making sure that the back-panel connectors on the motherboard are firmly in contact with the corresponding holes on the I/O template. Compare the positions of the motherboard mounting holes with the stand-off mounting positions in the case. If you simply look at the motherboard, it's easy to miss one of the mounting holes in all the clutter. We generally hold the motherboard up to a light, which makes the mounting holes stand out distinctly.

The Intel S875WP1 motherboard has nine mounting holes. The Intel SC5250-E, like many cases, is shipped with several standoffs preinstalled; unlike some cases, it labels all standoff mounting hole positions. The S875WP1 motherboard requires standoffs at positions A, E, and K, which have standoffs preinstalled, and at positions 1, 3, L, C, H, and M, which do not.

There is also a standoff preinstalled at position D. Ordinarily, it's necessary to remove superfluous standoffs to avoid shorting out the motherboard. However, the SC5250-E case is designed to accept oversized motherboards, which are the only ones that contact position D. In this case, the extra standoff does not interfere and can be removed or left in place at your option.

It is immediately apparent even to the casual eye that the mounting hardware supplied with the Intel case is a cut above the mounting hardware supplied with even top-notch cases like those from Antec and PC Power & Cooling. Rather than the typical 5mm brass standoffs, Intel supplies 6mm plated standoffs. All parts are separated by type in individual plastic baggies.

The standoffs are in Bag E. Remove six of them from the bag, and use a 6mm nut driver to install them at positions 1, 3, L, C, H, and M, as shown in Figure 4-12. Tighten the standoffs finger-tight, but no more.

After you install all the standoffs, verify that each motherboard mounting hole has a standoff, and that no standoffs are installed that don't correspond to a motherboard mounting hole. Then slide the motherboard into position, as shown in Figure 4-13, to verify that everything aligns properly.

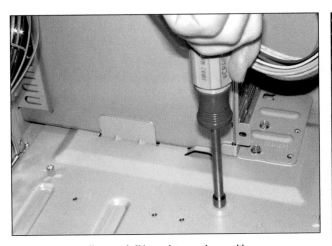

Figure 4-12. Install a standoff in each mounting position

Preparing and populating the motherboard

The steps detailed in the following sections prepare the motherboard by installing the processor, heatsink/fan unit, and memory.

WARNING

Before you handle the processor, memory, or other static-sensitive components, touch the power supply to ground yourself.

Figure 4-13. Verify that standoffs align with motherboard mounting holes

Figure 4-14. The retail-boxed Intel Pentium 4 processor and heatsink/fan

Figure 4-15. Lift the socket lever to prepare the socket to hold the processor

Figure 4-16. Align the processor with the socket and drop it into place

Installing the processor

For this system we used a retail-boxed Pentium 4 processor, which includes the processor itself and an Intel-branded heatsink/fan unit, as shown in Figure 4-14. The plastic bubble-wrap packaging Intel uses is truly obnoxious. We did eventually get the package open using scissors, but for a time we thought we'd have to resort to a chainsaw.

WARNING

Don't make the mistake of trying to pry the package open using just your fingers. Robert did that once with an Intel retail-boxed processor. When the package finally popped, the heatsink/fan unit went sailing across the room and the processor landed in his lap. (Thank goodness it wasn't the other way around.)

To install the Pentium 4 processor, lift the arm of the ZIF (zero insertion force) socket until it reaches vertical, as shown in Figure 4-15. With the arm vertical, there is no clamping force on the socket holes, which allows the processor to drop into place without requiring any pressure.

Correct orientation is indicated on the processor by a trimmed corner and on the socket by a small triangle, both visible in Figure 4-16 near the ZIF socket lever. With the socket lever vertical, align the processor with the socket and drop the processor into place, as shown in Figure 4-16. The processor should seat flush with the socket just from the force of gravity, or with at most a tiny push. If the processor doesn't simply drop into place, something is misaligned. Remove the processor and verify that it is aligned properly and that the pattern of pins on the processor corresponds to the pattern of holes on the socket.

WARNING

Never apply pressure to seat the processor—you'll bend the pins and destroy the processor. Note that closing the ZIF level may cause the processor to rise up slightly from the socket. After the processor is fully seated, it's safe to apply gentle pressure with your finger to keep it in place as you close the ZIF lever.

With the processor in place and seated flush with the socket, press the lever arm down and snap it into place, as shown in Figure 4-17. You may have to press the lever arm slightly away from the socket to allow it to snap into a locked position.

Installing the heatsink/fan (HSF)

To install the HSF unit, begin by polishing the heat spreader surface on top of the processor with a paper towel or soft cloth, as shown in Figure 4-18. Make sure to remove any grease, grit, or other material that might prevent the heatsink from making intimate contact with the processor surface.

Figure 4-17. Snap the ZIF lever into place to lock the processor in the socket

> If the processor has previously been used, clean off any remaining thermal compound or thermal-pad remnants before you install the heatsink/fan unit. You can remove old thermal compound using Goof-Off or isopropyl alcohol on a cloth, or by polishing the processor gently with 0000 steel wool. Steel wool is conductive, so make absolutely sure no stray bits of it remain after you finish polishing the processor. Even a tiny piece of steel wool can short out the processor or another motherboard component, with disastrous results.

Next, check the contact surface of the heatsink, shown in Figure 4-19. If the heatsink base is bare, that means it's intended to be used with thermal compound, usually called "thermal goop." In that case, polish the heatsink base as well.

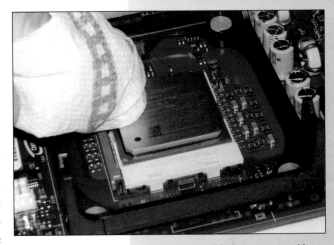

Figure 4-18. Polish the processor with a paper towel before installing the HSF

> The heatsink shown in Figure 4-19 is a so-called "AlCu" hybrid unit, for the chemical symbols for aluminum and copper. The body of the heatsink is made from aluminum, and the contact surface for the processor from copper. Copper has better thermal properties, but is much more costly than aluminum.
>
> Inexpensive heatsinks and those designed for slower, cooler-running processors use aluminum exclusively. Heatsinks designed for fast, hot-running processors (and for overclockers) use copper exclusively. Hybrid heatsinks balance cost and performance by using copper only where heat transfer properties are critical.

Figure 4-19. The base of the heatsink, showing the copper contact area

151

Alternately, some heatsinks have a square or rectangular pad made of a phase-change medium, which is a fancy term for a material that melts as the CPU heats and resolidifies as the CPU cools. This liquid/solid cycle ensures that the processor die maintains good thermal contact with the heatsink. If your heatsink includes such a pad, you needn't polish the base of the heatsink. (Heatsinks use either a thermal pad or thermal goop, not both.)

> Don't worry if your heatsink or thermal compound doesn't exactly match those we illustrate in this chapter. The type of heatsink and thermal compound supplied with Intel retail-boxed processors varies from model to model, and may also vary within a model line.

Intel never uses a cheap method when a better solution is available, and the packaging for their thermal compound is no exception. Rather than the usual single-serving plastic packet of thermal goop, Intel provides thermal goop in a syringe with a pre-measured dose. To apply the thermal goop, put the syringe tip near the center of the processor and squeeze the entire contents of the syringe onto the processor surface, as shown in Figure 4-20.

Figure 4-20. Apply the provided thermal compound

> Incidentally, the pre-measured thermal goop syringe shown here illustrates the proper amount of goop for a Pentium 4 processor. If you're applying goop from a bulk syringe, squeeze out only the amount shown here, about 0.1 milliliter (mL), which may also be referred to as 0.1 cubic centimeter (CC). Most people tend to use too much.
>
> If you apply too much thermal goop, the excess squooshes out from between the HSF base and the processor surface when you put the heatsink in place. Good practice suggests removing excess goop from around the socket, but that may be impossible with a large heatsink because the heatsink blocks access to the socket area. Standard silicone thermal goop does not conduct electricity, so there is no danger of excess goop shorting anything out.
>
> If you're a neatnik, use your finger (covered with a latex glove or plastic bag) to spread thin layers of goop on the processor surface and heatsink base before you install the HSF. We do that with silver-based thermal compounds, which we don't trust to be electrically non-conductive, despite manufacturers' claims to the contrary.

WARNING

If you remove the heatsink, you must replace the thermal compound or pad when you reinstall it. Before you reinstall, remove all remnants of the old thermal pad or compound. This can be difficult, particularly for a thermal pad, which can be very tenacious. We use an ordinary hair dryer to warm the thermal material enough to make it easy to remove. Sometimes the best way is to warm up the compound and rub it off with your thumb.

When we replace a heatsink, we use Antec Silver Thermal Compound, which works well and is widely available and inexpensive. Don't pay extra for "premium" brand names like Arctic Silver. They cost more than the Antec product, and our testing shows little or no difference in cooling efficiency.

Figure 4-21. Align the HSF unit over the processor, making sure the locking tabs on the HSF align with the corresponding slots on the HSF retaining bracket

The next step is to orient the HSF above the processor, as shown in Figure 4-21, keeping it as close to horizontal as possible. Slide the HSF unit down into the retaining bracket, making sure that the lock tabs on each of the four corners of the HSF assembly are aligned with the matching slots in the HSF retaining bracket on the motherboard. Press down gently and use a small circular motion to spread the thermal goop evenly over the surface of the processor.

Make sure that both of the white plastic cam levers (one is visible near Barbara's thumb in Figure 4-21) are in the open position, not applying any pressure to the HSF mechanism. With the HSF aligned properly, press down firmly, as shown in Figure 4-22, until all four HSF locking tabs snap into place in the corresponding slots on the HSF retaining bracket. This step requires applying significant pressure evenly to the top of the HSF mechanism, so it's generally easier to use your whole hand rather than just your fingers or thumb.

Figure 4-22. With the HSF aligned, press down firmly until it snaps into place

Figure 4-23. Clamp the HSF into place

With the HSF snapped into the HSF retaining bracket, the next step is to clamp the HSF tightly against the processor to ensure good thermal transfer between the CPU and heatsink. To do this, pivot the white plastic cam levers from their unlocked position to the locked position, as shown in Figure 4-23.

WARNING
The first lever is easy to lock into position because there is not yet any pressure on the mechanism. With the first lever cammed into its locked position, though, locking the second lever requires significant pressure. So significant, in fact, that the first time we tried to lock the second lever, we actually popped it out of the bracket. If that happens to you, unlock the first cam lever and snap the second one back into position. You may need to squeeze the pivot point with one hand to keep that lever from popping out of place again while you lock the first lever with the other hand.

The thermal mass of the heatsink draws heat away from the CPU, but the heat must be dissipated to prevent the CPU from overheating as the heatsink warms up. To dispose of excess heat as it is transferred to the heatsink, most CPU coolers use a small muffin fan to continuously draw air through the fins of the heatsink.

Some CPU fans attach to a drive power connector, but most (including this Intel unit) attach to a dedicated CPU fan connector on the motherboard. Using a motherboard fan power connector allows the motherboard to control the CPU fan, reducing speed for quieter operation when the processor is running under light load and not generating much heat, and increasing speed when the processor is running under heavy load and generating more heat. The motherboard can also monitor fan speed, which allows it to send an alert to the user if the fan fails or begins running sporadically.

Figure 4-24. Connect the CPU fan cable to the CPU fan connector

To connect the CPU fan, plug the keyed cable from the CPU fan into the three-pin header connector on the motherboard labeled "CPU Fan," as shown in Figure 4-24.

Installing the memory

Before you install memory modules, take a moment to determine the best memory configuration. The Intel S875WP1 motherboard supports dual-channel memory operation that doubles memory throughput relative to single-channel memory operation. Enabling dual-channel memory requires installing memory modules in pairs in specific DIMM slots, one per channel. Installing two DIMMs in one channel and none in the other channel forces single-channel operation.

Examining the S875WP1 motherboard, we see that it has four DIMM slots in two pairs. The slot nearest the processor is Channel A, DIMM 1, followed by Channel A, DIMM 2, Channel B, DIMM 1, and Channel B, DIMM 2. We want to install one memory module in Channel A and the other in Channel B. We could use either slot, but as a matter of good practice we decided to install our DIMMs in the first (DIMM 1) slot of each channel.

The S875WP1 numbers DIMM slots differently from other Intel motherboards—all other Intel motherboards we are familiar with number the first DIMM slot as 0 and the second as 1. The S875WP1 numbers the first DIMM slot as 1 and the second as 2. Best practice is to install DIMMs beginning with the first slot, whether it is numbered 0 or 1.

Locate the Channel A DIMM 1 socket and pivot the locking tabs on both sides outward. Align the edges of the first DIMM with the slots in the locking tabs and press firmly with both thumbs to seat the DIMM in the slot, as shown in Figure 4-25. Install the second DIMM in the Channel B DIMM 1 socket in the same manner.

Most DIMM sockets have two parts: a vertical post with an alignment slot, and a pivoting locking tab. Pressing the DIMM down into the alignment slot on the post automatically pivots the locking tab up into the locked position. The S875WP1 DIMM socket hardware is different. The alignment slot is part of the pivoting locking tab, which makes it a bit harder to get the DIMM aligned on both sides. We also found that it was more difficult to seat the DIMM because it was not in full contact with the alignment slot in the early part of its travel. The DIMM tended to wobble as we pressed down, and we were concerned that we might fracture the DIMM by pressing on it while it was unsupported. Be very careful installing DIMMs in this motherboard.

Figure 4-25. Align the DIMM with the socket and press it until it seats

Installing the motherboard

Installing the motherboard is usually the most time-consuming step in building a system because there are so many cables to connect. At times, it has taken us half an hour or more just to get all the cables connected and verified. The Intel S875WP1 reduces the effort needed by combining what would be individual cables on most systems into a monolithic connecting block. Plug in one connector, and you've connected all of the front-panel switches and indicators in one swell foop—if, that is, the case provides a matching connector cable. The SC5250-E case does provide that cable, thank goodness.

Seating and securing the motherboard

To begin installing the motherboard, slide it into the case. Carefully align the back-panel I/O connectors with the corresponding holes in the I/O template, and slide the motherboard toward the rear of the case until the motherboard mounting holes line up with the standoffs you installed earlier.

Before you insert any motherboard mounting screws, verify that the back-panel I/O connectors mate properly with the I/O template and that none of the grounding tabs on the I/O template is blocking a port connector. Then insert a screw through one mounting hole into the corresponding standoff, as shown in Figure 4-26. You may need to apply pressure to keep the motherboard positioned properly until you have inserted two or three screws. Use the screws from the bag labeled "A."

If you have trouble getting all the holes and standoffs aligned, insert two screws but don't tighten them completely. Use one hand to press the motherboard into alignment, with all holes matching the standoffs. Then insert one or two more screws and tighten them completely. Finish mounting the motherboard by inserting screws into all nine standoffs and tightening them.

Figure 4-26. Install screws in all mounting holes to secure the motherboard

Connecting the front-panel switch and indicator cable

Once the motherboard is secured, the next step is to connect the front-panel switch and indicator cable to the motherboard. The S875WP1 uses a 34-pin header to provide connections for all front-panel switches and indicators, including power, reset, and LED indicators. Table 4-4 lists the pinouts for this connector, which is located near the left front edge of the motherboard and is labeled J7J1. (We include these pinouts in case you install this motherboard in a different case.)

Table 4-4. Pinouts for front-panel connector block (J7J1)

Pin	Signal name	Pin	Signal name
1	Power LED Anode	2	5Vsb
3	Key (no pin)	4	Unused
5	GND	6	Unused
7	HDD Activity LED Anode	8	Unused
9	HDD Activity LED Cathode	10	Unused
11	Power Switch	12	NIC#1 Activity LED Anode
13	GND (Power Switch)	14	NIC#1 Activity LED Cathode
15	FP_RST	16	I1C SDA
17	GND (Reset Switch)	18	I2C SDA
19	ACPI Sleep Switch	20	Chassis Intrusion
21	GND (ACPI Sleep Switch)	22	NIC#2 Activity LED Anode
23	Unused	24	NIC#2 Activity LED Cathode
25	Key (no pin)	26	Key (no pin)
27	Unused	28	Unused
29	Unused	30	Unused
31	Unused	32	Unused
33	Unused	34	Unused

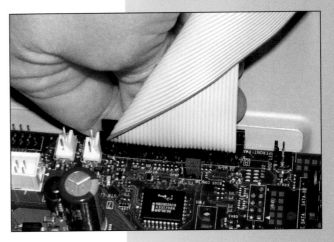

Figure 4-27. Attach the front-panel switch and indicator cable to the motherboard connector J7J1

The SC5250-E case has a connecting cable preinstalled on the front-panel side. The loose end of that cable is taped to the case near the left front edge of the motherboard. The cable looks exactly like a floppy drive cable, for which we mistook it when we first noticed it.

Peel the tape off to free the cable, align the cable connector with the motherboard front-panel connector (J7J1), and press the cable connector into place, as shown in Figure 4-27. Note that the cable connector is keyed with blocked holes that correspond to missing pins on the J7J1 connector.

Connecting the front-panel USB cable

The SC5250-E case includes a preinstalled front-panel USB connecting cable. The motherboard end of that cable is taped to the case near the left edge of the motherboard. The motherboard has a corresponding socket located between the AGP slot and the PCI slot nearest it. The connectors are keyed with a blocked hole and latch. Peel the tape off to free the cable, align the cable plug with the motherboard USB socket, and press the plug into place, as shown in Figure 4-28.

Installing the hard drives

The next step is to install the hard drives, all four of them. We removed the hard drive bay from the SC5250-E case and set it aside earlier. Locate the hard drive bay and the bag of screws labeled "A." These are the same screws you used to secure the motherboard.

The Intel SC5250-E drive bay has positions for six 3.5" drives. As shipped, the top and bottom positions are blocked by plastic spacers, leaving room for four drives. The plastic spacers channel the airflow from the drive bay fan around the drives to ensure proper cooling.

To mount the hard drives, slide them into the drive bay and secure each one with four screws from the "A" bag, as shown in Figure 4-29.

Figure 4-28. Attach the front-panel USB cable to the motherboard connector

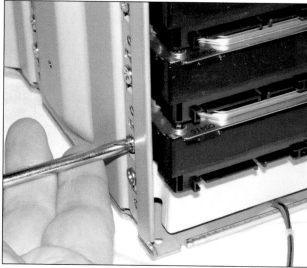

Figure 4-29. Slide the four hard drives into the drive bay and secure each of them with four screws (drive bay fan cable visible at bottom)

The Intel power supply provides only standard ("Molex") hard drive power connectors, and the Seagate S-ATA hard drives have only S-ATA power connectors. Therefore, an adapter is needed to power each hard drive. Connect the S-ATA end of an Antec S-ATA power adapter cable to each of the hard drives, as shown in Figure 4-30.

Skip this step if your power supply provides S-ATA power connectors, or if you are using S-ATA hard drives that provide standard Molex power connectors.

The next step is to connect an S-ATA data cable to each of the hard drives, as shown in Figure 4-31. Orient the cable connector so that its key is aligned with the key on the drive connector and then press the cable connector into place until you feel it seat.

Figure 4-30. If your power supply does not provide S-ATA power connectors, attach an S-ATA power adapter cable to each hard drive

We are configuring our four hard drives as a RAID 0+1 array to protect against data loss if a drive fails. When a drive fails, you need to know which drive to replace. The computer tells you which interface is connected to the problem drive, but you have to use that information to determine which physical drive has failed.

With the rats' nest of connecting cables inside the server, it can be difficult to determine which drive is connected to which interface, particularly after those cables are tied off and dressed. Accordingly, we always mark both ends of each cable. Use a felt-tip marker to draw a line across the end of each cable—one line on each end for Drive 1, two lines for Drive 2, and so on. (On dark cables, a white-out pen produces more visible markings.)

Figure 4-31. Connect an S-ATA data cable to each hard drive

WARNING

Be careful when connecting S-ATA power and data cables. The connectors, while not fragile, are not as robust as old-style parallel ATA power and data connectors. Install the cables by pressing straight in on the connectors, and remove them by pulling straight out. Avoid putting any lateral pressure on the connectors.

Figure 4-32. Slide the removable drive bay back into the chassis

With the drives secured in the bay and the S-ATA data cables and power adapters connected, the next step is to reinstall the drive bay in the case. Begin by feeding the cables through from the front of the case. Then position the drive bay as shown in Figure 4-32 and slide it into place, making sure than none of the cables jams.

Press the drive bay to seat it flush with the case, making sure that the screw holes immediately beneath the floppy disk drive bay align with the corresponding holes in the chassis. Locate the two screws you removed when you removed the drive bay and use them to secure the drive bay to the front of the case, as shown in Figure 4-33.

Then, locate the remaining two screws that you removed when you removed the drive bay, and use them to secure the drive bay to the side of the case, as shown in Figure 4-34.

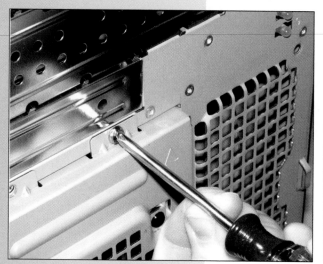

Figure 4-33. Press the removable drive bay flush with the chassis and drive two screws to secure it

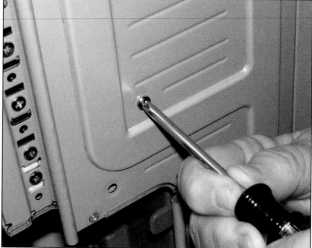

Figure 4-34. Drive the two remaining screws to secure the removable drive bay from the side

It's now time to connect the cables. Begin by locating the S-ATA data connectors near the left front corner of the motherboard (this might turn out to be more complicated than you think, so be sure to read the upcoming warning). Route the cables carefully to avoid tangling them with other cables. The goal is to have all four cables together so that you can later tie them off and dress them as a separate bundle. Place each S-ATA data cable connector on a motherboard connector, making sure the keying slots on the cable and motherboard port are aligned. Press the cable connector firmly until you feel it seat. Don't forget to use a felt-tip pen to label each cable.

Oops. Silly us. The S875WP1 motherboard is available in two versions, one with two Intel S-ATA connectors, and the second with two Intel S-ATA connectors and four additional S-ATA connectors driven by a Promise S-ATA RAID chip. Seeing four connectors in a row and two more off to the side, we assumed (doing that gets us every time) that the four together were the Promise RAID connectors and the two off by themselves were the standard Intel S-ATA connectors. Wrong. Figure 4-35 shows how we first connected the S-ATA cables. The two S-ATA connectors nearest the front of the motherboard (Barbara is pressing a cable onto one) are the "standard" S-ATA connectors, which are labeled "B." The Promise-based S-ATA RAID connectors are the four nearest the rear of the case, all labeled "A." Fortunately, we noticed and corrected our error before we reassembled the system. The correct connections are shown in Figure 4-36 (and yes, the connectors are in the order 1-3-2-4).

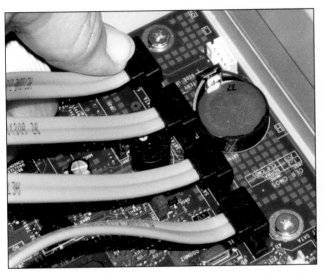

Figure 4-35. The wrong way to connect the S-ATA data cables to the motherboard S-ATA ports

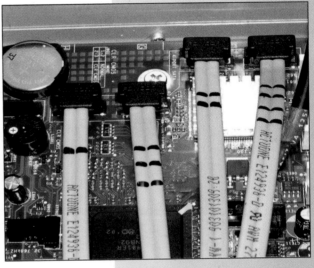

Figure 4-36. The right way to connect the S-ATA data cables to the motherboard S-ATA ports

The next step is to connect power to the hard drives. Locate four drive power ("Molex") connectors from the power supply, and route them carefully to the vicinity of the hard drives. You'll later tie these cables off and dress them as a group, so make sure that no other cables are intermingled with them. Press each Molex connector into the corresponding socket on the Antec S-ATA Power Adapter cable, as shown in Figure 4-37. It sometimes requires significant pressure to seat these connectors fully, so make sure you feel them snap into place.

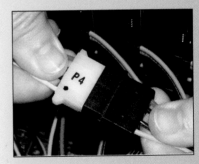

Figure 4-37. Connect a drive power connector from the power supply to each S-ATA drive

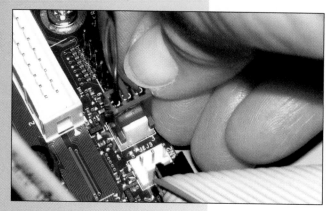

Figure 4-38. Connect the drive bay fan power cable to a motherboard fan connector

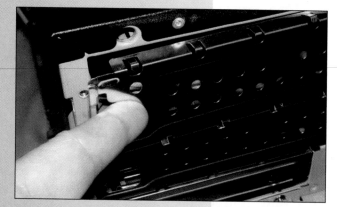

Figure 4-39. Remove the RF shield for the selected drive bay

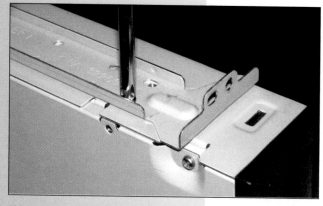

Figure 4-40. Install the drive rails

The final step in installing the hard drives is to connect the drive bay fan power cable. Locate that cable at the bottom rear of the drive bay (as shown back in Figure 4-29) and route it to one of the fan power headers at the front of the motherboard near the ATA interface connectors. The plug and socket are keyed with a slot and tab arrangement, as shown in Figure 4-38. Align the plug with the header pins, making sure the key slot is oriented correctly, and press the plug into the socket.

Installing the optical drive

The Intel SC5250-E case provides two external 5.25" bays, each of which is covered by a snap-in plastic bezel and a metal RF shield. We decided to install the optical drive in the top bay. Before installing the drive, you have to remove the bezel and the RF shield for the selected drive bay. To remove the drive bay bezel, simply lay the main system bezel facedown on the table. Working from the rear, press the plastic tabs on the drive bay bezel to release the tension and snap it out. To remove the RF shield, place a finger in one of the large holes near the side of the shield and tug on it until is snaps out, as shown in Figure 4-39.

Before you install the optical drive, verify the jumper settings. We plan to use the optical drive as the secondary master, leaving the primary ATA channel unused. Our optical drive was jumpered as master by default, so we didn't need to change the setting.

The Intel SC5250-E case uses something we haven't seen for a long time. Its drive rails come in Left and Right versions that are not interchangeable, and they secure both to the drive and to the case. Shades of the 1986-era IBM PC-AT. We had to search for the drive rails. We finally found them in an oblong white cardboard box with several other minor components, including rubber feet for the case.

Choose one of each type of drive rail and install them as shown in Figure 4-40, using screws from the plastic bag labeled "B." Align the rails as shown, with the bottom of the rail near the bottom of the drive and about 3/4" (19mm) of space between the front of the rail and the front of the drive. Getting the first part wrong means the drive won't fit into the bay. Getting the second part wrong means the drive won't seat flush with the main system bezel.

It's easier to connect the ATA cable to the optical drive before you install the drive in the case. The Intel S875WP1 motherboard included an ATA cable, which we used to connect the optical drive. That cable is an 80-wire UltraDMA cable, which is really intended for use with a fast hard drive, but works fine with any ATA/ATAPI drive. A standard 40-wire ATA cable would have been good enough for the optical drive, but we used what we had.

To connect the cable, locate pin 1 on the drive connector, which is usually nearest the power connector. The pin 1 side of the cable is indicated by a red stripe. Align the cable connector with the drive connector, making sure the red stripe is on the pin 1 side of the drive connector, and press the cable into place, as shown in Figure 4-41.

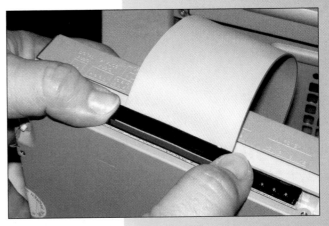

Figure 4-41. Connect the ATA cable to the optical drive

To mount the drive in the case, feed the loose end of the ATA cable through the drive bay from the front, align the drive rails with the corresponding slots in the case, and press the drive firmly into place, as shown in Figure 4-42. If you mounted the drive rails correctly, the drive should seat flush with the bezels that cover the vacant drive bays. It's worth taking a moment to verify proper fit by temporarily replacing the main drive bezel. You don't want to have to remove and reinstall the drive and all the cables if it turns out that the drive is seated too far in or too far out.

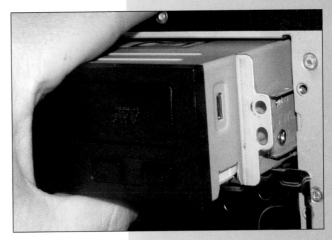

Figure 4-42. Slide the optical drive into the drive bay

With the optical drive seated fully, secure it to the chassis by driving one screw on either side, as shown in Figure 4-43.

The next step is to connect power to the optical drive. For some reason, we often forget to do this, which means that when we're ready to install the OS we often find ourselves shutting the system down, popping the cover, connecting power to the optical drive, and reassembling everything. It's not just us, either. We've watched other people build systems, and they often forget to connect power to the optical drive.

Figure 4-43. Secure the optical drive using one screw on either side

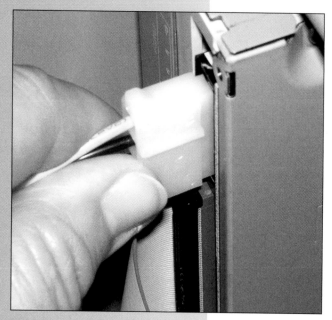

Figure 4-44. Connect a Molex drive power connector from the power supply to the optical drive

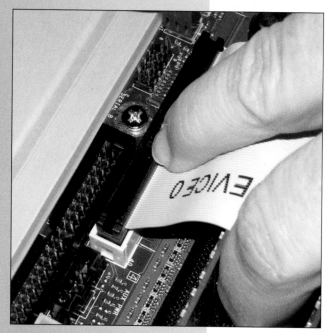

Figure 4-45. Connect the optical drive ATA cable to the secondary ATA interface on the motherboard

Locate a drive power ("Molex") connector coming from the power supply and route it to the back of the optical drive, making sure it is not tangled with or looped around other cables. Orient the cable connector properly—it's keyed with diagonal bevels on one side—and press it into the power connector on the drive, as shown in Figure 4-44.

It sometimes requires significant pressure to seat a Molex connector, so press until you feel it snap into place. It's quite possible to think you've seated the connector properly only to find out later that it's making partial or no contact. The Molex connector delivers both +5VDC and +12VDC. Many drives use 12V for the motor and 5V for the electronics. The usual symptom of a poor power connection is a dead optical drive, or one that spins up (because it is receiving 12V) but isn't recognized by the system (because it isn't receiving 5V).

Working from the rear of the drive, feed the ATA cable down into the case, placing the loose end near the front right edge of the motherboard. We want to connect the optical drive as the master device on the secondary ATA channel. The primary ATA and secondary ATA interfaces are located near the right front edge of the motherboard near the DIMM slots. The primary ATA interface is the black connector nearest the edge, and the secondary ATA interface is the white connector immediately adjacent. Locate pin 1 on the secondary ATA interface, align the ATA cable with its red stripe toward pin 1 on the interface, and press the connector into place, as shown in Figure 4-45.

Connecting power to the motherboard

The next step in assembling the system is to connect the two power connectors from the power supply to the motherboard. The Intel S875WP1 motherboard does not use a standard ATX12V power supply, although the connectors are similar. Instead, it uses an EPS12V power supply. The major differences between desktop-oriented ATX12V power supplies and server-oriented EPS12V power supplies are as follows:

Main power connector

Standard ATX12V power supplies use a 20-pin main power connector. EPS12V power supplies use a 24-pin main power connector. The pinouts for the first 20 pins are identical. The EPS12V power supply adds pins 21 through 24. Pins 21, 22, and 23 use red wires and supply additional +5VDC. Pin 24 uses a black wire and is an additional COM (ground) pin.

12V CPU power connector

The ATX12V provides a 4-pin (2X2) supplemental power connector that provides additional +12VDC on two pins and ground on the other two pins. The EPS12V power supply provides an 8-pin (4X2) supplemental power connector that provides additional +12VDC on pins 5 through 8 and ground on pins 1 through 4.

The main power connector on the S875WP1 motherboard can accept either an ATX12V or an EPS12V main power connector. That doesn't mean you can use an ATX12V power supply with this motherboard, though. The S875WP1 motherboard has an 8-pin socket for the EPS12V 12V CPU power connector. That socket is not compatible with the ATX12V 12V CPU power connector, and power must be connected to that socket for the motherboard to boot.

You can install the S875WP1 motherboard in some standard ATX cases, but you must replace the ATX12V power supply with an EPS12V power supply, such as one of those available from Antec or PC Power & Cooling. Before you attempt this, make sure the EPS12V power supply fits the ATX case.

To connect power to the motherboard, locate the main EPS12V power connector, a 24-pin socket located near the right front edge of the motherboard. Locate the corresponding cable coming from the power supply. The connectors are keyed, so verify that the plug is aligned properly with the socket before you attempt to seat it.

Once everything is aligned, press down firmly until the plug seats completely in the socket, as shown in Figure 4-46. It may take significant pressure to seat the plug, and you should feel it snap into place. The locking tab on the side of the plug should snap into place over the corresponding nub on the socket. Make sure the connector seats fully. A partially seated power connector may cause subtle problems that are very difficult to troubleshoot.

Figure 4-46. Connect the main EPS12V power connector

EPS12V motherboards require more +12VDC power than the 4-pin ATX12V connector supplies. For EPS12V, Intel substitutes the 8-pin 12V CPU power connector to route additional +12V current directly to the voltage regulator module that powers the processor(s). On most EPS12V motherboards, including the S875WP1, the 12V CPU power connector socket is located near the processor socket(s). The plug and socket are keyed. Orient the plug properly relative to the socket, and press the plug into place until the plastic tab locks, as shown in Figure 4-47.

Final assembly steps

Congratulations! You're almost finished building the system. Only a few final steps remain to be done, and those won't take long.

First, connect the supplemental case fan. The Intel SC5250-E has one rear-mounted 120mm supplemental fan. To enable it, connect its plug to a fan power connector on the motherboard, as shown in Figure 4-48.

Figure 4-47. Connect the 12V CPU power connector

Figure 4-48. Connect the rear case fan to a motherboard fan power connector

You might wonder why we connected the rear case fan to a fan power header at the front of the motherboard. It's because we failed to see one of the fan power headers.

The S875WP1-E provides five 3-pin fan headers. Four of the five—CPU_FAN, SYSFAN1, SYSFAN2, and SYSFAN4—connect to the tachometer input of the Hardware Management ASIC, which allows the system to monitor and control the fans. The fifth fan header, SYSFAN3, provides power but not monitor or control features. SYSFAN3 is located near the rear of the case, well positioned for the rear case fan. But we wanted to be able to monitor the rear case fan, so we connected it to one of the managed fan headers at the front of the case, not noticing that the SYSFAN4 managed fan header was even closer to the fan than SYSFAN3.

It did seem a bit odd that Intel would not provide a rear managed fan header in an otherwise well-engineered motherboard, so we went off in search of another fan header. Sure enough, we found SYSFAN4 lurking between the CPU and the rear I/O panel. We'll fix that when we tie off and dress the cables.

The final major step in assembling the system is to tie off and dress the cables. That simply means routing the cables away from the motherboard and other components and tying them off so they don't flop around inside the case. Chances are, no one but you will ever see the inside of your system, but dressing the cables has several advantages other than making the system appear neater. First and foremost, it improves cooling by keeping the cables from impeding airflow. It can also improve system reliability. More than once, we've seen a system overheat and crash because a loose cable jammed the CPU fan or case fan. Second, it makes it much easier to work on the system later on. Figure 4-49 shows what the SOHO server looked like before we dressed the cables.

You can use anything handy to tie off and dress the cables. We've used commercial tie-wraps, wire twist ties (be careful not to short anything out with the exposed wire at the ends), the yellow plastic ties that come with garbage bags, rubber bands, packing tape, and so on. Figure 4-50 shows the result of five minutes spent tying off and tucking the cables.

Note that the CPU cooling fan is unobstructed and that few cables intrude on the motherboard. The rear case fan and the power supply fan are both clear of obstructions, and there is a clear airway between the hard drive bay and the rear case fan. We tucked excess cable lengths into the nooks and crannies of the case to prevent them from flopping around.

The CPU fan cable and the 12V CPU power connector cable are wedged against the side of the HSF mounting bracket to keep them clear of the CPU fan. The unused cables from the power supply are tucked into a vacant external drive bay, as is the slack in the power supply cables that connect to the hard drive bay and the motherboard. Get your own server dressed this neatly, and you won't have to worry about obstructed airflow causing overheating.

You probably have the system on its side, so now is a good time to attach the rubber feet to the bottom of the case. Once that's done, return the case to its normal vertical orientation and remount the main system bezel. To do so, align the three plastic tabs on the right

Figure 4-49. Before: the typical rats' nest of cables

Figure 4-50. After: properly dressed and tucked cables

side of the bezel with the corresponding slots in the frame, and then swing the bezel closed until the two locking tabs on the left side of the bezel snap into place.

After you've completed these steps, double-check everything. Verify that all cables are connected properly, that all drives are secured, and that there's nothing loose inside the case. It's a good idea to pick up the system and tilt it gently from side to side to make sure there are no loose screws or other items that could cause a short. Use the following checklist:

__ No loose tools or screws (shake the case gently)
__ Heatsink/fan unit properly mounted; CPU fan connected
__ Memory modules fully seated and latched
__ Front-panel switch and indicator cable connected properly
__ Front-panel USB cable connected properly
__ Hard drive data cables connected to drives and motherboard
__ Hard drive power cables connected
__ Hard drive bay fan power cable connected
__ Optical drive data cable connected to drive and motherboard
__ Optical drive power cable connected
__ Optical drive audio cable(s) connected (if applicable)
__ Floppy drive data and power cables connected (if applicable)
__ All drives secured to drive bay or chassis
__ Expansion cards fully seated and secured to the chassis (if applicable)
__ Main EPS12V power cable and supplemental 12V power cable connected
__ Front and rear case fans installed and connected
__ All cables dressed and tucked

Start Small

As we've mentioned more than once, the first time you apply power to the system is the point of greatest danger. Accordingly, before we actually did the smoke test on the SOHO Server, we removed one of the memory modules and disconnected all but one of the hard drives. About 9,999 times in 10,000, that's a waste of time because everything works normally. The 10,000th time, though...

Once you're certain that everything is correct, it's time for the smoke test. Leave the side panel off for now. Connect the power cable to the wall receptacle and then to the system unit. The green LED near the center of the motherboard should illuminate as soon as you connect power to the power supply. Press the main power button on the top front of the case to start the system. Verify that the power supply fan, CPU fan, and case fan are spinning. At that point, everything should be working properly.

Turn off the system, disconnect the power cord, and take these final steps to prepare the system for use:

Set the BIOS Setup configuration jumper to Configure mode
The BIOS Setup configuration jumper block on the Intel S875WP1 motherboard is used to set the operation mode. This jumper is located on the left front of the motherboard, adjacent to the front-panel connector cable. By default, the jumper is in the 1-2 (Normal) position. Move the jumper block to the 2-3 (Configure) position.

Configure BIOS settings

After you set the configuration jumper to Configure mode, connect the monitor, keyboard, and mouse, reconnect the power cord, and start the system. BIOS Setup runs automatically and puts the system in maintenance mode. This step allows the motherboard to detect and configure the processor. When the BIOS Setup screen appears, clear all BIOS data and reset the system clock. Verify all other BIOS settings and change them as necessary to suit your preferences. Save the changes and exit. The system automatically shuts down. Disconnect the power cord.

> For details about BIOS configuration, refer to Chapter 7 of the *Intel Server Board S875WP1-E Technical Product Specification* and the latest *Specification Update*. These PDF documents can be downloaded from the Intel web site. (We can't give URLs because they change each time the documents are updated.)

Set the BIOS Setup configuration jumper to Normal mode

With the power cord disconnected, move the BIOS Setup configuration jumper block from 2-3 (Configure mode) to 1-2 (Normal mode).

Replace the side panel and reconnect power

With the jumper set for Normal operation, replace the side panel and reconnect the power cord. Your system is now completely assembled and ready for use.

> For most cases we've used, the side-panel latch alone is sufficient to secure the side panel, so we usually don't bother to reinsert the shipping screws. The Intel SC5250-E case has two blue plastic locking tabs on the rear of the side panel, but they didn't look sufficiently robust to secure the side panel reliably, so we reinserted both shipping screws.

Configure the RAID

Power up the system and press Ctrl-F to enter the Promise FastBuild Utility. (You may have to press Ctrl-F "blind" as the system boots, because the monitor may not display an image before the boot process passes the point where it prompts you to enter RAID setup.) By default, the array is configured in Performance mode, which stripes all four drives in a RAID 0. Use the down-arrow key to go to the first field, and press the spacebar to change "Performance" to "Security." The screen should now look similar to Figure 4-51. If you used hard drives with capacities other than 160 GB each, the array disk capacity figure will be different.

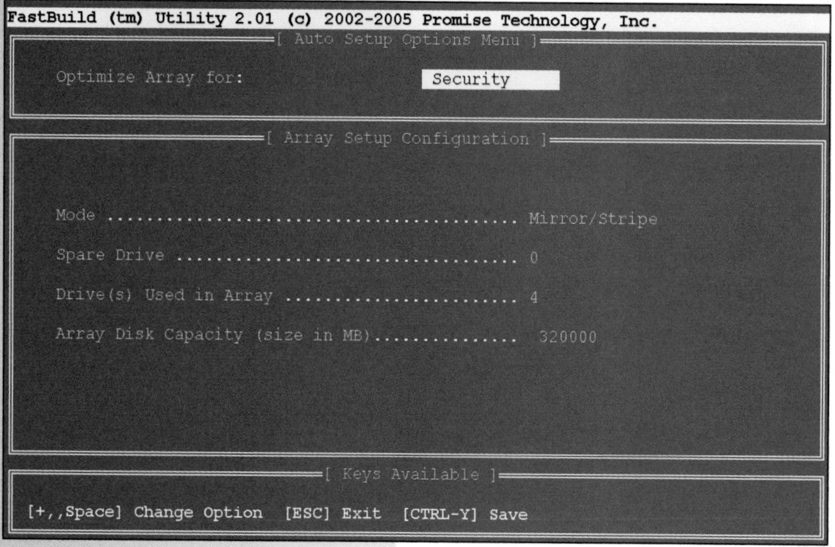

```
FastBuild (tm) Utility 2.01 (c) 2002-2005 Promise Technology, Inc.
============================[ Auto Setup Options Menu ]============================

  Optimize Array for:              Security

==========================[ Array Setup Configuration ]==========================



  Mode ...................................... Mirror/Stripe
  Spare Drive ............................... 0
  Drive(s) Used in Array .................... 4
  Array Disk Capacity (size in MB)........... 320000




==============================[ Keys Available ]==============================
  [+,,Space] Change Option   [ESC] Exit   [CTRL-Y] Save
```

Figure 4-51. Use the Promise FastBuild
Utility to configure the RAID

Press Ctrl-Y to save the array settings. The system prompts you to press "Y" to create the array and overwrite the Master Boot Record (MBR), or "N" to create the array without overwriting the MBR. Press "Y" to create the array and a new MBR. The system then prompts you to confirm that choice. Do so to create the array and then reboot the system.

Configure boot device priority

With the array defined, restart the system and press F1 to invoke the BIOS Setup utility. Again, you may have to press F1 "blind" because the monitor may not display the Boot screen quickly enough for you to see the BIOS Setup prompt. Pressing F1 repeatedly while the system boots does no harm.

When the BIOS Setup screen appears, use the right arrow to select the Boot Menu. Choose the Boot Device Priority to specify the boot sequence. Select the optical drive as the first boot device and the array as the second boot device. (You cannot do this earlier because the array is not listed as a boot option until you have configured it.) After you have configured the boot sequence properly, press F10 to save your changes and exit BIOS Setup.

At this point, the SOHO server is complete and ready to go.

Final Words

Plan to devote a weekend to building and configuring the SOHO server. Actual assembly takes only an hour or two; the rest of the time will be occupied with installing and configuring the server operating system.

Installing software

Well, we thought the system was complete and ready to go. We were wrong. Almost every time we build a system without a floppy drive—as Intel and Microsoft keep telling us to do—that decision bites us in the butt. This time was no exception. As it turned out, we needed a floppy drive not just once, but twice—once to update the BIOS, and a second time to install the RAID drivers during the OS install.

To download RAID drivers, visit the Intel web site and search for S875WP1. When you locate the main page for the motherboard, click on the link for drivers. Specify the OS for which you need drivers and download the appropriate ones. For Linux, the driver you want is the Promise PDC20319 SATA RAID Driver for Red Hat Linux 8.0, filename *RH8_RAID_PROMISE.EXE*.

Most people would probably just install an $8 floppy disk drive and have done with it. Not us. We're ornery. We weren't about to mess up our prettily dressed cables and stick an obsolete piece of technology into our shiny new server. Not us. No way.

So we did what we usually do. We popped the side panel, laid the floppy disk drive on top of the case, and connected the data cable and power cable just long enough to get done what we needed to do. Once we'd updated the BIOS and fed the Promise PDC20319 SATA RAID Driver to Red Hat Linux 8.0 setup, we shut down the system, disconnected the floppy drive, and put the side panel back on.

The good news is that the server works flawlessly with Red Hat Linux 8.0, and that's what we're running on it right now. The bad news is that RH8 is an aging and unsupported distribution, and as we wrote this Intel did not provide drivers for any later version.

We were deciding what to do when we were run over by the oncoming Deadline Train, so we didn't have time to explore the many possibilities. Intel may update their drivers. We may be able to use the Intel RH8 drivers with a later version. Promise provides Linux drivers, although they warn that those drivers are for use only with unmodified products supplied directly by Promise, and not with embedded controllers supplied by motherboard manufacturers. Still, they may work. Finally, there may be other distributions that support the S875WP1 natively. We're confident everything will work out. If not, we can always install Windows.

Possible future upgrades

Although we like our SOHO server overall, this is one seriously loud system. You won't want it sitting on your desk. You won't want it sitting under your desk. In fact, you may not want it in the same room with you. It's loud enough to be noticeable from across the room, and to intrude on normal conversation from a few feet away.

That's not Intel's fault. This is a server system, intended to sit in a server closet. As is proper when designing a server case, Intel gave great weight to system cooling and little consideration to noise level. And boy, does this system have good cooling. In the final stages of assembly, we had the server lying on its side on a table with a book two or three feet away. The rear case fan was blowing directly toward the book, and the book's pages were flipping in the breeze. After running the system for several hours, we found that the exhaust air was only a few degrees warmer than ambient, which is an excellent indication of good airflow and good cooling.

Still, we wish the server were a bit quieter. We may at some point replace the power supply with an Antec EPS12V TruePower unit, which should reduce the noise level significantly. We may also replace the rear case fan and the hard drive cooling fan with quieter units. Finally, the CPU cooler fan probably contributes more noise than any other component. We'll probably replace the HSF unit with a low-noise third-party unit.

For updated component recommendations, commentary, and other new material, visit *http://www.hardwareguys.com/guides/soho-server.html*.

Building a Kick-Ass LAN Party PC

5

Cost-effectiveness

Reliability

Compactness

Quietness

Expandability

Processor performance

Video performance

Disk capacity/performance

LAN parties came out of nowhere several years ago, and have become the rage amongst serious PC gamers. If you've never been to one, you have an experience in store. The basic idea of a LAN party is simple. Instead of gaming by yourself, or via the Internet with its latency problems, you get a bunch of people together in one room and run networked games on a LAN. A LAN party can be anything from three or four buddies playing networked FPS (First-Person Shooter) or air combat games in the basement rec room, to a formal event held at a hotel convention center with hundreds of gamers participating on a network that would be the envy of many businesses.

To locate a LAN party in your area or for information about running your own LAN party, visit *http://www.lanparty.com*.

Casual LAN partiers use standard desktop systems, but most serious LAN partiers build a PC optimized for LAN parties. In this chapter, we'll design and build the perfect *LAN Party PC* (LPPC).

Determining Functional Requirements

Our first thought was to build the LPPC around a Shuttle bare-bones SFF (Small Form Factor) system. These shoebox-size cubes are supposedly popular among LAN party gamers, at least if you believe what you read in the enthusiast magazines and web sites. Robert learned differently when he had the following exchange with a reader who attends LAN parties frequently:

> Robert: "So, are those shoebox PCs pretty popular among LAN party gamers?"
>
> Jason: "Not really. Some guys use them, sure, but most use regular mini-tower boxes."
>
> Robert: "Why is that?"
>
> Jason: "SFF cubes are expensive, have no expansion space, run hot, limit how much cool stuff like UV cables and fans you can add, and aren't really any more portable than a small mini-tower."

That pretty much confirmed our own suspicions. Several of our readers have reported reliability problems with the SFF cube systems, primarily power supply failures and overheating problems. Tom's Hardware Guide (*http://www.tomshardware.com*), an enthusiast site popular among gamers, had this to say in a review of several SFF systems:

> Only Shuttle's XPC on the P4 platform (SB65G2) has shown marginal lower temperatures of the processor (58°C), motherboard (44°C) and hard drive (43°C). The sound level, measured by a practical distance of 0.5 meter, was between 52 dB(A) and 58 dB(A).

In other words, shoebox PCs are hot and noisy. The temperatures that Tom's Hardware reports alarm us. When we design a system, we aim for a processor temperature at idle in the 30°C to 35°C range, increasing to perhaps 40°C under load. Running a processor at 58°C—and remember this was the *lowest* CPU temperature of all the systems tested—means shorter processor life and more frequent system crashes. No, thanks.

Another problem is that SFF PCs offer no flexibility. The case, motherboard, and power supply use proprietary or semi-proprietary form factors, so you're pretty much stuck with whatever the vendor decides to use. You install your own processor, memory, drives, and video adapter, but that's about it in terms of choosing your own components. Many SFF cases have only one or two expansion slots and accept only half-height expansion cards, which limits your choices severely. And then there's the price. At $350 or so for a case, power supply, and motherboard, we think the price of shoebox systems is excessive.

So we talked to some more serious gamers and sat down to rethink the project. Here's the list of functional requirements we came up with:

Portability

First and foremost, the LPPC must be easily portable. Size is one aspect, certainly, but weight is more important. A standard micro- or mini-tower box is small enough, but may weigh 20 pounds or more even before you install the power supply, drives, and other components. We wanted a system light enough for anyone to pick up with one hand, which mandated an aluminum case.

Durability

An LPPC naturally takes a beating compared to a traditional desktop system. It's constantly being transported, set up, and torn down. If you've traveled halfway across the country to attend a LAN party—or even if you've just driven over to a friend's house—the last thing you need is a DOA system because something vibrated loose. We also wanted a system that was resistant to minor dings and scratches. Painted cases accumulate scratches, which was another point in favor of an aluminum case with an anodized finish. The downside of an aluminum case is that it's easier to dent than a steel case. That shouldn't be a problem unless you toss the case around like the gorilla in the luggage commercial.

Uniqueness

Even the fastest LPPC loses coolness points if it looks stodgy. A beige case is definitely a non-starter. Black is good, and aluminum is better. A see-through side panel (or a transparent acrylic case) goes without saying, as do lighted fans and UV cables. The pinnacle of cool is a custom paint job and/or transfer-on images (assuming you can protect the surface against scratches). The goal is to make your LPPC unlike any other. If you do it right, other people should be at least a little afraid to touch it.

Robert plans to adorn his personal LPPC with images of the cast of his favorite TV show, the late, lamented *Buffy the Vampire Slayer* (with particular emphasis on the delightful Alyson Hannigan). Barbara is not amused.

Hardware Design Criteria

With the functional requirements determined, the next step was to establish design criteria for the LPPC hardware. To the right are the relative priorities we assigned for the LPPC.

Here's the breakdown:

Price

We'll keep price in mind, but it's not a major consideration for this system. Performance costs money, so we won't skimp on the processor, video adapter, and other components. We'll use only top-notch components in this system, particularly those that most affect gaming performance.

DESIGN PRIORITIES	
Price	★☆☆☆☆
Reliability	★★★★☆
Size	★★★☆☆
Noise level	★★☆☆☆
Expandability	★★☆☆☆
Processor performance	★★★★★
Video performance	★★★★★
Disk capacity/performance	★★★☆☆

Extreme Edition

When we started this project, we didn't understand why gamers were lining up to buy the Pentium 4 Extreme Edition (P4/EE). The P4/EE sold for several hundred dollars more than the fastest standard P4, which ran at the same clock speed and was itself an expensive processor. We found out why when we ran the P4 and the P4/EE processors side by side. In most applications, the P4/EE was faster than the standard P4, although not dramatically so. But in some games the P4/EE simply blew the doors off the standard P4. It was the difference between cruise and afterburner. It's amazing what adding a 2 MB L3 cache can do.

Reliability

Reliability is important for this system, but not the primary consideration. High performance and reliability are to some extent mutually exclusive. Fast processors and video adapters run hotter than mainstream components, and so are inherently less reliable. Accordingly, we'll design for reliability where possible, but we'll always give the nod to performance over reliability when the two are in conflict.

Size

Size is moderately important, weight and overall portability more so. Ultimately, what matters is that the LPPC be easy to move from one location to another, and that it be large enough to facilitate cooling the high-performance components it contains.

Noise level

Noise level is relatively unimportant for an LPPC. At a LAN party you're surrounded by other systems, so whatever noise your LPPC produces is just another drop in the bucket. Also, most people wear headphones at LAN parties—at some LAN parties it's mandatory—which muffles the din of many systems running in an enclosed space. We still give some consideration to noise level because an LPPC is, after all, also used at home.

Expandability

Expandability is fairly unimportant relative to other factors. An LPPC may be upgraded from time to time, but the usual upgrades are a faster processor and a faster video adapter, either of which simply replaces a component already installed. Furthermore, with BTX, PCI Express, and the Pentium 5 on the horizon, it's quite possible that this system will never be upgraded other than by wholesale replacement of components.

Processor performance

Processor performance is critical to any gaming PC. For typical applications, the difference between midrange and high-end processors may be nearly indistinguishable. Many games, however, use every bit of processor power they can get. Accordingly, we decided our LPPC would use the fastest processor we could get.

Video performance

Video performance is the *sine qua non* for a *ne plus ultra* gaming system. (Arrrghhh. Stop us before we Latin again!) Accordingly, we'll consider only high-end 3D graphics accelerators from *n*VIDIA and ATi. (ATi adapters have generally higher performance and superior bang for the buck, but *n*VIDIA adapters are faster with some games. Choose accordingly.)

Disk capacity/performance

Disk performance matters for some games. Disk capacity is less important. A SCSI adapter and a 15K RPM hard drive are overkill for a gaming system, so we'll stick with a mainstream 7,200 RPM ATA hard drive for our LPPC.

Component Considerations

With our design criteria in mind, we set out to choose the best components for the LPPC system. We took advice from our readers, because Barbara doesn't game at all and Tux Racer is Robert's idea of a challenging game. The following sections describe the components we chose, and why we chose them.

Case

Antec Super LANBOY (http://www.antec-inc.com)

We could have built the LPPC in just about any mini-tower case, but as usual Antec had exactly the right case for the purpose. The Antec Super LANBOY is a purpose-built aluminum mini-tower LAN party case. It even comes with a carrying strap.

The Super LANBOY is designed with portability in mind. At less than nine pounds without power supply, it is by far the lightest case we have ever used. In fact, when UPS dropped off the Super LANBOY and we first lifted the box, we honestly thought it was empty. But light doesn't have to mean flimsy. Although the Super LANBOY has a bit more flex than a heavy steel case, it is more than rigid enough to do the job.

The Super LANBOY accepts full ATX motherboards and standard ATX power supplies, and provides nine drive bays—four 3.5" internal bays and five external bays, three 5.25" and two 3.5". Because Antec expects this case to be used with a fast CPU and video adapter, it includes two large case fans to dissipate the heat, a standard rear-mounted fan, and a front-mounted fan with blue LED illumination. The case is also equipped with front-panel USB and audio jacks, and a clear side panel to show off your UV cables and other mods.

The Super LANBOY is also designed for quiet operation, which is a blessing when you're using it at home. The two case fans are 120mm, which spin slowly (and quietly) while still moving a lot of air. Antec also provides rubber grommet shock mounting for the drive bays, which both reduces hard drive noise and protects the hard drive if the system takes some hard knocks, as is likely to happen with an LPPC.

ALTERNATIVES: CASE

Although we think the Antec Super LANBOY is the best choice, almost any good aluminum ATX mini/mid-tower case can be used for an LPPC. Lian-Li (*http://www.lian-li.com*) makes several cases that are very popular among LAN partiers. We didn't choose a Lian-Li case because they sell at a significant premium over the Antec Super LANBOY, and we actually prefer the Antec case. Still, Lian-Li cases have an unquestionable cachet among LAN partiers, so we wouldn't argue with anyone who chose one.

**ALTERNATIVES:
POWER SUPPLY**

The Antec TruePower 430 or larger would suffice, as would a PC Power & Cooling (*http://www.pcpowercooling. com*) TurboCool 350 or larger. (PC Power & Cooling power supplies are much more conservatively rated than any other unit on the market.)

Power supply

Antec TrueControl 550 (http://www.antec-inc.com)

Unlike most Antec cases, the Super LANBOY comes without a power supply. We intended to use an Antec TrueBlue 480 power supply for this system, but our supplier was out of stock on that and several other Antec power supplies. The supplier did have two other candidates in stock, the Antec SmartBlue 350, which has blue LED illumination, and the TrueControl 550, which does not.

We ruled out the SmartBlue 350 for two reasons. First, a 350W power supply is marginal for this system, although it would suffice for a system with a slower processor and video card. Second, the SmartBlue 350 is a midrange Solution Series power supply, and we wanted one of Antec's high-end TruePower units. Accordingly, we chose the TrueControl 550, although the TrueBlue 480 would have done just as well.

Motherboard

Intel D875PBZ (http://www.intel.com)

As is almost always true, the processor decision drives the motherboard decision. The fastest AMD Athlon XPs are now midrange processors, so for high performance the choice was between the Intel Pentium 4 and the AMD Athlon 64. Although the Athlon 64 provides a lot of bang for the buck, we concluded at the time we were designing this system that Athlon 64 motherboards were not yet a sufficiently mature foundation for our LPPC, and so decided to go with a fast Pentium 4.

**ALTERNATIVES:
MOTHERBOARD**

If budget constraints forced us to use an AMD Athlon XP, we'd have chosen the superb ASUS A7N8X-E Deluxe motherboard, which has excellent performance, rock-solid stability, top-notch build quality, and an excellent feature set, including first-rate embedded audio. Even with the fastest Athlon XP processor available, that system would be noticeably slower than the Pentium 4 system we decided to build. However, it would have been considerably less expensive, and "slow" only when compared to the fastest Intel Pentium 4 and AMD Athlon 64 systems available.

> We should note that we were not alone in this decision. On paper, the Athlon 64 looks very attractive, offering comparable performance at half the price of a fast Pentium 4. However, the immaturity of the platform, concerns about the longevity of Socket 754, and other factors have caused the Athlon 64 to be largely ignored, even by the gamers whom one might reasonably expect to be its biggest boosters.

Having chosen the Intel Pentium 4, the next question became which motherboard to use. We looked at numerous Pentium 4 motherboards from Intel and other makers, and decided that the Intel D875PBZ was the optimum choice. It supports all current Pentium 4 processors, including the extraordinarily fast (and expensive) Pentium 4 Extreme Edition; it has all of the features we need, and it is immensely stable. Some motherboards are imperceptibly faster—although the difference is apparent only in benchmarks—and some have more features than the D875PBZ. Many cost a bit less. But the D875PBZ offers, in our opinion, the optimum combination of price, performance, build quality, and stability for our LPPC system.

Processor

Intel Pentium 4 Extreme Edition (http://www.intel.com)

Processor performance is critical for a gaming system, second only to 3D graphics performance. Although you can get by with a midrange processor for less processor-intensive games, for many games the difference between a fast processor and a midrange processor may be the difference between winning and losing.

We wanted our LPPC to put us on at least a level playing field with other gamers regardless of which games we happened to be playing—we need all the help we can get—and that meant choosing the fastest processor available. We considered using an Intel Northwood- or Prescott-core Pentium 4, but we concluded that the Pentium 4 Extreme Edition (P4/EE) was worth the extra cost.

The P4/EE is actually a relabeled Xeon server processor. In addition to the 512 KB or 1 MB of L2 cache used on standard Pentium 4 processors, the P4/EE includes 2 MB of L3 cache. In some applications, that extra cache makes little difference, but it pays off big-time when running many games. In our testing, the Intel P4/EE beat the AMD Athlon 64 in most gaming benchmarks, tied it in a few, and lost in only a couple by a very small margin. Clearly, the P4/EE is the processor of choice for a kick-ass gaming system. At the time we built the system, the P4/EE running at 3.4 GHz was the fastest available, so that's what we chose.

CPU cooler

Dynatron D25 (http://www.dynatron-corp.com)

Fast Pentium 4 processors dissipate significant heat, so it's important to install a CPU cooler that is rated for at least the speed of the processor you use. Retail-boxed Pentium 4 processors include an adequate heatsink/fan (HSF) unit. Our OEM processor came without a heatsink/fan. Intel no longer lists approved heatsink/fan units, so we went off in search of an appropriate cooler. We chose the Dynatron Dallas Series Model D25, which is rated for the 3.4 GHz Pentium 4/EE and slower.

Rather than using the standard mounting bracket that is preinstalled on most motherboards, the Dynatron cooler is supplied with a custom mounting bracket that replaces the standard bracket. The upside is that the Dynatron custom bracket provides a more secure mounting than the standard bracket. That's important for a system that will be lugged hither and yon—the last thing you want is a pound of heatsink flopping around inside the case. The downside is that installing the Dynatron cooler is a bit more involved and takes more time than simply clamping a heatsink to the stock bracket.

ALTERNATIVES: PROCESSOR

A 2.4 GHz or faster Northwood-core Pentium 4 or any Prescott-core Pentium 4 is fast enough for all but the most CPU-intensive games, as is an Athlon XP 2800+ or faster or any Athlon 64. If your goal is to build a truly kick-ass gaming system, you need the P4/EE or an Athlon 64 FX; otherwise, a $150 to $250 processor will suffice.

ALTERNATIVES: CPU COOLER

The Dynatron unit combines excellent price, cooling performance, and noise level, but nearly any heatsink/fan unit rated for the speed of processor you use will do the job, including the stock HSF bundled with retail-boxed processors. If we wanted a high-performance, quiet HSF—albeit at a premium price—we'd use the Zalman CPNS7000A-Cu (*http://www.zalman. co.kr*).

Memory

Crucial PC3200 DDR-SDRAM (http://www.crucial.com)

Top-quality memory is essential (we were about to say "crucial") to system performance and stability. We've used Crucial memory in scores of systems over the last decade or more, and it has never let us down. We can't say the same for most brands, and certainly not for commodity memory. Using cheap memory almost guarantees that your system will crash from time to time, and Murphy's Law says that it will always happen at the worst possible time.

Unlike memory packagers, Crucial actually manufactures memory, from the raw memory chips to the finished modules. In effect, sand goes in one end of a Crucial plant and memory modules come out the other. Because Crucial has absolute control over all phases of the manufacturing process, it produces extremely reliable memory and can sell it at very competitive prices.

We don't intend to overclock this system, and so decided to use standard Crucial PC3200 memory modules. Most games run happily in 256 MB, but many benefit from 512 MB. Few current games take advantage of more than 512 MB, but the potential is there and the cost of installing a full gigabyte is a minor consideration in a system of this class. Also, the operating system may be able to do a lot of things with the extra memory that benefit the game, such as using a lot of memory for disk cache and other buffers. Accordingly, we decided to install two Crucial 512 MB PC3200 DIMMs.

Why two 512 MB DIMMs rather than one 1 GB DIMM? Two reasons. First, one 1 GB DIMM costs significantly more than two 512 MB DIMMs. More important, the Intel 875P chipset supports dual-channel DDR memory if an even number of DIMMs are installed. Using two PC3200 DIMMs provides peak bandwidth of 6,400 MB/s, which matches the bandwidth of the processor. Using a single PC3200 DIMM limits peak bandwidth to 3,200 MB/s, causing the processor to waste time waiting on memory.

Video adapter

ATi RADEON 9800 XT (http://www.ati.com)

3D graphics performance is the single most important aspect of a gaming PC. For years, ATi and *n*VIDIA leapfrogged each other every few months to bring the fastest 3D graphics adapter to market and regain the gaming performance crown. During this period, gamers divided into two camps, ATi and *n*VIDIA. When ATi shipped a new high-end graphics adapter, *n*VIDIA fans gnashed their teeth and waited for *n*VIDIA to respond with something even faster. When *n*VIDIA shipped their new adapter, ATi fans did likewise.

Why "Performance" Memory Usually Isn't Worth Paying Extra For

Companies like Corsair and Muskin sell "high-performance" memory to the enthusiast market. We're sometimes asked if it's worth paying more for such memory rather than using Crucial modules. The short answer is that it's usually not.

Even nominally identical memory chips vary from one to the next. Some are faster than others, and performance memory packagers take advantage of that fact. They order large numbers of memory chips and use a process called binning to hand-select the fastest chips from that batch. After they've cherry-picked the fastest 5% or 10%, they resell the remaining chips to other memory packagers.

They assemble those hand-picked chips into high-performance modules and test the finished modules to verify that they function at higher speeds and tighter memory timings than standard memory. For example, when we wrote this, the fastest standard DDR memory was PC3200 with CL-3 memory timing, but some of these companies were selling PC3200 CL-2 modules as well as non-standard modules labeled as PC3500 or even PC4300.

Many gamers happily pay substantial premiums for such memory, on the assumption that faster memory must translate to faster system performance. Alas, that's not necessarily true. If one type of memory is fast enough to keep up with the processor, or nearly so, substituting faster memory has very little effect on overall system performance.

Some might object that the benchmarks show the difference. Sure they do, when they test memory subsystem performance in isolation. But memory performance is only one aspect of overall system performance, and using faster memory helps only if memory speed is the bottleneck. For most gaming systems, it is not.

The one exception is overclocked systems. If you boost the bus speed to run your CPU at higher than nominal speed, which we do not recommend, you're also pushing other system components, including the memory to speeds they were not designed to support. In such cases, it's a good idea to use hand-picked performance memory rather than depending on the tolerances built into standard memory modules.

The leapfrogging ended in mid-2002 when ATi shipped the RADEON 9700 adapter. The 9700 blew away the best *n*VIDIA could offer, and even when *n*VIDIA responded months later, the best their new adapter could do was to almost match the months-old ATi adapter. But ATi didn't rest on their laurels. They followed the RADEON 9700 with the 9700 Pro, 9800, 9800 Pro, and 9800 XT, all of which easily outperformed the best *n*VIDIA had to offer. Despite desperate attempts to counter ATi, *n*VIDIA kept coming up a day late and a dollar short. Low-end and midrange *n*VIDIA adapters continued to sell well, but ATi pretty much owned the high ground.

3D performance isn't the only thing that matters for a video adapter, even one used primarily for gaming. High-quality drivers are essential, not just for performance and display quality, but for system stability. ATi drivers used to have a bad reputation, but their current Catalyst drivers are fast, frequently updated, and stable. *n*VIDIA also supplies excellent drivers, but the advantage it used to have in driver quality disappeared years ago.

Unless you dedicate a system exclusively to gaming, 2D display quality also matters. When you use general Windows applications for word processing, email, web browsing, and so on, 2D display quality determines how good (or bad) the image looks. A card with good 2D display quality puts sharp, attractive text and images on your monitor; one with mediocre 2D display quality covers your monitor with ugliness.

ATi adapters have always had superb 2D display quality, only a half-step behind Matrox, which is the standard by which we judge all others. *n*VIDIA 3D accelerators have until recently had relatively poor 2D display quality, probably because *n*VIDIA optimized their drivers for 3D performance at the expense of all else. The most recent *n*VIDIA adapters have better 2D quality, but it remains a step behind that of ATi adapters.

ATi wins in every important respect, and therefore we opted to use an ATi RADEON video adapter. The question became, which one? Table 5-1 lists several ATi RADEON models available as of July 2004, with the key characteristics for each. The RADEON 9200, shown only for comparison, is an excellent general-purpose video card with competent 3D capabilities, but is not a card for a serious gamer. The 9600-series cards are appropriate for gamers who are on a budget, and the 9800-series cards for gamers willing to pay the price for the best 3D performance available.

Here's how to interpret these numbers:

- The amount of memory specifies memory installed on the video adapter itself, which determines how much data can be stored and manipulated locally without resorting to transferring data across the bus. Video memory that is not being used to render graphics can be used to cache video data for faster access. For current games, there is

At press time, ATi had announced but not yet shipped their new-generation video adapters, the X300-, X600-, and X800-series cards. Because we were unable to obtain samples by deadline, we built our Kick-Ass LAN Party PC around ATi's then-current flagship product, the RADEON 9800 XT. That adapter remains available, is just as fast as ever, and now sells for significantly less than ATi's new flagship, the RADEON X800 XT 256MB DDR video adapter. If we were building this system today, we'd probably use a RADEON X800 XT.

Table 5-1. Key characteristics of ATi RADEON video adapters

	9200	9600	9600 XT	9800	9800 XT
DDR memory (MB)	128	128	128	128	256
Memory interface	128-bit	128-bit	128-bit	256-bit	256-bit
Memory clock (MHz)	400	400	600	580	730
Engine clock (MHz)	250	325	500	325	412
Pixel pipelines	4	4	4	8	8
Pixel fill rate (gigapixels/s)	1.0	1.3	2.0	2.6	3.3
Geometry pipelines	1	2	2	2	2
Geometry rate (megatriangle/s)	125	.5	250	325	412
DirectX version	8.1	9.0	9.0	9.0	9.0
Retail price	$99	$169	$199	$299	$499

little advantage to having 256 MB of local video memory rather than 128 MB. However, a year or so ago, we'd have said the same about 128 MB versus 64 MB.

- The memory interface width and memory clock together determine how quickly data can be transferred between memory and the graphics processor unit (GPU). All other things being equal, doubling the memory interface width doubles the amount of data that can be transferred per second, as does doubling the memory clock speed. For example, a 128-bit interface running at 400 MHz transfers the same amount of data per second as a 256-bit interface running at only 200 MHz.

- The engine clock speed determines how fast the GPU can render graphics data. Note that this is true only within a GPU family. For example, the 9600 XT runs the engine clock at 500 MHz, versus "only" 412 MHz for the 9800 XT. The 9800 GPU, however, does much more work per clock tick than the 9600 GPU, and so provides much higher rendering performance even at lower clock speeds.

- The pixel and geometry pipelines and fill rates determine and specify how quickly graphics data can be rendered and transferred to the display.

- The DirectX version is important because it determines which games you can play. For example, attempting to play a new game that requires DX9 on the 9200 adapter is hopeless, because the 9200 supports only DX 8.1. You *can* use an earlier DirectX version with an adapter that supports a later version, but part of the reason for buying the more expensive adapter that supports the later DirectX version is to play later releases of games that require a recent DirectX version.

ALTERNATIVES: VIDEO ADAPTER

In the past, we sometimes used *n*VIDIA adapters in Linux systems, because *n*VIDIA had better Linux drivers. That's no longer true, so we seldom use *n*VIDIA adapters other than for comparison testing. If for some reason we wanted a high-end *n*VIDIA adapter for this system, we'd use an FX 5950 Ultra, although it costs more than the RADEON 9800 XT, is slower on most benchmarks, takes two slots, and has inferior video quality. If we were on a tighter budget, we'd use an ATi 9600 XT adapter.

- We list the retail price only to give a general idea of the relationship between price and performance. Retail prices will no doubt have fallen by the time you read this, and no one pays retail price anyway.

We didn't have a problem deciding which RADEON to use. We didn't even consider the 9200—it's simply not fast enough for a serious gaming system. The 9600-series cards offer tremendous bang for the buck, and we'd have chosen a 9600 if we were on a budget. But any self-respecting kick-ass gaming system has to use a high-end video adapter, so we limited our choices to the 9800-series cards. The standard 9800 is an extraordinarily fast card, but the 9800 XT is faster still, by as much as 25% or so in some games. So, despite its high price, we chose the 9800 XT.

Sound adapter

Turtle Beach Santa Cruz (http://www.turtlebeach.com)

The Intel D875PBZ motherboard is one of very few modern motherboards without embedded audio. That makes little difference, because we want the best audio available for our kick-ass gaming system. The Sound Blaster Audigy 2 is the gold standard in gaming audio, in terms of performance, features, and compatibility—if you're running Windows. If you also game under Linux, as we do, the limited Linux support for the Audigy 2 becomes problematic.

We chose a Turtle Beach Santa Cruz sound card for this system because of its excellent audio quality and its compatibility with Windows and Linux. The Santa Cruz, like the M-Audio Revolution 7.1, has better overall sound quality than the Sound Blaster Audigy 2, but is not quite as good a gaming card. It's not far behind, though, as most gamers will tell you, so using the Santa Cruz gives up little in terms of gaming features while gaining superior sound quality and Linux compatibility.

Hard disk drive

Maxtor DiamondMax Plus 9 160 GB ATA-133 (http://www.maxtor.com)

After many bad experiences with Western Digital and IBM ATA hard drives, we started using Seagate and Maxtor 7,200 RPM ATA drives exclusively. Our experience with both brands has been excellent, although each has its advantages. Seagate drives are much quieter, but Maxtor drives are a bit faster in some benchmarks. Because noise level isn't a major factor for the LPPC, we elected to go with a Maxtor drive.

Although the Santa Cruz is an excellent card, we would have chosen the Sound Blaster Audigy 2 if we ran Windows exclusively. If the Audigy 2 is a bit rich for your blood, there are several less expensive alternatives, including the Philips Sonic Edge and the M-Audio Revolution 7.1, both of which have good sound quality and good gaming support under Windows. (We have not yet had a chance to test the Turtle Beach Riviera and Catalina sound cards, both of which were announced as we were building this system.)

If you're on a tight budget, you needn't buy a standalone sound card at all. Instead, choose a motherboard with embedded audio suitable for gaming. For example, the Intel D865PERL is only slightly slower than the D875PBZ, costs less, and includes Intel's excellent SoundMax 4XL embedded audio. Similarly, nForce chipsets for the AMD Athlon family include superb embedded audio. Rather than spending more than $200 for a motherboard and standalone sound card, you can spend half that and give up very little in audio quality or features.

We've benchmarked various games in single-drive and RAID 0 configurations with 7,200 RPM and 10,000 RPM ATA and S-ATA drives and 15,000 RPM SCSI drives. We found that 7,200 RPM ATA drives provide the most bang for the buck. Few games perform noticeably better with even the fastest disk subsystems. They load faster on a 15K SCSI RAID 0, certainly, but during actual play we found little difference. Nor does the amount of cache make much difference. We've benchmarked various games on systems that were identical except that one used a Maxtor or Seagate hard drive with a 2 MB cache and the other the same model hard drive but with an 8 MB cache. There was no distinguishable difference. If you do want RAID 0, use two S-ATA drives with the RAID 0 support built into the Intel D875PBZ motherboard.

We chose the parallel (standard) ATA interface rather than serial ATA for two reasons, one of which will become clear in the next section. The major reason we chose standard ATA was that this system will dual-boot XP and Linux—not that Linux is a primo gaming platform as yet, but we wanted the option—and some Linux distros still have issues with S-ATA.

Disk capacity is relatively unimportant for an LPPC, in the sense that any current drive has more than enough capacity for most gaming systems. Although Maxtor was shipping a 200 GB model when we configured this system, the cost per gigabyte was very high. We could have saved a few bucks by going with a 60, 80, or 120 GB version, but the 160 GB model was reasonably priced, so that's what we chose.

ATA cable

Antec UV Cobra IDE cable (http://www.antec-inc.com)

Okay, we admit it. We're stodgy old farts who don't believe in rounded ATA cables. Sure, rounded cables improve airflow and look better, but the simple fact is that they don't comply with the ATA standard. Using them can cause data corruption, or at least make your hard drive work harder because of all the resends necessary when the rounded cable corrupts a transmission.

Still, showing up at a LAN party with flat ATA cables in your system loses coolness points, so we didn't have much choice. A rounded cable it was, and a UV fluorescent one at that. If we're going to do it, we'll go whole hog. The Antec UV Cobra cable was the snazziest rounded cable we saw at Best Buy, so that's what we went with.

Choose an optical drive for the LPPC system that meets your own requirements. At a minimum, you'll need a drive that reads CD-ROM and DVD-ROM discs, for which any DVD-ROM drive suffices. We consider current brand-name DVD-ROM drives, including units from NEC, Panasonic, Pioneer, Sony, or Toshiba, to be interchangeable except as noted below. Buy on availability and price. If you don't want a beige or black drive, consider the Sony DDU1621, which is available with a silver bezel. It doesn't exactly match most aluminum cases, but you may prefer it to a black bezel. If money is tight, consider a Lite-On DVD-ROM drive (*http://www.liteonit. com.tw*). We've found them to be reliable, and we've seen them on sale for $25.

Combo DVD-ROM/CD-RW drives are quite popular for LPPCs. Plextor, our favorite optical drive maker, no longer offers such a drive. We've looked at numerous combo drives, and we like the inexpensive Lite-On LTC48161 about as well as any of the others.

Note that our recommendation of inexpensive Lite-On drives does not extend to drives made by LG Electronics, another Korean manufacturer.

If you need to read burned DVDs, check compatibility. Most DVD drives read any type of DVD disc, except perhaps DVD-RAM. Others will not read DVD+R/RW or DVD-R/RW discs. Check the technical specs on the web site to verify that the drive you intend to buy is listed as compatible with the types of DVD discs you intend to use.

Optical drive

Plextor PX-708A DVD writer (*http://www.plextor.com*)

There wasn't much to decide here. We wanted a "do-it-all" optical drive for this system, and the Plextor PX-708A is the best such drive on the market. It writes CD-R/RW, DVD+R/RW, DVD-R/RW, and reads almost anything except DVD-RAM discs.

Keyboard and mouse

An LPPC really needs two keyboards and two mice, one set for home and one for away. Hey, sports teams have home and away jerseys, so there's really no reason not to have home and away input devices.

Home keyboard and mouse

Logitech Cordless MX Duo (*http://www.logitech.com*)

For home use, we don't know of a better keyboard/mouse combo than the Logitech Cordless MX Duo. The keyboard is a delight, with dedicated keys for various special functions. The iNav wheel on the left side of the keyboard allows you to use both hands for navigation and control. We've used a lot of keyboards over the years, and this is the best one we've found yet.

The Cordless MX Duo also includes Logitech's excellent MX700 cordless optical mouse, which nestles in a dedicated recharging cradle between sessions. For years, we used only Microsoft optical mice. Logitech MX-series mice are the first optical mice that we like better than Microsoft models.

Although we love the Logitech hardware, their drivers worry us a bit. One of our readers reported that installing the Logitech drivers also installed a program called BackWeb, which raises a warning flag. We believe Logitech uses BackWeb solely for support purposes, but we don't want possible spyware installed on our systems regardless of the source. For more information about this issue, see *http://www.backweb.com/services/html/spyware.html*.

This is really a non-issue for us, because we use the standard drivers supplied with Windows and Linux, and recommend that others do the same. If you want custom features supported by the Logitech driver, we suggest installing it and removing BackWeb manually.

Away keyboard and mouse

Zippy EL-715 illuminated keyboard (*http://www.hampton-technologies.com*)
Logitech MX 500 corded optical mouse (*http://www.logitech.com*)

We love the freedom of cordless for home use, but for away use corded devices are almost mandatory. Cordless keyboards and mice use radio frequency (RF) communications. Some provide an A-B switch to prevent conflicts by using different frequencies, but a choice of only two frequencies is wholly inadequate at a crowded LAN party. If you doubt that, just wait until the first time you watch the cursor moving across your screen in response to someone else's mouse movements. Until someone comes up with frequency-agile, stealthed cordless input devices, corded it is.

Portability is a major issue for an LPPC, as much for the keyboard as any other component. Also, LAN parties are often dimly illuminated, which makes a backlit keyboard desirable. We know of two portable keyboards with electroluminescent backlighting: the Auravision EluminX and the Hampton Technologies Zippy. Of the two, we prefer the Zippy EL-715, which also happens to cost less than the EluminX. The Zippy EL-715 is a medium-size notebook-style 105-key keyboard. At just over a pound and about 0.75" thick, the EL-715 is extremely portable. We find it a bit too cramped to use as our primary keyboard, but it's unsurpassed as a portable LAN party keyboard. The blue backlighting is bright enough to see what you're doing, but not so bright that it becomes intrusive in a dimly lit environment.

For a corded mouse, we chose the Logitech MX 500 optical mouse. We considered "travel-size" and "notebook" mice, but the small reduction in size and weight simply isn't worth the tradeoff in comfort and usability. The MX 500 is a premium full-size optical mouse with superb pointing accuracy. It's everything we want in a mouse for a gaming system, although serious gamers, many of whom prefer to use a five-button mouse instead of a game controller, may prefer Microsoft five-button mice or a similar model from another manufacturer.

Game controllers

Joystick: *Thrustmaster HOTAS Cougar* (*http://us.thrustmaster.com*)
Gamepad: *Logitech WingMan Rumblepad* (*http://www.logitech.com*)
Wheel: *Logitech MOMO Racing Force Feedback Wheel*

As with keyboards and mice, personal preference is the most important factor in selecting the best game controllers for your own needs. Cordless controllers are very nice for use at home or small LAN parties, but if you attend large LAN parties, corded is the only way to go.

One downside to cordless models is that none we know of incorporates full force feedback, which apparently requires too much juice to run from batteries. The best cordless controllers can provide is limited vibration feedback. Full force feedback uses small motors within the game controller to provide tactile response to gaming actions. For example, as you maneuver your F-16 Falcon onto the six of a MiG-29 Fulcrum and begin hosing him down with your Vulcan rotary cannon, a force feedback joystick jitters and jerks to simulate recoil. Games that implement force feedback well are much more immersive than games that do not.

ALTERNATIVES:
KEYBOARD & MOUSE

Thousands. Well, hundreds anyway. Personal preference is the most important factor in choosing a keyboard, mouse, game controller, display, or other I/O peripheral. What we hate you may love, and vice versa. For a cordless or corded mouse or keyboard, we suggest you try a Logitech model first. If you don't like it, exchange it for a similar model from Microsoft.

187

The first step is to decide which type or types of game controller you need, which is determined by the types of games you play. For example, we play mostly flight simulation and air combat games, so our primary controller is a joystick. For first-person shooter (FPS) games, most people consider a gamepad to be the optimum controller. For racing games, you'll want a wheel game controller. Although different types of controllers can substitute for each other to some extent, using an inappropriate game controller can put you at a severe disadvantage relative to players who are using controllers better suited to the type of game being played.

Once you determine which types of game controller you need, decide how to allocate your budget among them. If you regularly play games that require all three types of game controller, allocate your budget evenhandedly among them. That doesn't mean spending a third of your budget on each, because different types of controllers have different price points. It does mean you should buy all three high-end, all three midrange, or all three low-end, depending on your budget. When you play a racing game, for example, a $70 wheel controller is better than a $250 joystick. On the other hand, if you spend most of your time playing flight sims, play FPS games occasionally, and never play racing games, put most of your budget into the joystick and spend whatever is left on a decent gamepad. And so on.

Before you buy a game controller, see if you can play with someone else's for at least a short session. If you ask nicely, most gamers are happy to let you try their rigs. Of course, the flip side is that if you do buy that $250 joystick, you can expect to be very popular at LAN parties.

Speakers and headphones

Logitech Z-680 speaker system (*http://www.logitech.com*)
Zalman ZM-RS6F 5.1 Surround Headphones (*http://www.zalman.co.kr*)

A kick-ass gaming system needs kick-ass speakers, and the Logitech Z-680 5.1 speaker system is the best we know of for the purpose. With four 62W RMS satellite speakers, a 69W center-channel speaker, and a 188W sub-woofer, the Z-680 produces a wall-rattling 505W RMS. You don't just *hear* the bass, you *feel* the bass vibrating your internal organs. Nor is the Z-680 limited to gaming. At lower volume, it's also excellent for anything from listening to background music to playing DVDs.

As nice as the Logitech Z-680 is, it's overkill for a LAN party, not to mention for playing games at home while the spousal unit is trying to sleep. For those situations, you need headphones, and the Zalman ZM-RSF6F 5.1 Surround Headphones are the best we know of for gaming. They're light, they're durable enough to stand up to LAN party use, they fold up into a self-contained unit, and their three-meter cord gives you plenty of slack to move around.

The Zalman headphones use three separate drivers per ear to produce a surround sound field comparable to that provided by a 5.1 speaker system. The importance of positional audio may not be apparent at first glance, but it can mean the difference between winning and losing. When you play an FPS like UT2004, knowing where your opponents are is critical. Stereo headphones just don't cut it. By the time you figure out where shots are coming from, you're dead meat. The Zalman headphones make it easy to discriminate not just left and right but front and rear. The difference is amazing.

Displays

NEC MultiSync FP912SB 19" CRT (http://www.necmitsubishi.com)
ViewSonic P225f 22" CRT (http://www.viewsonic.com)
Samsung 152T 15" FPD (http://www.samsung.com)

Choosing a display is a major conundrum for a LAN partier. On the one hand, we want a big, sharp display, but on the other hand, we need portability. Ideally, the display should be affordable as well. Traditional CRT monitors meet the big, sharp, and affordable criteria, but they are also heavy, fragile, and awkward to carry around.

The obvious answer is a flat-panel display (FPD), which meets the portability requirement, but unfortunately a large, affordable FPD is an oxymoron. Worse still, while CRTs respond instantly as the image changes, FPD latency causes smearing and ghosting, especially at high frame rates. Inexpensive FPDs are simply unusable for fast-motion video, including gaming, while even the costliest FPDs are marginal for many games. Many LAN partiers conclude that the best solution is to buy a 19" or larger CRT for home use and an FPD for road trips.

The NEC MultiSync FP912SB is the 19" CRT we recommend. It supports high refresh rates at high resolutions. The colors are deep and saturated, the contrast is superb, and the images are as bright as you'll find in any CRT display.

If 19" isn't large enough, consider the 22" ViewSonic P225f. In the past, we rated ViewSonic as a second-tier monitor maker, but since their acquisition of Nokia's monitor business and engineering talent, high-end ViewSonic monitors are now as good as any available. With a street price over $500, the P225f ain't cheap, but it runs up to 2048 × 1536 at 79 Hz and has superb display quality. It doesn't quite require a forklift to move it, but given its size and weight you're unlikely to schlep it to LAN parties.

For an FPD, we think a 15" unit is the best choice in terms of price and portability. A 15" FPD provides an image only a bit smaller than a 17" CRT, which is acceptable if not optimum for many games. Good 15" FPDs aren't cheap by any means. You'll pay more for a 15" FPD fast enough for gaming

ALTERNATIVES: SPEAKERS & HEADPHONES

We had a hard time choosing between the Logitech Z-680 and the Klipsch ProMedia 5.1, which costs $100 or so more. Both are excellent for music and gaming. On balance, we slightly prefer the Z-680 for gaming and give the nod to the ProMedia 5.1 for music. If those options are a bit rich for your taste, go for the Logitech Z-5300, a 280W RMS 5.1 speaker system that sells for half the price of the Z-680.

We've found nothing we like nearly as much as Zalman ZM-RSF6F headphones for gaming. The bad news is that these are not general-purpose headphones. The bass is weak, although for gaming that is more than made up for by the excellent 3D imaging. Used for music and other stereo sources or for DVDs, the Zalman headphones boom and echo pretty badly. For general-purpose listening, buy a decent set of Grado or Sennheiser headphones.

Whatever floats your boat. As for other input/output peripherals, the choice of display is a very personal decision. We recommend a midrange or better 19" CRT from a first-tier maker for use at home. Any but the least expensive models from Hitachi, NEC/Mitsubishi, or ViewSonic is adequate. If you can't afford a good FPD, the best bet for road trips is a "disposable" CRT. Our favorite in that class is the NEC AccuSync AS700, which we've seen on sale for less than $125. If (when) you drop it, at least you won't be out much money.

than you would for a superb 19" CRT. It's difficult to choose a specific 15" FPD because none of them is perfect. On balance, we think the Samsung 152T is the best choice.

Although the 152T has been around for a while and its 25 millisecond pixel response time is slower than the fastest 20 ms and 16 ms units, we think the 152T still provides an excellent balance of price, image quality, and portability for a 15" gaming FPD. It runs 1024 × 768 resolution natively. Its brightness is rated at 330 nit, which is comparable to the brightest CRT monitors, and its 600:1 contrast ratio is excellent. It includes both standard analog VGA and DVI-D connectors, and so can be used with nearly any video adapter. It folds up for transport, and at less than seven pounds doesn't add much burden to a LAN partier's kit.

Component summary

Table 5-2 summarizes our component choices for the Kick-Ass LAN Party PC system.

Table 5-2. Bill of Materials for LPPC

Component	Product
Case	Antec Super LANBOY
Power supply	Antec TrueControl 550
Motherboard	Intel D875PBZ
Processor	Intel Pentium 4/3.4 Extreme Edition
CPU cooler	Dynatron D25
Memory	Crucial PC3200 DDR-SDRAM (two 512 MB DIMMs)
Video adapter	ATi RADEON 9800 XT
Sound adapter	Turtle Beach Santa Cruz
Hard drive	Maxtor DiamondMax Plus 9 160 GB ATA-133
ATA cable	Antec UV Cobra IDE cable
Optical drive	Plextor PX-708A DVD writer
Home keyboard and mouse	Logitech Cordless MX Duo
Away keyboard	Hampton Technologies Zippy EL-715 illuminated keyboard
Away mouse	Logitech MX 500 corded optical mouse
Game controller (joystick)	Thrustmaster HOTAS Cougar
Game controller (gamepad)	Logitech WingMan Rumblepad
Game controller (wheel)	Logitech MOMO Racing Force Feedback Wheel
Speakers	Logitech Z-680 5.1 speaker system
Headphones	Zalman ZM-RS6F Surround Headphones
Display (CRT monitor)	NEC MultiSync FP912SB 19" or ViewSonic P225f 22"
Flat-panel display	Samsung 152T 15"

Building the System

Figure 5-1 shows the major components of the Kick-Ass LAN Party PC. The Intel D875PBZ motherboard is in front of the Antec Super LANBOY case. Top row, left to right, are the Logitech Rumblepad game controller, the Turtle Beach Santa Cruz sound card, and the Antec TrueControl 550 power supply, with the Logitech Cordless MX Duo and the Plextor PX-708A DVD burner immediately beneath them. Center are the Maxtor DiamondMax Plus 9 hard drive and the ATi RADEON 9800 XT video adapter, with various LED fans and cables in front. The Pentium 4 Extreme Edition processor and the Crucial PC3200 memory modules are not shown.

We planned to build this system two ways, using a Sound Blaster Audigy 2 ZS in one version and a Turtle Beach Santa Cruz in the other. That would have allowed us to compare the two side by side for features, audio quality, and compatibility. But when we started to build the system, we couldn't find the Audigy 2 card. Robert says the card was misplaced (note the passive voice). Barbara says Robert lost it (note the very active voice). To promote domestic tranquility, Robert went for Plan B, blaming our younger border collie, Malcolm, who has been spotted in the past carrying around optical drives and other PC components in his mouth. We haven't found his cache yet.

We weren't about to buy another Audigy 2 ZS, so we built only the version with the Turtle Beach sound card. The Santa Cruz is an oldie but a goodie. The sound quality is superb, better than the Audigy 2 and better even than the M-Audio Revolution 7.1, which we have used on other systems. The Santa Cruz isn't as good a dedicated gaming sound card as the Audigy 2, but we actually prefer it overall. And it works with Linux.

Before you start building the system, verify that all components are present and accounted for. We always remind readers to do that, but for some reason always forget to do it ourselves.

Figure 5-1. Kick-Ass LAN Party PC components, awaiting construction

Although by necessity we describe building the system in a particular order, you don't need to follow that exact sequence when you build your own system. Some steps—for example, installing the processor and memory before installing the motherboard in the case—should be taken in the sequence we describe, because doing otherwise makes the task more difficult or risks damaging a component. Other steps—such as installing the video adapter after you install the motherboard in the case—must be taken in the order we describe, because completing one step is a prerequisite for completing another. But the exact sequence doesn't matter for most steps. As you build your system, it will be obvious when sequence matters.

Preparing the case

Before you do anything else, verify that the power supply is set to the correct input voltage. Some power supplies set themselves automatically. Others, including the Antec TrueControl 550 power supply we chose for this system, must be set manually. Check the position of the slide switch to make sure it's set for the correct voltage, as shown in Figure 5-2.

Figure 5-2. Verify that the power supply is set for the proper input voltage

---

WARNING

If you connect a power supply set for 230V to a 115V receptacle, no harm is done. The PC components receive half the voltage they require, and the system won't boot. But if you connect a power supply set for 115V to a 230V receptacle, the PC components receive *twice* the voltage they're designed to use. If you power up the system, that overvoltage destroys the system instantly in clouds of smoke and showers of sparks.

After you verify that the power supply is set correctly, remove the four thumbscrews, two per side, that secure the two side panels, as shown in Figure 5-3. Grasp the handle on each side panel and pull it to the rear until the panel slides off.

Ordinarily, we wouldn't remove the right-side panel, but Antec ships the Super LANBOY case with various items secured to the motherboard tray using long wire twist ties threaded through multiple holes. Rather than attempting to pull these twist ties through the motherboard tray, it's easier just to remove the second side panel and pull out the twist ties from the rear. Once

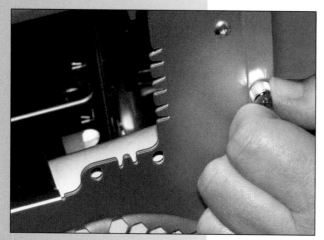

Figure 5-3. Remove the shipping screws

you've removed all the twist ties, reinstall the right-side panel and reinsert the two thumbscrews that secure it.

WARNING

Be careful when working on the Antec Super LANBOY case. It is robust for an aluminum case, but aluminum panels are inherently more fragile than the usual steel panels. It's easy to bend the panels or the chassis if you apply too much pressure.

When we started working on the Super LANBOY case, we were convinced that Antec had forgotten to include the usual package of screws, standoffs, and other small fasteners. Not so. They just hid them, which we'd have discovered sooner if we'd bothered to read the manual. To locate the fastener package, swing open the front bezel and locate the parts box, shown in Figure 5-4. Press and release the front of the box to release the catch, and then slide the parts box out of the chassis. Remove the sliding lid from the parts box and retrieve the package of fasteners, which you'll need soon.

Figure 5-4. Press to release the catch and slide the parts box out

---

At first, we thought the embedded parts box was simply a gimmick, but as we thought about it we realized that it's actually quite useful in a portable LAN Party PC. It's large enough to hold a selection of spare parts and small tools, which may come in handy when you're on the road. To prevent rattling, we inserted a piece of foam rubber on top of the tools and small parts we carry in the parts box.

Unlike many cases, the Antec Super LANBOY does not include a power supply. That means you don't have to pay for a power supply that may be useless to you. This system is heavily loaded, with a fast processor and video adapter, so we wanted a high-capacity power supply. We chose the Antec TrueControl 550, which provides front-panel control of voltages and fan speeds. Just the thing to make your LAN party buddies drool with envy.

To install the power supply, slide it into position from inside the case, as shown in Figure 5-5, placing it atop the shelf at the bottom of the cutout.

Figure 5-5. Slide the power supply into place

Hold the power supply in place with one hand while you drive at least one screw to hold it in place temporarily. Use the larger hex-head screws, four of which are provided in the parts bag. Once the power supply is aligned properly, drive the remaining screws to secure it completely, as shown in Figure 5-6.

Figure 5-6. Secure the power supply with the four screws provided

The Antec TrueControl 550 power supply has a busier rear panel than most power supplies. In addition to the standard fan, mains power connector, and voltage selector switch, the TrueControl 550 provides a manual on/off switch (just above the voltage selector switch) and a connector that can be used to provide +5V and +12V to external devices (between the manual on/off switch and the fan). Frankly, we're not sure what we'd connect here, but it certainly doesn't hurt to have it.

Nearly every case, including the Antec Super LANBOY, comes with an I/O template. So do most motherboards. The I/O template supplied with the case seldom fits the I/O panel of whatever motherboard you are using, so you need to remove the stock I/O template and replace it with the one supplied with the motherboard.

When we swap I/O templates, we usually worry about bending the template. With the Super LANBOY, we worried about bending the case. That's not a criticism of the Super LANBOY, which is very sturdy as aluminum cases go. Aluminum is much weaker than steel, and aluminum cases use very thin construction. Take extreme pains when you remove the old template and install the new one. If you're going to bend something, be sure it's the template rather than the case.

We played around for some time trying to determine the best way to remove the template without overflexing the case. Eventually, we decided that the safest method was to use a tool handle to press gently on the outside of the template, as shown in Figure 5-7, while maintaining counter-pressure with our fingers from inside the case in the area nearest to where we were applying pressure to the template.

Figure 5-7. Remove the I/O template supplied with the case

Most motherboards, including the Intel D875PBZ, include a custom ATX I/O template designed to match the motherboard I/O panel. Before you install the custom I/O template, compare it to the motherboard I/O panel to make sure the holes in the template correspond to the connectors on the motherboard.

Once you've done that, press the custom I/O template into place. Working from inside the case, align the bottom, right, and left edges of the I/O template with the matching case cutout. When the I/O template is positioned properly, press gently along the edges to seat it in the cutout, as shown in Figure 5-8. It should snap into place, although getting it to seat properly sometimes requires several attempts. It's often helpful to press gently against the edge of the template with the handle of a screwdriver or nut driver.

Figure 5-8. Snap the custom I/O template into place

WARNING

Again, be very careful not to bend the case when you seat the I/O template. Apply counter-pressure with a finger from outside the case as you press the template into place from inside the case, as shown in Figure 5-8.

After you install the I/O template, carefully slide the motherboard into place, making sure that the back panel connectors on the motherboard are firmly in contact with the corresponding holes on the I/O template. Compare the positions of the motherboard mounting holes with the standoff mounting positions in the case.

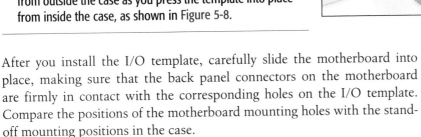

If you simply look at the motherboard, it's easy to miss one of the mounting holes in all the clutter. If you hold the motherboard up to a light, the mounting holes stand out distinctly.

The Intel D875PBZ motherboard has ten mounting holes. The Antec Super LANBOY, unlike most cases, arrives with no standoffs preinstalled. Count out the ten brass standoffs you need from the parts package and set them aside. Install all ten standoffs, making sure that each motherboard mounting hole has a corresponding standoff installed, and that each standoff corresponds to a mounting hole.

WARNING

If your case comes with preinstalled brass standoffs, make absolutely certain that each standoff matches a motherboard mounting hole. If you find one that doesn't, remove it. Leaving an "extra" standoff in place may cause a short circuit that could damage the motherboard and/or other components. One of our technical reviewers suggests a good method. After you locate the motherboard mounting holes, place the motherboard in position in the case and insert a felt-tip pen through each hole in turn to mark the hole positions on the motherboard tray that require a standoff.

Although you can screw in the standoffs using your fingers or needlenose pliers, it's much easier and faster to use a 5mm nut driver, as shown in Figure 5-9. Tighten the standoffs finger-tight, but do not overtighten them. It's easy to strip the threads by applying too much torque with a nut driver.

WARNING

Be very careful when installing standoffs. The Antec Super LANBOY has a thin aluminum motherboard tray. Aluminum is very soft, softer even than brass. It's extremely easy to strip a screw-hole if you apply too much pressure when installing the standoffs. Tighten the standoffs down only until you start to feel resistance.

Figure 5-9. Install a brass standoff in each mounting position

Once you've installed all the standoffs, verify that each motherboard mounting hole has a corresponding standoff and that each standoff has a corresponding mounting hole. As a final check, hold the motherboard in position above the case, as shown in Figure 5-10, and look down through each motherboard mounting hole to make sure there's a standoff installed below it.

Preparing and populating the motherboard

It is always easier to prepare and populate the motherboard (i.e., install the processor and memory) while the motherboard is outside the case. In fact, you must do so with some systems, because installing the heatsink/fan unit requires access to both sides of the motherboard. Even if it is possible to populate the motherboard while it is installed in the case, we always recommend that you have the motherboard outside the case and lying flat on the work surface. More than once, we've tried to save a few minutes by replacing the processor without removing the motherboard. Too often, the result has been bent pins and a destroyed processor.

Figure 5-10. Verify that a standoff is installed for each motherboard mounting hole and that no extra standoffs are installed

---

WARNING

Each time you handle the processor, memory, or other static-sensitive components, first touch the power supply to ground yourself. The system needn't be plugged in for this to be effective. The mass of the power supply itself provides a sufficient sink for static electricity charges.

Preparing the motherboard

Intel Socket 478 motherboards include a standard heat-sink/fan retaining bracket that fits HSF units supplied by Intel as well as many third-party HSF units. The Dynatron D25 heatsink/fan unit we chose uses its own bracket, which is better than the standard Intel bracket. This means that you must remove the standard Intel bracket; to do so, use a small flat-blade screwdriver to lift the four white posts, as shown in Figure 5-11.

> We detail the process of installing the Dynatron heat-sink/fan unit and its retaining bracket because this is the HSF we recommend if you use an OEM CPU rather than a retail-boxed model. If you use a retail-boxed CPU, the supplied HSF simply snaps into place in the standard Intel retaining bracket.

Figure 5-11. Lift the white plastic posts to release the standard bracket

Figure 5-12. With the posts raised, pull up gently to remove the standard bracket

Lifting the posts releases the pressure on the plastic expansion clamps on the underside of the motherboard. With all four posts raised as far as possible, grasp the standard bracket and pull straight up to release it, as shown in Figure 5-12. If the bracket does not pull free easily, use the flat part of the screwdriver blade to press gently on the expansion clamps from the back side of the motherboard until they release.

The Dynatron HSF includes a metal baseplate that mounts beneath the motherboard. The baseplate includes four threaded mounting posts that protrude through the mounting holes and provide a place to secure the Dynatron HSF. To mount the Dynatron base-plate, turn the motherboard over, align the threaded mounting studs with the mounting holes, and press the baseplate into place, as shown in Figure 5-13. With some motherboards, including the Intel D875PBZ we used, the baseplate fits snugly and stays in place against its own weight. With others, the baseplate is a loose fit, so you'll need to support its weight as you turn the motherboard face up, or the baseplate will drop out.

Figure 5-13. Working from the bottom of the motherboard, press the Dynatron baseplate into position

Figure 5-14. Lift the socket lever to prepare the socket to receive the processor

Figure 5-15. Drop the processor into place

Figure 5-16. Press down the ZIF lever to lock the processor into the socket

Installing the processor

To install the Pentium 4 processor, lift the arm of the ZIF (zero insertion force) socket until it reaches vertical, as shown in Figure 5-14. With the arm vertical, there is no clamping force on the socket holes, which allows the processor to drop into place without requiring any pressure.

Pin 1 is indicated on the processor and socket by a small triangle. With the socket lever vertical, align pin 1 of the processor with pin 1 of the socket and drop the processor into place, as shown in Figure 5-15. The processor should seat flush with the socket just from the force of gravity, or perhaps with very gentle pressure. If the processor resists being seated, something is misaligned. Remove the processor and verify that it is aligned properly and that the pattern of pins on the processor corresponds to the pattern of holes on the socket. *Never* force the processor to seat. You'll bend one or more pins, destroying the processor.

With the processor in place and seated flush with the socket, press the lever arm down and snap it into place, as shown in Figure 5-16. You may have to press the lever arm slightly away from the socket to allow it to snap into a locked position.

> Sometimes closing the ZIF lever lifts the processor slightly out of the socket. Once the processor is fully seated, it does no harm to use gentle pressure to keep it in place as you close the ZIF lever.

Installing the heatsink/fan (HSF)

Modern processors draw from 50W to more than 100W of power. Our Pentium 4 Extreme Edition is on the high end of the power consumption curve, and must dissipate the resulting heat over the surface of its heat spreader, which is about the size of a large postage stamp. Without a good heatsink/fan (HSF) unit, the processor would almost instantaneously shut itself down to prevent damage from overheating.

WARNING

Using a proper HSF is critical. Retail-boxed processors include an adequate HSF. If you buy an OEM processor, you must choose an HSF that allows the processor to operate within its acceptable temperature range. An HSF that fits the processor may or may not be usable. Faster processors consume more power and generate more heat. An HSF rated for a Pentium 4/2.4 physically fits a Pentium 4/3.4, but does not cool the faster processor adequately. HSFs designed for faster processors are generally larger, heavier, have more powerful fans, and cost more than HSFs designed for slower processors. The Dynatron D25 unit we used is rated for up to the 3.4 GHz Pentium 4 Extreme Edition.

To install the HSF unit, begin by polishing the heat spreader surface on top of the processor with a paper towel or soft cloth, as shown in Figure 5-17. The goal is to remove any grease, grit, or other material that might prevent the heatsink from making intimate contact with the processor surface.

As long as you're polishing, check the surface of the heatsink. If the heatsink base is bare, that means it's intended to be used with thermal compound, usually called "thermal goop." In that case, also polish the heatsink base. Some heatsinks have a square or rectangular pad made of a phase-change medium, which is a fancy term for a material that melts as the CPU heats and resolidifies as the CPU cools. This liquid/solid cycle ensures that the processor die maintains good thermal contact with the heatsink. If your heatsink includes such a pad, you needn't polish the base of the heatsink. (Heatsinks use *either* a thermal pad *or* thermal goop, not both.)

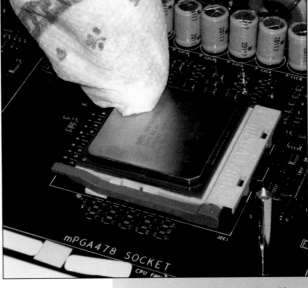

Figure 5-17. Polish the processor with a paper towel before installing the HSF

Although we really like the Dynatron D25 cooler, we can't say as much for the thermal goop supplied with it. Rather than the usual syringe or snip-top, squeezable plastic bag of thermal compound, the D25 included a small resealable plastic bag with a glop of thermal compound spread all over the inside. The compound itself looked like gray mud, and showed signs of drying soon after we applied it to the processor. We went ahead and used it, although we'll probably replace it with Antec Silver Thermal Compound the next time we remove the processor.

The Dynatron D25 we used was an early engineering sample that Dynatron sent directly to us. It may be that production models will include a superior thermal compound, or at least better packaging. If not, we suggest you discard the bundled thermal compound and use Antec Silver Thermal Compound or a similar product instead.

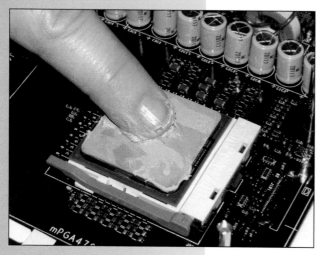

Figure 5-18. Apply the provided thermal compound

To apply the thermal compound, use your fingertip to spread a thin, even coating of compound over the entire surface of the processor die or heat spreader, as shown in Figure 5-18. Try to avoid letting compound run down over the edge of the processor. Best practice is to use a rubber glove or plastic bag to prevent skin oils from being deposited on the surface of the processor, but we've never bothered doing that and have never had a problem. Besides, applying the compound with a naked fingertip recalls the joy we had making mud pies when we were kids. Be careful, though. Some thermal compounds, particularly silver-based ones, are difficult to remove from clothes, fingers, and anything else they come into contact with.

CAUTION

Our editor comments that he has used thermal compound that was labeled as toxic and a skin irritant, and suggests that using rubber gloves is a good idea. By all means do so if you are at all concerned with safety.

WARNING

If you ever remove the heatsink, don't reuse the old thermal compound or pad when you reinstall it. Remove all remnants of the old thermal compound or pad, using a hair dryer or solvent if necessary, and reapply new thermal compound before you reinstall the heatsink.

Orient the HSF above the processor and slide it down over the mounting posts until it seats fully, as shown in Figure 5-19. Press down gently and wiggle the heatsink to make sure that the thermal compound is spread evenly over its base and the surface of the processor heat spreader.

Figure 5-19. Align the HSF unit over the processor and seat it

The Dynatron D25 heatsink can be installed in only two ways because its mounting holes form a rectangle rather than a square. We dithered for quite some time about which way to orient it; we didn't know if the fan blew or sucked, and even if we had it wasn't clear whether we'd be better off in one orientation or the other. Therefore, we plan to take temperature readings with the heatsink in the (random) orientation we chose.

Later, we'll remove it, reverse the orientation, and take more temperature readings. It probably won't make any difference at all, but we're anal that way.

With the HSF resting in position, the next step is to install the four screws that secure the heatsink to its mounting posts. The Dynatron D25 uses a unique mounting method. Rather than the usual cammed clamps, the D25 uses spring-loaded screws to provide the clamping force needed to ensure intimate contact between the heatsink base and the processor heat spreader.

To secure the D25, drop a spring into position over each mounting bracket post. Place the included washer on each screw and then drive the screw into place, as shown in Figure 5-20. To make sure the pressure is evenly applied, drive the four screws as you would install nuts when changing a tire. That is, tighten each screw only partially, and then alternate tightening the four screws in a diagonal sequence until all four are seated tightly.

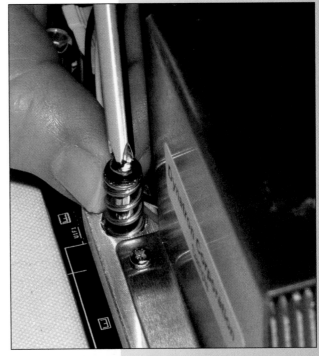

Figure 5-20. Secure the heatsink by driving screws into the four posts

The thermal mass of the heatsink draws heat away from the CPU, but the heat must be dissipated to prevent the CPU from eventually overheating as the heatsink warms up. To dispose of excess heat as it is transferred to the heatsink, most CPU coolers use a small muffin fan to continuously draw air through the fins of the heatsink. Some CPU fans use a drive power connector, but most are designed to attach to a dedicated CPU fan connector on the motherboard. Using a motherboard fan power connector allows the motherboard to control the CPU fan, reducing speed for quieter operation when the processor is running under light load and not generating much heat, and increasing fan speed when the processor is running under heavy load and generating more heat. The motherboard can also monitor fan speed, which allows it to send an alert to the user if the fan fails or begins running sporadically.

To connect the CPU fan, locate the three-pin header connector on the motherboard labeled CPU Fan and plug the keyed cable from the CPU fan into it, as shown in Figure 5-21.

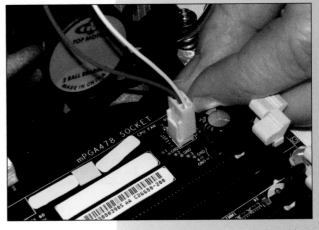

Figure 5-21. Connect the CPU fan cable to the CPU fan connector

Installing the memory

Installing memory is easy enough, but you need to install memory modules properly for the best performance. The dual-channel memory controller on the Intel D875PBZ motherboard provides better memory performance than a single-channel controller, but the motherboard defaults to single-channel mode unless you install memory modules in the proper slots.

The D875PBZ has four DIMM slots in two pairs. The slot nearest the processor is Channel A DIMM0, followed by Channel A DIMM1, Channel B DIMM0, and Channel B DIMM1. To enable dual-channel operation, one module must be installed in Channel A and the other in Channel B. Best practice is to install modules in the lowest-numbered slot first, leaving higher-numbered slots unpopulated, so we installed our two DIMMs in the first (DIMM0) slot of each channel.

To install a DIMM, pivot the locking tabs on both sides of the DIMM socket outward. Align the DIMM, making sure that the keying notch in the DIMM is oriented properly with the keying tab in the slot. Once the DIMM is aligned and vertical relative to the slot, use both thumbs to press down firmly until the DIMM seats, as shown in Figure 5-22. Both locking tabs should automatically pivot back into the locked position, engaging the notches in the side of the DIMM. If the tabs don't fully engage the notches, press the tabs into place manually. Install the second DIMM in the Channel B DIMM0 slot in the same manner.

Figure 5-22. Align the DIMM with the socket and press firmly until it seats

With the processor and memory installed, you're almost ready to install the motherboard in the case. Before you do that, though, check the motherboard documentation to determine if any configuration jumpers need to be set. The Intel D875PBZ has only one jumper, which sets operating mode and is located near the center of the front edge of the motherboard. (Look for the blue plastic jumper block with a small tab for a handle.) By default, the jumper is set to Normal mode, with pins 1 and 2 connected. The first time you start the system, the jumper must be set to Configure mode, with pins 2 and 3 connected. It's easier to set the jumper before you install the motherboard, so do so before you proceed to the next step.

One of our technical reviewers who builds many Intel systems himself notes that he never changes the configuration jumper from the default 1-2 (Normal) position, and that in his experience Intel motherboards automatically detect and set the proper processor speed and FSB settings with the configuration jumper set to Normal mode.

We have gotten in the habit of setting that jumper to Configure mode each time we set up a new system. It may be necessary in our case because most of the Intel processors we use are engineering samples, which are not multiplier-locked and can therefore be set to any supported core clock speed and multiplier setting that are within the ability of the processor to run. Standard retail-boxed and OEM Intel processors are multiplier-locked. With such a processor, changing the jumper may be superfluous. We still recommend setting the jumper to Configure for the initial boot and changing it to Normal later, because it does no harm and may at times be necessary.

Installing the motherboard

Installing the motherboard is the most time-consuming step in building this system because there are so many cables to connect. It's important to get them all connected right, so take your time and verify each connection before and after you make it.

Seating and securing the motherboard

To begin, slide the motherboard into the case, as shown in Figure 5-23. Carefully align the back-panel I/O connectors with the corresponding holes in the I/O template, and slide the motherboard toward the rear of the case until the motherboard mounting holes line up with the standoffs you installed earlier.

Figure 5-23. Slide the motherboard into position

Before you secure the motherboard, verify that the back-panel I/O connectors mate properly with the I/O template, as shown in Figure 5-24. The I/O template has metal tabs that ground the back-panel I/O connectors. Make sure none of these tabs intrudes into a port connector. An errant tab at best blocks the port, rendering it unusable, and at worst may short out the motherboard.

After you position the motherboard and verify that the back-panel I/O connectors mate cleanly with the I/O template, insert a screw through one mounting hole into the corresponding standoff. You may need to apply pressure to keep the motherboard positioned properly until you have inserted two or three screws.

Figure 5-24. Verify that the back-panel connectors mate cleanly with the I/O template

Figure 5-25. Install screws in all mounting holes to secure the motherboard

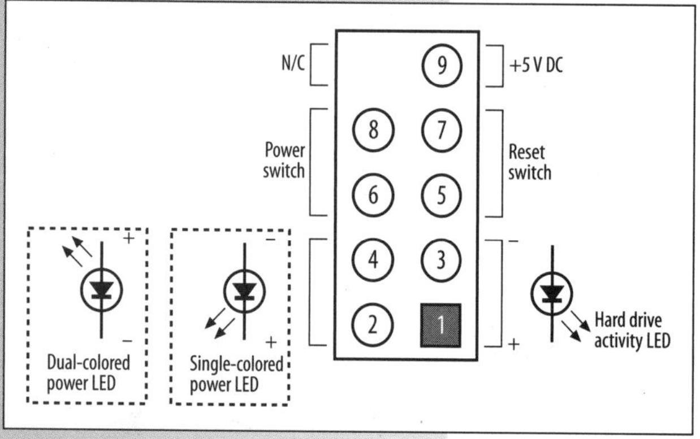

Figure 5-26. Front-panel connector pinouts (original graphic courtesy Intel Corporation)

If you have trouble getting all the holes and standoffs aligned, insert two screws but don't tighten them completely. Use one hand to press the motherboard into alignment, with all holes matching the standoffs. Then insert one or two more screws and tighten them completely. Finish mounting the motherboard by inserting screws into all standoffs and tightening them, as shown in Figure 5-25.

WARNING

When you install motherboard mounting screws, you're also putting torque on the standoffs. Tighten the motherboard screws gently, using a standard screwdriver. When you feel tension, stop turning the driver. The Antec Super LANBOY case is made of very soft aluminum, and if you overtorque the mounting screws, you're also overtorquing the standoffs, which will strip the motherboard tray threads. Don't even think about using a power screwdriver with an aluminum case.

Connecting the front-panel switch and indicator cables

Once the motherboard is secured, the next step is to connect the front-panel switch and indicator cables to the motherboard. Before you begin, examine the front-panel cables. Each is labeled descriptively, e.g., "Power," "Reset," and "H.D.D. LED." Match the descriptions with the front-panel connector pins on the motherboard to make sure you connect the correct cable to the appropriate pins. Figure 5-26 shows the pin assignments for the power switch, reset switch, power LED, and hard drive activity LED connectors.

It may be easier to connect the front-panel switch/indicator cables and the front-panel USB cables before you install the motherboard in the case. The tradeoff is that if you install the motherboard first, you have plenty of cable length, but the pins to which you must connect those cables are deep in the case and hard to get to. If you install the cables first, the pins are more easily accessible, but you have very little cable slack to work with, both when you connect the cables and when you slide the motherboard into the case.

Be sure to note the following:

- The power switch and reset switch connectors are not polarized, and can be connected in either orientation.

- The hard drive activity LED is polarized, and should be connected with the ground (white) wire on pin 3 and the signal (red) wire on pin 1.

The ground/common connection usually uses black wire. Apparently, Antec had a surplus of white wire when they built these cases, because that's what they used for ground/common on most of the front-panel cables.

- There are two power LED connectors on the Intel motherboard: one on the main front-panel connector block that accepts a two-position power LED cable, and a supplementary power LED connector adjacent to the main front-panel connector block that accepts a three-position power LED cable with wires in positions 1 and 3 (the latter being the type of power LED cable supplied with the Antec Super LANBOY case). The power LED connectors are dual-polarized and can support a single-color (usually green) power LED, as is provided with the Antec Super LANBOY case, or a dual-color (usually green/yellow) LED. For the Super LANBOY, connect the green wire to pin 1 on the supplementary power LED connector and the white wire to pin 3. If you are using a case that has a two-wire power LED cable and/or a dual-color power LED, check the case documentation to determine where and how to connect the Power LED cable.

Once you determine the proper orientation for each cable, connect the power switch, reset switch, power LED, and hard drive activity LED, as shown in Figure 5-27. Not all cases have cables for every connector on the motherboard, and not all motherboards have connectors for all cables provided by the case. For example, the Antec Super LANBOY case provides a speaker cable and a turbo LED cable. The Intel D875PBZ motherboard has a built-in speaker but no connectors for an external speaker or a turbo LED, so those cables go unused. Conversely, the D875PBZ has a chassis intrusion connector for which no corresponding cable exists on the Antec Super LANBOY case, so that connector goes unused.

When you're connecting front-panel cables, try to get it right the first time, but don't worry too much about getting it wrong. Other than the power switch cable, which must be connected properly for the system to start,

There Is a Standard, but...

Although Intel has defined a standard front-panel connector block and uses that standard for its own motherboards, few other motherboard makers adhere to that standard. Accordingly, rather than provide an Intel-standard monolithic connector block that would be useless for motherboards that do not follow the Intel standard, most case makers, including Antec, provide individual one-, two-, or three-pin connectors for each switch and indicator.

Figure 5-27. Connect the front-panel switch and indicator cables

Building the System

none of the other front-panel switch and indicator cables is essential, and connecting them wrong won't damage the system. Switch cables—power and reset—are not polarized. You can connect them in either orientation without worrying about which pin is signal and which is ground. LED cables may or may not be polarized, but if you connect a polarized LED cable backward, the worst that will happen is that the LED won't light.

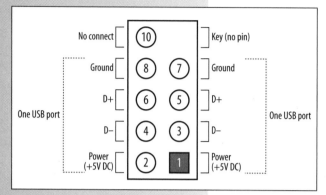

Figure 5-28. Front-panel USB connector pinouts (original graphic courtesy Intel Corporation)

Connecting the front-panel USB ports

The Antec Super LANBOY case provides two front-panel USB 2.0 ports, for which the Intel D875PBZ motherboard provides corresponding internal connectors. To route USB to the front panel, you must connect a cable from each front-panel USB port to the corresponding internal connector. Figure 5-28 shows the pin assignments for the dual front-panel internal USB connectors.

Some Antec cases, including the Overture case we used for the Home Theater PC, provide a monolithic ten-pin USB connector, which mates to motherboard USB header pins that use the standard Intel layout. With such a case, connecting the front-panel USB ports is a simple matter of plugging that monolithic connector into the header pins on the motherboard. Unfortunately, the Antec Super LANBOY front-panel USB connector cable provides ten individual wires, each with a single connector, although only eight of those wires are needed. Figure 5-29 shows Barbara sliding the eighth and final connector onto the proper pin.

Figure 5-29. Connect the front-panel USB cables

Getting those eight individual wires connected isn't easy. We tried connecting them one by one, both with our fingers and with bent-nose pliers. The problem with that method is that the individual wires are contained in a sheath, without much slack. When you get one wire on its pin, maneuvering the next wire into place tends to pull loose the one you just got seated.

The best way we found to get all the wires connected was to align the four wires as though they were a single connector, clamp them into position with our fingers, and then slide the connectors onto the header pins as a group. And even then we had problems. In Figure 5-29, Barbara is actually reinserting the ground wire, which had popped loose because it had less slack than the others.

206

Chapter 5, Building a Kick-Ass LAN Party PC

One of our technical reviewers suggests another method. Line up all eight of the individual connectors and hold them in place with your fingers. Slip a cable tie around them and tighten it sufficiently to hold the connectors in position. While you still have a bit of slack, press the group of connectors against a flat surface to square them up, and use your needlenose pliers to finish tightening the tie wrap to create a "monolithic block" that's more or less permanent. If you ever need to install a motherboard with a different pin arrangement in the case, you can simply snip the tie wrap and repeat the process.

A USB connection requires four wires. For some reason known only to Antec, the Super LANBOY case provides five wires for each of the two USB connections, ten wires total. Two of the wires in each group of five are black ground wires, one labeled "GND" and one "Ground 2." You can connect either one to the ground pin and leave the other unconnected. Working from the front of the motherboard toward the rear, the individual wires are as follows:

+5V (red wire) to pin 1 (first USB port) and pin 2 (second USB port)
D- (white wire) to pin 3 (first USB port) and pin 4 (second USB port)
D+ (green wire) to pin 5 (first USB port) and pin 6 (second USB port)
Ground (black wire) to pin 7 (first USB port) and pin 8 (second USB port)

Pin 9 is not present on the connector to provide keying. Pin 10 is present but not connected.

Connecting the front fan and setting the BIOS configuration jumper

As long as you're in the vicinity, you might as well connect the power cable for the front case fan and set the BIOS configuration jumper now. Locate the fan power header at the front edge of the motherboard, between the BIOS configuration jumper and the ATA connectors. Locate the front case fan power cable, which is bundled with the front-panel cables. Orient the keyed connector properly relative to the motherboard header pins, and press the connector into place, as shown in Figure 5-30.

The BIOS configuration jumper is visible in Figure 5-30 immediately to the right of the front case fan power header. By default, this jumper is set to 1-2 for Normal mode. When you first power on the system, you'll need to set this jumper to 2-3 for Configure mode, so do that now if you didn't do it earlier.

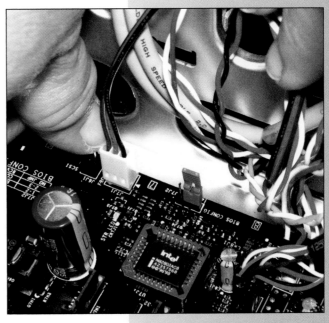

Figure 5-30. Connect the front fan to the fan power header

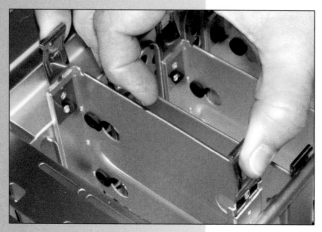

Figure 5-31. Remove an internal drive bay

One of the things we like about Intel motherboards is that they get even the small things right. The jumper block shown in Figure 5-30 has a small extension that allows you to easily grip it with your fingers and makes it much more convenient to change jumper settings. It probably only cost Intel an extra dollar per thousand jumper blocks to get that extra extension, but the point is that they were thoughtful enough to do it.

Similarly, the retail-boxed Intel motherboards we've seen that support S-ATA include not just an S-ATA data cable, but the S-ATA power adapter cable that is needed to connect some S-ATA drives to older power supplies. Including that cable cost Intel much more than a dollar, but they went ahead and included it anyway so that some poor guy attempting to build a system one Sunday afternoon wouldn't find himself dead in the water for lack of a cable.

Figure 5-32. Set the jumper to master

Installing the hard drive

The Antec Super LANBOY has three external 5.25" drive bays, two external 3.5" drive bays, and four internal 3.5" drive bays. The external bays are for devices like optical drives and floppy disk drives that use removable media. The four internal 3.5" bays can each hold one hard drive, and can be snapped in and out individually. To mount the hard drive, begin by removing an internal drive bay. As you press in on the two locking tabs, slide the bay out of the chassis, as shown in Figure 5-31.

Before you install the hard drive in the drive bay, verify that the drive is configured properly. We are using a parallel (standard) ATA hard drive in this system. By default, the drive is jumpered for cable select (CS). We prefer to jumper drives explicitly as master or slave devices. To set the drive to operate as a master, remove the jumper (as shown in Figure 5-32) and reinstall it on the set of pins nearest the ATA data connector. (Obviously, if you are using a different brand or model of hard drive, the jumper settings may differ.)

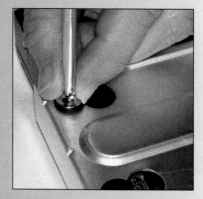

Figure 5-33. Secure the drive in the bay using four screws

The Antec drive bay uses rubber shock-mounting pads to isolate the drive, which reduces the amount of vibration and noise transferred from the hard drive to the chassis. One of those pads is partially visible as a small black circle at the bottom edge of Figure 5-33. Secure the drive to the bay by installing four of the provided screws with oversized heads, as shown in Figure 5-33. Drive the screws finger-tight, but no more. The rubber pads provide pressure on the screws to prevent them from loosening.

With the drive secured in the bay, the next step is to connect the Antec UV Cobra ATA data cable to the drive. One end of the cable has a black grounding wire extending from it. Connect that end of the cable to the Maxtor hard drive. (We'll connect the grounding cable to the chassis later.)

Verify the positions of pin 1 on the cable and drive connector (nearest the power connector). In this case, the drive connector and the cable are both keyed, so it's impossible to connect the cable backward. Align the cable connector to the drive connector and press down firmly until the cable connector slides into place, as shown in Figure 5-34.

Figure 5-34. Align pin 1 on the ATA cable with the drive connector and press the cable into place

The next step is to reinstall the bay in the chassis. To do so, align the drive bay rails with the chassis slots and slide the drive bay into the chassis. Press down firmly until the two locking tabs snap into place, as shown in Figure 5-35.

With the drive bay reinstalled, the next step is to connect power to the hard drive. To do so, select one of the hard drive power connectors on one of the multi-connector power cables coming out of the power supply. Don't use the cable with only yellow and black wires and connectors labeled "Fan Only"—we'll use that cable later for connecting the rear case fan. Use one of the cables with yellow, black, and red wires.

Figure 5-35. Slide the drive bay into the chassis and press until it snaps into place

The power connectors on the cable and hard drive are keyed with diagonal bevels on one side of the connector. Align the power cable with the drive power connector and press the cable connector firmly into place, as shown in Figure 5-36. You may have to exert significant pressure to force the cable connector to seat fully. Wiggle and tug gently on the connector to verify that it has in fact seated.

The final hard drive installation step is to connect the ATA data cable to the primary interface on the motherboard. The motherboard provides two ATA interfaces, labeled "Pri IDE" and "Sec IDE". The primary interface is the black connector near the right front edge of the motherboard. The secondary interface is the white connector immediately adjacent to the primary interface.

Figure 5-36. Connect the power cable to the drive

Figure 5-37. Connect the ATA data cable to the motherboard interface

Although any ATA or ATAPI drive will function properly connected to either interface, best practice is to connect the primary hard drive to the primary interface and use the secondary interface for optical drives, tape drives, and similar peripherals. The motherboard interfaces are keyed in the same manner as the cable and drive connectors. (The keying notch in the secondary interface connector is visible as a black square immediately in front of the cable.) Orient the ATA data cable so that its keying tab corresponds to the keying slot on the motherboard connector—pin 1 to pin 1—and press the cable connector into place, as shown in Figure 5-37.

Installing the expansion cards

As long as we have the system on its side, we might as well install the RADEON 9800 XT video adapter and Santa Cruz sound card now. To begin, align the RADEON with the motherboard AGP slot—the brown slot nearest the processor—to determine which slot cover you need to remove (it's not always obvious). For a D875PBZ motherboard installed in a Super LANBOY case, it's the slot cover next-to-nearest the processor.

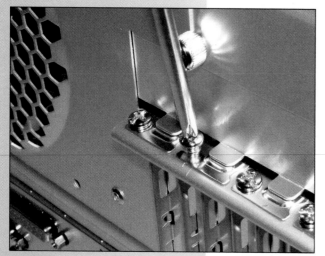

Figure 5-38. Remove the screw that secures the slot cover

The Antec Super LANBOY is unique among cases we have used in placing the slot cover screws outside the chassis. To begin installing the video adapter, remove the screw that secures the proper slot cover, as shown in Figure 5-38. Place the screw aside; you'll need it to secure the video adapter.

With the screw removed, the slot cover is still retained by a bracket. Loosen the thumbscrews that secure the bracket and slide the bracket upward, as shown in Figure 5-39. Once the bracket is out of the way, tighten the thumbscrews sufficiently to hold it in place.

With the retaining bracket raised, release the slot cover by squeezing the two sides and pressing inward, as shown in Figure 5-40 (facing page).

Figure 5-39. Loosen the thumbscrews that secure the retaining bracket and slide the bracket up and out of the way

It's probably a good idea to store the slot cover for future use. Standard slot covers are a dime a dozen, but the Super LANBOY uses a proprietary slot cover. If you ever want to remove a card and cover the slot, you'll want the original slot cover. If you're using a retail-boxed motherboard, the box it came in is a good place to store slot covers, unused cables, driver discs, and other small parts specific to that system.

Align the ATi RADEON 9800 XT video adapter with the AGP slot and press firmly with both thumbs until it snaps into place, as shown in Figure 5-41. Take care to verify that the video adapter is fully seated, not just partially. Even if you feel it snap into place, examine the slot and card-edge connector to verify that the card is seated fully and evenly.

Figure 5-40. Squeeze the sides of the slot cover and press inward to release it

Like many motherboards, the Intel D875PBZ has an AGP retaining mechanism at the rear of the AGP slot. Make sure that the tab on the AGP retaining mechanism is fully engaged with the corresponding cutout at the rear of the video adapter's connector.

The RADEON 9800 XT is a hot video card in every sense of the word. At the time we built this system, it was the fastest 3D graphics adapter on the market. But with speed comes heat, and the RADEON 9800 XT takes extraordinary measures to dissipate that heat. The large fan visible in Figure 5-41 draws cooling air through the array of ducts visible near the power connector and over the Graphics Processor Unit (GPU). Without that airflow, the GPU would quickly overheat and burn itself to a crisp (literally).

Figure 5-41. Use both thumbs to press the card firmly until it snaps into place

Some lesser graphics cards include fans that are powered from the AGP slot itself, but the RADEON 9800 XT draws nearly the maximum current a standard AGP slot can provide. Accordingly, the RADEON 9800 XT includes a standard Molex drive power connector that allows its fan to be powered directly by the power supply. Choose an available drive power connector—we used a spare connector on the same cable that we connected to the hard drive—and plug that connector into the power connector on the RADEON 9800 XT, as shown in Figure 5-42.

Figure 5-42. Connect power to the video adapter

Use a standard power connector to power the RADEON fan. The connectors labeled "Fan Only" are intended only for supplemental case fans. One of our technical reviewers recommends using a dedicated power connector for the RADEON fan rather than using a shared connector on the same power cable that connects to the hard drive.

Whatever you do, do not fail to connect power to the RADEON 9800 XT. If you turn on the system without the video adapter fan connected, you'll soon have a smoking heap of rubble that used to be a $400 video adapter. And, no, ATi won't replace the card under warranty. Running a RADEON 9800 XT without a fan is like running your car without oil.

Once you have seated the card and connected power to it, retrieve the screw you removed when you took off the slot cover and use it to secure the video adapter to the chassis, as shown in Figure 5-43.

Figure 5-43. Secure the video adapter to the chassis

If the system refuses to boot when you first apply power, check first to make sure the AGP adapter is fully seated. Some combinations of motherboard, adapter, and case make it difficult to seat the adapter completely. Even if the adapter seems to seat fully, always verify that the card contacts have fully penetrated the AGP slot, and that the base of the adapter is parallel to the slot and in full contact with it. Many motherboards, including the D875PBZ, have an AGP retaining bracket that mates with a corresponding notch on the video adapter. If you need to remove the adapter later, remember to press those tabs to unlock the retaining bracket before you attempt to pull the card.

With the RADEON 9800 XT installed, the next step is to install the Santa Cruz sound card. You face two conflicting priorities in choosing a PCI slot for the sound card. First, you want the sound card to be as far as possible from the video adapter, both to avoid heat buildup and to minimize RF interference between the two cards. On the other hand, the Santa Cruz card has connectors on the side of the card that faces the bottom of the chassis (as opposed to those visible in Figure 5-44 at the top edge of the card), and you'd like those connectors to be accessible.

Installing the Santa Cruz in the PCI slot nearest the bottom of the case provides the maximum possible separation between the RADEON 9800 XT and the Santa

Cruz, but the bottom of the chassis blocks the connectors on the Santa Cruz. Conversely, installing the Santa Cruz in the PCI slot nearest the RADEON 9800 XT makes the Santa Cruz connectors easily accessible, but puts the two adapters right next to each other.

We compromised by leaving three free slots between the RADEON 9800 XT and the Santa Cruz, and only one between the Santa Cruz and the bottom of the case. Once you have chosen a PCI slot, remove the slot cover as described in the previous section, align the Santa Cruz with the PCI, and press firmly until it seats completely, as shown in Figure 5-44.

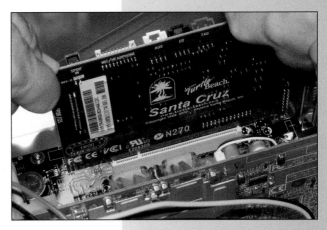

Figure 5-44. Align the sound card with the chosen slot and press firmly until it seats

> The Santa Cruz provides numerous input and output connectors, both on the slot bracket and on the card itself. We decided to use the rear-panel connectors for audio rather than routing audio to the front panel. If you prefer to use front-panel audio, refer to the sound card manual for detailed instructions.

With the sound card seated, secure it to the chassis by driving a screw through the slot bracket and into the chassis, as shown in Figure 5-45.

After you've installed and secured the video adapter and sound card, slide the retaining bracket back into place and tighten the thumbscrews (Figure 5-46).

Figure 5-45. Secure the sound card to the chassis

> There's one other expansion card you might consider installing: a LAN adapter. The Intel D875PBZ motherboard includes an embedded Intel PRO/1000 CT 10/100/1000 Ethernet adapter that should be able to connect to any Ethernet hub or switch, regardless of speed. Although Intel Ethernet adapters are among the most reliable and compatible adapters we've used, we have received a few reports of compatibility issues, usually with no-name network components.
>
> Because you seldom know what the network environment will be at a LAN party, installing a second LAN adapter of a different make, such as 3Com or D-Link, can be cheap insurance. If you can't connect with the Intel adapter, you should be able to connect with the secondary adapter. Of course, connectivity problems are often the result of a bad cable anyway, which is a good reason to carry a spare cable.

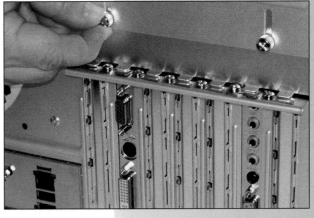

Figure 5-46. Slide the retaining bracket back into place and tighten the thumbscrews

Figure 5-47. Orient the rear case fan and thread the mounting studs through the case holes

Installing the rear fan

The Antec Super LANBOY case includes a clear acrylic rear case fan, but for some reason, rather than installing the fan at the factory, Antec simply straps the fan to the chassis with wire ties. To mount the fan properly, begin by locating the package containing four soft plastic mounting studs. Thread those studs through the corner mounting holes in the fan and then through the mounting holes in the case, as shown in Figure 5-47.

Mount the fan with the Antec hub logo toward the outside of the case, and the side with the wire-wrapped armatures visible inside the case.

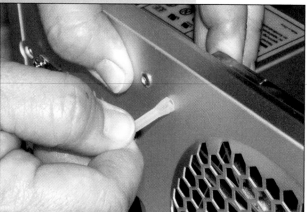

Figure 5-48. Pull each stud through its mounting hole until it snaps into place

The mounting studs are made of soft plastic with an expanded section that secures the fan to the case. Pull each stud through the corresponding case hole, as shown in Figure 5-48, until the expanded section of the stud snaps through the mounting hole.

After you have pulled all four studs into place, use your dykes, diagonal cutter, or needlenose pliers to trim the excess length from the studs, as shown in Figure 5-49.

When you finish mounting the fan, connect power to it. Locate the cable coming from the power supply that has two connectors labeled "Fan Only." This cable has only yellow and black wires, rather than the yellow, black, and red wires used by the drive power cables. Locate the keying bevels on the two connectors, orient them properly, and snap the two connectors together, as shown in Figure 5-50.

Figure 5-49. Trim the excess length from the rear fan mounting studs

Figure 5-50. Connect power to the rear case fan

The "Fan Only" power connectors allow the power supply to control the speed of the fan in response to temperature variations. If you prefer to have the rear case fan run at full speed all the time, simply use a standard power connector instead of the "Fan Only" connector.

Connecting the ATX power connectors

The next step in assembling the system is to connect the two power connectors from the power supply to the motherboard. The main ATX power connector is a 20-pin connector located near the right front edge of the motherboard. Locate the corresponding cable coming from the power supply. The main ATX power connector is keyed, so verify that it is aligned properly before you attempt to seat it.

Once everything is aligned, press down firmly until the connector seats, as shown in Figure 5-51. It may take significant pressure to seat the connector, and you should feel it snap into place. The locking tab on the side of the connector should snap into place over the corresponding nub on the socket. Make sure the connector seats fully. A partially seated main ATX power connector may cause subtle problems that are very difficult to troubleshoot.

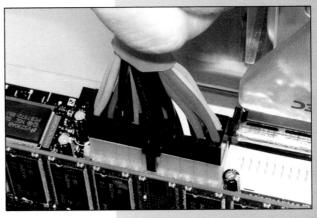

Figure 5-51. Connect the main ATX power connector

Pentium 4 systems require more power to the motherboard than the standard main ATX power connector supplies. Intel developed a supplementary four-pin connector, called the ATX12V connector, that routes additional +12V current directly to the voltage regulator module (VRM) that powers the processor. On most Pentium 4 motherboards, including the D875PBZ, the ATX12V connector is located very near the processor socket. The ATX12V connector is keyed. Orient the cable connector properly relative to the motherboard connector and press it into place until the plastic tab locks, as shown in Figure 5-52.

WARNING

Failing to connect the ATX12V power connector is a common cause of initial boot failures on newly built Pentium 4 systems. The processor requires more +12V power than the main ATX power connector can provide. Without that additional power, the system simply refuses to boot.

Figure 5-52. Connect the ATX12V power connector

Installing the optical drive and voltage/fan control panel

Figure 5-53. Remove the plastic bezel that covers the drive bay

The Antec Super LANBOY case provides three external 5.25" bays, each of which is covered by a snap-in plastic bezel. We have two 5.25" devices to mount, the Plextor PX-708A DVD burner and the voltage/fan control panel provided with the TrueControl 550 power supply. We decided to install the voltage/fan control panel in the top bay and the Plextor PX-708A in the middle bay.

The first step required to install a 5.25" device is to remove the bezel for the selected drive bay. To do that, pull one edge of the bezel from the front while you press on the center of the bezel from the rear until it snaps out, as shown in Figure 5-53. Remove the bezel and store it in the motherboard box. If you ever change the drive configuration on the Super LANBOY, you'll want the original bezel, which matches the case color and finish.

The lower two 5.25" drive bays are blocked by metal RF shields. To remove a shield, grasp it as shown in Figure 5-54 and twist back and forth until the shield breaks free. Be careful working on this area of the case later. Removing the RF shield leaves two sharp metal burrs that can cut you if you're not careful.

The TrueControl 550 power supply includes a voltage/fan control panel bezel that mounts in an unused external drive bay. You can use the controls located on that bezel to control the power supply fan speed and various voltage rails directly from the front of the system without opening the case.

Figure 5-54. Twist the metal RF shield back and forth until it snaps out

The fan control aspect is self-explanatory, but the voltage control deserves a bit of explanation. Voltage control is done using the set of trim potentiometers on the bezel. These require a screwdriver to adjust (as opposed to the ordinary knob for fan-speed control), because you shouldn't have to adjust them often and you shouldn't adjust them arbitrarily. By tweaking the trim pots while you watch a monitoring utility such as Intel's Active Monitor, you can fine-tune the voltage that the power supply delivers on the +3.3V, +5V, and +12V rails. For example, if the nominal +12V rail is actually delivering +11.945V, you can adjust the trim pot to bring the +12V rail to exactly +12.000V. Having the voltage as close as possible to nominal on these three critical voltage rails increases system stability.

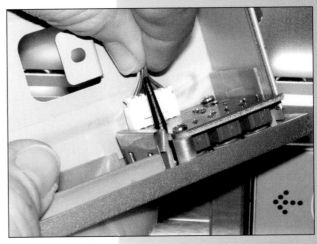

Locate the voltage/fan control panel cable coming from the power supply. It's the one with the keyed white connector. Pull that cable through the drive bay to the front of the case and press it into place on the corresponding connector on the rear of the voltage/fan control panel bezel, as shown in Figure 5-55.

Rather than requiring a dedicated drive bay, the voltage/fan control panel bezel is designed to allow mounting a 3.5" device, such as a floppy disk drive or a tape drive.

Figure 5-55. Connect the voltage/fan control panel cable to the header pins

Slide the voltage/fan control panel into the drive bay, as shown in Figure 5-56. Press it into place until the front of the bezel is flush with the front of the chassis.

The Antec 5.25" drive bays do not use rails. Instead, the drive bays themselves are formed with truncated shelves to help you guide the drives into position and to support them until you secure them with screws. When the drive rests on these shelves, it is automatically positioned properly in the vertical plane. Verify that the control panel is flush with the front bezel, and then drive four screws to secure it, as shown in Figure 5-57.

Figure 5-56. Slide the voltage/fan control panel into the drive bay

Although there are eight screw holes in both the bay and the voltage/fan control panel bezel, four screws is more than sufficient to retain it securely. As long as you put two screws into each side, one front and one back, it makes no difference which holes you use. We chose the two lower screw holes because they were more accessible. However, to minimize the possibility of torquing, we recommend that you use the same holes on either side. For example, if you drive the screws into the upper front and lower back holes on one side, do the same on the other. In other words, all four screws should be containable in a single plane.

In contrast, one of our technical reviewers recommends "cross-hatching" the screws to distribute stress over more than one plane, for example, by installing screws top-front/bottom-rear on one side and bottom-front/top-rear on the other. It probably doesn't make much difference, as long as you drive two screws into each side of the drive.

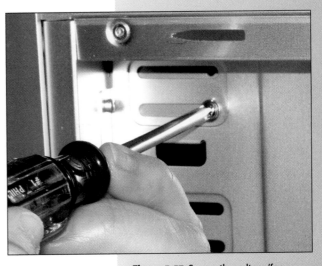

Before you install the optical drive, verify the jumper settings against the sticker or embossed markings on

Figure 5-57. Secure the voltage/fan control panel bezel with four screws

the drive itself. Taking the time to double-check little things like this will make troubleshooting much easier if you encounter problems. The Plextor PX-708A DVD writer ships with a jumper installed in the rightmost position, which configures the drive as master. We plan to use the optical drive as the secondary master, so the default jumper setting is correct.

It's usually easier to connect the ATA cable to the drive before you install the drive in the case. We used the standard 40-wire ATA cable included with the Plextor PX-708A. Because optical drives have relatively slow transfer rates, they can use the older 40-wire ATA cable rather than the 80-wire Ultra-ATA cable used for ATA hard drives. To connect the cable, locate pin 1 on the drive connector, which is usually nearest the power connector. The pin 1 side of the cable is indicated by a red stripe. Align the cable connector with the drive connector, making sure the red stripe is on the pin 1 side of the drive connector, and press the cable into place, as shown in Figure 5-58.

Figure 5-58. Connect the ATA cable to the optical drive

> You can always substitute an 80-wire ATA cable for a 40-wire ATA cable, but the converse is not true. Hard drives require an 80-wire cable for best performance. A hard drive operates properly with a 40-wire cable, but with decreased throughput. Optical drives, tape drives, and similar ATA/ATAPI devices with slower transfer rates operate properly and at maximum performance with either a 40-wire or an 80-wire cable.

To mount the drive in the case, feed the loose end of the ATA cable through the drive bay from the front, align the drive with the truncated shelves built into the drive bay, and press the drive firmly into place until the front bezel of the drive is flush with the front panel, as shown in Figure 5-59. Working from the rear of the drive, feed the ATA cable down into the case, placing the loose end near the front right edge of the motherboard.

Figure 5-59. Slide the optical drive into the bay

Secure the Plextor PX-708A DVD writer using four screws in the same manner you used to secure the voltage/fan control panel bezel, but with one additional step. Remember that thin black wire coming out one end of the Antec Cobra ATA cable we used to connect the hard drive (Figure 5-34)? That is a grounding cable.

The grounding cable connects to the wire braid and the aluminum foil sheath that are used to shield the individual wires and the cable itself against RF interference. For that shield to function properly, it must be grounded. The best way to ground the shield is to connect that black wire directly to the chassis. Connect the grounding cable to the chassis using one of the screws that secure the optical drive, as shown in Figure 5-60.

The next step in installing the optical drive is to connect one end of an ATA data cable to the drive and the other end to the motherboard ATA interface. We connected the Plextor PX-708A optical drive as the master device on the secondary ATA interface. (We used the primary ATA interface for the hard drive, and it's good practice to put your hard drive and optical drive on separate interfaces whenever possible.)

The primary and secondary ATA interfaces are located near the right front edge of the motherboard near the DIMM slots. The primary ATA interface is the black connector nearest the edge, already occupied by the Antec Cobra cable that connects the hard drive. The secondary ATA interface is the white connector immediately adjacent. Locate pin 1 on the secondary ATA interface and align the ATA cable with its red stripe toward pin 1 on the interface.

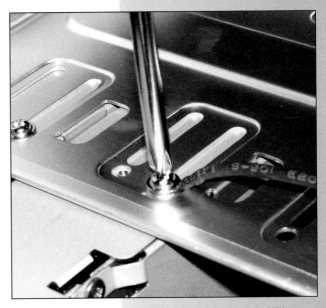

Figure 5-60. Secure the optical drive to the chassis, using one of the screws to connect the grounding wire from the hard drive ATA cable

---

After you connect the ATA cable, don't just leave it flopping around loose. That not only looks amateurish, but can impede airflow and cause overheating. Tuck the cable neatly out of the way, using tape, cable ties, or tie wraps to secure it to the case. If necessary, temporarily disconnect the cable to route it around other cables and obstructions, and reconnect it once you have it positioned properly.

The final step in installing the optical drive (and one we often forget) is to connect power to the drive. Choose one of the power cables coming from the power supply and press the Molex connector onto the drive power connector, as shown in Figure 5-61. It may require significant pressure to get the power connector to seat, so use care to avoid hurting your fingers if the connector seats suddenly. The Molex power connector is keyed, so verify that it is oriented properly before you apply pressure to seat the power cable.

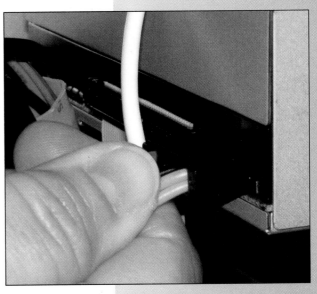

Figure 5-61. Connect the power cable to the optical drive

WARNING

You may have to wiggle the connector slightly to get the contacts aligned, and it's sometimes necessary to press quite firmly to seat the connector. Be careful, though, because too much force or wiggling can cause the contacts to pop out of the connector.

Final assembly steps

Congratulations! You're almost finished building the LAN Party PC. Only a couple steps remain to be done, and those won't take long.

Connect the fan-signal connector (optional)

The TrueControl 550 power supply has a fan-signal connector cable that allows the power supply to report its current fan speed to the motherboard. That speed can be monitored by the BIOS and reported by the Intel Active Monitor software that is bundled with the motherboard. The fan-signal connector cable is the one with a three-pin connector with just two wires, one black and one blue.

To enable this function, connect the fan-signal connector cable to a fan connector on the motherboard. We chose the VRM fan connector, which is a standard three-pin fan connector located near the edge of the motherboard between the processor socket and the rear I/O panel. With the processor installed and the motherboard already in place, it's hard to get to this connector. Your best bet is to use your needlenose pliers to install the connector.

WARNING

You may not want to enable this function. The TrueControl 550 power supply fan spins slowly when the power supply is lightly loaded. The BIOS may misinterpret low speed as a fan failure and generate false alarms.

Figure 5-62. Dress and tuck the cables to prevent them from interfering with airflow or fans

Dress the cables

The final step in assembling the system is to dress and tuck the cables, as shown in Figure 5-62. This simply means routing the cables so they don't block airflow and won't become entangled in the CPU or case fan. All you really need to do is untangle the cables (temporarily disconnect them if you need to), group them according to their source and destination within the case, and then tie them off and tuck them into whatever nooks and crannies are available. Unused 5.25" drive bays are a particularly handy place to stuff excess cable lengths, particularly the rats' nest of cables that come out of the power supply.

After you've completed these steps, take a few minutes to double-check everything. Verify that all cables are connected properly, that all drives are secured, and that there's nothing loose inside the case. Check one last time to verify that the power supply is set for the correct input voltage. It's a good idea to pick up the system and tilt it gently from side to side to make sure there are no loose screws or other items that could cause a short. Use the following checklist:

- __ Power supply set to proper input voltage
- __ No loose tools or screws (shake the case gently)
- __ Heatsink/fan unit properly mounted; CPU fan connected
- __ Memory modules fully seated and latched
- __ Front-panel switch and indicator cables connected properly
- __ Front-panel I/O cables connected properly
- __ Hard drive data cable connected to drive and motherboard
- __ Hard drive power cable connected
- __ Optical drive data cable connected to drive and motherboard
- __ Optical drive power cable connected
- __ Optical drive audio cable(s) connected (if applicable)
- __ Front-panel voltage/fan controller connected (if applicable)
- __ Floppy drive data and power cables connected (if applicable)
- __ All drives secured to drive bay or chassis
- __ Expansion cards fully seated and secured to the chassis
- __ Video adapter fan connected (if applicable)
- __ Main ATX power cable and ATX12V power cable connected
- __ Front and rear case fans installed and connected (if applicable)
- __ All cables dressed and tucked

Once you're certain that all is as it should be, it's time for the smoke test. Leave the cover off for now. Connect the power cable to the wall receptacle and then to the system unit. Unlike many power supplies, the Antec TrueControl 550 has a separate rocker switch on the back that controls power to the power supply. By default, it's in the 0 or off position, which means the power supply is not receiving power from the wall receptacle. Move that switch to the 1 or on position. Press the main power button on the front of the case, and the system should start up. Check to make sure that the power supply fan, CPU fan, and case fan are spinning. You should also hear the hard drive spin up and the happy beep that tells you the system is starting normally. At that point, everything should be working properly.

When you turn on the rear power switch, the system will come to life momentarily and then die. That's perfectly normal behavior. When the power supply receives power, it begins to start up. It quickly notices that the motherboard hasn't told it to start, and so it shuts down again. All you need to do is press the front-panel power switch and the system will start normally.

It Should Have Worked...

Well, it should have worked properly, but it didn't. When we applied power to the system, it didn't boot. Did you catch the showstopper? We left a subtle hint. Check Figure 5-21, and you'll see that the AA (Altered Assembly) number on the motherboard is C26680-200. Intel says that a D875PBZ motherboard with an AA number of C27085-207 or later or C26680-206 or later is compatible with the Pentium 4 Extreme Edition processor. Our board was too old to support that processor.

We were actually lucky. Our system failed to boot, but it could have been much worse. The high current draw of the P4/EE processor could have overloaded and burned out the voltage regulator module (VRM), destroying the motherboard and perhaps even the processor.

Like all motherboard manufacturers, Intel "slipstreams" motherboard revisions without changing the model number of the product. As it happened, we had three Intel D875PBZ motherboards in inventory, one brand new, one only a month or so old, and one several months old. The one we pulled to build this system happened to be the oldest one, and it wasn't compatible with the processor we wanted to use.

(continued)

It Should Have Worked... *(continued)*

You probably won't encounter a similar problem if you buy your components at about the same time. Most online vendors turn their inventory very quickly, and any product you get is likely to have a recent production date. There is a lesson here, though. It's always worth verifying that the exact motherboard you use is compatible with the exact processor model you use.

In particular, this problem often rears its ugly head during upgrades. You may have a year-old motherboard model that is still in production. If you check the web site, you may find that the manufacturer lists that motherboard as compatible with the processor you plan to install. Unfortunately, the processor compatibility list almost always refers to the current revision of the motherboard. A year-old model may be (and probably is) incompatible with a fast recent processor. Intel is very good about listing CPU compatibility by revision level. Most motherboard makers bury that information deep in their technical documents, if indeed they publish it at all. Be very, very careful about installing a hot new processor in an older-model motherboard.

For us, it was easy enough to solve the problem. We simply pulled the earlier D875PBZ motherboard and replaced it with the latest AA model. But that was an hour's work that we could have avoided by checking first.

Turn off the system, disconnect the power cord, and take these final steps to prepare the system for use:

Set the BIOS Setup configuration jumper to Configure mode
The BIOS Setup configuration jumper block on the Intel D875PBZ motherboard is used to set the operation mode. This jumper is located on the left front of the motherboard. By default, the jumper is in the 1-2 (Normal) position. If you didn't do so earlier, move the jumper block to the 2-3 (Configure) position.

Reconnect the power cord and restart the system
When the configuration jumper is set to Configure mode, starting the system automatically runs BIOS Setup and puts the system in maintenance mode. This step allows the motherboard to detect the type of processor installed and configure it automatically. When the BIOS Setup screen appears, clear all BIOS data and reset the system clock. Save your changes and exit. The system automatically shuts down. Disconnect the power cord.

Set the BIOS Setup configuration jumper to Normal mode
With the power cord disconnected, move the BIOS Setup configuration jumper block from 2-3 (Configure mode) to 1-2 (Normal mode).

Replace the side panel and reconnect power
With the jumper set for Normal operation, replace the side panel and reconnect the power cord. Your system is now completely assembled and ready for use.

Figure 5-63 shows our friend, Dr. Mary Chervenak, with the Kick-Ass LAN Party PC in its finished state—except for the Alyson Hannigan images. The fabric tote-strap is supplied by Antec. The clear side panel makes the system impressive even in full daylight, but it really shines in the dark (literally). Mary wanted to take it home with her, but we wouldn't let her.

Figure 5-63. The completed Kick-Ass LAN Party PC (have gun, will travel)

Lugging All This Stuff

The Kick-Ass LAN Party PC is easily luggable, but that raises the question "What about all my other stuff?" You need a lot of accessories when you attend a LAN party, and it makes sense to organize them in one place. The best solution we know of—albeit an expensive one—is to use a deep, oversize aluminum case with cut-to-fit foam liners, such as those available from Zero Halliburton. You can arrange the interior so that every accessory has its own place, making it evident at a glance if something is missing. Such cases are expensive, particularly in large sizes, so those on a budget may have to settle for a large nylon backpack, such as those available from L. L. Bean and Lands' End. (You can also buy purpose-built LAN party accessory cases from many online vendors. Google for "LAN party accessories" and you'll turn up a bunch of hits. We have no experience with any of those, though, so we can't comment.)

As to what to carry, here's our list:

- Flat-panel display (wrapped in foam unless you use a rigid case).

- Display cable (and a spare).

- Keyboard, mouse, and game controllers (with spare batteries, if applicable).

- Wrist-rest, mousepad, and any other ergonomic accessories you use.

- Headphones and/or speakers.

- Category 5 or 6 Ethernet drop cable, 10-foot (and a spare).

- Extra USB cable.

- Power cables for the PC and display (and spares). An outlet-strip surge protector is also handy. There are seldom enough electrical receptacles.

- Cable ties to keep everything neat. The last thing you want is someone tripping over your power cable.

- Copies of all the games you plan to play, including any that you haven't installed on the hard drive. The best way to carry CDs and DVDs is in a zippered nylon audio CD case, available at Best Buy and similar retailers. Make sure you also have patches, cheat sheets, and similar items, either on the hard drive or on CD.

- A minimal toolkit. Include at least a #2 Phillips screwdriver, needlenose pliers, a flashlight with batteries, and spare screws and other small connectors. It's also a good idea to include a small first-aid kit, with adhesive bandages, disinfectant, and so on.

- Spare glasses or contact lenses, medications, etc.

- Emergency stock of munchies and caffeinated beverages.

That's a lot of stuff, including some things you may never need, but Murphy's Law says that whatever you leave at home will turn out to be what you need at the LAN party.

Final Words

This system went together easily, or would have if we'd used the right motherboard revision. Actual construction took about 90 minutes, which we spread out over several days as we photographed each step. If this is the first time you've built a system, leave yourself a full weekend to build it, install software, and so on.

One thing we did wonder about. The Antec Super LANBOY case is so light that we worried about its strength and durability. Well, there's only one way to find out, and better us than you. After we'd shot several images of Mary lifting and toting and holding the LPPC, we decided to see just how it would stand up to some weight.

Robert had little doubt that, at 110 kilos, if he stood on top of the case he'd crush it flat. Mary, at about 50 kilos, might be a different story. So Robert suggested to Mary that she stand on top of the case. Mary hesitated at first, thinking that anything that light wouldn't be able to hold her weight. It did, though, as you can see in Figure 5-64, without so much as a crinkle in the case or even a slightly bowed panel. This is a tough case.

Figure 5-64. Mary Chervenak atop the LAN Party PC

We did all the usual stuff—updating the BIOS, installing the OS and service packs, updating the drivers, installing applications, and so on. But what we really wanted to know was how fast the system would run. It's a screamer, both for general use and for running UT, Quake, and other graphics-intensive games. We're still rotten gamers, but at least now we'll lose with panache.

Robert wanted to use the LPPC as his den system, but the lights and the clear side panel scare the dogs. Oh, well.

For updated component recommendations, commentary, and other new material, visit *http://www.hardwareguys.com/guides/lppc.html*.

Building a Home Theater PC

6

Cost-effectiveness

Reliability

Compactness

Quietness

Expandability

Processor performance

Video performance

Disk capacity/performance

We admit it—we're audio/video Luddites. Our den audio system is a decade old. The receiver has Dolby Pro Logic, but we've never gotten around to hooking more than two speakers to it. We use it only for playing CDs and occasionally an elderly cassette tape. We have a standard 27" Panasonic television, analog cable, no premium channels, and no satellite receiver, and we have never owned a DVD player. TiVo? We've heard of it.

The only movies we generally watch are old ones on PBS, Turner Classic Movies, MoviePlex, and similar commercial-free channels. Barbara watches *The West Wing* (which Robert calls *The Left Wing*) regularly. We sometimes watch *Mystery!*, *Masterpiece Theatre*, or other PBS programs. Other than news, sports, and the Weather Channel, that's about it.

For 15 years, we've made it a practice never to watch television in real time if we can avoid it. We tape everything, including commercial-free programs, and watch them later at our convenience. That way, we can watch multipart programs without waiting a week between episodes, and if the phone rings we can simply pause the VCR.

Despite the limited amount of time we devote to watching television, it sometimes happens that two programs we want to record are on simultaneously or that we want to watch a tape at the same time another program needs to be recorded. To avoid such conflicts, we have VCRs all over the house. One in the den. One in the master bedroom. One in the guest suite downstairs.

The trouble with VCRs (and videotapes) is that they die. Over the years, as each VCR died, we bought another to replace it. Robert, being a "keeper," has a stack of dead VCRs that he believes may one day live again as advances are made in consumer-electronics medical science. Barbara, being a "thrower-away," argues that these old VCRs deserve only a decent burial.

One day in late 2003, the den VCR began making ominous squeaking noises as it was recording or playing a tape. Things went downhill fast. It soon began randomly failing to record scheduled programs. Then it started eating tapes. Time to add it to the stack of dead ones and buy a new VCR, obviously. But wait!

As we searched the Sunday paper's advertising circulars for VCRs, we noticed a TiVo *Personal Video Recorder* (PVR). Hmmm. VCRs are a dying '80s technology, and recording television programs to a hard drive is an attractive concept. Some of our friends had been TiVo users for years, and had waxed lyrical about the joys of pausing live television, having an online program guide, and so on. So we decided to look into buying a TiVo.

What we found didn't please us. A TiVo Series2 with an 80 GB hard drive and a supposed 80-hour capacity could in fact record 80 hours only at the lowest quality setting, which noticeably degrades image quality. At the highest-quality setting, the so-called 80-hour unit records only about 25 hours. And, although there are ways to add a second hard drive to the TiVo unit to expand its capacity (see *http://www.tivofaq.com*), doing so voids the warranty.

Still, we considered buying the 80-hour TiVo Series2. At $350 or so, the TiVo unit itself was expensive, but not outrageously so. But then we learned that the online programming guide, which is mandatory for the newer TiVo Series2 units, cost $12.95 a month or $299 for a lifetime Subscription. The latter didn't sound too bad until we learned that "lifetime" referred to the unit's lifetime, not ours. If we ended up replacing the TiVo with an upgraded unit a few years down the line—or if the TiVo failed outside its 90-day warranty—we'd have to pay the $299 Subscription again for the new unit. This was beginning to sound expensive.

The final straw came when Barbara asked a key question. We archive programs we think we might want to watch again—our VHS tape library includes *Upstairs, Downstairs*, *I Clavdivs*, James Herriot's *All Creatures Great and Small* series, and so on. How, Barbara asked, could we archive stuff that we recorded on the TiVo? Good question. The short answer is, we couldn't, at least not without using some kludgey workarounds. TiVo records video in a proprietary format. Getting the video from the TiVo hard drive to a writable DVD would be a struggle, to say the least.

One possible solution was to buy a combination TiVo/DVD recorder unit, but decent ones started at $1,000 and went up from there. That didn't include the program guide Subscription, either, so we'd be spending $1,300+ to get TiVo plus archiving functionality. And, even after spending that much, we'd end up with a dedicated single-purpose appliance loaded with all kinds of nasty *Digital Restrictions Management* (DRM) features that would restrict how we could store and use the video we'd recorded.

Time for Plan B: building our own *Home Theater PC* (HTPC). For the $1,300 cost of a TiVo with archiving capabilities, we figured we could build one heck of a system for our entertainment center. So we sat down to decide exactly what features and functions we wanted our new HTPC to provide.

Determining Functional Requirements

We started out thinking about the HTPC as a supplement to our current home-audio components, but as our design progressed we realized that with the right components the HTPC could actually *replace* all the existing home-audio components—not only the VCR and the TiVo we'd decided not to buy, but the CD player and our nonexistent DVD player as well.

Here's the list of functional requirements we came up with:

Analog cable-ready 125-channel tuner
> Our cable TV service is standard analog that uses no channels above 99, but our televisions can tune channels through 125. Because our cable company sometimes adds channels—and sometimes adds higher-numbered channels while leaving lower channels unused—we wanted a tuner card that supported analog cable channels at least through channel 125.

VCR replacement functions
> We use our VCRs primarily for time-shifting. Other than sporting events, news, weather, and similar live programming, we haven't watched a program in real time for 15 years. We record everything and zap the commercials, if any. It was essential that the HTPC provide similar functionality, including commercial zapping.

Video recording quality
> We record everything in VHS SP mode unless we're recording a movie that won't fit on a T-160 tape in SP mode. We consider VHS SP mode the minimum acceptable video quality, and would prefer to record everything in DVD quality. Accordingly, although lower-quality recording modes are desirable for additional flexibility, DVD-quality mode is essential.

Capacity
> We tend to accumulate recorded programs and watch them in batches. For example, if *Masterpiece Theatre* is running a four-part series,

we don't start watching it until we've recorded all four episodes. Considering our television viewing habits, we decided we needed an absolute minimum of 20 hours of video storage, and 40 hours would be better.

Watch-while-record

The system must allow us to watch a live program while recording another. The ability to watch a recorded program while recording another program is an advantage, but is not essential.

Live-pause and real-time commercial zapping

The system must allow us to "live-pause" a program while it is being recorded. That is, if we begin watching a program in real time, the system must allow us to press a pause button when the phone rings and continue recording the program. When we have dealt with the interruption, the system must then allow us to resume watching the program at the point at which we paused it. Because live-pause buffers video for later viewing, this feature would also allow us to zap commercials in a live program merely by waiting several minutes after the program starts to begin watching it.

Online program guide

The system must feature a free, interactive program guide, customized to the channels provided by our cable system. Selecting a program to be recorded should be a simple matter of pointing to that program on the guide menu and pressing a button. Ideally, the program guide should be customizable to hide channels we never watch.

Video archiving

The HTPC must make provision for archiving recorded programs to writable CD and DVD discs that can later be played back in the HTPC or on an ordinary DVD player. Ideally, the HTPC would also allow us to transfer our existing VHS tapes to optical discs.

Standard file formats

The HTPC must record video data as standard file formats without DRM copy protection or other impediments to copying and editing those recordings. Ideally, the HTPC would also be able to translate various standard file formats to other file formats.

CD and DVD player

The HTPC must function as a standard CD player and DVD player, capable of playing CD-DA audio discs and DVD-Video discs. Ideally, the HTPC should also be capable of ripping the content of CD and DVD discs to its hard drive.

Media library and audio/video server

The HTPC should provide a media library management function, allowing us to store and organize video and audio data, including the downloadable .MP3 and .OGG music/audio file formats. Ideally, the media library should support CDDB for audio data. The HTPC should also function as a multimedia server for other systems throughout the house, either by delivering streaming audio/video or by allowing those other systems to access stored audio/video files via a network share.

Gaming console replacement

The HTPC should function as a gaming PC within the limitations of using a standard television for display.

Casual PC replacement

The HTPC should be usable for casual PC functions such as checking email or browsing the Web, again within the limitations of using a television as a display device.

Extensibility

As we thought about the functions an HTPC could provide, we realized that it could support other unrelated functions in the future. For example, we may eventually use the HTPC to control a home weather station or provide automated-attendant and voicemail functions for our home telephone system. Because the HTPC is a standard PC, making provision for these possible future functions is a simple matter of making sure that the HTPC has plenty of processor, memory, hard drive capacity, USB ports, and so on.

Ease of use

Although the HTPC is a PC and will sometimes be used as such, ease of use is a major consideration for the core multimedia functions. For example, scheduling a program to be recorded or playing a DVD should be a matter of punching a few buttons on a remote control rather than navigating Windows menus with a keyboard and mouse.

That's a lot to ask of a system, but even at that two of our original wish-list items didn't make the final cut:

Record multiple programs simultaneously

We originally intended the HTPC to be capable of recording two programs simultaneously, but we concluded that building in that functionality would involve more cost and trouble than it was worth. Recording a second program simultaneously requires a second tuner card. Basic tuner cards are relatively inexpensive, but a basic tuner card wouldn't do the job. Recording two programs simultaneously also means compressing two programs simultaneously. Real-time video compression is extremely demanding. We either would have had to install a second tuner card with hardware compression, which is relatively expensive, or use a much faster main system processor, with all that implies for noise and heat.

We realized that we already had other systems with RADEON All-In-Wonder cards installed, which could function as "satellite" PVRs. Rather than overbuilding the main HTPC system, we could simply use

RF Distribution

If you want to distribute RF through-out your home, you can do so by using an RF modulator. In theory, it is possible to distribute that signal on the existing cable by filtering the channel used by the RF modulator at the cable demarc, but in practice, attempting to do so risks poor image quality and interference on that chan-nel—and not just for you, but for your neighbors. If that happens, expect a visit from an angry cable company employee.

The alternative, which we would choose, is to run a separate coax cable to each TV and provide some means of switching between the two RF inputs. We decided that wasn't worth the trouble. It's easier just to transfer video files, either on a DVD or across the network to a set-top PC connected to the remote TV.

DESIGN PRIORITIES	
Price	★★★☆☆
Reliability	★★★★★
Size	★★☆☆☆
Noise level	★★★★☆
Expandability	★★★☆☆
Processor performance	★★★☆☆
Video performance	★★★★☆
Disk capacity/performance	★★★★☆

one of those other systems to record a second program on those rare occasions when there was a scheduling conflict.

Streaming video/RF-out

We originally intended to design an HTPC capable of outputting an RF signal that could be received by any television in the house. However, we concluded that, although it was possible, it would require signifi-cant cost and effort for little return. As an alternative, we decided that it would be easy enough to burn any programs we wanted to watch elsewhere to a CD-RW or DVD+RW and watch them on a standard DVD player.

Hardware Design Criteria

With the functional requirements determined, the next step was to estab-lish design criteria for the HTPC hardware. To the lower left are the relative priorities we assigned for the HTPC.

Here's the breakdown:

Price

Price is an issue, but only in the sense that we'd like the total price of the system to be the same or lower than the cumulative price of the several components it replaces. Accordingly, we'll use only first-rate components in this system, and if spending a few extra dollars buys us additional performance, reliability, or functionality, we'll spend the extra money.

Reliability

Reliability is paramount for this system. Not, perhaps, in the same sense that reliability is critical for a departmental file server, but Robert never wants to have to explain to Barbara that she can't watch President Bartlett save the world again because the fancy new HTPC failed to record the latest episode of *The Left Wing*. We won't use RAID disk storage, ECC memory, and other server technologies for cost, space, and other reasons, but we will attempt to design as reliable a system as possible within those constraints by using top-notch components, emphasizing cooling even at the expense of noise level, using an over-size power supply, and so on.

Size

Size is relatively unimportant for our HTPC, except in the sense that we'd like it to resemble a standard home-audio component in size, shape, and appearance. Accordingly, rather than simply using the smallest available case, we decided to consider larger cases that accept full-size ATX motherboards, have more drive bays, and so on. Larger cases also run cooler and are generally quieter than the smallest cases.

Older Standards Make Life Easier

Sometimes the old ways are the good ways, and this is certainly true for someone who wants to build an HTPC. Broadly speaking, there are two types of television signaling protocols and two delivery methods.

The current standard television signaling protocols are *NTSC* (National Television System Committee), which is used in North America and Japan, and *PAL* (Phase Alternating Line), which is used in most of Europe, China, and Africa. NTSC and PAL are analog protocols. They may be transmitted over-the-air or via cable using analog transmission, or via cable or satellite using digital transmission. The second type of signaling protocol is called *HDTV* (High-Definition TeleVision), which is purely digital and may be transmitted over-the-air or via cable or satellite, using digital transmission methods.

There are several other standards in limited use. France uses *SECAM* (a French acronym for Sequential Color with Memory). Brazil uses a hybrid of NTSC and PAL called *M-PAL*. Argentina, Paraguay, and Uruguay use a lower-bandwidth version of PAL called *N-PAL*. Many former Soviet-bloc and Middle Eastern countries use a variant of SECAM called *MESECAM*. But if you're reading the English-language version of this book, you're almost certainly using NTSC or PAL, and most capture cards are available in versions for either of those standards.

Although digital transmission and HDTV have real advantages in terms of bandwidth and image quality, both have severe drawbacks for anyone contemplating building an HTPC. A standard NTSC signal delivered by analog cable is easy for an HTPC to deal with. You can simply connect the cable to the tuner card and allow the PC to change channels as needed.

Using digital cable or satellite as a program source makes matters more complex. At the time we wrote this, there were no (legal) digital tuner cards for PCs, mostly because the movie industry is paranoid about "piracy" and wants to keep its content locked up as tightly as possible. If you use digital cable or satellite as a program source, you must therefore change channels on the satellite box or digital cable receiver rather than on

the HTPC. That makes it difficult, although not impossible, to select the channel to be recorded under programmatic control.

The best solutions to the digital tuning problem are Rube Goldberg arrangements.

One solution is a programmable remote control for your satellite receiver or digital cable box. To record a program, you set the remote control to change to the proper channel at the proper time and leave it pointed at the satellite receiver or digital cable box. You also set the HTPC to begin recording at the proper time. The HTPC records whatever signal the satellite box or digital cable box happens to be delivering, so if someone moves the remote or the dog walks in front of it at just the wrong time, you may end up recording something other than what you intended.

Another solution is to equip the HTPC with an IR emitter that can mimic the remote control for your satellite receiver or digital cable box. The IR emitter works under the control of a scheduling program running on the HTPC. When it's time to record a program, the HTPC sends a series of commands to the IR emitter, which turns on the satellite receiver or digital cable box and tunes it to the correct channel.

These methods are awkward and unreliable at best. We hate to say it, but if you're stuck with satellite or digital cable, the best solution is to buy a box with built-in TiVo functionality. Either that, or "downgrade" to analog cable.

HDTV is another problem. Not only is HDTV mired in changing standards—many HDTV receivers bought recently may be useless in a year or two—but in our opinion the technology itself is not ready for prime time, even if you use a top-quality name-brand HDTV receiver. We know of no reliable way to record and display HDTV signals on an HTPC. That is likely to change over the next year or two, but for now we recommend that you build an HTPC only if your television signal is NTSC or PAL, delivered by analog cable or over-the-air.

Many HTPCs have been built in standard mini-tower cases, and we've even seen one or two in full-tower cases standing beside the television. If your HTPC will reside in an existing home-audio rack, make sure that the case you use fits the rack. In particular, if your home-audio rack has an enclosed back, make sure the case is not too deep to fit.

Noise level

Noise level is important, but not critically so. Our HTPC is destined to reside in a home-audio rack across the room from the sofa. Achieving low noise levels always involves tradeoffs among cost, performance, cooling, and reliability. All other things being equal, a quiet system either costs more, is slower, runs hotter, or is less reliable—or it may have all of those undesirable qualities. Accordingly, we decided to compromise by using quiet standard components, but not by using radical quiet-PC technologies such as a very slow processor, an insulated enclosure, fanless coolers, water cooling, and so on.

Expandability

Expandability is relatively important because the home entertainment landscape is changing rapidly. HDTV is imminent, and the venerable DVD will eventually be replaced by Blu-Ray or a similar high-capacity DVD standard. We also wanted to make provision for adding additional unrelated functions to the system, such as controlling a home weather station or functioning as an automated attendant and voice-mail controller for our telephone system.

Processor performance

Processor performance is moderately important. Simple functions such as playing a CD or DVD or playing recorded video make few demands on the processor. The slowest available mainstream processor would more than suffice for such functions. Recording video is a different matter, because real-time video compression is extremely CPU intensive, but we intend to use a video adapter with hardware compression support. Because the HTPC will at times function as a normal PC—for gaming, web browsing, and so on—we decided that it needed a moderately fast processor.

Video performance

Video performance is nearly as important as reliability. Several aspects of video performance are crucial, including video capture, video processing and compression, and 3D acceleration (for gaming). Accordingly, we wanted a video adapter that provided top-notch video capture and compression features, along with competent gaming performance.

Disk capacity/performance

Disk capacity and performance are as important as video performance. The HTPC will store massive amounts of audio and video data, so capacity is important. Performance is equally important, because the HTPC may be called upon to do many things simultaneously, all of which may involve disk activity.

Choosing Software

The traditional advice is to choose software before choosing the hardware to run it on, and that advice remains valid. The PVR and related software applications that will run on the HTPC are fundamental. So, before we made specific hardware selections, we had to decide which PVR software we'd run.

The working title of this chapter was *Building a Linux-Based PVR System*, as this was our original intention. It seemed reasonable at the time. TiVo is based on Linux, of course, and so we assumed Linux would be a good foundation for our PVR/HTPC system. As it turned out, such was not the case.

Linux PVR applications

The two primary Linux-based PVR applications, MythTV (*http://www. mythtv.org*) and Freevo (*http://freevo.sourceforge.net*), are, like many Linux applications, a strange combination of crude and elegant, polished and rough, and powerful yet missing major functions. At the time we looked at it, for example, Freevo lacked such basic functions as TV Live Pause (time-shifting) and DVD menus.

Installing and configuring these Linux-based applications from scratch is not for the faint of heart. We're sure a Linux guru could get either of them up and running eventually, but we're not Linux gurus. And, as is clear from reading numerous online forums and message boards, even Linux gurus frequently run into problems getting these applications to work properly.

One of our goals for this system was that it be easy to configure and easy to use. In other words, we wanted it to work as an appliance. Even if we were Linux gurus, most of our readers are not, so we reluctantly discarded the idea of building a Linux-based system. Both MythTV and Freevo are under active development, and we don't doubt that in a year or two either or both of them will be powerful, full-featured, easy-to-use PVR applications. But for now we decided they were simply insufficient for our purposes.

Windows PVR applications

Having considered and rejected Linux applications, we resigned ourselves to using Windows and began looking at Windows-based PVR applications. We downloaded evaluation versions of each of the major PVR applications and played with them on a testbed system.

Two types of Windows-based PVR applications are available. Standalone applications, such as myHTPC, Sage, ShowShifter, and SnapStream, are distributed separately, and are designed to work with a range of hardware. Bundled applications, such as the ATi Multimedia Center and Windows XP Media Center Edition, are bundled with specific hardware. We ruled out

MythTV the Easy Way

There is an easy way to install MythTV. KnoppMyth (*http://mysettop-box.tv*) is a version of Knoppix Linux optimized for MythTV. We down-loaded the ISO, burned it to CD, and booted a system with the KnoppMyth CD. Within an hour, we had a func-tioning MythTV PVR system. Well, kind of. The basics were there, but there were a lot of functions we couldn't make work, including the remote control, which apparently wasn't recognized as being connected to the USB port.

Windows XP Media Center Edition on philosophic grounds, and decided to take a closer look at the "big four" standalone applications and ATi's Multimedia Center.

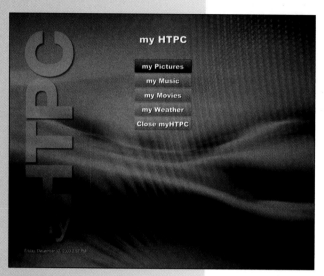

Figure 6-1. myHTPC main menu

myHTPC

myHTPC *(http://myhtpc.net)* is the most Linux-like of the four standalone applications we evaluated. In effect, myHTPC is a bunch of XML-based scripts rather than a monolithic application. There's a lot to like about myHTPC, not least that it's free. myHTPC uses a plug-in architecture, which makes it very configurable and flexible, and is well supported by a very active user community.

Those are the good points. Alas, there's also a lot to dislike about myHTPC. Running the installer extracts the program files and creates directories, and then fires up a configuration wizard. When that wizard completed, we were surprised to find that we had only a menu system installed, as shown in Figure 6-1.

We looked around for such basic features as the online program guide and recording menu, only to eventually realize that myHTPC did not provide those functions by default. Instead, we had to download, install, and configure plug-ins for these basic features. We tried several of the available recording plug-ins and were able to get them working, more or less, but we never did succeed in getting the online program guide to function. At first, it appeared to work, but it never downloaded the program data. Finally, after waiting nearly an hour, we concluded that it never was going to work.

myHTPC is also missing several key functions, including such basics as time-shifting and skipping commercials. Some other important features, such as support for the ATi Remote Wonder, require various workarounds or are unavailable.

We concluded that myHTPC is a toolkit rather than a turn-key application. We don't doubt that a tinkerer could make it work, after a fashion, but myHTPC was clearly not the application we wanted to use for a production HTPC.

Sage

We next looked at Sage *(http://www.sage.tv)*, which enjoys an excellent reputation among HTPC enthusiasts. The Sage PVR software is very good. It meets most of our functional requirements, and includes some features not available with other PVR software. Intelligent Recording, for example, has the TiVo-like ability to track the programs that you choose to record and on that basis automatically record other programs that it considers similar. (We prefer to make our own decisions about which programs to record, so we discounted this feature.)

Unfortunately, Sage has some weak points. The Sage online program guide uses data that is *screen-scraped*—pulled straight from dynamically generated web pages, with or without the permission of the web site owner—from Zap2It (*http://www.zap2it.com*). That concerned us, because there have already been lawsuits about screen-scraping, and we were loath to depend on a program guide gleaned in that fashion. Also, the program-guide features of Sage are relatively weak compared to some of the other applications we looked at.

The real killer, though, is that Sage supports very few tuner cards. When we checked, the Sage web site listed only four Hauppage models, the Adaptec VideOh!, and the Provideo PV256C/PV256T. Two discontinued products, the Creative Labs Video Blaster Digital VCR and the AVerMedia M179, were also listed, along with a note that other MPEG-2 encoding cards based on the Conexant IVAC-15, IVAC-16, CX23415, or StreamMachineCodec should function, but had not been tested. That's a pretty sparse selection.

Incredibly, none of the popular ATi All-In-Wonder or TV Wonder cards is among those supported. We considered that sufficient to eliminate Sage from further consideration.

ShowShifter

ShowShifter (*http://www.showshifter.com*) is another PVR application with a wide following among HTPC builders. It is functionally complete. with the exception of its reliance on an external online program guide provided by TitanTV. It has excellent support for the ATi RADEON series of capture/ tuner cards, and explicit support for the ATi Remote Wonder. Looking at the specifications, we decided that ShowShifter belonged on our shortlist.

Alas, we found the reality to be different. ShowShifter has all the right pieces, but it simply felt crude to us. We found the online programming guide particularly disconcerting. Press the button to bring up the program guide, and BAM! ShowShifter goes away, and Mozilla pops up in its place. Geez.

Still, ShowShifter is fully featured, easy to install, and easy to use. We eventually put ShowShifter in the "possible" column, hoping for something better but satisfied that it would do the job. We plan to keep an eye on ShowShifter. If a new version includes an integrated program guide, we may well decide to use it in the future.

SnapStream Personal Video Station

The specs looked good, so we downloaded the SnapStream Personal Video Station (PVS) 3.1 demo (*http://www.snapstream.com*), installed it, and fired it up. That was when the trouble started.

The demo setup procedure locked up reproducibly at the "Setup free TV listings" screen. That screen warned us that "To receive your FREE TV listings you need to sign up for a FREE SnapStream.Net account," so Robert was quite concerned when, after filling in his email address and password and clicking Next, nothing happened. He waited a moment and clicked Next again, with no result. One definition of insanity is doing the same thing repeatedly while expecting a different outcome, but he kept trying regardless. Finally, Robert went and took a shower. When he returned 20 minutes later, the screen remained unchanged.

Another definition of insanity is installing a bunch of demo programs on your main system, and that turned out to be the problem. Robert finally realized that in addition to the SnapStream demo, his main system also had myHTPC and the ShowShifter demo running. After killing and removing those programs and eradicating all mention of them in the registry, he reinstalled the SnapStream demo and all was well.

Figure 6-2. SnapStream PVS main menu

SnapStream PVS, shown in Figure 6-2, is the most polished of the four independent PVR programs we looked at and has what we consider to be the best interface. Functionally, SnapStream PVS lacks several features provided by other programs, including a DVD player, digital music playback, and the ability to display digital images. We considered those minor failings, as all of those functions are easily implemented with third-party applications.

The SnapStream setup utility makes it easy to install and configure the software. It leads you through selecting a remote control and then installs the software and invokes a setup wizard. After you provide your location and program source (Antenna, Standard Cable, External Cable Box, or Satellite), you're taken to SnapStream.net Setup, where you can configure the online program guide. You then select your capture device, scan your channels, and configure audio.

When you start SnapStream, you can choose among the following modes:

Full Screen
> Full Screen is the normal operating mode for an HTPC. It provides a clear, easy-to-use GUI that is visible at across-the-room distances and is easy to control with the navigation keys on the ATi Remote Wonder.

Windowed
> Windowed mode presents the standard GUI in a window. We found this mode to be of limited use on the HTPC because of the lim-

ited resolution of the television, but it might be useful when running SnapStream on a computer monitor.

Web Admin

Web Admin mode is used for all administration and configuration tasks, including TV display, recording options, program guide options, and maintenance. If you enable remote administration, you can access administrative functions from any PC on the home network or remotely via the Internet. You ordinarily use Web Admin mode only for initial setup and subsequent configuration changes; the HTPC routinely runs in Full Screen mode.

Log

SnapStream logs all program activities, including recording start/stop/ channel details, program startup/shutdown, online program guide updates, and so on. This feature is useful primarily for troubleshooting. We had no problems with the program, and so no opportunity to evaluate the usefulness of the log. Still, better to have it than not.

Functionally, SnapStream provides the core PVR functions necessary for the HTPC. Recording functions are well implemented, and the online program guide is fully integrated. With one click, you can choose to record the highlighted program one time only, record all occurrences of that program, or record only new episodes of that program. Playback functions also worked well, except that we were unable to make fast-forward work reliably or rewind work at all. At first we thought there was a configuration problem with the ATi Remote Wonder, but eventually we concluded that these features were simply broken. Having no desire to sit through commercials, we decided that SnapStream wasn't a good choice.

ATi Multimedia Center (MMC)

The ATi Multimedia Center (MMC) was the last application we looked at, and we wish we'd looked at it first. Unlike Sage, ShowShifter, and SnapStream, all of which sell for $60 or more, ATi MMC is "free" in the sense that it is bundled with ATi RADEON All-In-Wonder cards. MMC uses a unique "floating" control panel, shown in Figure 6-3, that hovers over the desktop, with options and buttons that change according to the function you select.

Figure 6-3. ATi Multimedia Center floating control panel

As you might expect from a bundled application, integration and functionality are both excellent. All of the core functions are there, and all of them work as expected. MMC includes TV-ON-DEMAND (live pause), a polished PVR module with all the functions we require, the excellent Gemstar GUIDE Plus+ online program guide, full-featured players for CD, DVD, VCD, and other multimedia types, and the MMC Library file management module. It also includes the VideoSoap filtering function, which uses the power of the RADEON graphics processor to filter and clean up video.

We concluded that the ATi Multimedia Center was the best fit for our requirements. (Alas, the MMC software works only with ATi RADEON All-In-Wonder cards, so if you choose a different tuner card you'll have to use some other software.)

Component Considerations

With our design criteria in mind, we set out to choose the best components for the HTPC system. Although we've designed and built many PCs over the years, the HTPC was a new experience for us because the special purposes it serves were outside our general experience. For example, although we understand PC audio and video quite well, the different standards used for television video and home-theater audio were largely a mystery to us. Accordingly, we made a few false starts, but we think we ended up choosing optimal hardware components for the HTPC environment. The following sections describe the components we chose, and why we chose them.

Case and power supply

Antec Overture (http://www.antec-inc.com)

You can, of course, build an HTPC in a standard mini-tower case like the Antec Sonata. But the critical Spousal-Unit Approval (SUA) criterion (otherwise known as, "You're not putting *that* in my den!") demands a case that matches standard home-audio components in size and appearance as closely as possible. Barbara has a sense of humor about these things, but many spouses do not, so it's worth checking before you purchase a case. As we learned, there are a lot of HTPC cases available, but most have one or more drawbacks.

Many HTPC builders use the Cooler Master ATC-610-GX1 case (*http://www.coolermaster.com*). Although it is attractive, it accepts only micro-ATX motherboards. We wanted an HTPC case that accommodates full ATX motherboards, and those are surprisingly hard to find. Projection Systems, Inc. sells the beautiful Nexus and Vision II HTPC cases (*http://www.crtcinema.com*). Both accept full ATX motherboards and have such niceties as built-in IR windows, but they cost $249 and $399 respectively, not including power supply. We decided to keep looking.

Our search for the perfect HTPC case turned up several other candidates, but none came close to the Antec Overture case we eventually chose. The standard home-audio component size is 17" wide by 4" to 6" high by 12" to 14" deep. The Antec Overture is 17" wide by 5.25" high, which matches standard home-audio components perfectly. The Overture is nicely finished in black gloss and brushed chrome.

The Overture is designed from the ground up as an HTPC case. In addition to such quiet-PC features as an oversized, thermally controlled case fan and rubber shock mounting for the hard drives, the Overture has such niceties as front-panel USB, FireWire, audio connectors, and a filtered air intake that doesn't require opening the case to clean the filter.

A full-blown HTPC needs a powerful, quiet power supply. The Antec Overture includes a special single-fan version of the well-regarded Antec TruePower 380W power supply. In addition to providing lots of well-regulated power, the True380XR is so quiet that we were unable to hear it running.

We don't know of a better HTPC case and power supply at anything near the $100 or so price of the Antec Overture.

Motherboard

ASUS A7N8X Deluxe (http://usa.asus.com)

For this system, stability and reliability are key considerations. The last thing we need is the system shooting craps when it's supposed to be recording the final episode of a multipart *Masterpiece Theater* or while we're watching a severe weather alert on the Weather Channel.

With stability and reliability as the prime requirements, the question became whether to use an AMD Athlon motherboard or an Intel Pentium 4 motherboard. Fortunately, superb motherboards are available for both processors. On the AMD side, the *n*VIDIA nForce2 chipset has proven in our testing to be as robust and reliable as the best Intel chipsets. On the Intel side, the 865/875-series chipsets are the standard by which we judge other chipsets.

We had two final motherboard candidates, the ASUS A7N8X Deluxe and the Intel D865PERL. Both are immensely stable, have very high build quality, provide all the features we need, and cost about the same. We elected to go with the ASUS board for two reasons:

Performance
> An AMD Athlon with performance appropriate for an HTPC is significantly less expensive than a comparable Intel Pentium 4 processor.

Audio
> Embedded Intel SoundMax audio is excellent, but the embedded *n*VIDIA SoundStorm audio is stunning. If possible, we wanted to avoid buying a $100+ audio adapter like the Creative Audigy2. Although the embedded Intel SoundMax audio might have served the purpose, we were certain that the embedded *n*VIDIA SoundStorm audio would suffice.

ALTERNATIVES: MOTHERBOARD

The ASUS A7N8X Deluxe and Intel D865PERL motherboards are full ATX. If you use a microATX case, such as the Antec Aria, choose a motherboard that fits the case. We know of no microATX Athlon motherboard that meets our requirements for the HTPC system, which was one of the major reasons we used a full-ATX case for this system. If you use a microATX case, we recommend the Intel D865GLC motherboard. If you are building a full-ATX Intel system, consider the superb ASUS P4P800 Deluxe as an alternative to the Intel D865PERL.

Processor Temperatures

Until recently, Intel processors ran cooler than AMD processors with similar performance levels. That remains true for low-end and midrange processors. A Northwood-core Intel P4 processor with performance comparable to the AMD Athlon XP processor we used in this system indeed runs cooler. That situation has recently changed dramatically, though. Intel's fastest P4 processors, based on the new Prescott core, dissipate nearly twice the wattage of comparable AMD Athlon 64 processors and run much hotter than AMD models.

Buy Enough Horsepower

A subtle point to remember when choosing a processor is that an HTPC is likely to be upgraded much less frequently than a desktop PC. Once an HTPC system is built, configured, connected, and tested, it should reasonably be expected to live quietly in the home-audio rack for several years between upgrades. Accordingly, when the choice is between "just enough" and "more than I'll ever need," we suggest you choose the latter.

Ours is a special situation because we know we'll be tweaking this system over the coming months, but we'd really rather not be swapping processors in and out. For example, we settled for one medium-size hard drive in this testbed HTPC, but if we were building it as a production model we'd have installed two of the largest hard drives we could find.

SoundStorm audio, also used in the Microsoft Xbox, has a unique feature. It accepts any audio input, including Windows systems sounds and other stereo sources, and outputs an AC3 Dolby Digital 5.1 digital signal to a compatible receiver or amplifier. That meant we could simply connect the SoundStorm output to a 5.1 speaker system and allow the system to take care of audio routing automatically.

One problem is that Athlon XP processors, while fast and inexpensive, produce more heat than Intel processors of comparable performance, and therefore require larger (and noisier) fans. An HTPC needs to be quiet, so the noise level of the CPU fan was of concern to us. We concluded that, if necessary, we could reduce the noise level by substituting one of the various quieter (albeit more expensive) Athlon cooling solutions.

Despite our choice of the ASUS A7N8X motherboard, we have no argument with anyone who weighs the options and chooses an Intel D865PERL motherboard instead. The Intel motherboard is an excellent choice, and has the advantage of using a cooler and quieter Pentium 4 processor.

Processor

AMD Athlon XP 2600+ (http://www.amd.com)

There are two schools of thought regarding appropriate processor performance for an HTPC. Simple playback (real-time video decoding) puts minimal demands on the processor, but recording (real-time video encoding) demands either a fast processor or a video adapter with hardware-encoding support. Accordingly, a dedicated PVR system can use a mini-ITX motherboard with a slow VIA processor as long as the video adapter provides hardware encoding.

But we are building a general-purpose HTPC system rather than a simple PVR. We want to leave our options open for the future. For example, although we are satisfied to record only one stream for now, it's possible that in the future we would want to upgrade our HTPC to allow it to record two or more simultaneous video streams. Also, our HTPC will do much more than simple PVR tasks. It will serve audio and video throughout the house, and be used as a substitute for a game console. Using a fast processor is inexpensive insurance for future flexibility.

After reading everything we could get our hands on about video encoding and playing around with some encoding software, we concluded that a processor in the 2+ GHz range made the most sense. We didn't need the fastest processor available, but the slower models weren't all that much less expensive than mid-speed models, so we settled on something in the 2.5 GHz range as a first approximation. Looking at price versus speed, it was clear that at the time we built this system an AMD Athlon XP 2600+ was the "sweet spot" in terms of price and performance, so that's what we chose.

Some HTPC applications, such as ATi Multimedia Center (MMC) EazyShare, need all the processor power they can get. An EazyShare server is happiest with a 3+ GHz Intel Pentium 4 or an Opteron/Athlon64, which are expensive processors. EazyShare needs all that power not just to stream video to remote PCs, but because it distributes programming and control functions to those remote PCs.

For our HTPC system, we decided that streaming video was unnecessary. If we want to play recorded video on other PCs, it's easy enough to copy the video files to the remote systems or to access them directly on the HTPC via a Windows share. Most of the time, though, we'll play recorded video remotely with a DVD player rather than a PC. For that, it's a simple matter to archive the video to a writable DVD or VCD and sneakernet it back to the bedroom. We may later build a low-end PVR system for the bedroom and use it to access video files stored on the main HTPC (and vice versa).

The Intel Pentium 4/2.4 processor has about the same performance as the Athlon XP 2600+, but was selling at a 70% premium. Frankly, we would have preferred the Intel processor. It runs cooler, uses a quieter cooling fan, and the Pentium 4 architecture is superior for video processing. But the higher cost of the Intel processor and the prospect of losing the SoundStorm audio on the ASUS motherboard was enough to tip us toward the AMD Athlon XP 2600+.

Memory

Corsair XMS PC3200 DDR-SDRAM (http://www.corsairmemory.com)

The HTPC must perform various functions, so it's important that it have sufficient memory. We decided that, although 256 MB might suffice, 512 MB was a safer bet. We don't yet know all of the functions we may expect this system to provide, so installing 512 MB is cheap insurance. We actually considered installing a gigabyte, but that would have been conspicuous consumption.

The A7N8X Deluxe motherboard supports dual-channel PC3200 DDR memory. Dual-channel memory outperforms single-channel memory but requires installing DIMMs in pairs, so we chose two 256 MB DIMMs rather than one 512 MB DIMM. Ordinarily, we'd have chosen Crucial or Kingston memory for this system, but we found a special deal on the motherboard that bundled two 256 MB Corsair XMS modules at an unbeatable price, so that's what we chose.

Like Mushkin and others, Corsair is an "enthusiast" memory brand that is popular among the overclocking crowd. Corsair is referred to as a packager or an assembler rather than a manufacturer, because they don't actually make memory chips. Instead, Corsair buys premium memory chips from actual producers like Micron and Samsung, and then assembles those chips into memory modules. By

Use the Right CPU Cooler

Athlon XP processors require a CPU cooler rated for at least the speed of the CPU you are using. We happened to have a Dynatron (*http://www.dynatron-corp.com*) DC1207BM-L Chicago Series heatsink/fan on the shelf that was rated for the Athlon XP 2600+. Our contacts at AMD have recommended Dynatron coolers to us, and our experience with them has been excellent, so we decided to use that cooler. It's inexpensive, efficient, and, at 36 dBA, relatively quiet for a standard cooler. Because our HTPC will reside across the room from the sofa, we decided that the fan noise would not be intrusive. If experience proves otherwise, we'll substitute a quiet cooler such as the Zalman Ultra Quiet CPU Cooler (*http://www.zalman.co.kr/english/intro.htm*).

ALTERNATIVES: MEMORY

If it had not been for the special bundling/rebate deal that included the Corsair memory modules at a price we couldn't refuse, we'd have used Crucial memory for this system, as we do for nearly every system we build. After you choose your motherboard, visit *http://www.crucial.com* and use their Memory Configurator to select memory modules that are compatible with your motherboard.

hand-selecting ("binning") memory chips, Corsair can produce premium modules and matched pairs that operate reliably with very fast memory timings.

For standard systems there's no reason to pay a premium for such "overclockable" memory. Unless you happen to find a deal on Corsair or other premium modules, we recommend standard Crucial or Kingston memory for your HTPC.

Video adapter and capture/tuner card

ATi RADEON All-In-Wonder 9600 Pro (http://www.ati.com)

An HTPC system requires four separate video functions:

Display

The HTPC must display computer output on a television. That requires a standard PCI or AGP video adapter or a motherboard with embedded graphics that is capable of outputting a video signal that can be displayed by a television set (rather than a computer monitor).

TV tuning

Because our television signal is delivered via analog cable, we need some means to select the channel to be viewed or recorded and to convert it from the RF signal present on the cable TV connector to video usable by the HTPC.

Video capture

Television video uses standards and protocols that differ from those used by PC video. The HTPC must have the ability to capture a television video stream and process it into a form that can be stored and played back by the PC.

Video encoding/decoding

A raw, uncompressed video stream would fill even the largest hard disk very quickly. All practical video storage methods use some form of compression, such as MPEG-1, MPEG-2, or MPEG-4, to reduce the size of stored video data. In order to make playback practical in devices with limited processing power, such as DVD players, MPEG compression algorithms place the processing burden on compression (encoding), while making decompression (decoding) as easy as possible. So, although even a slow processor can decode and play video without straining, the process of capturing, encoding, and storing video requires a lot of CPU ticks.

Some adapters simply deliver a raw video stream to the main system processor, which must compress the data itself. Because real-time video compression is extremely demanding, using such an adapter means the HTPC must have a very fast CPU, and even the fastest CPU

ALTERNATIVES: VIDEO ADAPTER & CAPTURE/TUNER CARD

If you prefer to use PVR software other than ATi MMC, consider using a Hauppage video capture/tuner card. Hauppage makes several models. The one you want is the WinTV-PVR-350, which includes hardware support for MPEG encoding and decoding and includes video output to allow you to watch recordings on a TV (rather than just on your computer monitor). Most standalone PVR software supports the Hauppage WinTV-PVR-350. Note, however, that this is a dedicated PCI video capture/tuner card and does not replace a standard video adapter. You'll need to install a separate AGP graphics card in addition to the Hauppage video capture/tuning card (*http://www.hauppage.com*).

may drop frames during real-time encoding. Other adapters use the video GPU to encode locally, delivering a precompressed video stream to the HTPC for storage.

TV adapters may provide any combination of these functions. For example, some adapters provide video capture and TV tuning functions, but require a separate graphics card to display the video. Other adapters provide display and capture functions but have no tuner, and so are useful only for capturing direct video signals such as the output from a camcorder. Still other adapters may provide display, tuning, and capture functions, but offload encoding functions to the main system processor. Adapters such as the ATi RADEON All-In-Wonder 9600 Pro combine all four functions in one card.

Based on previous experience as well as on intensive reading of HTPC newsgroups and forums, we knew we wanted to use an ATi RADEON All-In-Wonder adapter with onboard MPEG encoding support. In fact, its lack of support for the RADEON was sufficient grounds for us to rule out using the Sage PVR software, despite its excellent reputation.

The ATi RADEON All-In-Wonder series cards are well supported by third-party PVR software vendors such as ShowShifter and SnapStream, and are also bundled with ATi's well-regarded Multimedia Center (MCC) software. MCC includes PVR functionality as well as most or all of the other functions we want an HTPC to provide, so in the interests of simplicity and compatibility we decided to use MCC as the standard against which we could judge other software.

ATi makes several All-In-Wonder models based on various RADEON chipsets. At the time we were designing the HTPC, these models included the All-In-Wonder (AIW) 9000 Pro, the AIW 9600 Pro, and the AIW 9800 Pro. We ruled out the AIW 9000 Pro because it does not include hardware MPEG encoding support and because we wanted better graphics performance for console gaming on the television. And although we'd love to have its graphics performance, we also ruled out the AIW 9800 Pro based on its very high price.

That left us with the AIW 9600 Pro, which does everything we need and at a reasonable price. Apart from slower 3D graphics performance, the AIW 9600 Pro matches the AIW 9800 Pro in all important respects. Also, unlike the AIW 9800 Pro, the AIW 9600 Pro includes an FM input connector and tuner that allows us to dispense with our receiver. The AIW 9600 Pro does not include the HDTV support that is standard with the AIW 9800 Pro, but ATi offers a $30 optional adapter that adds HDTV support to the AIW 9600 Pro.

Overall, we consider the ATi RADEON AIW 9600 Pro the standout choice among capture/tuner cards for an HTPC.

We can't give specific URLs for HTPC newsgroups and forums because there are so many of them and they change frequently. A quick Google search for some key terms—such as *htpc, pvr, dvr, radeon, sage, show-shifter*, and *snapstream*—turns up hundreds of useful pages.

Hard disk drive

Seagate Barracuda 7200.7 ST3160023AS 160 GB Serial ATA
(http://www.seagate.com)

Hard drive capacity, performance, noise level, and reliability are critical for an HTPC system.

Capacity

The most obvious consideration is capacity. Depending on the characteristics of the video stream and the compression type used, video eats disk space at a rate of 700 MB to 5 GB per hour. At the low end, 700 MB/hour stores only VHS-quality video. We'll probably want to store most of what we record at DVD quality, which means we have to plan for the 2.5 to 5 GB/hour rate that typical DVD-quality video streams require. That means 100 GB of disk space translates to only 20 to 40 hours of video storage.

But we need to store more than just video. The HTPC will also store and serve CD audio discs ripped and compressed in OGG format at a high-quality setting. OGG uses variable bit-rate compression, but it's safe to assume that an average audio CD will require at least 150 MB of storage space when compressed at a quality level acceptable to us. Barbara has several hundred CDs she'll want to rip, which may require another 100 GB or more of storage space.

Performance

Hard drive performance is another important criterion. The HTPC will spend much of its time idling, but at times it may need to do many things simultaneously, such as recording one video stream while playing back another while serving an audio stream at the same time. Accordingly, a large cache and fast rotation rate are important. On that basis, we concluded that we needed a 7,200 RPM hard drive with an 8 MB buffer.

Noise level

Modern 7,200 RPM hard drives differ greatly in noise level. We considered models from Seagate and Maxtor. The Maxtor drives, although fast and reliable, are significantly louder than the Seagate Barracuda models, both at idle and when seeking, reading, or writing. We decided on that basis to go with the Seagate.

Reliability

Seagate drives are extremely reliable, but even so we were concerned about the possibility of drive failure. As Barbara sometimes points out, Robert has to sleep sometime, and the thought of losing a week's or a month's worth of stored programs to a drive failure was not a pleasant one. Our first thought was to install two Serial ATA drives and mirror them using RAID 1. The obvious downside to that is that mirroring cuts drive capacity in half, and we need all the capacity we can get.

Then we realized we already had a solution. The HTPC system will be connected to our internal network and, via our firewall, to the Internet. It has to be connected so that it can download program guide updates, periodically reset its clock against an SNTP time server, and so on. We have literally terabytes of disk spinning elsewhere on our network, so it'd be easy enough to set up a cron job to periodically check the HTPC's hard drives and copy any new files to a hard drive elsewhere on the network. Problem solved.

We concluded that we needed at least 200 GB of available drive space on the HTPC system, and more would be better. We decided to use serial ATA drives rather than standard parallel models because S-ATA cables are thin and allow for better airflow. At the time we designed the system, Seagate had just begun shipping 200 GB S-ATA models, but these were not yet widely available. Accordingly, we decided to install two 160 GB S-ATA Seagate Barracudas.

What we decided to do and what we actually did are two different things. We built the HTPC system on a Sunday. The two Seagate S-ATA drives arrived bare, with only mounting screws. The ASUS A7N8X Deluxe motherboard included two S-ATA data cables, but no S-ATA power adapters. We assumed—always a danger-ous thing to do—that the Antec power supply would include S-ATA power con-nectors. Unfortunately, Antec was in the process of transitioning to an updated power supply that included S-ATA power connectors, but the Overture case we used was an early model that had only standard Molex connectors. We knew we had a bunch of S-ATA power adapters around somewhere, but were unable to find them. As a result, we had no way to use the Seagate S-ATA drives. We ended up installing an older P-ATA 120 GB Seagate Barracuda ATA V drive, which served for testing purposes. Before we bring up the system live, we'll pull the P-ATA drive and install the two S-ATA drives we'd originally planned to use.

Optical drive

Plextor PX-504A DVD+R/RW writer (http://www.plextor.com)

We dithered about what type of optical drive to install in our HTPC system. Obviously, the HTPC must be able to read CD, DVD-ROM, and DVD-Video discs, but that left us to choose among a DVD-ROM drive, a combination DVD-ROM/CD-RW drive, and a DVD writer. The funda-mental question was whether we wanted the ability to write discs on the HTPC system and, if so, what type of discs.

Our first thought was to install a DVD-ROM drive, on the theory that if we wanted to archive something we'd recorded, we could simply copy that file across the network to one of our desktop systems and burn the disc there. We were concerned that mastering and burning a CD or DVD on the HTPC system would be difficult because of the limited resolution of the television screen.

ALTERNATIVES: OPTICAL DRIVE

We got our Plextor PX-504A while a $30 rebate was in effect, so it cost us less than $80. That made it the most cost-effective high-quality DVD writer we could find at that moment. As the 4X Plextor drive now has 8X and 12X Plextor siblings, it's likely that the PX-504A may no longer be available when you read this. In that case, the 8X PX-708A and the 12X PX-712A are the best choices, depending on your budget. If you want a Serial ATA DVD burner, choose the Plextor PX-712SA.

For a DVD±R/RW drive, our second choice is the Sony DRU-530A. If you're on a tight budget, the NEC ND-2500A is an excellent inexpensive DVD±R/RW drive, which provides 8X DVD+R writes to boot. If you can't find the NEC unit, any one of the widely distributed inexpensive Lite-On 8X DVD writers should suffice. They're not as reliable or durable as Plextor units, but they are excellent low-end choices.

If your HTPC is connected to your network, as it should be, it may not need an optical writer at all. In that case, choose any current DVD-ROM drive made by Lite-On, Mitsumi, NEC, Samsung, Sony, or Toshiba. Make sure the model you choose explicitly lists compatibility with the writable DVD formats you use. Otherwise, buy on price.

We concluded that the only way to find out was to try, so we decided to install a DVD writer in the initial iteration of our HTPC. If it turns out that burning discs is too clumsy at television-screen resolution, we'll replace the DVD writer with a DVD-ROM drive and transfer any files we want to archive across the network to one of our desktop systems for burning.

Having decided to install a DVD writer, we were faced with the decision of which model to choose. Other than for testing purposes, we have used Plextor optical drives almost exclusively for years. We have found Plextor drives to be reliable, robust, compatible, and reasonably priced, so we decided to install a Plextor DVD burner in the HTPC system.

At the time we built the system, Plextor offered two DVD burners. The PX-504A supports only DVD+R/RW formats and writes DVD+R at 4X. The PX-708A supports DVD+R/RW and DVD-R/RW formats, and writes DVD+R at 8X. Although the PX-708A would have been the faster and more flexible choice, it also cost significantly more than the PX-504A.

The less expensive Plextor drive does everything we needed the optical drive in our HTPC to do, so we decided to install a PX-504A rather than the more expensive PX-708A. Had this been our only system with a DVD writer, we would probably have chosen the PX-708A despite its higher price, if only for the 8X burning support. The PX-708A burns a full DVD+R disc in about eight minutes versus twice that for the PX-504A, so if you're impatient the PX-708A may be the better choice.

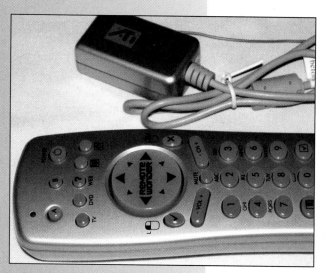

Figure 6-4. The ATi Remote Wonder and receiver

Remote control

ATi Remote Wonder (http://www.ati.com)

At first glance, the ATi Remote Wonder, shown in Figure 6-4, looks like an ordinary universal remote control with extra buttons for controlling PC functions. It's not. The Remote Wonder is designed solely to control a PC to which the USB Remote Wonder receiver is connected. The Remote Wonder includes dedicated buttons for controlling the TV, DVD, and other functions of an HTPC, six programmable buttons that can be used to control Windows functions, and a jog/shuttle dial that emulates all functions of a standard two-button mouse. The Remote Wonder is optimized to control the "fifteen-foot interface" used by HTPC applications running on low-resolution television displays at across-the-room distances.

The Remote Wonder is bundled with ATi RADEON All-In-Wonder video adapters, but if it hadn't been, we'd have bought one separately. With the exception of entering text, the Remote Wonder provides all of the functions for which we'd otherwise have to use a keyboard and mouse, making it

Compatibility Bit Setting and the Book Type Field

There's a bit of nastiness playing out in the background of the writable DVD format wars. The issue has to do with compatibility between discs written using the + formats and some DVD-ROM drives and DVD players.

In theory, any DVD player or DVD-ROM drive should be able to read a DVD+R/RW or DVD-R/RW disc because the reflectivity and contrast characteristics of writable discs are similar to those of stamped dual-layer DVD discs, which any player should be able to read. In practice, some older DVD-ROM drives and DVD players refuse to play DVD+R/RW discs but will play DVD-R/RW discs. Others refuse to play DVD-R/RW discs but will play DVD+R/RW discs. As annoying as that can be, it is a natural consequence of the age of the device.

If "natural" incompatibilities are annoying, "artificial" incompatibilities are infuriating. These artificial incompatibilities result from the fact that the DVD+R/RW format is not sanctioned by the DVD Forum, which controls the patents, trademarks, and other rights for the DVD standard. Accordingly, the DVD Forum does everything possible to ensure that its approved standards, DVD-R/RW and DVD-RAM, succeed, and that the DVD+R/RW standard, sponsored by the rival DVD+RW Alliance, fails.

The DVD Forum has a problem, though, because DVD+R/RW is superior in every respect to DVD-R/RW. Even Pioneer, which stood to profit hugely if DVD-R/RW became the standard, has since shipped hybrid DVD burners that can write either DVD+R/RW or DVD-R/RW discs. Pioneer's backhanded endorsement of the + formats was about as shocking as Pepsi endorsing Coke, and is indisputable evidence of the superiority of the + formats.

DVD discs, whether pressed or burned, have a media descriptor in the lead-in area. This descriptor, called the Book Type Field, identifies the disc explicitly by type—DVD-ROM, DVD+R, DVD-R, and so on. For writable DVD discs, the Book Type Field is not intrinsic to the media, but is written under the control of the DVD writer firmware and the burning software.

DVD drives and players that fully comply with the DVD Forum specifications may refuse to recognize discs with a Book Type Field of DVD+R or DVD+RW. That is, the drive or player could play the disc if it tried, but because the media descriptor byte is "foreign" the drive or player rejects it without even attempting to play it.

It is possible to fool a DVD-ROM drive or player by writing an incorrect Book Type Field to the disc. For example, a DVD+R disc can be written with a Book Type Field of "DVD-ROM" rather than the correct "DVD+R," a process known as changing the compatibility bit settings. Most "problem" DVD players and drives will read such discs successfully. There is no real disadvantage to changing compatibility bit settings routinely, although most DVD writer makers recommend using a false Book Type Field only if needed for compatibility with other DVD players and drives.

So why don't DVD writers routinely set the Book Type Field to "DVD-ROM" when writing DVD+R/RW discs? Some do, including some Hewlett-Packard models that do so automatically. Some other DVD writers allow changing the Book Type Field, but require it to be done manually for each disc. Still other DVD writers, including Plextor and Philips models, forbid resetting the Book Type Field. Changing the Book Type Field requires support in firmware, and these models simply make no provision for it.

The reason they don't support changing the Book Type Field is an ugly story. In essence, Plextor, Philips, and other manufacturers that do not permit changing the Book Type Field are playing by the rules, presumably in the hopes of avoiding a lawsuit by the DVD Forum. The DVD Forum sees the inability of some DVD players and drives to read DVD+R/RW discs as a competitive advantage for DVD-R/RW and therefore "requests" that DVD writer manufacturers not support changing the Book Type Field. In effect, the DVD Forum intentionally enforces this incompatibility for its own benefit and at the expense of consumers.

Fortunately, Book Type Field is unimportant unless you have one of the relatively few models of DVD players and drives that refuse to read DVD+R/RW discs. If all of your DVD drives and players can read DVD+R/RW discs, the compatibility bit setting issue need not concern you. To avoid this problem, we recommend buying only DVD-ROM drives and DVD players that explicitly support DVD+R and +RW discs.

For more information about which specific DVD players and drives are compatible with DVD+R/RW discs, visit *http://www. dvdplusrw.org* and click the Compatibility List link.

We think the ATi Remote Wonder (or the enhanced Remote Wonder II) is the best choice for HTPC applications. It is well designed, incorporates every necessary function, and is well supported by most PVR software. In fact, the ATi Remote Wonder is so good that we see no reason to choose anything else. However, we should mention the Snapstream Firefly PC Remote, which appears to be essentially a clone of the ATi product. The Firefly PC Remote shipped in May 2004, and we have not yet had an opportunity to evaluate it.

very easy to control the routine functions of our HTPC. (We still installed a wireless keyboard and mouse, of course, but it's very nice to be able to use just the Remote Wonder for most HTPC functions.)

The bad news is that the Remote Wonder is useless for controlling your television and other components, because it uses RF instead of IR. The good news is that using RF gives the Remote Wonder extended range and removes the line-of-sight requirement of IR remotes. We were able to use the Remote Wonder from more than 30 feet away and through two residential walls to control the functions of our HTPC.

Nor is the Remote Wonder limited to use with ATi video adapters or with the ATi Multimedia Center software. Most major PVR software, including Sage, ShowShifter, and SnapStream, supports the Remote Wonder, at least partially, and the Remote Wonder can be used for remote control of any PC merely by connecting the receiver to a USB port and installing the driver software. ATi sells the Remote Wonder separately, and has recently introduced the Remote Wonder II, an enhanced version with longer range and additional programmable keys.

Keyboard and mouse

Logitech diNovo Media Desktop (http://www.logitech.com)

Our original plan was to connect a standard keyboard and mouse temporarily to the HTPC and remove it after we'd finished installing and configuring software. We'd use the ATi Remote Wonder exclusively for routine operation, or so we thought. When we started using the system, though, we realized that there were times when we really needed a standard keyboard and mouse, not least when we wanted to use the system as a gaming console, for checking email, or for surfing the Web.

Any wireless keyboard/mouse combo with sufficient range for your needs. Unless you sit within three to five feet of the HTPC, standard IR and RF wireless products are unlikely to have sufficient range. Bluetooth RF devices, on the other hand, are typically rated for a 30-foot range (although 15 to 20 feet is more realistic). We prefer the Logitech diNovo Media Desktop, but the Microsoft Wireless Optical Desktop for Bluetooth is also an excellent choice.

Robert, being cheap, thought we could simply leave a standard keyboard and mouse connected to the HTPC, and store them on top of the system. Barbara, being tidy, ruled that out. Clearly, we needed a wireless keyboard and mouse that were usable at across-the-room distances. That was a problem, because most of the wireless keyboards and mice we've seen are intended to be used on a desktop at no more than three to five feet from the receiver, not a dozen feet or more.

Keeping our fingers crossed, we tried several standard wireless keyboard/mouse combos, and found that none of them would reliably work across the room. We also tried a Gyration wireless RF keyboard/mouse combo. Although it claims a 30-foot range, we found it didn't work reliably at much more than a dozen feet in our environment.

We decided to give the Logitech diNovo Media Desktop a try. Although not inexpensive, it incorporates an excellent programmable keyboard, the detachable MediaPad Bluetooth command center, a Bluetooth hub, and

Logitech's superb MX900 rechargeable cordless optical mouse. This is one of those products with hidden depths. The more we use it, the more features and applications we discover.

Speakers

Logitech Z-680 speaker system (http://www.logitech.com)

We originally intended to connect the HTPC to our aging JVC receiver and speakers, but as the project unfolded we realized that the HTPC could replace every component in our home-audio rack except the television. We'd been considering buying an audio system for our downstairs guest suite, and Robert was struck by a cunning plan.

Why not simply relocate all of the existing home-audio equipment downstairs and make the HTPC a standalone system? Our old receiver supported only Dolby Pro Logic, and we had only two speakers connected to it. We wanted a modern system, with front and rear channels, center channel, and an LFE (low-frequency emitter, usually called a subwoofer) anyway, so now seemed the time to do it. All we needed to add to the HTPC was an amplifier and a set of six speakers, so we set out to learn what was available.

We checked the Crutchfield catalog (*http://www.crutchfield.com*) and found that even their least expensive home theater receiver and speaker system cost more than we wanted to spend. But the HTPC is, after all, a PC rather than a home-audio component, so we decided to look at PC speaker systems, the best of which are very good indeed. A true audiophile would no doubt sneer at the idea of using a PC speaker system for a home theater setup, but to our admittedly uneducated ears there is little or no difference in sound quality.

After considerable research, we settled on the Logitech Z-680 5.1 speaker system. The Z-680 incorporates four satellite speakers for left/right and front/rear audio, a center-channel speaker, and an LFE subwoofer. The satellite speakers are rated at 62W RMS each, the center-channel speaker at 69W RMS, and the LFE at a massive 188W RMS, for a total RMS output of 505W. At a street price of $300 or so, the Z-680 speakers match the performance and specifications of traditional home-audio systems that sell for two to three times the price.

Two methods are commonly used to specify the output power of amplifiers. Peak Power is often specified for computer speakers, particularly inexpensive ones, but is essentially meaningless. Peak Power specifies the maximum instantaneous power an amplifier can deliver, but says nothing about how much power it can deliver continuously. The RMS (root mean square) Power rating is more useful because it specifies how much power the amplifier can deliver continuously.

One of our technical reviewers makes a good point. He writes:

"Speakers are probably the most subjective elements of the system. While I certainly have no argument with your selection, there are many fine alternatives in the same price range. It's also an area where more dollars doesn't always mean better performance or better sound. I think it appropriate to urge readers to make the effort to personally audition speakers where possible rather than rely solely on reviews and recommendations...and given that room interactions play such a major role in speaker performance, [readers] should buy from an outlet with a liberal return policy."

ALTERNATIVES: SPEAKERS

Also consider the $325 Klipsch Promedia Ultra 5.1 set, which provides five 60W satellites (any can be used as the center-channel speaker) and a 170W subwoofer. The Z-680 and Promedia Ultra 5.1 are both top-quality speaker systems, with superb sound quality and as much power as anyone could need. We slightly prefer the Klipsch speakers for listening to classical music and we slightly prefer the Logitech speakers for HTPC use and gaming.

If the Z-680 and Promedia Ultra 5.1 are a bit much for your budget, consider the $150 THX-certified Logitech Z-5300 set, which provides 35.25W to each of the four satellites, 39W to the center-channel speaker, and 100W to the subwoofer. Although it doesn't quite match the Z-680 or the Promedia Ultra 5.1, the sound quality is excellent for this price level.

The Z-680 speaker system includes Dolby Digital & DTS hardware decoding and is THX certified. We confess that we don't understand what all that means, but our audiophile friends tell us those are Good Things. And, although admitting it may label us as audio barbarians, we have to say that the audio from the Z-680 speaker system sounds as good to us as anything else we've listened to.

Component summary

Table 6-1 summarizes our component choices for the home theater PC system.

Table 6-1. Bill of Materials for HTPC

Component	Product
Case	Antec Overture
Power supply	Antec True380 (included)
Motherboard	ASUS A7N8X Deluxe
Processor	AMD Athlon XP 2600+
Memory	Corsair XMS PC3200 DDR-SDRAM (two 256 MB DIMMs)
Video/capture/ tuner adapter	ATi RADEON All-In-Wonder 9600 Pro
Hard drive	Seagate Barracuda 7200.7 ST3160023AS 160 GB Serial ATA (two)
Optical drive	Plextor PX-504A DVD+R/RW writer
Remote control	ATi Remote Wonder
Keyboard/mouse	Logitech diNovo Media Desktop
Speakers	Logitech Z-680 speaker system

Figure 6-5. HTPC components, awaiting construction

Building the System

Figure 6-5 shows the major components of the HTPC. The ASUS A7N8X Deluxe motherboard and the Logitech DiNovo Media Desktop keyboard and mouse are on top of the Antec Overture case, with the Plextor PX-504A DVD burner and the ATi All-In-Wonder 9600 Pro video adapter to the right. In front, from left to right, are two 256 MB sticks of Corsair PC3200 memory, the Athlon XP processor, the Seagate Barracuda hard drive, and the Dynatron CPU cooler.

We build systems on the kitchen table because it provides plenty of work room, easy access from front and rear, and plenty of light, all of which are important. Barbara isn't happy about having her kitchen table thus occupied, but when Robert explained that the alternative was using her antique dining room table, she grudgingly agreed that the kitchen table was the better choice. Wherever you choose to build your system, make sure it provides sufficient workspace, easy access, and good lighting. Spousal approval is optional, but highly recommended.

You needn't follow the exact sequence we describe when building your own system. For example, some people prefer to install the drives before installing the motherboard, while others prefer the converse. The best sequence may depend on the case you use and the components you are installing. For example, some case and motherboard combinations make it difficult or impossible to connect the ATX power cable after drives have been installed. Use your best judgment while building the system and you won't go far wrong.

Before you proceed, verify that you have all of the necessary components. Open each box and confirm that all items on the packing list are present. We didn't bother to do that, and it came back to bite us more than once, as you'll see.

Preparing the case

Before you do *anything* else, verify that the power supply is set to the correct input voltage. Some power supplies auto-detect input voltage and set themselves automatically. Other power supplies, including the Antec unit we're using, require moving a slide switch to indicate the correct input voltage, as shown in Figure 6-6.

WARNING

If your mains voltage is 115V and the power supply is set for 230V, no damage occurs. The system simply won't start. However, if your mains voltage is 230V and the power supply expects 115V, you will see a very short and expensive fireworks show the first time you plug the system in. The motherboard, processor, memory, expansion cards, and drives will all be burnt to a crisp within a fraction of a second.

Figure 6-6. Verify that the power supply is set for the current input voltage

Most motherboards come with a custom ATX I/O template designed to match their I/O panel. The ASUS A7N8X Deluxe has many I/O ports and an accordingly complex template, shown in Figure 6-7. Before proceeding, verify that the template supplied with the motherboard matches the actual I/O connectors present.

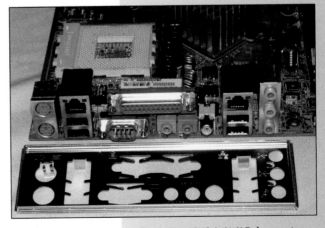

Figure 6-7. ASUS A7N8X Deluxe custom I/O template

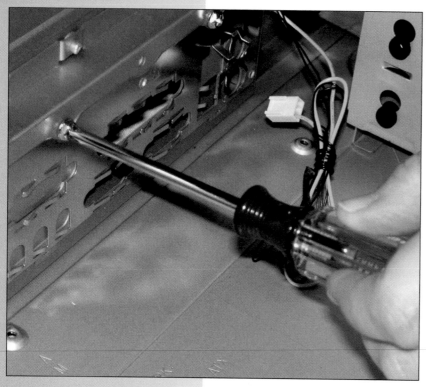

Figure 6-8. Remove the stock I/O template

Figure 6-9. Align the custom I/O template

Most cases use simple snap-in ATX I/O templates. The standard I/O template supplied with the Antec Overture case mounts with screws, rather than simply snapping in. Because the standard template doesn't match the I/O connectors on the A7N8X Deluxe motherboard, we need to remove the standard I/O template, as shown in Figure 6-8.

After removing the standard I/O template, position the A7N8X Deluxe template as shown in Figure 6-9. Working from inside the case, align the bottom, right, and left edges of the I/O template with the matching case cutout.

When the I/O template is positioned properly, press gently to seat it in the cutout. You should feel the template snap into place. Be careful while seating the template—it is made of thin metal and is easy to bend. We generally find that it's easier to seat the template by pressing gently against the edge with the handle of a screwdriver or nut driver, as shown in Figure 6-10.

After seating the I/O template, carefully slide the motherboard into place. Compare the positions of the motherboard mounting holes with the standoff mounting positions in the case. The ASUS A7N8X has nine mounting holes. Install a brass standoff in each corresponding position, and then slide the motherboard back into place temporarily to verify that you have installed a standoff at each of those nine positions. Although you can screw in the standoffs using just your fingers, it's much easier and faster to use a 5mm nut driver, as shown in Figure 6-11.

WARNING

Make absolutely sure that every standoff installed corresponds to a motherboard mounting hole. An extra standoff can contact the bottom of the motherboard, causing it to short and possibly damaging or destroying the motherboard and other components.

Populating the motherboard

It is always easier to populate the motherboard (i.e., install the processor and memory) while the motherboard is outside the case. In fact, you must do so with some systems, because installing the heatsink/fan unit requires access to both sides of the motherboard. Even if it is possible to populate the motherboard while it is installed in the case, we always recommend having the motherboard outside the case and lying flat on the work surface. More than

Figure 6-10. Seat the I/O template

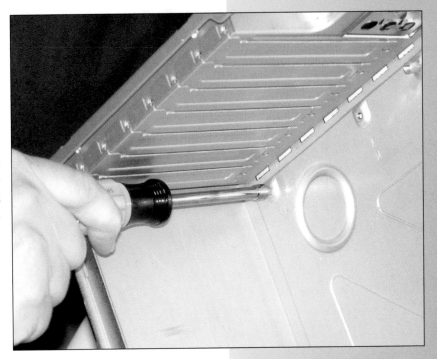

Figure 6-11. Install standoffs in each position needed by the motherboard

once, we've tried to save a few minutes by replacing the processor without removing the motherboard. Too often, the result has been bent pins and a destroyed processor.

WARNING

Each time you handle the processor, memory, or other static-sensitive components, first touch the power supply to ground yourself. The power supply needn't be connected to a receptacle for this to be effective; the power supply itself has sufficient mass to serve as a sink for static charges.

Installing the processor

To install the Athlon XP 2600+ processor, begin by lifting the arm of the ZIF (zero insertion force) socket to a vertical position, as shown in Figure 6-12. Doing so removes the clamping force from the socket holes (whence the ZIF name), allowing the processor simply to drop into place.

With the socket lever vertical, align pin 1 of the processor with pin 1 of the socket and drop the processor into place, as shown in Figure 6-13. The processor should seat flush with the socket just from the force of gravity; if it doesn't, something is misaligned. Remove the processor and verify that it is aligned properly and that the pattern of pins on the processor corresponds to the pattern of holes on the socket. *Never* apply pressure to the processor—you'll end up bending the pins and destroying it.

Figure 6-12. Lift the socket lever to prepare the socket to receive the processor

Figure 6-13. Drop the processor into place

With the processor in place and seated flush with the socket, press the lever arm down and snap it into place, as shown in Figure 6-14. You may have to press the lever arm slightly away from the socket to allow it to snap into a locked position.

> Seating the ZIF level arm may cause the processor to rise slightly from the socket. Once the processor is fully seated, it does no harm to maintain slight pressure on it with your finger while you lock the ZIF lever arm.

Installing the heatsink/fan (HSF)

Modern processors draw a lot of power—sometimes 60W to 100W or more—and dissipate a correspondingly large amount of heat. Our Athlon XP 2600+ draws more than 60W—as much as some light bulbs—and must dissipate the resulting heat over the surface of the processor die, which is less than half the size of a small postage stamp. Without a good heatsink/fan (HSF) unit, the processor die would literally burn itself to a crisp almost instantly.

It is therefore critical that you install an appropriate HSF to keep your processor cool. Note that not just any HSF that fits will suffice. HSF units are rated for the fastest processor they can be used with. If you buy a retail-boxed processor, it will come with an adequate HSF; however, it may not be the best HSF in terms of cooling efficiency, noise level, or both. Accordingly, we decided to install a third-party HSF for our HTPC system. We chose the Dynatron unit shown in Figure 6-15, which is rated for faster processors than the one we're using, and is quieter than the stock HSF as well.

The large white square on the base of the Dynatron HSF is a thermal pad, which aids in heat transfer between the processor die and the heatsink itself. Technically, such thermal pads are known as *phase-change media*, which is a fancy way of saying that they melt when they get hot and resolidify when they cool down again. This melt/cool cycle ensures that the processor die maintains good thermal contact with the heatsink.

Figure 6-14. Lock the processor into the socket

Figure 6-15. The Dynatron Chicago-series HSF, base upward

255

Make sure to use only approved thermal solutions with AMD processors. For years, we've been in the habit of using "thermal goop" to aid heat transfer. AMD does not approve any type of thermal goop, instead insisting that only approved phase-change media are acceptable for use with their processors. They're serious, too, because their warranty excludes processor damage if it occurred while using anything other than an approved phase-change media. So much for Arctic Silver and the other premium thermal goops so beloved of overclockers.

Most AMD HSF units have a preinstalled thermal pad. That pad may be bare, or it may be covered by a strip of paper attached with gum; if so, remove the paper covering before using the HSF. (The discolorations on each side of the thermal pad in Figure 6-15 are adhesive left over from the paper cover. We polished the copper surface gently with a paper towel dampened with isopropyl alcohol to remove the gummy deposits before we installed the HSF.)

After making sure the thermal pad is uncovered, orient the HSF above the processor, as shown in Figure 6-16. Note that it fits in only one orientation, with the cutout on the base of the HSF aligned with the raised portion of the socket, and with the two locking tabs on the socket aligned with the locking mechanism on the HSF.

With the HSF oriented correctly, the next step is to lock the two ends of the HSF clamp into place on the corresponding socket tabs. Installing one end of the clamp will be easy, but the other end will be difficult; you get to choose which is which. In this case, the locking tab to the right of the processor (in the middle of the photo) is the less accessible of the two. The other locking tab, not shown, is to the left of the processor and is easily accessible. The first locking tab you connect is easy because there is no pressure on the clamp, so we recommend connecting the less accessible locking tab first.

Figure 6-16. Align the HSF unit over the processor and socket

WARNING
We really hate installing HSF units on AMD processors. The AMD design is deficient, using two relatively fragile plastic locking tabs that are built into the socket itself. Intel, by contrast, designed an excellent HSF locking method for the Pentium 4, which locks the HSF to a bracket connected to the motherboard itself rather than to the relatively fragile plastic processor socket. Also, because the processor die itself is exposed, it's possible to literally crush the processor if you're not careful while clamping the HSF to the socket. We recommend using extreme caution any time you install or remove an HSF from an AMD processor.

With the first locking tab in place, now comes the fun part. Getting the second tab locked can be a major pain in the ass, because you have to fight against the pressure of the clamping mechanism while snapping the second locking tab into position. The best way we've found to do that is to press down on the top of the clamping bracket with one screwdriver while using a second small screwdriver to bend the bracket slightly outward until it snaps into place, as shown in Figure 6-17. Make absolutely certain during this process that the HSF unit is seated squarely and level on the processor. Otherwise, you risk crushing the processor die.

Figure 6-17. Lock the HSF into place

The raw thermal mass of the heatsink draws heat away from the CPU die, but unless that heat is disposed of the heatsink will eventually overheat, causing the processor to burn up (or at least to shut down). A passive heatsink—one that uses only convection cooling—is possible in theory, but a passive heatsink that is usable with modern hot-running processors is too large, heavy, and costly to be practical in most environments. Accordingly, most heatsinks for modern processors use a built-in fan to draw air through the heatsink fins, keeping the temperature of the heatsink itself near the ambient air temperature in the case.

Although it would be possible to power the CPU fan with a standard power connector, most CPU fans use a special three-pin connector that plugs into a dedicated CPU fan connector on the motherboard. This allows the motherboard to control and monitor the CPU fan. The motherboard can control the fan speed, reducing fan speed for quieter operation when the processor is running under light load and not generating much heat, and increasing fan speed when the processor is running under heavy load and generating more heat. The motherboard can also monitor fan speed, which allows it to send an alert to the user if the fan fails or begins running sporadically.

To connect the CPU fan, locate the three-pin header connector on the motherboard labeled CPU Fan or something similar, and plug the keyed cable from the CPU fan into it, as shown in Figure 6-18.

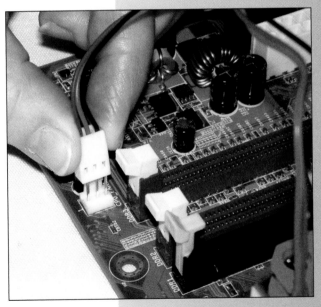

Figure 6-18. Connect the CPU fan cable to the CPU fan connector

Installing the memory

Physically installing memory is easy enough, but it's worth taking a moment to determine how your motherboard handles memory before you actually plug in the modules. The ASUS A7N8X Deluxe motherboard has a dual-channel memory controller that substantially increases memory throughput compared to a single-channel memory controller. With a dual-channel memory controller, DIMMs must be installed in pairs, so we thought it odd when we noticed that the ASUS A7N8X had three DIMM slots—not two, not four, but three. It's hard to add DIMMs in pairs to a motherboard with an odd number of DIMM slots. Hmm.

Figure 6-19. Orient the DIMM with the notch aligned properly with the socket

Reading the documents, we learned that we could configure dual-channel operation by installing our two 256 MB DIMMs in slots 1 and 3 or slots 2 and 3, but installing DIMMs in slots 1 and 2 would configure single-channel operation. In theory, dual-channel memory doubles memory throughput relative to single-channel memory. In practice, it doesn't matter much with an Athlon processor, because even single-channel PC3200 DDR memory is fast enough to match the memory bandwidth of the Athlon XP processor. Still, dual-channel must be better than single-channel, and the motherboard didn't seem to care, so we decided to install our DIMMs in slots 2 and 3.

To install a DIMM, pivot the locking tabs on both sides of the DIMM socket outward. Orient the DIMM so that the notch in the contact area of the DIMM is aligned with the raised plastic tab in the DIMM socket, as shown in Figure 6-19.

With the DIMM properly aligned with the DIMM socket and oriented vertically relative to the socket, use both thumbs to press down on the DIMM until it snaps into place, as shown in Figure 6-20. The locking tabs should automatically pivot back up into the locked position; if they don't, pivot the locking tabs into place manually to lock the DIMM in the socket.

Figure 6-20. Seat the DIMM

After you install the processor and memory, check the motherboard manual to determine if any configuration jumpers need to be set. The ASUS A7N8X has only one such jumper, which sets processor FSB speed and was set correctly for our processor by default.

Installing the motherboard

Installing the motherboard may take as long as all the other assembly steps combined because there are so many cables to connect. It's important to get all of them connected right, so take your time and verify each connection before and after you make it.

Seating and securing the motherboard

To begin, slide the motherboard into the case, as shown in Figure 6-21. Carefully align the back-panel I/O connectors with the corresponding holes in the I/O template, and slide the motherboard toward the rear of the case until the motherboard mounting holes line up with the standoffs you installed earlier.

The I/O template has metal grounding tabs that make contact with various back-panel I/O connectors. Make certain that the tabs are positioned correctly and that they do not intrude into one or more of the port connectors. More than once, we've mounted a motherboard, inserted all the screws, and connected all the cables before we noticed that there was a metal tab sticking into one of our USB or LAN ports. Before you secure the motherboard in place, verify that the back-panel I/O connectors are mated properly with the I/O template, as shown in Figure 6-22.

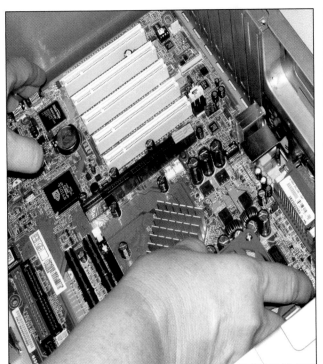

Figure 6-21. Slide the motherboard into position

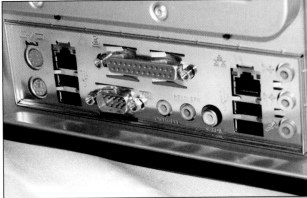

Figure 6-22. Back-panel connectors should mate cleanly with the I/O template

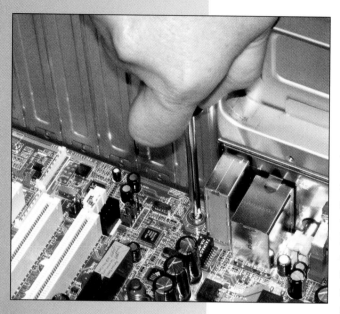

Figure 6-23. Secure the motherboard

Once the motherboard is positioned properly and you have verified that the back-panel I/O port connectors are mated cleanly with the I/O template, insert a screw through each motherboard mounting hole into the corresponding standoff, as shown in Figure 6-23. For the first two or three screws, you may have to apply pressure with one hand to keep the holes and standoffs aligned while driving the screw with the other.

At times it's difficult to get all the holes and standoffs aligned. If you're having trouble, insert two screws into easily accessible positions but don't tighten the screws completely. You should then be able to force the motherboard into complete alignment, with all holes matching the standoffs. At that point, insert one or two more screws into less accessible standoffs and tighten them completely. Finish mounting the motherboard by inserting screws into all standoffs and tightening them. Don't put excessive force on the screws, or you may crack the motherboard. Finger-tight is plenty.

With cheap motherboards and cases, it's sometimes impossible to get all of the mounting holes aligned with the standoffs. With high-quality products like the Antec case and ASUS motherboard, everything usually lines up perfectly. But if you do find that you're unable to insert all the motherboard mounting screws, don't despair. We like to get all the screws installed, both for physical support and to ensure that all grounding points on the motherboard are grounded, but getting most of the screws installed—say seven or eight of the nine—is normally good enough.

If you are unable to install all the screws, take the time to remove the brass standoffs where no screw will be installed. A misaligned standoff may short something out. In positions where you cannot use brass standoffs because of alignment problems, you can substitute white nylon standoffs, a few of which are usually included in the parts package. (If not, you can get them at most computer stores.) You may have to trim the nylon standoffs to length to make them fit. It's particularly important to provide some support for the motherboard near the expansion slots, where significant pressure may be applied when installing cards. If the motherboard is unsupported, pressing down may crack it.

Connecting the front-panel cables

Once the motherboard is secured, the next step is to connect the front-panel switch and indicator cables to the motherboard, as shown in Figure 6-24. Although Intel has defined a standard front-panel connector block and uses that standard on its own motherboards, few other motherboard makers adhere to it. Accordingly, rather than provide an Intel-standard monolithic connector block that would be useless for motherboards that do not follow the Intel standard, most case makers provide individual two- or three-pin connectors for each switch and indicator.

The only essential front-panel connector is the power switch, which must be connected for you to be able to start the system. You'll probably also want to connect the reset switch, the power LED, and the hard disk activity (HDD) LED (shown in Figure 6-24). Your case may have front-panel cables for which no corresponding pins exist on the motherboard; for example, many cases include a speaker cable, but most motherboards have embedded speakers and so may not include pins to connect to the case speaker. Conversely, your motherboard may have pins for which the case has no corresponding cable; for example, the ASUS A7N8X Deluxe motherboard has pins for a keyboard lock, which the Antec case does not support.

Figure 6-24. Connect the front-panel switch and indicator cables

Before you begin connecting front-panel cables, examine the cables. Each should be labeled descriptively, e.g., "Power," "Reset," and "HDD LED." Match those descriptions with the front-panel connector pins on the motherboard to make sure you connect the correct cable to the appropriate pins. Switch cables—power and reset—are not polarized; you can connect them in either orientation without worrying about which pin is signal and which is ground. LED cables may or may not be polarized, but if you connect a polarized LED cable backward the worst that will happen is that the LED won't light. Most cases use a common wire color, usually black, for ground, and a colored wire for signal.

When you're connecting front-panel cables, try to get it right the first time, but don't worry too much about getting it wrong. Other than the power switch cable, which must be connected properly for the system to start, none of the other front-panel switch and indicator cables is essential, and connecting them wrong won't damage the system.

Connecting the internal I/O cables

The Antec Overture case has front-panel ports for USB, FireWire (IEEE-1394), and audio. The ASUS A7N8X Deluxe motherboard has corresponding internal connectors. To route these I/O functions to the front panel, you must connect a cable from each front-panel I/O port to the corresponding internal connector.

Figure 6-25. Connect the front-panel USB port

Earlier Antec cases used eight individual wires for the front-panel USB port. That meant you had to connect eight separate wires, but it did have the advantage of allowing the port to be connected regardless of how the pins on the internal USB connector happened to be arranged. The Overture case has a monolithic USB connector; fortunately, that connector mates to the USB pins on the ASUS motherboard, and the pinouts are correct. Routing USB from the ASUS A7N8X Deluxe to the Antec Overture front panel is thus a simple matter of pressing the front-panel cable onto the internal pins, as shown in Figure 6-25.

The next step is to route audio to the front-panel audio ports. Fortunately for us, the Antec front-panel audio cable connector physically matched the internal front-panel audio connector on the ASUS motherboard, and it appeared that the wires also connected to the correct pins. Unfortunately, the internal connector had two jumpers installed on it, which prevented the front-panel audio cable from seating.

Even more unfortunately, we could find nothing in the manual or on the ASUS web site to tell us about these jumpers. We assumed that the jumpers were installed to disable front-panel audio and to route all audio functions to the back-panel I/O connectors. We wanted audio available at both the front and back panels. Would removing those jumpers disable audio at the back panel and route it only to the front panel? Could we have audio both places, or did we have to choose one? Who knew? The only way to find out was to try it, so we removed the jumpers, noting carefully their original positions.

Figure 6-26. Remove the jumpers from the front-panel audio connector

The internal front-panel audio connector was in an awkward location, so we used our bent needlenose pliers to pull the jumpers, as shown in Figure 6-26, and set them aside for possible future reinstallation.

With the jumpers removed, we snapped the Antec front-panel audio cable into place, as shown in Figure 6-27.

With USB and audio connected to the front panel, we next attempted to route FireWire (IEEE-1394) to the front-panel connector. We ran into a problem doing that. The Antec FireWire front-panel cable terminates in a 5X2 connector block similar to the one used for USB, but the ASUS internal FireWire ports use an inline 8X1 connector. Short of building a custom adapter cable, there was therefore no way to route the internal FireWire connectors to the front panel.

Installing cliffhanger connectors

Despite the plethora of ports on the rear I/O panel, the ASUS A7N8X has additional ports that appear only internally. Because there is no room on the rear I/O panel for these ports, the only convenient solution is to route the internal ports to external port connectors on expansion slot covers. These slot covers, called *cliffhanger brackets*, are shown in Figure 6-28. The top cliffhanger is a dual-FireWire (IEEE-1394) port connector. The middle cliffhanger has two additional USB 2.0 ports on the left and an old-style 15-pin game connector on the right. The bottom cliffhanger provides a second DB-9 serial connector.

We had no need of a second serial port, so we decided not to install that cliffhanger. Similarly, we'd already routed the internal USB ports to the front panel of the Overture case and we didn't need the DB-15 game port, so we decided not to install that cliffhanger either.

The third cliffhanger, though, was a lifesaver. Because of incompatible connectors, we'd been unable to route the two internal FireWire ports to the Antec front panel. The ASUS A7N8X Deluxe motherboard includes two FireWire routing cables. One end of each of those cables connects to one of the internal FireWire connectors, and the other end connects to one of the external FireWire connectors on the cliffhanger bracket.

Figure 6-27. Connect the front panel audio cable

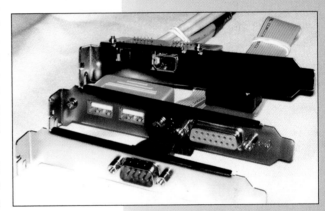

Figure 6-28. Cliffhanger brackets supplied with the ASUS A7N8X Deluxe

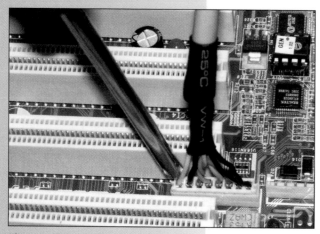

Figure 6-29. Connect a routing cable to a FireWire port

Figure 6-29 shows one of those routing cables being connected to an internal port. These inline connectors can be difficult to seat, particularly when other motherboard components prevent you from using your fingers to apply pressure. In such situations, use the tip of a screwdriver to press gently until the connector snaps into place.

With the cable connected to the internal FireWire port, connect the cable to the cliffhanger, as shown in Figure 6-30.

Once both ends of both FireWire routing cables are connected, remove a slot cover, insert the cliffhanger, and secure it with a screw, as shown in Figure 6-31.

Figure 6-30. Connect the FireWire cable to the cliffhanger

Figure 6-31. Secure the cliffhanger bracket

Installing the drives

The Antec Overture has two external 5.25" drive bays, two external 3.5" drive bays, and three internal 3.5" drive bays. The external bays are for devices like optical drives and floppy disk drives that use removable media. The internal 3.5" bays are for hard drives.

To mount the hard drive, begin by removing the internal drive bay, as shown in Figure 6-32.

Before you install the hard drive in the drive bay, verify that the drive is configured properly. We had intended to install two Serial ATA Seagate Barracuda drives in this system, but we had to go to Plan B when we found that we had no way to power the S-ATA drives. Fortunately, we had a spare 120 GB P-ATA Barracuda on the shelf, so that's what we used to build the first iteration of the HTPC system.

S-ATA drives do not require setting master/slave jumpers because each S-ATA drive connects to a dedicated interface. P-ATA drives like the one we were forced to use temporarily do require setting the master/slave jumper. The P-ATA Barracuda was jumpered by default to use Cable Select. We prefer to set master/slave status explicitly, so we rejumpered the drive to master, as shown in Figure 6-33.

With the hard drive configured properly, the next step is to mount it in the removable drive bay, as shown in Figure 6-34. The dark circles in the photograph are rubber shock-mounting pads, which reduce the amount of vibration and noise transferred from the hard drive to the chassis. Note that because we are mounting only one drive, we've chosen to mount it in the central position to maximize cooling airflow around the drive. If we were mounting two drives in this bay, as we will do later, we'd mount them in the top and bottom positions with a gap between them, again to maximize cooling airflow.

Figure 6-32. Remove the internal drive bay

Figure 6-33. Set the master/slave jumper on a hard drive

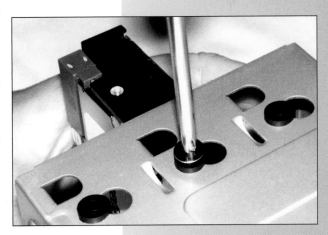

Figure 6-34. Secure the hard drive to the drive bay

Once the drive is mounted in the bay, connect the ATA cable to the drive, as shown in Figure 6-35. Make sure that the red stripe on the cable corresponds to pin 1 on the drive connector. Pin 1 is always labeled—sometimes on the connector itself, sometimes on the circuit board, and sometimes on a label on top of the drive. If there's no obvious label, it's generally safe to assume that pin 1 is on the side of the ATA connector nearest the power connector. If you do happen to connect the cable backward, it won't work, but no damage will occur. In our case, there was no possibility of connecting the cable incorrectly, because both the cable and the connector were keyed with a notch and slot arrangement.

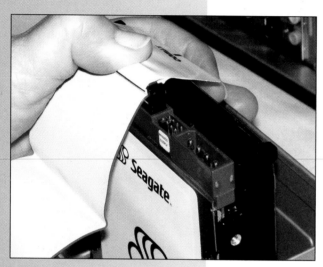

Figure 6-35. Connect the ATA cable to the hard drive

A standards-compliant Ultra-ATA cable has three connectors. The blue connector at one end of the cable connects to the ATA interface on the motherboard; the black connector at the other end of the cable connects the master device; and the gray connector in the middle connects the slave device, if present. Serial ATA connects only one drive per interface. S-ATA cables have an identical keyed connector at each end, and it doesn't matter which end connects to the drive and which to the interface.

With the hard drive secured in the bay and the ATA cable connected, replace the removable drive bay, as shown in Figure 6-36. Slide the drive bay back into position, making sure that the locking tabs on the bottom of the drive bay mate with the matching slots on the case.

With the drive bay in place, maintain pressure against it with one hand to keep the screw holes aligned, and insert the two retaining screws, as in Figure 6-37.

Figure 6-36. Replace the drive bay

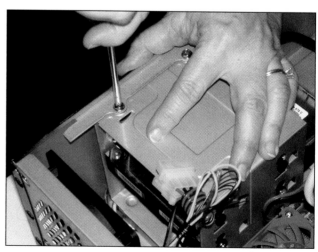

Figure 6-37. Secure the removable drive bay

The next step is to connect the hard drive ATA cable to the primary ATA interface on the motherboard, as shown in Figure 6-38. Make certain to connect the hard drive to the primary interface rather than to the secondary interface, or the system may not boot. On most motherboards, the primary and secondary ATA interfaces are adjacent and clearly labeled. Some motherboards, including the ASUS A7N8X Deluxe, use different colors for the two connectors. Again, make sure that the red stripe on the cable connects to the pin 1 side of the interface.

The final installation step for the hard drive is connecting the power cable, as shown in Figure 6-39. Parallel (standard) ATA drives use a Molex connector, which is keyed with two missing corners on the connector. Verify that the power cable is oriented properly relative to the power connector on the drive, and press until the cable seats completely. You may have to wiggle the connector and apply significant pressure to seat the power cable.

The Antec Overture case also uses a removable drive bay for the two external 5.25" bays. To remove the drive bay, press down on the locking button and pivot the locking arm away from the post, as shown in Figure 6-40. Slide the removable drive bay backward, and lift it up and out of the case.

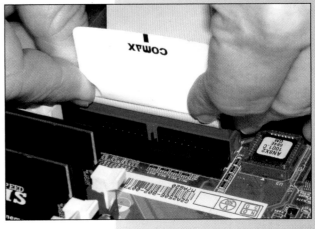

Figure 6-38. Connect the hard drive ATA cable to the primary ATA interface

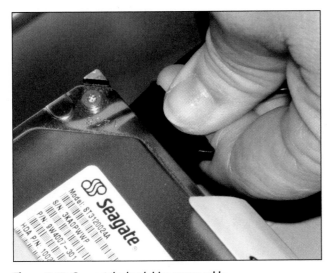

Figure 6-39. Connect the hard drive power cable

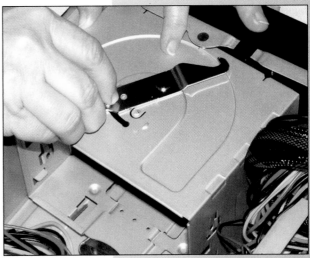

Figure 6-40. Remove the 5.25" drive bay

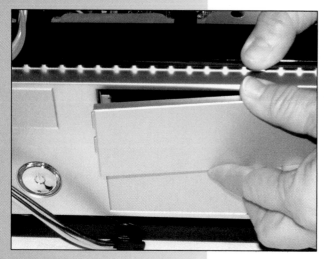

Figure 6-41. Remove the 5.25" bezel cover

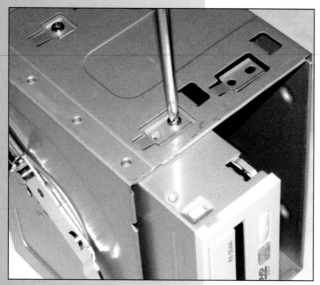

Figure 6-42. Secure the optical drive in the drive bay

The Antec Overture case uses plastic snap-in drive bay bezel covers. We decided to mount the DVD writer in the top position, and so removed that bezel cover. To remove the bezel cover, use one hand inside the case to put pressure on the center of the bezel cover until it bows outward in the middle. Then grasp the edge of the bezel cover with the other hand and pull it free, as shown in Figure 6-41.

Secure the optical drive to the drive bay, as shown in Figure 6-42. We suggest you use only two screws initially, because you'll want to verify correct positioning of the drive before you insert all the screws. After you've inserted two screws, temporarily replace the drive bay in the case to verify that the front of the optical drive is flush with the front bezel. Once you've verified that and corrected the drive position if necessary, insert four screws to secure the drive to the drive bay.

Verify the master/slave jumper for the optical drive, just as you did for the hard drive. In this case, the Plextor drive is jumpered as master by default. We want the optical drive to be the secondary master, so the default jumpering is correct. With that verified, connect the ATA cable to the drive, as shown in Figure 6-43. Because optical drives are relatively slow devices, they can use the older 40-wire ATA cable rather than the 80-wire Ultra-ATA cable we used for the hard drive. Again, make sure that the red stripe on the cable corresponds to pin 1 on the drive.

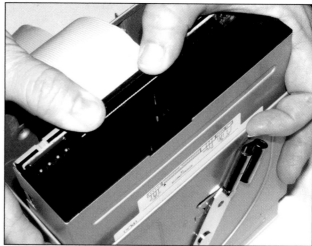

Figure 6-43. Connect the ATA data cable to the optical drive

Chapter 6, Building a Home Theater PC

For the hard drive, we connected the power cable after replacing the drive bay in the case. For the optical drive, it was easier to connect the power cable before replacing the drive bay, as shown in Figure 6-44. Again, the Molex power connector is keyed, so verify that it is oriented properly before you apply pressure to seat the power cable.

Slide the removable 5.25" drive bay back into position, as shown in Figure 6-45, making sure that the locking tabs and notches mate. Once the bay is in position, pivot the locking arm into place, making sure that the hook on the locking arm mates with the post and that the locking button snaps back into the locked position.

The next step is to connect the optical drive ATA cable to the secondary ATA interface on the motherboard, as shown in Figure 6-46. Again, make sure that the red stripe on the cable connects to the pin 1 side of the interface.

After you connect the ATA cables to the drives, don't just leave them flopping around loose in the case. That not only looks amateurish, but can actually cause overheating and other system problems by impeding airflow. Tuck the cables neatly out of the way, using cable ties or tie wraps to secure them to the chassis. (One of our technical editors suggests using large plastic-coated hairpins to secure ribbon cables such as standard ATA cables.) If necessary, temporarily disconnect the cables to route them around other cables and obstructions, and reconnect them once you're satisfied that you've done everything possible to keep them neatly out of the way.

Installing the video adapter

To install the RADEON All-In-Wonder 9600 Pro video adapter, first align it with the AGP slot on the motherboard to verify which slot cover needs to be removed (it's not always obvious). Remove the correct slot cover and carefully slide the rear bracket of the RADEON into place, making sure that the external connectors on the bracket clear the edges of the slot. Carefully

Figure 6-44. Seat the power cable for the optical drive

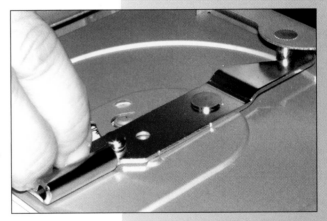

Figure 6-45. Lock the 5.25" drive bay into place

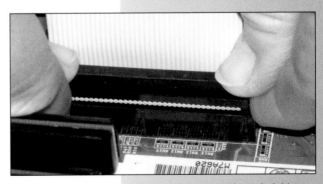

Figure 6-46. Connect the optical drive ATA cable to the secondary ATA interface

align the AGP connector on the RADEON with the AGP slot and use both thumbs to press the RADEON down until it snaps into the slot, as shown in Figure 6-47. Make certain that the card is fully seated, and then secure it by inserting a screw through the bracket into the chassis.

Figure 6-47. Seat the RADEON All-In-Wonder 9600 Pro video adapter

> **WARNING**
>
> The RADEON All-In-Wonder 9600 Pro adapter uses a fan to cool the video chipset, but that fan is powered internally by the AGP slot. Some video adapters, including the RADEON All-In-Wonder 9800 Pro, use a larger fan that must be connected to a Molex power connector from the main power supply. If the video card you install has such a fan, be very sure to connect power to the fan. Otherwise, your expensive new video card may burn itself to a crisp seconds after you apply power to the system.

The RADEON All-In-Wonder 9600 Pro has only four external connectors, as shown in Figure 6-48. The top f-connector is FM-In. The second f-connector is TV-In. The square white connector that resembles a DVI connector is AV-Out, and connects to a special "hydra" cable that includes numerous audio and video connectors. The bottom connector is AV-In, and connects to the ATi Input Adapter.

Figure 6-49 shows the incredible number of audio and video input and output connectors supported by the RADEON All-In-Wonder 9600 Pro. The hydra AV-Out cable on the left includes, from left to right, VGA-2, S-Video Out, Composite Video Out, VGA-1, S/P-DIF, and Audio Out (at lower center). The box at the right is the ATi Input Adapter, which connects to the AV-In connector on the RADEON. The four connectors on the ATi Input Adapter are, from left to right, S-Video In, Composite Video In, Left Audio In, and Right Audio In. ATi also offers the optional ATi HDTV Component Video Adapter, which connects to VGA-2 and allows the RADEON to output directly to an HDTV.

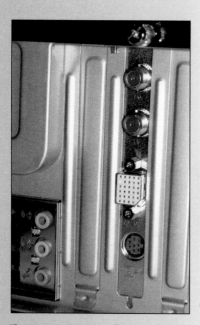

Figure 6-48. RADEON All-In-Wonder 9600 Pro external connectors

Gulp. We're no audio/video experts, and we confess that we found this array of connectors somewhat intimidating. Robert lived in fear that he'd connect everything up, turn on the power, and have water spurt out of the television while the speakers burned down. Still, everything worked out in the end, and that's all that matters.

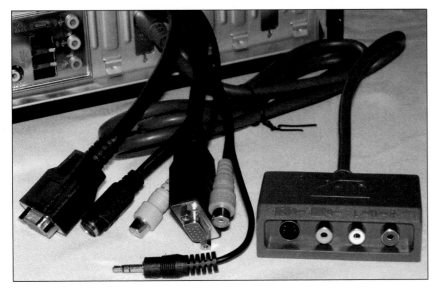

Figure 6-49. The input and output connectors supported by the RADEON All-In-Wonder 9600 Pro video adapter

Connecting the main ATX power connector

The final step in assembling the HTPC is to connect the main ATX power connector to the motherboard. We were so used to building Intel Pentium 4 systems that we searched long and hard for the ATX12V connector on the motherboard, only to finally realize that there wasn't one. The ASUS A7N8X Deluxe gets along just fine with only the original main ATX power connector.

The main ATX power connector is keyed, so verify that you have it aligned properly before proceeding. Once you're sure everything is lined up, press down firmly until the connector seats, as shown in Figure 6-50. It may take significant pressure to seat the connector, and you should feel it snap into place. The locking tab on the side of the connector should snap into place over the corresponding nub on the socket. Make sure the connector seats fully; a partially seated main ATX power connector may cause subtle problems that are very difficult to troubleshoot.

Figure 6-50. Connect the main ATX power connector

Now, take a few minutes to double-check everything. Verify that all cables are connected properly, that all drives are secured, and that you haven't left a tool or a loose screw in the patient. Check one more time to make sure that the power supply is set for the correct input voltage. We generally pick up the system and tilt it from side to side to make sure there are no loose screws, tools, or other items that could cause a short.

Once you've verified that everything is as it should be, it's time for the smoke test. Leave the cover off for now. Connect the power cable to the wall receptacle and then to the system unit. Press the power button, and the system should start up. Verify that the power supply fan, CPU fan, and case fan are spinning freely. You should also hear the hard drive spin up and the happy beep that tells you the system is starting normally. At that point, everything should be working properly.

Disconnect the power cable at the wall, replace the cover, and move the system to your entertainment center. Connect the keyboard, mouse, and the various A/V and other cables. Connect a computer monitor temporarily until you have installed and configured the operating system and applications. Connect power to the system, and turn the system on. Now comes the fun part.

Final Words

With the HTPC built, the final steps are to install and configure software, connect the HTPC to the cable and TV, and learn how to use the thing. Or at least we thought those would be the final steps. As it turned out, we needed to make a few changes before we could use the system.

Installing and configuring software

We opted out of the Microsoft upgrade merry-go-round with Windows 2000, so we never install Windows XP except on testbed systems. We knew from experience with other systems that the ATi Multimedia Center (MMC) software runs well on Windows 2000, so to begin we installed Windows 2000. Ordinarily, we're very choosy about which Windows updates to apply, but the ATi MMC software requires the latest everything from Microsoft, so we fired up Windows Update and told it to have its way with us. A couple hours and many reboots later, we had a fully updated Windows 2000 system, with the current versions of DirectX, Media Player, and so on.

Installing the ATi software is straightforward. Insert the CD in the drive and let 'er rip. ATi provides installation wizards to configure the software appropriately for your environment using sane defaults. For example, Figure 6-51 shows one of the ATi wizard screens prompting us to choose a recording format. In each case, the wizard presents a sane default choice and explains the reason for that selection. Selecting a different option displays a concise explanation of when and why you might want to choose it.

Even with the wizards, it took us an hour or so to install the software. There are many modules and each of them requires configuration—everything from specifying preferences for the DVD player to scanning and selecting cable TV channels to specifying where your data is stored and how it is organized. Still, it required no special expertise to configure the software, and at the end of the process we had a functioning HTPC.

> ATi updates RADEON drivers often, but be careful—updated drivers can be a double-edged sword. Installing them may fix one problem but break something that had been working. Resist the urge to update drivers unless you have a specific problem that the driver-release notes or ATi tech support tells you is fixed by the newer drivers. This is especially true for a Windows 2000 system.

Figure 6-51. The ATI Multimedia Center wizard prompts for recording format

Hardware changes

When we actually started to use the HTPC, it became clear that a couple of changes were needed. One was cosmetic. After we installed the HTPC in our entertainment center, Robert decided that the combination of a white DVD writer bezel and a brushed chrome system bezel, shown in Figure 6-52, was unattractive. He decided to swap the white DVD writer for a black DVD writer and to spray-paint the main system bezel flat black. Barbara talked him out of that, fearing that the paint would flake.

Functional considerations drove the two other changes we decided to make. First, using the DVD writer with only a television screen for a display was awkward at best. Because the HTPC links to our home network, there is no real need to write DVDs locally anyway—we can simply copy captured data over the network to one of our desktop systems and write the DVD on that system. On that basis, we concluded that leaving the DVD writer in the HTPC wasted a valuable resource. We decided to pull it for use elsewhere and replace it with an inexpensive DVD-ROM drive.

Figure 6-52. The HTPC as we first built it

The second change we made was adding wireless networking to the HTPC. Originally, we planned to run a 100BaseT network cable to the rear of the entertainment center and connect the HTPC to our wired network via its embedded Ethernet adapter. That turned out to be a bad idea. Our entertainment center is on an exterior wall, and running cable through exterior walls is notoriously difficult. At best, we'd end up with insulation bunched up and scattered all over the place. At worst, we might drill through something important. It also didn't help matters that the basement area immediately beneath our den is finished and provides no access to the ceiling or wall immediately under the entertainment center.

At that point, one of our readers suggested using wireless. The thought had crossed our minds earlier, but our only experience with wireless had been with some early 802.11b adapters, which were much too slow for our needs. On that basis, we'd discounted wireless, but it sounded like it was worth another look.

Checking into the current state of wireless, we found that standard 802.11g components provide 54 megabit/s throughput and that enhanced 802.11g components provide 108 megabit/s. Although that bandwidth might (or might not) be adequate for streaming video, it would certainly suffice for transferring video files back and forth between the HTPC and other machines on our network.

Installing wireless would have other advantages as well. At some point, we will probably build some "satellite" PVR systems—inexpensive, small, quiet PCs that we can use in the master bedroom and the downstairs guest suite to access stored programs on the main HTPC. Robert had also been thinking for years about installing a desktop system in the guest suite, but hadn't done so because of the difficulty in running cable.

Faced with choosing components about which we knew little, we did what we usually do. We asked our readers and others who were familiar with the current state of wireless technology for their advice. "Should we go with D-Link, Linksys, NETGEAR, or something else? Or are they all about the same?"

The feedback was pretty much what we expected. Some people had no strong opinion, and suggested that just about any brand would do. Most people had opinions, though, some of them very strong. Each company was loved by at least one person. "The only one worth buying is <fill-in-the-blank>. All the rest are junk." And each company was absolutely hated by at least one person. "Whatever you do, don't buy <fill-in-the-blank>. Anything else will work." Overall, although it was an unscientific sample, D-Link was clearly the most loved and least hated, with NETGEAR in second place, and Linksys a distant third.

We had just about decided to use D-Link components when Robert's colleague Jerry Pournelle called one day to talk about his upcoming Chaos Manor column for BYTE magazine. Robert asked him in passing what he thought about wireless components. "Go with D-Link," said Jerry. Knowing Jerry, he probably bought one of everything and tried them all before he decided what to use. So we went ahead and ordered the Lite-On DVD-ROM drive and the D-Link 802.11g wireless components shown in Figure 6-53.

Figure 6-53. Lite-On DVD-ROM drive and D-Link 802.11g wireless components

So far, our experience bears out the advice that Jerry and our readers gave us. We experienced some aggravating problems during setup, none of which were really D-Link's fault, but we've found the D-Link DWL-2100AP 802.11g wireless access point and the D-Link DWL-G520 802.11g PCI adapter to be fast and reliable.

With the new components in hand, we pulled the HTPC from our entertainment center, popped the lid, and removed the external drive bay. Figure 6-54 shows the Plextor DVD writer still in the drive bay, with the Lite-On DVD-ROM drive above it. Note the difference in depth. The Plextor DVD writer is about an inch (25mm) longer than the DVD-ROM drive. That additional depth isn't a problem with the Antec Overture case (or with standard mini/mid-tower cases), but the depth of the optical drive may be a factor with some small cases.

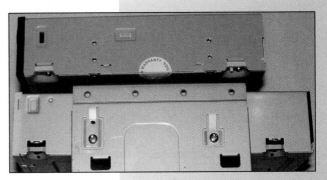

Figure 6-54. Plextor DVD writer (bottom) versus Lite-On DVD-ROM drive (top)

With the Plextor DVD writer removed and the Lite-On DVD-ROM drive installed, the next step was to install the D-Link DWL-G520 802.11g PCI adapter, shown in Figure 6-55. The DWL-G520 adapter provides two brackets. The standard bracket, shown attached to the adapter, is used in standard PC cases. If your case accepts only half-height PCI cards, you can remove the screws that secure the adapter to the standard bracket and replace it with the half-height bracket shown between the adapter and the rubber-duck antenna.

Figure 6-55. The D-Link DWL-G520 802.11g PCI adapter and brackets

Chapter 6, Building a Home Theater PC

To install the D-Link DWL-G520 802.11g PCI adapter, select an available PCI slot and remove the slot cover. Align the adapter carefully with the slot and press it into place, as shown in Figure 6-56, and reinstall the screw to secure the adapter.

With the D-Link DWL-G520 802.11g PCI adapter seated and secured, screw in the rubber-duck antenna, as shown in Figure 6-57. Rotate the black collar to adjust the angle of the antenna, and then pivot the antenna into a vertical position.

Figure 6-56. Seat the D-Link DWL-G520 802.11g PCI adapter

Figure 6-57. Connect the D-Link DWL-G520 802.11g PCI adapter antenna

Connecting the HTPC

With the hardware assembled, the software installed and configured, and network connectivity working, the only remaining task was to move the HTPC back to our entertainment center and connect it. We'd forgotten what a maze of wires existed behind that entertainment center. It took some time to get those untangled, and then we began to install the HTPC.

As usual, we'd forgotten something. Although we wanted to be able to watch a live program while recording another, we'd decided not to install a second tuner card on the theory that we'd simply watch live programs via the RF cable TV input on the TV, and recorded programs via a video connection from the HTPC to the TV.

But when we started to connect the HTPC, we got clubbed upside the head with the duh stick. Holding the cable TV cable in one hand, we belatedly realized that we needed to connect that one cable to two connectors. It had to connect to the TV if we wanted to watch live programs, and to the HTPC if we wanted to record programs. Duh. So it was off to Radio Shack in search of an amplified cable TV splitter. With that in hand, the connections went quickly.

A better way to transfer VHS tapes

We have hundreds of VHS videotapes in our library, accumulated over the last 20 years. Nearly all of them were recorded at SP for best quality, and they've been stored vertically (like books), so we weren't surprised when a random check showed that these tapes were as good as ever. Still, tapes do age, and there's a very real possibility that in a few years we'll no longer have a VCR capable of playing them back, so we wanted to transfer them to optical disc.

We originally planned to use the HTPC to do the transfer, simply by hooking up a VCR and feeding the audio/video signal from the VCR to the HTPC. That would have worked, too, but thinking it through we realized that it wasn't the best solution. We have hundreds of hours of programs on VHS tapes, and while the HTPC was doing transfers it wouldn't be able to perform its primary functions. Transferring tapes in "off time" could literally take a year or more.

Looking for alternatives, we found the Plextor ConvertX. The ConvertX is a dedicated audio/video converter box that converts analog video input to digital video output on the fly. A VCR or other analog video source connects to the input. The output is a USB 2.0 port that connects to a standard desktop PC that runs the Plextor capture software. Capturing video with the ConvertX couldn't be easier. You fire up the Plextor capture software, start the VCR playing, and let 'er rip. Captured video is stored to the hard drive. It can be written directly to a CD or DVD disc, or can be edited first to remove commercials and other extraneous material.

The ConvertX supports MPEG-1 (VCD) compression, which provides VHS-like video quality and stores about one hour of video on a recordable CD. It also supports MPEG-2 (DVD-Video) compression, which provides DVD-like video quality and stores between 12 and 27 minutes on a recordable CD or 81 to 173 minutes on a recordable DVD. Finally, the ConvertX supports two forms of MPEG-4 compression, ISO and DiVX, which provide video quality ranging from sub-VHS to near-DVD, and store between 22 and 104 minutes on a recordable CD or 146 to 665 minutes on a recordable DVD.

In the past, we'd looked at several supposedly "turn-key" solutions for transferring video from VHS tapes. All of them were deficient in video quality, ease of use, or both. The Plextor ConvertX is the first truly turn-key video transfer solution we've seen. It just works. And at a street price of $150 or so it's also an inexpensive solution, particularly if you have a lot of tapes to transfer.

Robert decided to set up a "conversion station" on his credenza, using the ConvertX, a spare VCR, and a testbed system with USB 2.0 ports and a large hard drive. That conversion station runs quietly all day long, transferring three or four VHS tapes a day to digital video. Many of our archive tapes contain two one-hour programs each, which we split and write in VCD format to two $0.25 CD-R discs. The video quality is acceptable, no worse than SP VHS, and it's a convenient way to use up our remaining stock of CD-R discs. We reserve our more expensive DVD+R discs for writing full-length movies and other programs that we don't want to split across multiple discs.

Although there have been questions raised from time to time about the archival stability of optical discs, we're comfortable using high-quality CD-R and DVD+R discs for archiving our video. We store the discs in Tyvek sleeves, where we expect that they'll outlive us.

If you have a VHS tape archive that you want to convert to optical discs, do yourself a favor and buy a Plextor ConvertX. You won't regret it.

Going forward

Surprisingly enough, everything works. (We know we shouldn't admit to being surprised, but it's the truth.) The HTPC records and plays back video. Recorded video quality is indistinguishable from the live signal and distinctly better than TiVo recordings even at its best video quality. The HTPC functions as a top-notch DVD player, with video quality as good as the best commercial units (aided in no small part by the video processing provided by the RADEON adapter). The Logitech speakers provide first-rate sound quality and enough volume to rattle the walls, literally. Now, if only there were something on worth watching...

Things remain to be done. We're using the Logitech Z-680 speakers in 2.1 mode. Implementing the full multichannel sound supported by the nVIDIA audio adapter and Logitech speakers will mean crawling around the attic for a few hours to run speaker cables, and Robert hasn't had time to do that yet. Although copying video data to one of our desktop systems is easy, Robert hasn't yet attempted to produce a video DVD from that data. We plan to build a couple of inexpensive, small, quiet satellite systems that will allow us to watch recorded programs in our bedroom and in the downstairs guest suite. Eventually, we'll look into upgrading to HDTV and replacing our cable feed with a satellite feed. And, although we really like the ATi MMC software, we'll be keeping a close watch on its competitors with an eye to eventually giving them another trial.

The HTPC provides a solid foundation for future expansion. After using it for only a short time, we'll never use a VCR again. If you build an HTPC, we think you'll feel the same.

For updated component recommendations, commentary, and other new material, visit *http://www.hardwareguys.com/guides/htpc.html*.

Building a Small Form Factor PC

7

Cost-effectiveness	**Expandability**
████████████░░░░░░░	░░░░░░░░░░░░░░░░░░
Reliability	**Processor performance**
███████████████░░░	████████████░░░░░░
Compactness	**Video performance**
███████████████░░░	████████░░░░░░░░░░
Quietness	**Disk capacity/performance**
███████████░░░░░░░	███████████░░░░░░░

When the discussion turns to *Small Form Factor* (SFF) PCs, the first question that comes to our minds is how the term is being used. SFF means different things to different people. For some, it's any PC smaller than the norm. For others, it's specifically the "shoebox" form factor—the so-called "cube" systems—pioneered by Shuttle. (In fact, Shuttle says SFF means *Shuttle Form Factor*.) Still others consider any PC built around a microATX motherboard and case to be an SFF system. And some True Believers claim that only systems based on Mini-ITX motherboards—which are so small they can be built into a teddy bear or cigar humidor—qualify as SFF PCs.

We think the best way to define SFF is by case volume. The cubic capacity of standard mini/mid-tower ATX cases ranges from 30 to 50 liters. Typical microATX cases range from 10 to 20 liters. The standard Shuttle SFF case is 200mm × 300mm × 185mm (just under 8" × 8" × 12"), and has a volume of about 11 liters. Cases designed for Mini-ITX motherboards are smaller still, from 6 to 9 liters. Most people perceive a 20-liter or smaller case as "small" and a 10-liter or smaller case as "tiny." Any case with a volume of 20 liters or less fits our definition of SFF.

To provide an idea of scale, a cube that contains 20 liters is about 27 cm (10.7″) on a side. A cube that contains 6 liters is about 18 cm (7.2″) on a side. An NBA basketball has a volume of just under 7.5 liters.

Intel heavily promoted at least two FlexATX computers, although they probably now wish they hadn't. An arrangement with Mattel resulted in the Hot Wheels PC and the Barbie PC, neither of which set any sales records.

Although Shuttle introduced the "shoebox" form factor, it was by no means the first company to produce SFF computers. Soon after Intel introduced the ATX form factor in the mid-1990s, they recognized the need for smaller systems. ATX was soon followed by smaller variants—Mini-ATX, microATX, and finally FlexATX. Although Intel produced some Mini-ATX and FlexATX motherboards, those form factors were generally ignored by third-party manufacturers, leaving ATX as Intel's answer for standard-size systems, and microATX for small systems.

Shuttle's first shoebox PC immediately struck a chord with gamers, hobbyists, and other PC enthusiasts. It was expensive, ran hot, didn't have much room for drives or expansion cards, and was noisy. But it was *small*.

Shuttle followed that first SFF system with a continuing stream of new SFF systems based on various proprietary motherboards for the Athlon XP, Pentium 4, and, most recently, the Athlon 64. Shuttle devotes significant engineering and design resources to their SFF systems, and it shows. Until recently, Shuttle SFF systems were the standard by which all other SFF systems were judged.

In the last year or two, many manufacturers have jumped on the SFF bandwagon, trying to horn in on the market niche that Shuttle developed. Until recently, most of these clones were pale imitations of the original product. Recently, however, several of these other makers, including ASUS, Biostar, and EPoX, have begun shipping SFF systems comparable in quality and features to those made by Shuttle. Shuttle no longer has the SFF market to itself.

A lot of people love Shuttle SFF PCs and their clones. We don't, for several reasons. Most of them use proprietary (or at least semi-proprietary) components, including the motherboard and power supply. So if you want to upgrade your motherboard or power supply, tough luck—you're stuck with whatever the system manufacturer offers in the way of upgrade options, which often isn't much. We might have been able to live with that, but what we couldn't live with was the very high cost of proprietary SFF "barebones" systems. SFF systems typically sell for a 50% to 100% premium over the price of an industry-standard motherboard, case, and power supply of comparable quality.

But merely because we don't much like SFF barebones systems doesn't mean we think there is no place for small systems. On the contrary, small systems are perfect for many situations, namely anywhere you need a PC that a standard mini-tower system won't fit or would be intrusive. An SFF system is an ideal candidate for a dorm room, a bedroom set-top box, a home theater system, or a portable LAN party system.

In this chapter, we'll design and build the perfect SFF PC.

Determining Functional Requirements

The problem with determining functional requirements for an SFF PC is that the SFF umbrella covers a broad range of systems. An SFF PC can be anything from an inexpensive "appliance" PC with a slow processor and embedded video to a fire-breathing gaming system with a $1,000 processor and a $500 video card—or anything in between. The only thing these systems have in common is small size.

Accordingly, although we had to choose one SFF PC configuration to build for ourselves and to illustrate this chapter, we specify numerous alternative choices in components that we might have used if we had been designing the SFF PC for a different purpose. When we sat down to think through our own requirements for an SFF PC, here's what we came up with:

Size

> Well, that's the whole point, isn't it? A large SFF PC is an oxymoron. Still, although we wanted a small system, we didn't want to make too many compromises in features, performance, cooling, or reliability. We decided that we'd settle for "medium-small."

Reliability

> One of our concerns about SFF PCs is that the small case volume makes it difficult to cool the system properly. Running components at high temperatures reduces their service life and makes them less reliable and more crash-prone. The keys to building a reliable system are to choose top-quality components—particularly motherboard, memory, hard drive, and power supply—and to keep them cool. In the interests of keeping the system as cool and therefore as reliable as possible, we considered the thermal characteristics of the various components and chose accordingly.

Performance

> We wanted our SFF PC to be small, but not slow. High performance goes hand in hand with higher temperatures, of course, so we had to strike a balance between performance and cooling/reliability. We decided that 3D graphics performance was unimportant for our particular SFF PC, so we elected to use embedded graphics. That allowed us to spend some of our heat budget on a faster processor. We did, however, want a system that would support a fast 3D graphics card (if we decide to install one later), which meant the case must accept full-size cards and have sufficient cooling to run at reasonable temperatures with a midrange or faster CPU and a hot-running graphics adapter installed.

Noise level

> SFF PCs are popular because they are unobtrusive. But unobtrusiveness requires more than small size. A tiny PC that sounds like a leaf blower fails the unobtrusiveness test. The SFF PC must be quiet as

well as small. Unfortunately, that introduces yet another tradeoff. Quiet PCs are quiet because they minimize fan noise, which impedes cooling, or because they use insulation to deaden sound, which also impedes cooling. Once again, we'll need to strike a balance between sound level, performance, and cooling/reliability. We decided that it was a reasonable goal to build a system that was quiet (but not inaudible) while providing midrange or better performance and reasonable temperature levels.

This is a very demanding set of requirements, and one we weren't sure we'd be able to meet. Small, fast, cool, quiet, and reliable. Pick any four. Achieving all five in one system wouldn't be easy.

Hardware Design Criteria

With the functional requirements determined, the next step was to establish design criteria for the SFF PC hardware. At left are the relative priorities we assigned for our SFF PC. Your priorities may of course differ.

Our SFF PC configuration is a well-balanced system. Other than expandability and video performance, which are unimportant to us for this system, all of the other criteria are of similar priority. Here's the breakdown:

DESIGN PRIORITIES

Price	☆☆☆☆☆
Reliability	☆☆☆☆☆
Size	☆☆☆☆☆
Noise level	☆☆☆☆☆
Expandability	☆☆☆☆☆
Processor performance	☆☆☆☆☆
Video performance	☆☆☆☆☆
Disk capacity/performance	☆☆☆☆☆

Price

Price is moderately important for this system, but value is more so. We won't try to match the price of mass-market consumer-grade systems, but we won't spend money needlessly, either. If spending a bit more noticeably improves performance, reliability, or cooling, we won't begrudge the extra few dollars.

Reliability

Reliability ties for top importance with size. We'll make compromises in cost, performance, noise level, or any other criterion to make this system as reliable as it is possible to make an SFF PC. The case volume of an SFF PC makes it difficult to achieve reliability comparable to a larger system using similar components, but we'll do everything possible to build the most reliable system we can within the inherent limits of the small case.

Size

Size is matched in importance only by reliability. If it isn't small, the whole exercise is rather pointless. Still, we didn't award this category the absolute highest possible priority, because there are some compromises we simply won't make. Barebones "shoebox" PCs are available that have literally half the case volume of the SFF system we eventually decided to build, but those tiny systems simply give up too much in return for saving a few inches.

Noise level

Noise level is moderately important for an SFF PC. Our goal is a system that is unobtrusive in both size and noise level. Accordingly, we'll choose the quietest available mainstream components that otherwise meet our requirements for performance, thermal characteristics, and reliability.

Expandability

Expandability is unimportant for our SFF PC. We may at some point want to make minor system upgrades, such as adding an AGP video adapter, an expansion card or two, more memory, and perhaps a second hard drive. To the extent that we can provide for such future expansion without compromising higher-priority considerations, we'll do so. But we consider expandability to be dead last in priority.

Processor performance

Processor performance is moderately important for our SFF PC. Our performance goal for this system required a processor in the 3.0 GHz range, if possible. Heat concerns limited our processor choices to Northwood-core Pentium 4 processors, which consume much less power and run cooler than newer Prescott-core Pentium 4 models. During the design phase, we had no data about the temperatures different processors might reach in a small case, so we built three test configurations, using 1.8, 2.6, and 3.2 GHz processors, and measured operating temperatures for each.

Video performance

3D video performance is relatively unimportant for our SFF PC because we do not intend to use it for gaming. Embedded video suffices for general use, and produces much less heat than a high-performance AGP adapter. We recognize that many people may decide to build an SFF gaming system, though, so we tested various video configurations, from basic embedded video to an ATi RADEON 9800XT. (We concluded that it was possible to use *either* a high-end video card *or* a fast processor in an SFF system, not both, unless we were willing to accept very high system temperatures.)

Disk capacity/performance

Disk capacity and performance are moderately important for an SFF PC. This is an easy criterion to meet because current ATA hard drives are huge, fast, cheap, and reliable. Fortunately, the best models are also relatively quiet and produce little heat.

The best way to determine whether a Pentium 4 processor uses the Northwood core or the Prescott core is to check the size of the L2 cache, which is always specified. Northwood processors have 512 KB of L2 cache. Prescott processors have 1 MB of L2 cache. Also, Northwood processors are made with the 0.13 μ process, whereas Prescott uses the 0.09 μ process, which is usually stated as 90 nanometer.

Component Considerations

With our design criteria in mind, we set out to choose the best components for the SFF PC. The following sections describe the components we chose, and why we chose them. For the SFF PC, we had to reverse our usual practice of choosing the components and then building the system. As strange as it sounds, we had to build the SFF PC and then choose the components.

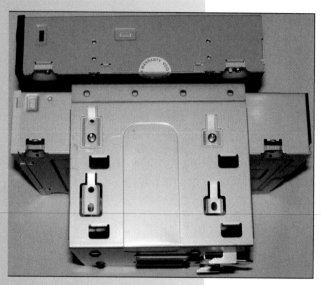

Figure 7-1. Plextor PX-708A DVD writer (bottom) and Lite-On DVD-ROM drive

What we mean is that component choice is constrained when you build a small system. With a standard system, you needn't worry about components fitting the case. With an SFF PC, component size is a constant concern. For example, the CPU cooler you really want to use may be too tall to fit between the motherboard and the drive bay, the ideal optical drive may be half an inch too deep to seat fully in the drive bay, or the fan on your video adapter may intrude on the PCI slot.

For example, Figure 7-1 (yes, we stole it from the Home Theater PC chapter) shows two optical drives, a Plextor PX-708A DVD writer on the bottom and a Lite-On DVD-ROM drive on top. In a standard case, the inch or so difference in depth is immaterial. In an SFF case, that extra inch may mean the larger drive won't fit the case. (As it happened, we were able to use the Plextor PX-708A optical drive, but it was a tight fit.)

Such factors as motherboard layout and cable flexibility may also come into play. For example, the motherboard you want to use may have the front-panel connectors in an inaccessible location, or the S-ATA connectors may have insufficient clearance to allow the S-ATA cable to be seated without breaking off the connector.

If you use components other than those we specify, you may encounter problems with fit or function. To minimize potential problems, buy the case before you buy other components. Measure the available space, and compare your measurements carefully against the component sizes listed on their web sites. Note that the sizes given for components are usually accurate, but do not include clearances required for cables. With the case in front of you, you can also get a reasonably good idea of layout issues, component clearance issues, and so on. Without the case, you'll find that it's impossible to make even reasonable guesses about whether particular components will fit.

Configuring any PC involves tradeoffs, but this is doubly true when you configure an SFF PC. The small case volume makes cooling more difficult and component dimensions critical, and the smaller power supply limits your choices for high-current devices like fast processors and video adapters. Any PC requires compromises between performance and noise, but this is even more apparent with an SFF PC. Many "quiet PC" technologies—such as using large passive heatsinks and multiple large, slow fans—simply cannot be used with an SFF PC because there isn't room for them. If you want a fast SFF PC, it's going to be loud. If you want a quiet SFF PC, it's going to be slow.

WARNING

Although we tested the configuration we used to build our own SFF PC, we did not test permutations with the listed alternatives. Those alternatives are simply the components we would have considered if our requirements had been different. We would still have had to verify fit and function and perhaps would have been forced to substitute other components. Therefore, we can't guarantee that these alternative components will fit or function reliably, individually or together.

Case and power supply

Antec Aria microATX Case (http://www.antec-inc.com)

We almost didn't write an SFF chapter for this book because we couldn't find SFF components that met our (admittedly very high) standards. So what changed our minds? In April 2004, Antec introduced their Aria "shoebox" case, shown in Figure 7-2 sitting on top of an Antec Minuet microATX case. Until we learned of the Aria, we had decided that if we built an SFF PC, we'd build it around the slimline Antec Minuet case. But as soon as we saw the preliminary specification sheet for the Aria, we knew we had to get our hands on one.

Figure 7-2. Antec Aria case (top) and Antec Minuet case

The Aria addressed all our objections to SFF systems in one swell foop. It accepts any microATX motherboard and full-height expansion cards. It has a robust 300W ATX12V power supply rather than the marginal 160W to 220W power supplies provided with most barebones "shoebox" SFF systems. It is the quietest case we have ever used, and yet it provides cooling sufficient to run midrange or faster components at reasonable temperatures. Finally, the Aria's reasonable price meant we could build an SFF system without breaking the bank to buy an overpriced proprietary SFF barebones system.

The Aria is not the first case designed for microATX, FlexATX, or Mini-ITX motherboards, but most such cases are slimline "pizza-box" designs rather than the "shoebox" or "toaster" design made popular by Shuttle. Slimline cases are useful for some "appliance" applications, but have too many limitations for a general-purpose system—e.g., they accept only two or three disk drives, have a low-wattage SFX power supply, accept only half-height expansion cards, and so on. In the past, if you wanted a general-purpose shoebox system, the only alternative was to buy a barebones system from Shuttle or one of its competitors. With the Aria, system builders who want a cube-style system finally have the case they need to build it.

The Aria is larger than a typical shoebox SFF PC—about half an inch taller and an inch or so deeper. But the real difference is width. The Aria is nearly three inches wider than most SFF PCs, but don't blame Antec. The additional width is needed to accommodate a microATX motherboard, with its full complement of expansion slots. The relatively small increase in linear dimensions pays off in case volume. The volume of the Antec Aria is about 18 liters, nearly twice the 11-liter volume of typical SFF cases. That additional volume makes the Aria easier to work on, and contributes to more efficient cooling and a lower noise level.

Table 7-1 compares the Antec Aria and Minuet with the Shuttle SB62G2, a typical barebones SFF system.

Table 7-1. Antec Aria and Minuet cases versus Shuttle SB62G2

	Antec Aria	Antec Minuet	Shuttle SB62G2
Shape	Shoebox/toaster	Slimline	Shoebox
Height	7.9" / 200mm	3.8" / 96mm	7.3" / 185mm
Width	10.6" / 269mm	12.75" / 324mm	7.9" / 200mm
Depth	13.2" / 335mm	16.8" / 427mm	11.8" / 300mm
Weight (pounds/kilograms)	10.00 / 4.55	12.6 / 5.71	6.27 / 2.85
Case volume (liters/cubic inches)	18.0 / 1,105	13.2 / 814	11.1 / 681
External drive bays (5.25"/3.5")	1 / 0	1 / 1	1 / 1
Internal drive bays (5.25"/3.5")	0 / 3	0 / 1	0 / 1
Expansion slots	AGP + 3 PCI	AGP + 6 PCI	AGP + 1 PCI
Motherboard included	None	None	FB62 (proprietary Intel 865G)
Other motherboards accepted	Any microATX	Any microATX	Not applicable
Power supply	300W	220W	220W
Front-panel ports	USB, FireWire, audio	USB, FireWire, audio	USB, FireWire, audio
Street price (case and power supply)	$119	$60	Not available
Street price (with motherboard)	~ $200	~ $165	$325

The Antec Aria wins the comparison easily. Relative to the Shuttle barebones system, the Aria is a bit larger and heavier, but uses industry-standard components, has a better power supply, much more flexibility, and better cooling, and costs much less. Relative to the Minuet, the Aria has a better power supply, has room for more drives, and is a sexy "cube" style case rather than a vanilla "pizza-box" slimline.

The Antec Aria also includes an 8-in-1 card reader that connects to an internal USB port. This is a useful peripheral if you own a digital camera—and who doesn't nowadays? The card reader accepts most popular card formats, including CompactFlash Card (I and II), MicroDrive, Memory Stick, Memory Stick Pro, MultiMedia Card, Secure Digital Card, and SmartMedia Card. About the only thing it doesn't read is the relatively obscure xD-Picture Card, used by Olympus and Fujifilm digital cameras. (You can read xD-Picture Cards by using an adapter. Inexpensive adapters are readily available wherever xD-Picture Card media are sold.)

We got our hands on two of the first Aria cases that arrived in the United States, and put them through some pretty rigorous testing. We were quite pleased with what we found. Fit and finish are excellent. There are no sharp edges or burrs, so you don't have to worry about getting cut.

The Aria includes the AR300, a 300W ATX12V power supply. This power supply is robust enough to support just about any combination of components you could physically install in the Aria case, and so quiet you can barely tell it's running. It uses a 120mm fan that varies its speed according to temperature.

> Although the AR300 power supply has standard ATX12V connectors, its physical form factor is proprietary. Although we'd prefer a fully standard ATX12V power supply, there's simply no way to fit one into such a small case. Our objection to proprietary power supplies is that they can be very expensive to replace when they fail. We don't expect that to be an issue with the Antec AR300 unit, however, both because we expect it to be quite reliable and because we expect Antec to provide replacement units at reasonable prices.

Most SFF barebones systems we've seen use thin aluminum panels, which weigh little and help cooling but do nothing to reduce sound emissions. In fact, most of them seem to resonate with a high-pitched buzz or whine that originates in the power supply fan and CPU fan. The Aria is different. Its side panels use composite construction, with two thin aluminum plates sandwiching a central plastic layer. The top panel is similar, but uses one aluminum plate facing the inside of the system, with an exposed corrugated plastic layer on the outside.

Although Antec gave up the minor cooling advantage of using thin single aluminum panels, their composite panels are acoustically inert. When we tapped on them, all we heard was a dull thud, rather than the metallic sound generated by simple aluminum panels. We suspect that these composite panels contribute a great deal to the low noise level of the Aria.

If you want to build an SFF system, we don't know of a better case than the Antec Aria.

ALTERNATIVES: CASE & POWER SUPPLY

None we'd choose. We considered several other models, including microATX "micro-towers" like the Athenatech A106 (*http://www.athenatech.us*), the Enermax CS-10073-B (*http://www.enermax.com.tw*), and the WaveSonic CS-3107 (*http://www.wavesonic.com*). They're all nice cases, but we wanted a "cube" case rather than a tower or "pizza-box" case. All of these cases had other drawbacks as well, such as small power supplies or the inability to accept full-size expansion cards.

We were intrigued by the Monarch Hornet (*http://www.monarchcomputer.com*), a cube-style case that accepts microATX motherboards. We might have built our SFF PC around it, too, if the Aria hadn't come along. Although the Hornet case isn't available by itself, you can order it with a variety of standard motherboards, including various Intel and ASUS models. Unfortunately, the Monarch Hornet is quite expensive. The Hornet case with a basic power supply and Intel D865GLC motherboard costs nearly twice as much as the Aria with the same motherboard.

We concluded that the Antec Aria (*http://www.antec-inc.com*) is the standout choice for an SFF PC case.

Motherboard

Intel D865GRH or D865GLC (http://www.intel.com)

We require a microATX motherboard for our system, but motherboards that use this form factor are relatively rare. A manufacturer that produces a score of Pentium 4 motherboard models might offer only one or two of those in microATX. Quite often, those microATX models use older chipsets or have fewer features than the full ATX models. Still, although the selection is limited, there are good microATX motherboards available for the Celeron, Pentium 4, Athlon XP, and Athlon 64 processors.

For our SFF PC, we wanted a Pentium 4 motherboard made by Intel. Intel motherboards set the standards by which we judge all other motherboards for construction quality, stability, and reliability. Intel produces two microATX motherboards that use the 865 chipset, the D865GRH and the D865GLC. The two are essentially identical except that the D865GRH includes *Digital Restrictions Management* (DRM) hardware.

Anyone who knows our position on DRM–we oppose the RIAA, the MPAA, and Microsoft using it to violate consumers' fair use rights and to hamper Linux and other open source software–may find it odd that we would consider a motherboard with DRM features. We did so for two reasons. First, we don't object to our data being under lock and key–as long as *we* control the key. Second, we think DRM will continue to proliferate, and we wanted to learn more about it. Know Your Enemy.

We built test configurations using the Intel D865GRH and the D865GLC. Both support any current Intel Pentium 4 or Celeron processor that uses a 400, 533, or 800 MHz FSB. They have four DIMM slots—which makes future memory upgrades easy—and support up to 4 GB of PC3200 DDR-SDRAM. They provide numerous interfaces and ports, including three PCI slots, a Universal 0.8/1.5 V AGP 3.0 (4X/8X) slot, two parallel ATA-100 interfaces, two Serial ATA interfaces, an FDD interface, PS/2 mouse and keyboard ports, serial and parallel ports for compatibility with legacy peripherals, and eight USB 2.0 ports. Both motherboards are rock-solid and feature Intel's traditional top-notch build quality. The GLC sells for $15 or $20 less than the GRH, and is the best choice for an SFF PC.

If you buy a D865GRH or D865GLC, make sure you know exactly what you're getting. Like many Intel motherboards, they are available in retail-boxed or OEM versions, and with different features. The GRH is available in two models, with Audio or with Audio and Gigabit LAN. The GLC is available in three models, with Audio, with Audio and 10/100 LAN, and with Audio and Gigabit LAN. For available configurations and product codes for the D865GLC, see *http://developer. intel.com/design/motherbd/lc/lc_available.htm*; for the D865GRH, see *http:// developer.intel.com/design/motherbd/rh/rh_available.htm*.

ALTERNATIVES: MOTHERBOARD

For an Athlon XP processor, try the ASUS A7N8X-VM, which uses the *n*VIDIA *n*Force2 chipset, has embedded GeForce4 MX video, an AGP 8X slot, and a full complement of modern features, lacking only S-ATA support. For an Athlon 64 processor, try the Aopen MK89-L, which is the only microATX Socket 754 motherboard we know of that uses the *n*VIDIA *n*Force3 150 chipset.

Processor

Intel Pentium 4/3.2 (http://www.intel.com)

Just because our SFF PC is small doesn't mean it has to be slow. For our configuration, we chose a relatively fast processor—a 3.2 GHz Intel Pentium 4. We were concerned at first that the Aria case would not provide sufficient cooling for such a fast processor, but our testing showed that it does. We chose an older Northwood-core Pentium 4/3.2 because Northwood-core processors consume less power than the newer Prescott-core processors, and accordingly dissipate less heat.

We would not hesitate to install an AMD Athlon XP or Athlon 64 with thermal characteristics similar to the Northwood-core Pentium 4/3.2, which is to say one that dissipates 89W or less. We would consider using a Prescott-core Pentium 4, but only with the understanding that doing so would cost us some of our heat budget that we might otherwise have allocated to faster video, a second hard drive, more memory, or another heat-generating component.

> The power consumption delta between Northwood and Prescott is profound. For example, a 3.2 GHz Northwood consumes 89W, whereas a 3.2 GHz Prescott consumes 106W. That extra 17W translates to significant additional heat, as much as might be produced by a midrange video adapter or two additional hard drives. In other words, if you install a Prescott, the additional power and cooling burden relative to a Northwood may restrict what other components you can install.

The best processor to use depends on the purpose of the system. Our SFF configuration will be used as a general-purpose system, so we chose a relatively fast Pentium 4. If your SFF PC will be used for less demanding tasks, such as an appliance PC or a home theater PC, use a slower (and less expensive) processor. The sound level produced by the SFF PC is linked to the amount of heat the processor produces. A fast, hot processor requires a CPU cooler with a fast, loud fan. It also forces the power supply fan to run constantly at high speed. For a quiet configuration, use a slow, cool-running processor.

Whichever processor you choose, buy the retail-boxed version rather than the OEM version. The retail-boxed version costs only a few dollars more, and includes a three-year warranty and a bundled processor cooler.

Memory

Crucial PC3200 DDR-SDRAM (http://www.crucial.com)

Memory is inexpensive enough that it is senseless to hamper a system by installing too little. We consider 256 MB appropriate for most appliance

---

ALTERNATIVES: PROCESSOR

Alternatives: For an appliance PC or other system that need not be extremely fast, use a low-end or midrange Athlon XP. If you have been seduced by the 64-bitness of the AMD Athlon 64, use the fastest retail-boxed model you can find for less than $200. Note, however, that Socket 754 is not long for this world, so you'll be buying into a dead-end product line. Of course, some might argue the same is true of Intel Socket 478, which Intel is striving mightily to replace with Socket 775.

PCs, 512 MB for most mainstream PCs, and 1 or 2 GB for most "power-user" systems.

The Intel D865GRH and GLC motherboards have four DIMM slots and a dual-channel memory controller that provides faster memory performance when DIMMs are installed in pairs. If you are installing 256 MB of system memory, use two 128 MB DIMMs. If you are installing 512 MB, use two 256 MB DIMMs. If you are installing 1 GB, install two 512 MB DIMMs. If you are installing 2 GB, install four 512 MB DIMMs rather than two 1 GB DIMMs (1 GB DIMMs are very expensive per MB compared to 512 MB DIMMs).

Crucial memory is fast, reliable, inexpensive, and readily available. We've used Crucial memory for more than a decade in hundreds of systems, and it's never let us down. Accordingly, we chose two Crucial PC3200 256 MB DIMMs for this system. If you run memory-intensive applications or many applications simultaneously, install a pair of Crucial PC3200 512 MB DIMMs instead.

Video adapter

Embedded video;
ATi RADEON 9200 or 9600 video adapter (http://www.ati.com)

Choose your video adapter according to the purpose of the system. Embedded video suffices for most purposes. If you need better 3D graphics performance, choose one of the ATi RADEON video adapters, according to your needs and budget. For entry-level 3D graphics, a RADEON 9200-series adapter is an excellent choice. If you need better 3D performance and are willing to spend a bit more to get it, go with a RADEON 9600-series adapter.

The RADEON 9200- and 9600-series adapters are fanless and generate relatively little heat. The 9800-series, X800Pro, and X800XT adapters run very hot, and are not ideal for use in an SFF case. We used a RADEON 9800Pro and a 9800XT in our SFF PC with a Pentium 4/3.2 processor, and found that the CPU and case temperatures were high enough to alarm us. Accordingly, if you need the higher 3D performance of these very fast video adapters, we recommend that you choose something other than an SFF case for your system.

If you need TV recording functions, choose an ATi RADEON All-In-Wonder adapter. The AIW 9200 is relatively inexpensive, but offloads video compression to the CPU. Accordingly, use the AIW 9200 only if you also use a reasonably fast processor. The AIW 9600 costs a bit more, but provides hardware-accelerated video compression, which means that it can record and compress video in real time even if the system uses a slow processor. Using either of these adapters in the Aria provides a good foundation for an SFF home theater PC.

Hard disk drive

Seagate Barracuda 7200.7 SATA 160 GB (http://www.seagate.com)

An SFF PC needs a quiet, cool-running hard drive with mainstream performance. Serial ATA is a better choice for an SFF system than parallel (standard) ATA, because S-ATA drives use thin cables rather than wide ribbon cables. This simplifies working on the system and aids cooling.

We think the best S-ATA drives are the Seagate Barracuda 7200.7 SATA models. The Barracuda 7200.7 is inexpensive, fast, quiet, and extremely reliable, and is available in 80, 120, 160, and 200 GB capacities. At the time we built this system, the 200 GB model was still selling at a substantial premium, so we went with the 160 GB unit.

Optical drive

Plextor PX-708A DVD writer (http://www.plextor.com)

We debated the best type of optical drive to use in our SFF PC. We considered installing a DVD-ROM drive, a CD writer, a combo DVD-ROM/CD-RW drive, or a DVD writer. We ruled out the CD writer because we wanted the ability to read DVD discs. The SFF PC is small and portable enough that we may carry it along on vacations or use it in other places where our network is not available; that meant we needed some sort of writable optical drive to make backups, which ruled out the DVD-ROM drive. Although a combo DVD-ROM/CD-RW drive might suffice for backups when the SFF PC is disconnected from the network, we decided that the higher capacity of a DVD writer was worth the small additional cost.

We chose the Plextor PX-708A DVD writer for its high speed, reliability, and flexibility. It writes all common optical formats, including CD-R/RW, DVD+R/RW, and DVD-R/RW, and reads nearly any optical disc except DVD-RAM. Unlike many DVD writers, which are very picky about media, the PX-708A happily accepts just about any blank disc you give it. We've successfully used everything from premium name-brand writable DVD discs to no-name stuff we've found on sale in the bargain bins. The PX-708A even does 8X writes on some no-name 4X DVD+R discs.

In May 2004, Plextor began shipping the 12X PX-712A DVD writer. We thought about using that drive rather than the 8X PX-708A for this and the other systems in this book, but the PX-712A sells at a significant premium over the PX-708A, and 12X media will be expensive and difficult to find for quite some time. If you want the best DVD drive available, by all means use the Plextor PX-712A, but we think most people will be happy with the Plextor PX-708A.

Any DVD writer you choose should support 8X DVD+R writes. The 8X units cost little more than obsolescent 4X units, and for most people their performance is worth the small additional cost. Although 12X DVD writers

ALTERNATIVES: HARD DISK DRIVE

Any ATA or Serial ATA Seagate or Maxtor 7,200 RPM ATA drive, in any capacity. S-ATA is a better choice than P-ATA because S-ATA uses thin cables that impede airflow less than the wide ribbon cables used by P-ATA drives. Also note that the superior performance of S-ATA is achieved only with native S-ATA drives, which are currently made only by Seagate. Bridged S-ATA drives, such as those made by Maxtor, use protocol translation, which reduces performance.

ALTERNATIVES: OPTICAL DRIVE

If you prefer an external DVD writer, choose the Plextor PX-708UF. It provides USB 2.0 and FireWire interfaces, and is easily portable from system to system. We prefer Plextor drives to any competing models, but we also recognize that not everyone wants to spend that much on an optical drive. If you'd prefer a less expensive DVD writer, use the NEC ND-2500A or the Lite-On LDW-811S, which sell for well under $100.

The 52X Plextor Premium is the best CD writer available, although it costs nearly as much as a low-end DVD writer. If you're on a tight budget, choose the Lite-On LTR-52327S 52X CD-RW drive. If you need a combo DVD-ROM/CD-RW drive, choose the 48X Lite-On LTC48161H or the 52X Lite-On SOHC-5232K.

are now available, they sell at a significant premium over 8X models, their 50% write speed advantage over 8X units is less noticeable than the 100% write speed advantage that 8X units provide relative to 4X units, and 12X discs are difficult to find and expensive. When 12X writers approach price parity with 8X writers, we'll start using 12X writers routinely. Until then, we think 8X DVD writers are the best choice.

WARNING

If you need to read burned DVDs, check compatibility. Most recent DVD drives and DVD players read any type of DVD disc, except perhaps DVD-RAM. Others will not read DVD+R/RW or DVD-R/RW discs. Check the technical specs on the web site to verify that your DVD drive or player is listed as compatible with the types of DVD discs you intend to use.

External peripherals

We're going to wimp out here. Rather than make specific recommendations for keyboard, mouse, speakers, display, and other external peripherals, we'll refer you to the other project system chapters in this book and to our web site (*http://www.hardwareguys.com*).

It's not that we don't want to provide a list of recommended external peripherals for the SFF PC. It's that we can't, because an SFF PC can be built as anything from a $500 appliance system to a $1,200 mainstream system to a $3,000 gaming system. Accordingly, all we can recommend is that you choose external peripherals according to your budget and the purpose of the system.

Component summary

Table 7-2 summarizes our component choices for the core SFF PC system.

Table 7-2. Bill of Materials for SFF PC

Component	Product
Case	Antec Aria microATX Case
Power supply	Antec AR300 (bundled)
Motherboard	Intel D865GLC or D865GRH
Processor	Intel Pentium 4/1.8, /2.6, or /3.2 (Northwood-core)
CPU cooler	(Bundled with retail-boxed CPU)
Memory	Crucial PC3200 DDR-SDRAM
Video adapter	Embedded video ATi RADEON 9200- or 9600-series video adapter ATi RADEON All-In-Wonder (9200- or 9600-series)
Hard disk drive	Seagate Barracuda 7200.7 SATA
Optical drive	Plextor PX-708A DVD writer

Building the System

Figure 7-3 shows the major internal components of the SFF PC. The Seagate 7200.7 Barracuda SATA hard drive and the Plextor PX-708A DVD burner are on top of the Antec Aria case, with the Intel D865GRH motherboard at the lower left. To its right, front to back, are the two 256 MB sticks of Crucial PC3200 memory, the Pentium 4 processor, and the stock Intel CPU cooler.

Before you proceed, make sure you have everything you need. Open each box and verify the contents against the packing list. Make sure all driver discs, cables, screws, and other small components are present.

Figure 7-3. SFF PC components, awaiting construction

Preparing the case

The first step in building any system is always to make sure that the power supply is set to the correct input voltage. Some power supplies, including the unit supplied with the Antec Aria, set themselves automatically. Others must be set manually, using a slide switch to select the proper input voltage.

Size Does Matter

When you build a standard PC, the exact component installation sequence usually doesn't matter much. With an SFF PC, that's often not true. The small case means there's little room to work, and one component may be inaccessible after you install another component. If you forget to connect a cable to the motherboard, for example, you may later have to partially disassemble the system to get to it.

The Antec Aria case is much better than most SFF cases in this respect. The top panel and both side panels are removable, which means the interior is quite accessible, albeit a bit cramped. The disadvantage of the Aria is that it doesn't include custom-length cables preinstalled and routed, as is the case with most "barebones" SFF systems. That means you need to take particular care to route cables appropriately to avoid restricting airflow.

If your case uses such a power supply, make sure that it's set to the proper input voltage before you proceed.

WARNING

If you connect a PC set for 230V to a 115V receptacle, nothing is damaged. The PC components receive half the voltage they require, and the system won't boot. But if you connect a power supply set for 115V to a 230V receptacle, the PC components receive *twice* the voltage they're designed to use. If you power up the system, that overvoltage will destroy the system instantly in clouds of smoke and showers of sparks.

To begin preparing the Antec Aria case, remove the thumbscrew that secures the top panel, as shown in Figure 7-4.

WARNING

Be careful when working on the Antec Aria case. Although it is solidly built for an aluminum case, it is still much more fragile than a standard steel case.

Figure 7-4. Remove the thumbscrew that secures the top panel

After you remove the thumbscrew, slide the top panel back slightly until the hooks that secure it disengage. Lift the panel off, as shown in Figure 7-5.

The Antec Aria uses a swing-up removable drive bay that secures to the chassis via four posts that mate with corresponding notches in the chassis. To remove the drive bay, pivot the rear end upward and lift the drive bay free of the chassis, as shown in Figure 7-6.

Figure 7-5. Slide the top panel back slightly and lift it off

Figure 7-6. Pivot the drive bay upward and lift it free of the chassis

Chapter 7, Building a Small Form Factor PC

WARNING

The drive bay is made of thin sheet aluminum, which is very easy to bend. We found that out the hard way when we started working on the Aria case. As we tugged and pulled on the bay, trying to figure out how to remove it, we squeezed too hard on the central portion and were horrified when the sheet metal bent noticeably. Fortunately, it was just as easy to bend the sheet aluminum back into place. To avoid bending your drive bay, pivot the rear of the bay upward toward the front of the case until the rear two posts come free. Then lift the bay straight up, sliding the front two posts out of the matching slots in the chassis.

With the drive bay removed, the inside of the case is visible, as shown in Figure 7-7. The brown cardboard box contains mounting screws and other hardware. The white box contains the Cyclone Blower, a supplementary cooling fan that mounts in place of a PCI expansion card.

The black rectangle visible at the top is a universal 5.25" drive bezel. Its purpose is to conceal the front of the optical drive. In theory, that allows you to use an optical drive with a mismatched bezel color because the optical drive bezel is concealed by the universal bezel. In practice, it didn't work out that way for us, so we removed the universal bezel. The problem was that the universal bezel provides a slot for the drive tray and the eject button, but makes no provision for accessing the front-panel volume control and audio jacks on the drive. Worse still, the universal bezel conceals the activity LED on the drive, which we wanted to remain visible.

Figure 7-7. The interior of the Aria case with the top panel removed

WARNING

The circuit card visible beneath the universal bezel controls the 8-in-1 card reader. Be very careful of this circuit board when you work inside the case. It sticks out into the case interior, where it can easily be damaged, and is unsupported other than by the bezel of the 8-in-1 card reader. During a thumb-fingered moment while we were building our system, we almost knocked the circuit board off by dropping the power supply on it.

Both side panels of the Aria case are removable, which provides excellent access to the interior of the case while you are working on it. To remove a side panel, locate the black plastic latch at the center rear of the panel, shown in Figure 7-8.

While squeezing the side-panel latch, slide the side panel slightly forward to release the hooks that secure it to the chassis and then pivot the side panel away from the case, as shown in Figure 7-9.

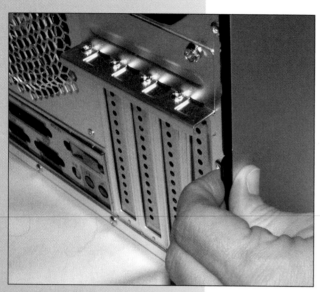

Figure 7-8. Locate the latch at the center rear of the side panel

Figure 7-9. While squeezing the latch, slide the side panel forward slightly and then pull it away from the case

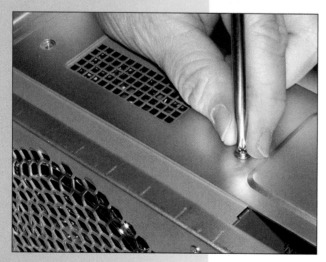

Figure 7-10. Remove the screws that secure the power supply

Antec says you needn't remove the power supply to work on the system. We're sure they're right, but we decided it would be worthwhile to remove the power supply temporarily to improve access to the inside of the case during the initial assembly steps. The Antec power supply is secured by six screws, two on the top and four in the rear. To remove the power supply, begin by removing the two top screws, as shown in Figure 7-10. Once those are removed, support the power supply with one hand and remove the four rear screws.

The Aria power supply is unusual in that the mains AC power connector is built into the case rather than the power supply unit itself. The power supply connects to the main power receptacle using three wires with spade-lug connectors. We thought about removing the power supply completely, but decided against it because there was enough slack in the wires to allow us to set the power supply on the top rear of the case, as shown in Figure 7-11.

WARNING

If we were doing it again, we'd pull the power supply completely, carefully noting (or shooting an image of) the connections between the power supply and the main power receptacle. As we worked on the system with the power supply balanced precariously, we managed to jostle it slightly. That was enough to make the power supply come crashing down into the interior of the case, nearly decapitating the circuit board for the 8-in-1 card reader.

Figure 7-11. Balance the power supply on top of the case to gain more working room (but see the text for a warning)

Nearly every case we've used, including the Antec Aria, comes with an I/O template. So does nearly every motherboard. The generic I/O template supplied with the case never seems to fit the I/O panel of the motherboard, so you need to remove the stock I/O template and replace it with the one supplied with the motherboard.

I/O templates are made of thin metal that is easily bent. Making matters worse, aluminum cases like the Antec Aria are easily bent as well. The best way we found to remove the standard I/O template without damaging it or the case is to apply gentle finger pressure to the template from outside the case while supporting the case structure from inside using the other hand, as shown in Figure 7-12.

> If you must make a choice, bend the stock I/O template rather than the case. You'll probably never need the stock I/O template again, but if you bend the case in the area around the I/O template cutout, you'll find it difficult or impossible to get the new I/O template installed properly.

Figure 7-12. Remove the I/O template supplied with the case

Most motherboards, including the Intel D865GRH, come with a custom ATX I/O template that matches the motherboard I/O panel. Before you install the custom I/O template, compare it to the motherboard I/O panel to make sure the holes in the template correspond to the connectors on the motherboard.

Once you've done that, press the custom I/O template into place. Working from inside the case, align the bottom, right, and left edges of the I/O template with the matching case cutout. When the I/O template is positioned properly, press gently along the edges to seat it in the cutout, as shown in Figure 7-13. It should snap into place, although getting it to seat properly sometimes requires several attempts. As you apply pressure against the template from inside the case, use your finger to apply offsetting pressure on the outside to support the case structure.

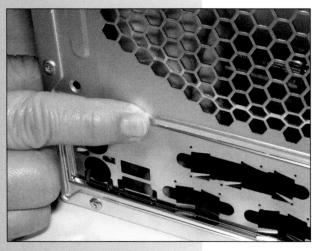

Figure 7-13. Snap the custom I/O template into place

> **WARNING**
> Be careful not to bend the I/O template or the case when you seat the template. The template holes need to line up with the external port connectors on the motherboard I/O panel. If the template or the case is bent even slightly, it may be difficult to seat the motherboard properly.

After you install the I/O template, carefully slide the motherboard into place temporarily, as shown in Figure 7-14. Make sure that the back-panel connectors on the motherboard are firmly in contact with the corresponding holes on the I/O template. Compare the positions of the motherboard mounting holes with the standoff mounting positions in the case. One easy way to do this is to place the motherboard in position and insert a felt-tip pen through each motherboard mounting hole to mark the corresponding standoff position beneath it.

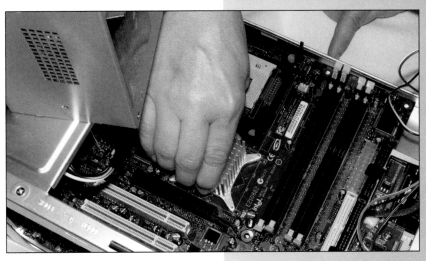

Figure 7-14. Slide the motherboard into place temporarily to verify standoff mounting positions

The Intel D865GRH motherboard has eight mounting holes. The Antec Aria, like many cases, is shipped with several standoffs preinstalled. All six of the standoffs preinstalled in the Aria corresponded with motherboard mounting holes, so we needed to install only two standoffs.

WARNING

If your case comes with preinstalled brass standoffs, make absolutely certain that each standoff matches a motherboard mounting hole. If you find one that doesn't, remove it. Leaving an "extra" brass standoff in place may cause a short circuit that could damage the motherboard and/or other components.

If you simply look at the motherboard, it's easy to miss one of the mounting holes in all the clutter. It helps to hold the motherboard up to a light, which makes the mounting holes stand out distinctly.

The Antec Aria uses a mixture of standard brass standoffs and chrome-plated steel motherboard clips, shown in Figure 7-15. The top of each clip has a small bent protruding nipple that is small enough to pass through a motherboard mounting hole. Once the motherboard is dropped into place over these clips, sliding the motherboard slightly toward the back of the case causes the clips to clamp down on the top surface of the motherboard, securing it in place.

As shipped, the Aria has brass standoffs in two positions and motherboard clips in four positions. For the two remaining required standoffs, we decided to use motherboard clips. They appear to secure the motherboard quite well, and we decided two screws were sufficient to lock the motherboard into place against the clips. If you're uncomfortable depending on the clips—for example, if this is to be a portable system—you can replace the motherboard clips with standard brass standoffs, which are provided in the parts bag.

Figure 7-15. Insert a motherboard mounting clip in each position that corresponds to a motherboard mounting hole

To install the clips, press gently on the sides of the clip and slide it into the mounting position. Make sure that the bent nipple on the clip faces the same direction as the nipples on the clips that are already installed. Robert was able to insert the clips using only finger pressure to compress them, but

Barbara found it easier to compress the clips with bent needlenose pliers. Whichever method you use, make sure each clip snaps securely into the motherboard tray.

Once you've installed all the standoffs and motherboard clips, do a final check to verify that each motherboard mounting hole has a corresponding standoff or clip, and that no standoffs or clips are installed that don't correspond to a motherboard mounting hole. If you've removed the power supply, you can as a final check hold the motherboard in position above the case and look down through each motherboard mounting hole to make sure there's a standoff installed below it.

Installing the processor and memory

Even for a full-size system, it's easier to install the processor and memory while the motherboard is outside the case. An SFF system has so little working room that it's almost mandatory to do so.

Installing the processor

To install the Pentium 4 processor, place the motherboard on a flat surface. Lift the arm of the ZIF (zero insertion force) socket until it reaches vertical, as shown in Figure 7-16. With the arm vertical, there is no clamping force on the socket holes, which allows the processor to drop into place without requiring any pressure.

Figure 7-16. Lift the socket lever to prepare the socket to receive the processor

Pin 1 is indicated on the processor and socket by a small triangle. With the socket lever vertical, align pin 1 of the processor with pin 1 of the socket and drop the processor into place, as shown in Figure 7-17. The processor should seat flush with the socket just from the force of gravity. If seating the processor requires anything more than a very gentle nudge, something is misaligned. Remove the processor and verify that it is aligned properly and that the pattern of pins on the processor corresponds to the pattern of holes on the socket.

Figure 7-17. Drop the processor into place

WARNING

Never apply significant pressure to the processor—you'll bend one or more pins and destroy it. If despite everything you do bend a pin, you may be able to straighten it sufficiently to allow the processor to seat by running a thin credit card in both directions along the rows and columns of unbent pins.

With the processor in place and seated flush with the socket, press the ZIF lever arm down and snap it into place to secure the processor. You may have to press the lever arm slightly away from the socket to allow it to snap into a locked position.

Closing the ZIF lever sometimes causes the processor to lift slightly out of its socket. Once you are sure the processor is fully seated, it's safe to maintain gentle finger pressure on it to keep it in place as you close the ZIF lever.

Installing the heatsink/fan (HSF)

Modern processors draw from 50W to more than 100W of power. That power must be dissipated as heat over the surface of the processor heat spreader, which is about the size of a large postage stamp. To visualize the scale of heat production, imagine a 50W to 100W incandescent light bulb the size of the processor running continuously. That heat must be drawn away from the processor and eventually exhausted from the case. Otherwise, the processor would almost instantaneously shut itself down to prevent damage from overheating.

Drawing heat away from the processor is the job of the heatsink, which is a heavy mass of metal with fins to provide a large surface area. Most heatsinks are made of aluminum, which has good heat transfer characteristics, or of copper, which has even better thermal characteristics but is much heavier and more expensive than aluminum. Standard heatsinks use a small embedded fan to draw cool air over the surface of the heatsink, transferring the heat produced by the processor to the air inside the case. In conjunction, those two components are referred to as a heatsink/fan (HSF) unit or a processor cooler.

WARNING

Using a proper HSF is critical. Retail-boxed processors include an HSF unit that is perfectly adequate for the task. For this system, that's what we used.

If you buy an OEM processor, you must choose an HSF unit that is sufficient to keep the processor operating within its design temperature range. Just because an HSF fits doesn't guarantee that it's usable. Faster processors consume more power and generate more heat. An HSF rated for a Pentium 4/2.4 will physically fit a Pentium 4/3.2, but is grossly inadequate for the faster processor. HSFs designed for faster processors are generally larger, heavier, use copper instead of aluminum fins, and have more powerful fans.

To install the HSF unit, begin by polishing the heat spreader surface on top of the processor with a paper towel or soft cloth, as shown in Figure 7-18. The goal is to remove any grease, grit, or other material that might prevent the heatsink from making intimate contact with the processor surface.

After you polish the processor, check the surface of the heatsink. If the heatsink base is bare, that means it's intended to be used with thermal compound, usually called "thermal goop." In that case, also polish the heatsink base, as shown in Figure 7-19. Some heatsinks have a square or rectangular pad made of a phase-change medium, which is a fancy term for a material

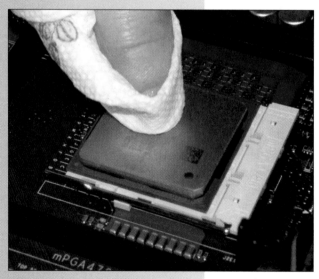

Figure 7-18. Polish the processor with a paper towel before installing the HSF

Figure 7-19. Polish the heatsink base with a paper towel

that melts as the CPU heats and resolidifies as the CPU cools. This liquid/solid cycle ensures that the processor die maintains good thermal contact with the heatsink. If your heatsink includes such a pad you needn't polish the base of the heatsink. (Heatsinks use *either* a thermal pad *or* thermal goop, not both.)

The retail-boxed Pentium 4 processor we used for the SFF system includes a heatsink/fan unit designed for use with thermal compound. This HSF is a hybrid unit. The body of the heatsink is made of aluminum, but the area that the processor contacts is made of copper. Such hybrid heatsinks are lighter and less expensive than solid copper units and provide similar cooling efficiency.

The Intel heatsink/fan unit includes a syringe with a premeasured amount of thermal compound. Remove the cap from the syringe and squeeze the thermal compound into a pile on the center of the processor, as shown in Figure 7-20. You don't have to get all of the thermal compound out of the syringe; getting most of it is enough.

Figure 7-20. Apply the provided thermal compound

If you apply thermal compound too liberally, excess compound may squeeze out between the HSF base and the processor surface when you put the heatsink in place. Good practice suggests removing excess compound from around the socket, but that may be impossible with a large heatsink because the heatsink blocks access to the socket area. Silicone thermal compound like that provided with the stock Intel HSF does not conduct electricity, so there is no danger of excess compound shorting anything out.

Some people recommend using your finger (covered with a latex glove or plastic bag) to spread the thermal compound evenly over the surface of the heat spreader. With the Intel stock HSF and its premeasured dose of thermal compound, we just leave the little pile of thermal compound in place near the center of the heat spreader. Placing the heatsink on top of the processor squooshes out the compound evenly, allowing it to fill all gaps between the heat spreader surface and the heatsink base with no great danger of excess compound gooping things up. With third-party silver-based thermal compounds—which we don't trust to be electrically nonconductive, despite manufacturers' claims to the contrary—we use our finger to spread just enough compound to cover the heat spreader with a thin, even layer.

WARNING

If you remove the heatsink, you must replace the thermal compound or pad when you reinstall it. Be sure to remove all remnants of the old thermal pad or compound. This can be difficult, particularly for a thermal pad, which can be very tenacious. We use a hair dryer to warm the thermal material enough to make it easy to remove. Try warming up the compound and rubbing it off with your thumb. (Use rubber gloves or a plastic bag to keep the gunk off your skin.)

Alternatively, one of our technical reviewers says that rubbing gently with 0000 steel wool works wonders in removing the gunk, and is fine enough not to damage the surface. Another reviewer tells us that he uses Goof-Off or isopropyl alcohol to remove the remnants of the thermal goop or thermal pad. Whatever works for you is fine. Just make sure to remove the old thermal compound and replace it with new compound each time you remove and reinstall the processor.

When we replace a heatsink, we use Antec Silver Thermal Compound, which works well and is widely available and inexpensive. Don't pay extra for "premium" brand names like Arctic Silver. They cost more than the Antec product, and our testing shows little or no difference in cooling efficiency.

Figure 7-21. Align the HSF unit over the processor and seat it

Before you proceed, check the orientation of the two white plastic clamps on the heatsink bracket. (One is visible at the center of Figure 7-21.) Each of the clamps has a cam that presses the heatsink into close contact with the processor. Make sure that both clamps are in the relaxed position, with the cammed portion upward (away from the processor). In that state, the two clamps point to opposite sides of the heatsink bracket.

Orient the HSF above the processor as shown in Figure 7-21, keeping it as close to horizontal as possible. Slide the HSF unit down into the retaining bracket, making sure that the locking hooks on all four corners of the HSF snap into place over the corresponding posts on the motherboard bracket. Press down gently and use a small circular motion to spread the thermal goop evenly over the surface of the processor.

WARNING

Before you clamp it into place, the metal heatsink has some play within the plastic bracket that contains it. That's good in the sense that it allows you to move the heatsink around slightly to distribute the thermal compound. But it's bad in the sense that it allows the heatsink itself to be misaligned within its bracket when you attempt to clamp it down. If that happens, you may break the bracket. Figure 7-21 shows the fins of the heatsink overlapping the edge of the motherboard retaining bracket. This image was not staged. We didn't realize that the heatsink was misaligned until we attempted to clamp it into place. If we'd persisted without correcting the misalignment, we'd have snapped off the clamping arm. Figure 7-22 shows the heatsink fins properly aligned inside the bracket.

With the HSF resting loosely in place, the next step is to clamp it tightly against the processor to ensure good thermal transfer between the CPU and heatsink. Rotate one of the cammed clamps 180 degrees to the opposite side of the bracket until it seats, and then do the same for the other clamp. It's easier to press the first clamp into place because there isn't yet any pressure on the HSF, so we generally do the less accessible clamp first—in this case, the clamp nearer the center of the motherboard. The clamp at the edge of the motherboard, shown in Figure 7-22, is more easily accessible, so we locked that one into place second. (The cammed portion of the clamping arm is visible at center, beneath the center of the bracket.)

Figure 7-22. Clamp the HSF into place

The thermal mass of the heatsink draws heat away from the CPU, but the heat must be dissipated to prevent the CPU from eventually overheating as the heatsink warms up. To dispose of excess heat as it is transferred to the heatsink, most CPU coolers use a small muffin fan to continuously draw air through the fins of the heatsink. Some CPU fans use a drive power connector, but most are designed to attach to the dedicated CPU fan connector on the motherboard. Using a motherboard fan power connector allows the motherboard to control the CPU fan, reducing speed for quieter operation when the processor is running under light load and not generating much heat, and increasing fan speed when the processor is running under heavy load and generating more heat. The motherboard can also monitor fan speed, which allows it to send an alert to the user if the fan fails or begins running sporadically.

To connect the CPU fan, locate the three-pin header connector on the motherboard labeled CPU Fan, and plug the keyed cable from the CPU fan into it, as shown in Figure 7-23.

Installing the memory

Before you begin plugging in memory modules, take a moment to determine the best memory configuration. The Intel D865GRH motherboard supports dual-channel memory operation, but unless you install memory modules in the proper sockets, the motherboard operates in the slower single-channel mode. Dual-channel operation requires using DIMMs in pairs, one per channel.

Figure 7-23. Connect the CPU fan cable to the CPU fan connector

The D865GRH motherboard has four DIMM slots in two pairs. The slot nearest the processor is Channel A DIMM0, followed by Channel A DIMM1, Channel B DIMM0, and Channel B DIMM1. To enable dual-channel memory operation, we need to install one of our 256 MB memory modules in Channel A and the other in Channel B. We could use either slot, but as a matter of good practice we decided to install our DIMMs in the first (DIMM0) slot of each channel. Also, the Channel B DIMM1 slot is nearer the main ATX power connector, so using it reduces the clearance available when you connect power to the motherboard.

After you identify the proper memory slots, pivot the white plastic locking tabs on both sides of the DIMM sockets outward to prepare the slot to receive a DIMM. Orient each DIMM so that the notch in the contact area of the DIMM is aligned with the raised plastic tab in the slot and slide the DIMM into place, as shown in Figure 7-24.

Figure 7-24. Orient the DIMM with the notch aligned properly with the socket

Figure 7-25. Seat the DIMM by pressing firmly until it snaps into place

With the DIMM properly aligned with the Channel A DIMM0 slot and oriented vertically relative to the slot, use both thumbs to press down on the DIMM until it snaps into place. The locking tabs should automatically pivot back up into the locked position when the DIMM snaps into place, as shown in Figure 7-25. If they don't, close them manually to lock the DIMM into the socket.

With the processor and memory installed, you're almost ready to install the motherboard in the case. Before you do that, check the motherboard documentation to determine if any configuration jumpers need to be set. The Intel D865GRH has only one jumper, which sets the operating mode. On our motherboard, that jumper was set correctly by default.

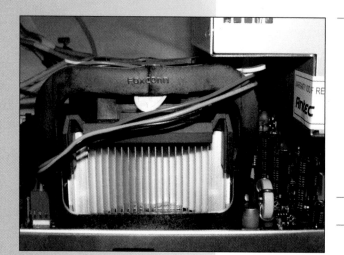

Figure 7-26. The limited clearance between the HSF and the power supply makes it impossible to install the power supply with the motherboard already in place

WARNING

If you removed the power supply, reinstall it before you install the motherboard. We neglected to do that the first time we built the SFF system, and after installing the motherboard and connecting all the cables, we found that the power supply couldn't be reinstalled with the motherboard already in place. The problem, as shown in Figure 7-26, is that there is very little clearance between the top of the HSF clamping bracket and the bottom of the power supply.

Figure 7-26 shows one of the small touches that contribute to a well-built system. We have looped the fan power cable around the HSF clamp and thence to the CPU Fan power connector, keeping the cable from flopping around loose in the case and possibly fouling the fan.

Installing the motherboard

Installing the motherboard is the most time-consuming step in building the system because there are so many cables to connect. It's important to get them all connected right, so take your time and verify each connection before and after you make it.

Seating and securing the motherboard

To begin, slide the motherboard into the case, carefully aligning the back-panel I/O connectors with the corresponding holes in the I/O template. As the motherboard I/O connectors seat, the protruding nipples on the motherboard clips should grasp the motherboard. Keeping pressure on the motherboard to align the two brass standoffs with the corresponding mounting holes, drive screws into the two brass standoffs to secure the motherboard in place, as shown in Figure 7-27.

Figure 7-27. Secure the motherboard by driving screws into the brass standoffs

> Before you install the motherboard, tie off the front-panel and other cables to keep them out of the way. The limited working space inside an SFF case makes it easy to lose track of a cable and later find that it's caught beneath the mounted motherboard and can't be pulled free because the connector jams it in place.

After you secure the motherboard, verify that the back-panel I/O connectors mate properly with the I/O template, as shown in Figure 7-28. The I/O template has metal tabs that ground the back-panel I/O connectors; make sure none of these tabs intrudes into a port connector. An errant tab at best blocks the port, rendering it unusable, and at worst may short out the motherboard.

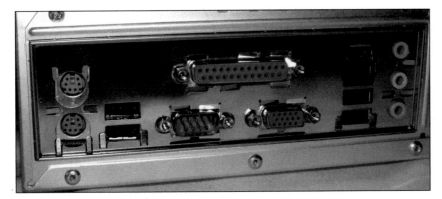

Figure 7-28. Verify that the back-panel connectors mate cleanly with the I/O template

Connecting the front-panel USB ports

The Antec Aria case provides two front-panel USB 2.0 ports and the 8-in-1 card reader, which also uses a USB connection. If the ports and card reader are to function, each must be connected to an individual motherboard USB port. The Intel D865GRH motherboard provides four internal USB ports, so we expected to have no problems connecting the front-panel USB ports and the card reader.

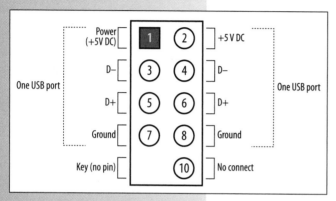

Figure 7-29. Front-panel USB connector pin assignments (original graphic courtesy Intel Corporation)

We did encounter a problem, though. The Intel motherboard provides four USB ports in two sets of two, using a 5×2 connector block with the pin assignments shown in Figure 7-29. The front-panel USB ports and card reader on our early-model Aria have individual cables, each of which terminates in a 5×1 inline connector, with the fifth position blocked. Current Aria cases have 5×1 inline USB connectors with no positions blocked and a 4×1 reader connector.

Those cables can connect to the first USB port on each motherboard USB block (shown on the left in Figure 7-29) because there is no pin present at the fifth position. The second (right-hand) USB port on each connector has a pin in position 10, which prevents the Antec cable from seating. That meant we could use only two of the four available internal USB ports. We needed three—one for the card reader and two for the front-panel USB ports. Hmmm.

Incredibly, Antec recognizes the problem and even mentions it in the manual, saying "Note: Due to the blocked 'key' pin, you will need to use a motherboard USB header row with only 4 pins." Duh. Why not just give us a four-pin connector, or a five-pin connector that doesn't have pin 5 blocked?

Pin 10 doesn't carry any signal, so our temporary solution was to use our needlenose pliers to bend pin 10 out of the way enough to allow the Antec cable to seat. We're not pleased with that solution, because the bent pin doesn't allow the connector to seat fully. The next time we tear this system down, we'll use our dykes to nip off pin 10 completely, allowing the connector to seat fully.

WARNING
If you do choose to remove the pin, make absolutely certain you know which pin you're clipping off, and make sure you remove the clipped pin so that it doesn't short something out. Pin 10 is dispensable. If you accidentally clip off one of the others, you render that USB port useless. Also note that such unauthorized surgery voids the warranty on the motherboard. Alternatively, you may be able to remove the block in the cable connector by prying it out with a safety pin or other sharp object, or by melting it with a heated safety pin.

It makes no difference which of the three cables you connect to which of the four USB ports. Once you've decided which to connect where, slide each of the three cable connectors onto a motherboard USB connector, as shown in Figure 7-30.

Figure 7-30. Connect the front-panel USB cables

WARNING

If you use Windows 98, Windows 98SE, or Windows 2000 SP2 or earlier, Antec specifically warns *not to connect the 8-in-1 card reader cable* until you install the operating system and the driver contained on the CD that is supplied with the Aria case. Windows ME, Windows 2000 SP3 or higher, Windows XP, and Linux with the 2.4.0 or higher kernel do not require a separate driver, so you can connect the card reader before you install the operating system.

Connecting the front-panel switch and indicator cables

The next step is to connect the front-panel switch and indicator cables to the motherboard. Each of the front-panel cables is labeled descriptively, e.g., "Power," "Reset," and "HDD LED." Match those descriptions with the front-panel connector pins on the motherboard to make sure you connect the correct cable to the appropriate pins. Figure 7-31 shows the pin assignments for the Power Switch, Reset Switch, Power LED, and Hard Drive Activity LED connectors.

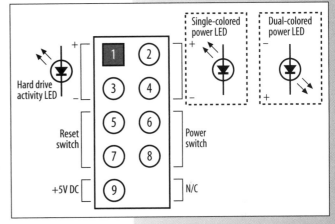

Figure 7-31. Front-panel connector pin assignments (original graphic courtesy Intel Corporation)

- The Power Switch and Reset Switch connectors are not polarized, and can be connected in either orientation.

- The Hard Drive Activity LED is polarized, and should be connected with the signal (red) wire on pin 1 and the ground (black) wire on pin 3.

Although the Intel motherboard provides two power LED connectors—one on the main front-panel connector block that accepts a two-position power LED cable, and a supplementary power LED connector adjacent to the main front-panel connector block that accepts a three-position power LED cable with wires in positions 1 and 3—the Antec Aria case does not provide a standard power LED. Instead, the Aria provides this function using two blue LEDs that connect directly to a Molex power connector from the power supply. If you choose to connect these LEDs, they are illuminated as long as the system is powered up.

Once you have sorted out the front-panel cables, connect the Power Switch, Reset Switch, and Hard Drive Activity LED, as shown in Figure 7-32.

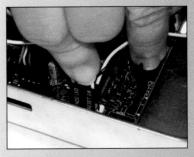

Figure 7-32. Connect the front-panel switch and indicator cables

Connecting the front-panel audio ports

The next decision is whether to enable the front-panel audio connectors. The Intel D865GRH motherboard has a set of header pins, the front panel audio connector/jumper block, that serves two functions:

- With jumpers installed, the pins serve as a jumper block that routes audio line-out to the rear-panel audio line-out connector, and mic-in to the rear-panel mic-in connector.

- With jumpers removed, the pins serve as a connecting block for the front-panel audio cable, routing audio line-out and mic-in signals to the front-panel audio connectors. In this configuration, the rear-panel audio line-out and mic-in connectors are disabled.

We decided to leave all audio functions connected to the rear panel, both because we find it disconcerting to have cables dangling from the front of the system and because enabling front-panel audio disables audio features that are available only if the back-panel audio connectors are enabled. If you prefer to have front-panel audio, remove the jumpers and install the front-panel audio connecting cable supplied with the Aria case. This cable has a monolithic, keyed, 10-pin connecting block that is compatible with the standard Intel front-panel audio connector.

For more information about configuring the front-panel audio connector/jumper block, see Table 39 in section 2.9.1 on page 85 of the *Intel Desktop Board D865GRH Technical Product Specification*, available on the Intel web site at *http://www.intel.com*.

Figure 7-33. Connect the S-ATA hard drive cable

Connecting the drive cables to the motherboard

The next step is to connect the Serial ATA data cable to the motherboard Serial ATA interface. The motherboard provides two Serial ATA interfaces, labeled SATA 0 and SATA 1. Although the drive functions properly connected to either interface, best practice is to connect the primary hard drive to the first interface, which is SATA 0. The motherboard SATA connector is keyed to fit in only one direction. Orient the Serial ATA data cable with its keying slot corresponding to the keying tab on the motherboard connector, and press the cable into place, as shown in Figure 7-33.

The next step is to connect the ATA cable for the optical drive to the motherboard. We want the Plextor PX-708A optical drive to be the master device on the secondary ATA channel. (We'll leave the primary ATA channel unused, because Windows can become confused if the primary hard drive is Serial ATA and there is a master device on the primary ATA channel.)

The primary ATA and secondary ATA interfaces are located near the right front edge of the motherboard, close to the DIMM slots. The primary ATA interface is the black connector nearest the edge, and the secondary ATA interface is a white connector immediately adjacent. Locate pin 1 on the secondary ATA interface, align the ATA cable with its red stripe toward pin 1 on the interface, and press the connector into place, as shown in Figure 7-34.

Figure 7-34. Connect the P-ATA optical drive cable

> The ATA cable shown is the Antec Cobra ATA cable that was included with the Aria case. Ordinarily, we are not enamored of rounded ATA cables, which do not comply with the ATA specification. Because the conductors in a round cable are not separated by ground wires, as they are in an Ultra-ATA 80-wire ribbon cable, crosstalk between signal lines may cause frequent read and write retries, and data corruption is possible. These problems are more likely to occur with Ultra-ATA hard drives, and are less likely to occur with devices that use relatively low data transfer rates, such as optical drives. Rounded cables are indisputably better than ribbon cables in terms of air-flow, however, so we decided to use the supplied Cobra cable for our optical drive.

Locate the fan sensor cable coming from the power supply. It's the short two-conductor cable with blue and black wires that terminates in a three-pin jumper block. Connect this cable to the fan power header located near the rear I/O panel, as shown in Figure 7-35.

The next step is to connect the two power connectors from the power supply to the motherboard. The main ATX power connector is a 20-pin connector located near the right front edge of the motherboard. Locate the corresponding cable coming from the power supply. The main ATX power connector is keyed, so verify that it is aligned properly before you attempt to seat it.

Figure 7-35. Connect the fan to the fan power header

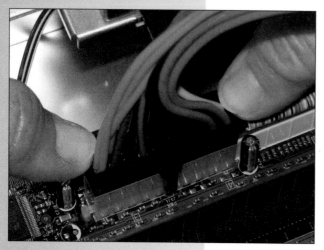

Figure 7-36. Connect the main ATX power connector

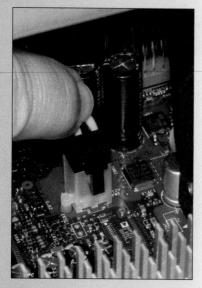

Figure 7-37. Connect the ATX12V power connector

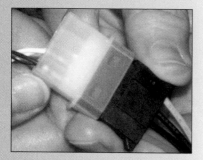

Figure 7-38. Connect the front-panel blue LEDs to a power cable

Once everything is aligned, press down firmly until the connector seats, as shown in Figure 7-36. It may take significant pressure to seat the connector, and you should feel it snap into place. The locking tab on the side of the connector should snap into place over the corresponding nub on the socket. Make sure the connector seats fully. A partially seated main ATX power connector may cause subtle problems that are very difficult to troubleshoot.

Pentium 4 systems require more power to the motherboard than the standard main ATX power connector supplies. Intel developed a supplementary connector, called the ATX12V connector, that routes additional +12V current directly to the VRM (Voltage Regulator Module) that powers the processor. On most Pentium 4 motherboards, including the D865GRH, the ATX12V connector is located very near the processor socket. The ATX12V connector is keyed. Orient the cable connector properly relative to the motherboard connector and press it into place until the plastic tab locks, as shown in Figure 7-37.

WARNING

If you forget to connect the ATX12V cable, the system won't boot. For six months after the Pentium 4 first shipped, we always forgot to connect the ATX12V cable on P4 systems, which meant we always had to open up the system and connect the cable. Connecting the ATX12V is now such ingrained behavior that we search for the ATX12V connector even on Athlon XP motherboards that don't have it.

As long as you're connecting power cables, you might as well connect the cable that powers the two LEDs on the Aria front panel. Locate the Molex connector with blue and white wires that comes from the front panel and connect it to one of the drive power connectors, as shown in Figure 7-38.

Like many computer component makers, Antec uses blue LEDs in many of its products. If you're wondering why this fad has seemingly caught on with every manufacturer simultaneously, it's because blue LEDs are finally available at a reasonable price. Green, red, and yellow LEDs have been common and cheap for many years. Blue LEDs were the Holy Grail among semiconductor manufacturers. A couple of years ago, someone finally developed a manufacturing process to produce blue LEDs cheaply, and now they're ubiquitous.

Installing the drives

The Antec Aria has one external 5.25" drive bay and three internal 3.5" drive bays. The external bay is for an optical drive, and the three internal 3.5" bays can each hold one hard drive.

> This is the first time we've built a system with a case that makes no provision for a floppy disk drive (FDD). We half expected Windows XP Setup to demand a driver floppy before it would allow us to format the S-ATA hard drive. If it had, we'd have popped the lid and plugged in an FDD temporarily, but as it happened Windows XP installed without requiring a driver floppy.

Antec provides a universal drive bezel for the 5.25" bay. This bezel is intended to conceal the optical drive. A hinged flapper allows the tray of the optical drive to extend and retract; pressure on the push button of the universal bezel is transferred to the eject button on the drive itself. The idea is that because the universal bezel conceals the optical drive bezel, you needn't worry about matching the color of the optical drive bezel to the front bezel of the Aria. When we built this system, we had several Plextor PX-708A optical drives with white bezels in inventory, but had run short of black models. Accordingly, we decided to use a white PX-708A in conjunction with the universal bezel.

As we were building the system, we changed our minds about using the universal bezel. Why? Because in addition to concealing the white bezel of the drive, the universal bezel also concealed the front audio jacks on the drive, the volume control, and (most important) the LED indicator. We wanted all of those to be accessible, and so decided to remove the universal bezel. We suggest you do the same, so you'll probably want to use a black Plextor PX-708A drive rather than the white one we ended up using. To remove the universal bezel, apply pressure on one side to release the hooks and snap the bezel out, as shown in Figure 7-39.

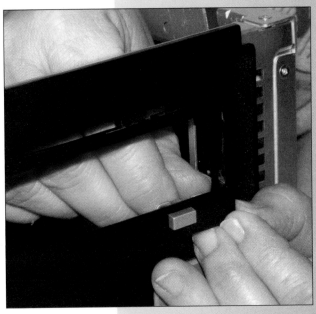

Figure 7-39. Remove the universal optical drive bezel

Figure 7-40. Secure the hard drive in the bay

The next step is to mount the hard drive and optical drive. Retrieve the drive bay assembly that you removed and set aside earlier. To mount the hard drive, place the drive bay assembly face-down on the table, with the 3.5" drive bays at the top. Slide the Seagate 7200.7 Barracuda SATA hard drive into the center 3.5" drive bay and secure it using four of the screws with rubber grommets supplied with the case, as shown in Figure 7-40.

Figure 7-41. Secure the optical drive in the bay

S-ATA supports only one device per interface, so S-ATA drives do not have the master/slave jumper used on parallel (standard) ATA drives. We used an S-ATA hard drive for this system. If you install a P-ATA hard drive, verify that its jumper is set to master before or immediately after you install it in the drive bay.

With the hard drive secured, slide the optical drive into the 5.25" bay and secure it with four screws, as shown in Figure 7-41. If you are using the universal bezel, use the set of screw holes nearest the rear of the drive bay, which recesses the drive to allow clearance for the universal bezel. If you are not using the universal bezel, use the screw holes nearest the front of the drive bay to seat the drive further forward, flush with the main case bezel.

The Plextor PX-708A optical drive is jumpered by default as the master device. We intend to connect the optical drive as the secondary master, so the default jumpering is correct. If for some reason you need to install the optical drive as a slave device, adjust the jumper before or immediately after you install the drive in the drive bay.

Figure 7-42. Install the drive bay in the chassis

With both drives mounted and secured, slide the drive bay assembly partially into position, as shown in Figure 7-42. Don't seat it fully yet—you still need to connect the data and power cables to the drives. At this point, the sequence in which you do things becomes important.

To begin connecting drive cables, locate the free ends of the S-ATA cable, the P-ATA cable, and a Molex power connector from the power supply. Feed these three cables up between the back of the drive bay assembly and the front of the power supply. Locate the S-ATA power cable coming from the power supply, but for now leave it down inside the case.

With the drive bay assembly partially in position, the hard drive is now below the optical drive. The optical drive is considerably deeper than the hard drive, which means the hard drive data and power connectors are relatively inaccessible. Begin by connecting the S-ATA data cable to the hard drive. The cable and drive connectors are keyed, so note the orientations of the L-shaped keys on the drive and cable before you proceed. Position the cable connector over the drive connector in the correct orientation and press firmly until the cable connector seats, as shown in Figure 7-43.

WARNING

Use care when you connect or disconnect S-ATA data and power cables. S-ATA connectors are small, constructed of brittle plastic, and relatively fragile. It's easy to snap one off accidentally by applying too much pressure.

Figure 7-43. Connect the S-ATA data cable to the hard drive

The next step is to connect the ATA data cable to the optical drive, as shown in Figure 7-44. Locate pin 1 on the optical drive, which is nearly always adjacent to the power connector, as it is on the Plextor PX-708A. If you are using a standard ribbon cable, orient the red strip on the cable with pin 1 on the drive connector and press the cable firmly into place. We used the Antec Cobra ATA cable supplied with the case, which uses a red wire for pin 1 and is also keyed on the body of the cable connector.

The next step is to connect power to the optical drive. Like most optical drives, the Plextor PX-708A uses a standard Molex drive power connector. Orient the power cable connector with the two beveled corners corresponding to the matching bevels on the drive connector, and press the power connector firmly into place, as shown in Figure 7-45. Make sure the power connector seats fully, which may require significant pressure.

Figure 7-44. Connect the ATA cable to the optical drive

The final step in connecting the drives is to connect power to the S-ATA hard drive. The Antec AR300 power supply provides one S-ATA power connector, but the cable is too short to reach the drive unless the drive bay assembly is pivoted into its fully seated position. That means you'll have to connect that cable "blind," so knowing the proper orientation is helpful. Accordingly, note the orientation of the L-shaped key on the power connector of the S-ATA drive before you seat the drive bay assembly.

Figure 7-45. Connect power to the optical drive

Figure 7-46. Connect power to the hard drive

Once you're sure you know how and where the cable connects, pivot the drive bay assembly into its seated position, with all four posts fully engaged in the corresponding notches in the chassis. Orient and align the S-ATA power cable with the hard drive power connector and press the cable firmly into place, as shown in Figure 7-46.

> The drive power connector is very inaccessible—it is surrounded by the rear of the optical drive, the front of the power supply, and the CPU cooler, leaving almost no working room. We found it helpful to turn the case on its side; using a flashlight can help as well. If you have large hands, as Robert does, you may need to find someone with small hands to seat the S-ATA power cable. We hope Antec addresses this problem in later production of this case; all they'd need to do is make the S-ATA power cable a few inches longer.

Figure 7-47. Verify that the optical drive is seated flush with the front bezel

After you've connected both data cables and both power cables, the system is nearly complete. Verify that the optical drive is seated flush with the front bezel, as shown in Figure 7-47. Once again, we've somehow ended up with a white drive bezel in a black case. We'll swap out the white Plextor PX-708A for a black unit once we get some more of those in stock, but for now it works fine.

Installing the Low-Speed Cyclone Blower

Antec bundles the Low-Speed Cyclone Blower with the Aria case. ("Low-speed cyclone" sounds like an oxymoron to us, but there it is.) The Cyclone Blower occupies an expansion slot, exhausting warm air through the slot cover. It uses a low-speed fan that is so quiet it is difficult to hear it running even with your ear right up against the unit. Antec recommends the following placement for the Cyclone Blower:

- If no AGP card is installed, install the Cyclone Blower in the first slot (the slot that would otherwise be occupied by the AGP card).

- If an AGP card is installed but no other expansion card is installed, install the Cyclone Blower in the third slot, leaving one slot open between the AGP card and the Cyclone Blower.

- If an AGP card and one other expansion card are installed, install the Cyclone Blower in the third slot and the other expansion card in the fourth (last) slot.

- If an AGP card and two other expansion cards are installed, install the Cyclone Blower in the second slot, adjacent to the AGP card, and install the two other expansion cards in the third and fourth slots.

Installing the Cyclone Blower is optional. Antec provides it for configurations that require more cooling than the power supply fan can provide. We decided to install it, because our final system configuration uses a relatively hot 3.2 GHz Pentium 4, and we may at some point install a fast, hot video adapter. With a slow processor and embedded video, the Cyclone Blower may not be needed. On the other hand, it adds so little noise that we'd probably use it even on a cool-running system. Every little bit of cooling helps, particularly in an SFF case.

To install the Cyclone Blower, use the same procedure you would use to install an expansion card. Begin by removing the two screws that secure the expansion slot cover bracket, as shown in Figure 7-48.

With those two screws removed, the expansion slot cover bracket is still retained by the four screws that secure the four expansion slot covers. Remove all four of those screws, as shown in Figure 7-49, and pull the expansion slot cover bracket free.

With the expansion slot cover bracket removed, remove the appropriate slot cover, as shown in Figure 7-50. Our final configuration for the SFF system did not use an AGP adapter, so we chose to install the Cyclone Blower in the first slot.

Figure 7-48. Remove the expansion slot cover bracket

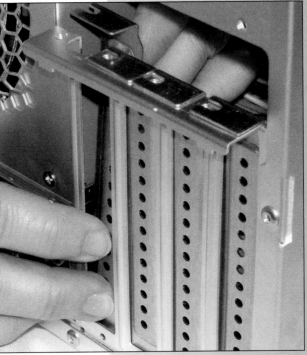

Figure 7-50. Remove the appropriate expansion slot cover

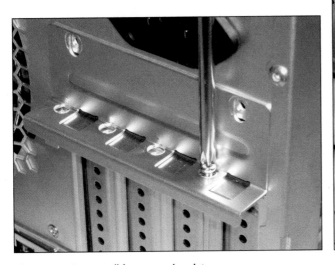

Figure 7-49. Remove all four expansion slot cover screws

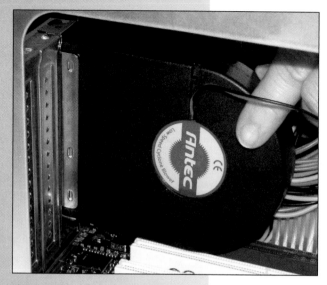

Figure 7-51. Install the Low-Speed Cyclone Blower

Save the Aria slot cover in case you later change the system configuration. The Aria slot covers are unique. The holes contribute to system cooling, so it's a bad idea to use a standard solid slot cover rather than the ventilated Aria slot cover. We taped our slot cover to the inside of a side panel so it would be handy if we ever remove the Cyclone Blower.

Slide the Cyclone Blower into place, as shown in Figure 7-51. Unlike some PCI slot fans, the Cyclone Blower doesn't use a dummy card edge connector that mates with an expansion slot, so it is secured in place only by the slot cover screw.

Holding the Cyclone Blower in position with one hand, drive a screw through the slot cover bracket to secure the blower in place, as shown in Figure 7-52.

With the Cyclone Blower and the slot cover bracket held in place by one screw, reinsert the two screws that secure the slot cover bracket to the chassis, as shown in Figure 7-53. After you've done that, reinsert the slot cover screws in the three remaining slot covers.

Figure 7-52. Reinstall the expansion slot cover bracket

Figure 7-53. Secure the expansion slot cover bracket

With the Cyclone Blower secured, locate an available power connector from the power supply. Orient the keying bevels on both connectors and press the connectors until they mate firmly, as shown in Figure 7-54. You can use any available Molex power connector. The Cyclone Blower draws so little current that it can share the power lead with a drive or video adapter.

Final assembly steps

Congratulations! You're almost finished building the system. About all that remains is to dress the cables, configure BIOS Setup, and reinstall the top and side panels.

Figure 7-54. Connect power to the Cyclone Blower

Ordinarily, we spend a few minutes tying off the cables and tucking them neatly out of the way. We planned to do the same for the SFF system. In fact, we planned to do a better job than usual of dressing the cables because the small case volume makes airflow critical. However, we found that it is quite difficult to dress the cables in an SFF system because there's so little room to work. After 15 minutes or so, we'd finally gotten the cables dressed as best we could, and were satisfied with the job.

And there it stood until we needed to open the system to reshoot a couple of images. We attempted to pivot the drive bay assembly upward, but it wouldn't move. Arrrghhh. With the cables dressed, it's impossible to work on the system. We spent another few minutes *un*dressing the cables so that we could get into the system to shoot our images. When we reassembled the system, we reluctantly concluded that it was best to leave the cables undressed, merely tucking them out of the way as best we could. That's true for us because we frequently need to open up systems to work on them, swap components, and so on. If this were a relatively static system, we'd probably dress the cables formally as the final assembly step.

By "formal" we don't mean dressing the cables in tuxedos and long gowns, as one of our editors wryly suggested. We mean using tie wraps to bundle the cables and secure them to the chassis.

Whether or not you choose to dress your cables, take a few minutes to double-check everything one last time before you apply power to the system. Use the following checklist:

___ No loose tools or screws (shake the case gently)
___ Heatsink/fan unit properly mounted; CPU fan connected
___ Memory modules fully seated and latched
___ Front-panel switch and indicator cables connected properly
___ Front-panel I/O cables connected properly
___ Hard drive data cable connected to drive and motherboard
___ Hard drive power cable connected
___ Optical drive data cable connected to drive and motherboard
___ Optical drive power cable connected
___ Optical drive audio cable(s) connected, if applicable
___ All drives secured to drive bay or chassis
___ Expansion cards fully seated and secured to the chassis
___ Main ATX power cable and ATX12V power cable connected
___ All cables dressed and tucked, if you choose to do that

Once you're certain that all is as it should be, it's time for the smoke test. Leave the cover off for now. Connect the power cable to the wall receptacle and then to the system unit. Press the main power button on the front of the case, and the system should start up. Check to make sure that the power supply fan and CPU fan are spinning. You should also hear the hard drive spin up and the happy beep that tells you the system is starting normally. At that point, everything should be working properly.

When you turn on the rear power switch, the system will come to life momentarily and then die. That's perfectly normal behavior. When the power supply receives power, it begins to start up. It quickly notices that the motherboard hasn't told it to start, and so it shuts down again. All you need to do is press the front-panel power switch and the system will start normally.

Turn off the system, disconnect the power cord, and take these final steps to prepare the system for use:

1. *Set the BIOS Setup configuration jumper to Configure mode*
   The BIOS Setup configuration jumper block on the Intel D865GRH motherboard is used to set the operation mode. This jumper is located near the left front edge of the motherboard. By default, the jumper is in the 1-2 or Normal position. Move the jumper block to the 2-3 or Configure position.

2. *Reconnect the power cord and restart the system*
   When the configuration jumper is set to Configure mode, starting the system automatically runs BIOS Setup and puts the system in maintenance mode. This step allows the motherboard to detect the type

of processor installed and configure it automatically. When the BIOS Setup screen appears, choose the menu option to clear all BIOS data and then reset the system clock. Save your changes and exit. The system automatically shuts down. Disconnect the power cord.

3. *Set the BIOS Setup configuration jumper to normal mode*
With the power cord disconnected, move the BIOS Setup configuration jumper block from 2-3 (Configure mode) to 1-2 (Normal mode).

4. *Replace the side panel and reconnect power*
With the jumper set for Normal operation, replace the side panel and reconnect the power cord. Your system is now completely assembled and ready for use.

Final Words

We actually built several permutations of the SFF PC to see how various configurations affected noise level and heat production. We used the Intel D865GRH and D865GLC motherboards with Northwood-core Pentium 4 processors running at 1.8, 2.6, and 3.2 GHz. We tried various CPU coolers, using either the embedded fan or a separate 80mm or 92mm low-speed fan with the supplemental fan bracket supplied with the Aria. We used the embedded video, and also tried installing low-end (ATi RADEON 9200), midrange (RADEON 9600), and high-end (RADEON 9800XT) video adapters. We even briefly installed an old microATX Pentium III motherboard just to say we'd done it.

We learned that the Antec Aria case is sufficiently flexible to use for anything from a "silent" PC to a fire-breathing gaming system. As you might expect, the system was noisier and ran hotter with faster processors and video adapters.

In a minimal configuration—using a Pentium 4/1.8, a very quiet 80mm CPU fan in the optional bracket, and embedded video—the system was inaudible from a few feet away even in a very quiet room. Such a configuration could serve as a Home Theater PC or in another application where low noise was an important consideration. With the slower processor, the CPU and case temperatures remained at low levels, only a degree or two warmer than we would expect in a standard mini-tower case. At an ambient temperature of 22°C, the CPU idled at 29°C and reached 43°C under load.

In a midrange configuration—a Pentium 4/2.6, stock CPU cooler, and embedded video or the RADEON 9600—the system was audible but not intrusive. Such a configuration would be an excellent mainstream system. Again, the Aria case provided good cooling at reasonably low noise levels. At an ambient temperature of 22°C and using embedded video, the CPU idled at 32°C and reached 49°C under load. Adding the RADEON 9600 bumped that up by a degree or two.

321

Linux on the Aria SFF PC

The Aria SFF PC we built for this chapter has found a permanent home as Robert's den system, sitting beneath his end table. Even with the 3.2 GHz processor, the Aria is quiet enough not to be intrusive.

For several years, Robert has wanted to migrate to Linux as his primary desktop operating system, but always found that traditional Linux distros came up short in usability. But Robert is nothing if not persistent, and in June 2004 he decided to install Xandros Business Desktop OS Business Edition (*http://www.xandros. com*).

This time, he was not disappointed. Xandros is what a desktop Linux distro should be. Everything just works. Connecting a Xandros client to our Windows-based network is as easy as connecting a Windows client. Burning CDs is easier than with Windows. Fonts are gorgeous. Xandros even runs some Windows programs, including Word 2000 and Excel 2000, which we use every day. Xandros is the first Linux distro we've seen that can realistically replace desktop Windows.

The only important feature Xandros lacks is DVD writing support, but we're sure they'll fix that soon. Otherwise, it's just about perfect. Enough so that most of our desktop systems will soon be running Xandros Desktop OS.

In a maxed-out gaming configuration—a Pentium 4/3.2 and the RADEON 9800XT—the system was noticeably louder and ran much hotter: so much so that we were concerned about system stability. At an ambient temperature of 22°C, the CPU idled at 41°C and reached 62°C under load. Still, gamers cheerfully accept temperatures that worry us to death, so we won't rule out the Aria for a gaming or LAN Party PC. Even in a maximum configuration, the Aria is not loud for a gaming system. The primary noise is a high-pitched whine produced by the CPU cooler and the video adapter fan.

Testing made clear to us that using both a fast processor and a fast video card would be pushing our luck. Either one produces significant heat, and both together simply produce more heat than the small volume of the Aria case can handle at reasonable temperature levels. In the configuration we finally settled on—a Pentium 4/3.2, stock CPU cooler, and embedded video—the system produced about the same noise level as the midrange configuration, and ran only a few degrees warmer. At an ambient temperature of 22°C, the CPU idled at 36°C and reached 55°C under load, which are acceptable temperatures for routine use.

After working with this system, we concluded that an SFF system built with proper components can be perfectly serviceable in all but the highest-performance configurations if small size is an important consideration. But if size is not critical, we suggest avoiding the compromises in cooling, noise, and expandability that are inherent in SFF systems, and building a standard mini-tower system instead.

All of that said, though, we have to admit that the Antec Aria is a snazzy case, and the system we built around it is definitely sexier than a vanilla mini-tower. (If it's any indication, Robert and Barbara both wanted to replace their primary office systems with the SFF system. Fortunately, we had the parts to build a second one...)

For updated component recommendations, commentary, and other new material, visit *http://www.hardwareguys.com/guides/sff.html*.

Index

Index

About the Authors

Robert Bruce Thompson is the author or coauthor of numerous online training courses and computer books. Robert built his first computer in 1976 from discrete chips. It had 256 *bytes* of memory, used toggle switches and LEDs for I/O, ran at less than 1 MHz, and had no operating system. Since then, he has bought, built, upgraded, and repaired hundreds of PCs for himself, employers, customers, friends, and clients. Robert reads mysteries and nonfiction for relaxation, but only on cloudy nights. He spends most clear, moonless nights outdoors with his 10" Dobsonian reflector telescope, hunting down faint fuzzies, and is currently designing a larger truss-tube Dobsonian (computerized, of course) that he plans to build.

Barbara Fritchman Thompson worked for 20 years as a librarian before starting her own home-based consulting practice, Research Solutions (*http://www.researchsolutions.net*), and is also a researcher for the law firm Womble Carlyle Sandridge & Rice, PLLC. Barbara, who has been a PC power user for more than 15 years, researched and tested much of the hardware reviewed for this book. During her leisure hours, Barbara reads, works out, plays golf, and, like Robert, is an avid amateur astronomer.

Colophon

Our look is the result of reader comments, our own experimentation, and feedback from distribution channels. Distinctive covers complement our distinctive approach to technical topics, breathing personality and life into potentially dry subjects.

Emily Quill was the production editor and copyeditor for *Building the Perfect PC*. Nancy Reinhardt was the proofreader. David Futato and Melanie Wang did the typesetting and page makeup, with assistance from Emily Quill. Colleen Gorman, Matt Hutchinson, and Claire Cloutier provided quality control. Julie Hawks wrote the index.

Ellie Volckhausen designed the cover of this book using Photoshop 5.5 and QuarkXPress 4.1. The cover image is a photograph by David Reavis. Emma Colby produced the cover layout with QuarkXPress 4.1 using Adobe's Formata Condensed font.

David Futato and Melanie Wang designed the interior layout using InDesign CS, based on a series design by David Futato. This book was converted from Microsoft Word to InDesign CS by Julie Hawks and Joe Wizda. The text and heading fonts are Linotype Birka and Adobe Formata Condensed, and the code font is TheSans Mono Condensed from LucasFont. The illustrations and screenshots that appear in the book were produced by Robert Romano and Jessamyn Read using Macromedia Freehand MX and Adobe Photoshop 7.